African American Women Writers in New Jersey, 1836–2000

Abdus-Samad, Nihmat Mujahid   Ahmad, Ameerah Hasin   Ali,
Islah Samirah Beyah see Beyah, Islah Amos, Gloria Lucille   Baraka,
Amina   Bartel, Carole see Haynes, Oona'o   Benyard, Daphne Haygood
Beyah, Islah   Biggs, Hudra Elissa Clay   Blanks, Louise Scott
Thompson   Booker, Sue see Thandeka   Brown, Denise Michele see
Beyah, Islah   Brown, Margery Wheeler   Brown, Martha Hursey
Brown, Vashti Proctor Bryant, Irene Martin Burnett, Gracie Diane
Butler, Anna Land   Butler, Rebecca Batt   Butler, Sally Central
Campbell, Bertha Georgetta Merritt   Campbell, Georgetta see
Campbell, Bertha Georgetta Merritt   Carmichael, Mary Elizabeth
Cornish   Clarke, Cheryl Lynn Clyburn, Evelyn   Coleman, Chrisena
Anne   Collins, Elsie McIntosh   Darden, Carole see Lloyd, Carole
Darden   Darden, Norma Jean   Davis-Thompson, Esther Louis
Dorin, Lenora Allen Downing, Theresa Bowman   Drewry, Cecelia
Hodges   Dudley, Frankie W.   Edge, Sylvia Clark   Fauset, Jessie
Redmon Flagg, E. Alma Williams Flournoy, Valerie Rose   Flournoy,
Vanessa   Freeland, Annabelle Robinson Fullilove, Mindy Thompson
Gaines, Kathryn Elizabeth   Gilmore-Scott, Monique   Grant,
Gwendolyn Goldsby Greene, Carolyn Jetter Guyton, Diana Brenda see
Karriem, Jaleelah Hailstock, Shirley T. Hall, Valerie see Ahmad,
Ameerah   Hayes, Leola Grant   Haynes, Oona'o   Hendley, Essie Lee
Kirkland Hinton, Maurita Miles   Holley, Mary Rose   Holmes,
Linda Janet   Hooks, Helen Shaw see Shaw, Helen Howell, Christine
Moore   Hudson, Cheryl Audril Willis Hughes, Sally Page   Hunter-

African American
Women Writers
in New Jersey,
1836–2000

A Biographical Dictionary
and
Bibliographic Guide

Sibyl E. Moses

Rutgers University Press
New Brunswick, New Jersey, and London

Publication of this book was assisted by a
grant from the New Jersey Historical Commission

First paperback edition 2006

Library of Congress Cataloging-in-Publication Data

Moses, Sibyl E.
African American women writers in New Jersey, 1836–2000 : a biographical dic-
tionary and bibliographic guide / by Sibyl E. Moses.
p.   cm.
Includes bibliographical references.
ISBN 0-8135-4019-4 (pbk.: alk. paper)
ISBN 0-8135-3183-7 (hardcover: alk. paper)
1. American literature—New Jersey—Bio-bibliography—Dictionaries.
2. American literature—African American authors—Bio-bibliography—
Dictionaries.   3. American literature—Women authors—Bio-bibliography—
Dictionaries.   4. African American women—New Jersey—Biography—
Dictionaries.   5. Authors, American—New Jersey—Biography—Dictionaries.
6. African American women authors—Biography—Dictionaries.   7. African
American authors—Biography—Dictionaries.   8. African American women in
literature—Dictionaries.   9. Women and literature—New Jersey—Dictionaries.
10. New Jersey—In literature—Bibliography.   11. New Jersey—Biography—
Dictionaries.   I. Title.

PS253.N5 M67 2003
810.9'9287'089960730749—dc21   2002068383

British Cataloging-in-Publication information is available from the British
Library.

Perms t/k

Manufactured in the United States of America

For my parents,
Sibyl Chambliss Moses
and
John Edison Moses

Contents

Preface

In 1984 I volunteered to write a short article on African American women writers in New Jersey for *About Ourselves,* a community newsletter published by the Seton Hall University Department of African American Studies. I assumed that it would be an easy task, for as an African American woman who lived in New Jersey for more than twenty years, I knew a few of the writers: E. Alma Flagg, Ntozake Shange, the Darden sisters, Carole and Norma Jean. However, when I visited libraries that house special collections of New Jersey materials, such as the Newark Public Library and those of Rutgers University and the New Jersey Historical Society, I discovered that there was no published work specifically on New Jersey African American women writers. Librarians tried to be helpful by mentioning the names of a few writers (who unfortunately were already known to me) and by suggesting reference books, notably *New Jersey and the Negro: A Bibliography, 1750–1966,* developed by the Librarians' Committee on the Negro in New Jersey and published in 1967 by the New Jersey Library Association.[1]

New Jersey and the Negro is interesting for several reasons.[2] First, this bibliography reveals the state of research on the African American in New Jersey at that particular time. Donald A. Sinclair quotes in the preface, "Owing to the relative neglect of this subject in past years, New Jersey has no history of its Negroes, or even adequate slavery studies. Except for recent surveys concerned with his economic or social difficulties, little research has been devoted to the Negro as a human being, his home and community life, his thoughts, feelings, and customs. Clearly there is work to be done. Research is necessarily involved with the problem of source material. As regards to the Negro in New Jersey it is a problem indeed. The sources that exist, printed or manuscript, are comparatively scanty, obscure and scattered."[3] Also of interest is that the bibliographers restricted their research to the identification and location of published works in only three areas: (a) Negro life in New Jersey, (b) New Jersey's role in the history of American Negroes, and (c) attitudes and behavior of white New Jerseyans toward Negroes. Although this bibliography was a tremendous feat, the subcommittee clearly indicated that they made no effort to fully "identify the miscellany of works written by Negroes resident in New Jersey."[4] Nevertheless, some prominent African American New Jersey authors were mentioned, such as William Still, Paul Robeson, E. Frederick Morrow, LeRoi Jones (now Amiri Baraka), and four women writers: Anna Land Butler, Rebecca Batts Butler, Deborah Cannon Partridge Wolfe, and Marion Thompson Wright. I now knew seven New Jersey African

American women writers. I wrote the article, but to repeat Donald A. Sinclair, "clearly there is work to be done."[5]

Obviously, a state such as New Jersey with its huge African American population, especially in its urban areas near New York City and Philadelphia, would surely produce more than seven African American women writers. Who are they? Is it merely a matter of identifying African American women writers listed in reference works as New Jerseyans? What of those not cited in these published sources? How is one to uncover them? These questions prompted me to undertake this investigation of African American women writers in New Jersey, a project covering nearly twenty years.

DESIGNATING REGIONAL WRITERS

Prior to considering the process, strengths, and weaknesses of using published sources to identify such authors, I examined the criteria used to designate a regional writer. Alice Marple, for example, in her study of Iowa authors, states that "when an author has been intelligently mentioned as an Iowa author, or was of Iowa birth, or worked in Iowa, he [she] is, for the purpose of our collections and of this list, an Iowa author." Ralph Janeway identifies Ohio authors as "only those persons who were born in Ohio, who have lived in the state for a period of time long enough to be considered an Ohioan." Mary E. Hazeltine describes a Wisconsin author as "(1) one who was born in Wisconsin or has had long residence in the state; (2) one who can claim residence for a considerable period; (3) one who has lived in Wisconsin long enough to have used Wisconsin material effectively, or to reflect its spirit, or to have made a contribution to its life or institutions. . . ."[6]

Although all three agree that birth is one criterion to identify a person as a regional author, there is a problem of interpreting the other criterion involving time of residence. Such phases as "long residence in the state" and "residence for a considerable period" are vague and are open to numerous interpretations. To avoid this problem, I have defined a New Jersey African American woman writer as a woman of African descent, living or dead, who was born in New Jersey or resided in the state for at least fifteen years, either continuously or during different periods of her life. Fifteen years, I felt, was a sufficient amount of time to become part of the culture of the state, but please note that this is an arbitrary decision. Similarly, I have defined a writer to be one who has written, edited, or completed at least one monographic publication. A publication is a printed literary work that is publicly distributed as a book, pamphlet, or report. Novels, short stories, poetry, juvenile literature, essays, anthologies, coloring books containing text,[7] autobiographies, biographies, bibliographies, government reports, encyclopedias, textbooks, and cookbooks are among the specific genres that were included in this study.

Using Written Sources to Identify African American Women Writers in New Jersey

Consulting published sources to identify African American women writers in New Jersey required examining pertinent reference works: (1) Ora Williams' *American Black Women in the Arts and Social Sciences: A Bibliographical Survey;* (2) Casper Leroy Jordan's *A Bibliographical Guide to African-American Women Writers;* (3) James A. Page and Jae Min Roh's *Selected Black American, African, and Caribbean Authors: A Bio-Bibliography;* (4) Theressa G. Rush, Carol F. Myers, and Esther S. Arata's *Black American Writers Past and Present: A Biographical and Bibliographical Dictionary;* (5) Ann Allen Shockley and Sue P. Chandler's *Living Black American Authors: A Biographical Dictionary;* (6) Barbara Rollock's *Black Authors and Illustrators of Children's Books: A Biographical Dictionary;* (7) Rebecca Batts Butler's *Profiles of Outstanding Blacks in South Jersey during the 1950's, 1960's, 1970's;* and (8) *Who's Who Among Black Americans, 1980–1981.*[8] In addition to these sources, I used the Research Libraries Group's *Research Libraries Information Network* and the Online Computer Library Center, Inc.'s *WorldCat,* both indispensable reference tools that enable users to identify bibliographic records of works by individual authors and other items relevant to the study. Though these reference works were used to identify African American women writers in New Jersey, the results were limited. All this effort produced only thirteen names.

Using Oral Sources to Identify African American Women Writers in New Jersey

Because the published sources were of such limited use, I turned to the African American community for help, as did earlier investigators, notably Edward Clarke,[9] who was concerned with identifying African American writers in New England, and Patrick Kay Bidelman and Darlene Clark Hine, who collected primary source material for a history of African American women in Indiana and Illinois.[9] The question facing me was: Who, then, in the African American community would know African American women writers in New Jersey and/or could refer an investigator to other members of the community who might know one or more of these writers? One group consists of those whose political or social position within the African American community entailed knowing fairly well a considerable number of people: ministers, elected officials, and leaders of prominent women's social or civic organizations. To request their help, I used the standard academic research strategy: a letter. Thus, more than four hundred letters were sent to ministers whose congregations were predominantly African Americans. Letters were also sent to more than two hundred African American federal, state, county, and municipal officers in New Jersey, including school board members, after their names were gleaned from *Black Elected Officials,* a yearly publication of the Joint Center for Political and Economic Studies in Washington, D.C.[10] And more than forty letters were mailed to the New Jersey chapters of four national African American women's organizations: the National Sorority of Phi Delta Kappa, Inc., whose membership is composed of African American teachers; Alpha Kappa Alpha Sorority, Inc.; Sigma Gamma Rho Sorority, Inc.; and the Daughters of Isis, the auxiliary to the Ancient Egyptian Arabic Order of Nobles of the Mystic Shrine (A.E.A.O.N.M.S.), a Prince Hall Masonic organization.

Unfortunately, from all these groups, there were only eleven responses to the written request, and beyond the identification of a small number of writers, these letters served primarily as a form of publicity for the project and a means of educating the community and promoting an awareness of African American women writers in the state.

Why was there such a poor response? Rather than assume that the aforementioned members of the African American community did not know any more writers in their political or school districts, congregations, and social organizations, or that they were unable, even unwilling, to notify others of my request for help in identifying these particular writers, I wonder if the fault was the lack of my personal contact except a letter written by a stranger, or in other terms, an unknown person. I base this assumption on the fact that several individuals who received my letter offered no assistance until I personally met them at a conference or other social event and introduced myself as the writer of the letter.

Moreover, that the poor response to the letters was partly due to such an impersonal relationship is borne out by the enormous success with the second group within the African American community who could and did identify a large number of African American women writers in New Jersey. This group consisted of my relatives, personal friends, and acquaintances, and they encompassed library colleagues, bookstore owners, fellow church members, sorority sisters, activists in the arts community, elementary, secondary, and college educators as well as other professional and business people whom I interviewed. Although these relatives, close friends, and acquaintances usually had direct knowledge of local writers, some of them also suggested others who might know other possible African American women writers in New Jersey. In some cases, my task necessitated interviewing a chain of two or three or four or even five or more people before the New Jersey writer was identified.

Potential informants for this project, within the African American community, consist of more than religious, social, and political leaders and my relatives, friends, and acquaintances. To meet the other members of the community, I had to embark upon a third strategy—field work. This involved such activities as systematic personal visits to public libraries, local historical societies, schools, publishing houses, and other institutions, as well as attending public lectures, poetry readings, professional meetings and conferences, and social events of African Americans in New Jersey, such as the meetings and banquets of the New Jersey Black Issues Conference, the Marion Thompson Wright Lecture (jointly sponsored by the New Jersey Historical Commission, Newark Public Library, and Rutgers University), and the luncheon of the New Jersey Federation of Colored Women's Clubs, as well as those of Alpha Kappa Alpha, Phi Delta Kappa, and Zeta Phi Beta sororities. Attendance, of course, provided opportunities to meet new African American women writers in New Jersey as well as network with people who might know such writers.

The identification of African American women writers in New Jersey is practically completed, thanks in part to the limitations of existing biographical and bibliographic reference works which forced me to rely on oral sources within the African American community to uncover the majority of these writers. At the time I wrote my dissertation in 1995, I had located only seventy writers.[11] Since that time I have added more than forty-eight writers, and I am still involved in this research. Here, then, are the biographies of 118 African American women writers in New Jersey, accompanied by a list of their publications and in many cases, autobiographical narratives wherein a writer discusses influences that helped shape her life, writings, and or desire to write.

FORMAT AND CONTENT

The typical format for each entry includes seven paragraphs labeled with descriptor fields under the following headings: Personal; Residence in New Jersey; Career; Memberships; Awards, Honors, Other Certificates; Reflections; Publications; and Bio-Bibliographical Sources. The entry is structured as follows:

Personal: full name (former names, if any); dates and places of birth and death; parents' names, occupations, and birthplaces, when known and provided; maternal and paternal grandparents' names, as well as their occupations, and birthplaces, when known and provided; names of siblings; name of spouse(s)/partner(s); names of children; elementary, secondary, and post secondary institutions attended, and degrees earned with dates; religious affiliation.

Residence in New Jersey: names of cities and towns in New Jersey where author has lived, with dates.

Career: name of employer, position, dates, where provided.

Memberships: names of various community, social, and professional organizations, with offices held.

Awards and Honors: community, literary, and other awards or forms of recognition, with dates, if provided.

Reflections: author's response to query about memorable experiences, influences on her life, and her decision to write.

Publications: chronological list of books/monographs written, edited, or compiled by the author; list of works in other books, journals, newspapers, and so forth.

Bio-Bibliographical Sources: primary and secondary sources consulted (e.g., correspondence, interviews, books, articles, reviews, etc.) to obtain information about the author.

Two appendices facilitate access to specific writers, by geographic affiliation and by genre: Appendix A: Distribution of African American Women Writers in New Jersey by Geographical Affiliation (City/Town), and Appendix B: Distribution of African American Women Writers in New Jersey by Genre.

I have not attempted to summarize, analyze, or evaluate any of their works. My primary purpose was to uncover the names of these African American women and the titles of their publications so that literary scholars could perform that task. It is important to realize that this is one of the earliest studies that concentrates on African American women writers of a particular state, and I hope that there will be others who will undertake similar studies in other states with large African American populations, because all of this is extremely important in recording and preserving the contributions of African American women in the literary world.

Sibyl E. Moses

NOTES TO PREFACE

1. New Jersey Library Association, Bibliography Committee, comp., *New Jersey and the Negro: A Bibliography, 1715–1966* ([Trenton, N.J.]: New Jersey Library Association, 1967).

2. Another interesting fact is that this special subcommittee comprised twenty-one librarians and two "Negro" citizen consultants who "represented the active interest of the Negro community in its own history." These consultants were Mrs. Vera Brantley McMillon of Newark and Dr. Myra Smith Kearse of Vaux Hall, both of whom were eminently qualified. Mrs. McMillon had earned her degree in economics from Howard University and was Supervisor of Case Workers in Newark's Welfare Department. It was she who presented a paper on three centuries of Negro history in New Jersey at the New Jersey Historical Society's Annual Professional Conference in 1964, a paper that prompted the creation of the Librarians' Committee on the Negro in New Jersey, the subcommittee responsible for the compilation of the bibliography. Dr. Kearse, also a Howard University graduate, was a physician and a prominent civil rights advocate in Newark and Vaux Hall. (See *Past and Promise: Lives of New Jersey Women,* The Women in New Jersey Project, comp. [Metuchen, N.J.: Scarecrow Press, 1990].) Both women, members of the local chapter of Alpha Kappa Alpha Sorority, Inc., were obviously influenced by this sorority that had as its national mandate the promotion of African American history on the local level. These women, hence, were actively involved in the African American community in New Jersey.

3. Quoted from Donald Sinclair's *The Negro and New Jersey,* a preliminary check-

list of Rutgers University Library's holdings, as cited in New Jersey Library Association, Bibliography Committee, comp., *New Jersey and the Negro,* 5.

4. *Ibid.,* 5.

5. It is interesting to note that this work did not include other early African American women writers in New Jersey such as Jessie Redmond Fauset, Gertrude Pitts, and Jarena Lee. Within the past twenty years, several new publications about African Americans in New Jersey have appeared; the primary focus, however, is not New Jersey's writers. See, for example, Ernest Lyght's *Path of Freedom: The Black Presence in New Jersey's Burlington County, 1659–1900* (Cherry Hill, N.J.: E. & E. Publishing House, 1978); Giles R. Wright's *Afro-Americans in New Jersey: A Short History* (Trenton, N.J.: New Jersey Historical Commission, Department of State, 1988); Spenser R. Crew's *Black Life in Secondary Cities: A Comparative Analysis of the Black Communities of Camden and Elizabeth, N.J., 1860–1920* (New York: Garland, 1993); Jack Washington's *In Search of a Community's Past: The Story of the Black Community of Trenton, New Jersey, 1860–1900* (Trenton, N.J.: Africa World Press, 1990).

6. Alice Marple, *Iowa Authors and Their Works: A Contribution Toward a Bibliography* (Des Moines, Iowa: Historical Department of Iowa, 1918), viii; W. Ralph Janeway, *A Selected List of Ohio Authors, and Their Books* (Columbus, Ohio: H. L. Hedrick Mimeographed Publications, 1933), 3; Mary E. Hazeltine, *One Hundred Years of Wisconsin Authorship, 1836–1937; A Contribution to a Bibliography of Books of Wisconsin Authors* (Madison, Wisc.: Wisconsin Library Association, 1937), 1–2.

7. There is a considerable number of African Americans who are Muslims, many of whom belong to the Nation of Islam and frequently send their children to Muslim schools in which all the curricular materials, with the exception of dictionaries, are directed to be written by Muslims. See Warith Deen Mohammed, "Educational Concerns of Imam Warith Deen Mohammed" Sedalia, North Carolina, 9 April 1982 as quoted in Ummil-Khair Zakiyyah Sharif's *IQRAA! A Qur'an-Based Curriculum Guide* [Jersey City, N.J.: New Mind Productions, 1989] 3. Some African American Muslim women teachers wrote curricular material such as coloring books used to instruct children to learn the alphabet by using examples from the Koran to illustrate the text. See Ummil-Khair Zakiyyah Sharif's *ABC's in Al Quran* ([Jersey City, N.J.]: New Mind Productions, 1983).

8. Ora Williams, *American Black Women in the Arts and Social Sciences: A Bibliographic Survey,* rev. and expanded ed. (Metuchen, N.J.: Scarecrow Press, 1978); Casper Leroy Jordan, comp., *A Bibliographical Guide to African-American Women Writers* (Westport, Conn.: Greenwood Press, 1993); James A. Page and Jae Min Roh, *Selected Black American, African, and Caribbean Authors: A Bio-Bibliography* (Littleton, Colo.: Libraries Unlimited, 1985); Theressa G. Rush, Carol F. Myers, and Esther S. Arata, *Black American Writers Past and Present: A Biographical and Bibliographical Dictionary* (Metuchen, N.J.: Scarecrow Press, 1975); Ann Allen Shockley and Sue P. Chandler, *Living Black American Authors: A Biographical Dictionary* (New York: R. R. Bowker, 1973); Barbara Rollock, *Black Authors and Illustrators of Children's Books: A Biographical Dictionary,* 2nd ed. (New York: Garland, 1992); Rebecca Batts Butler, *Profiles of Outstanding Blacks in South Jersey during the 1950's, 1960's, 1970's* (Camden, N.J.: Reynolds Publishers, 1980); *Who's Who Among Black Americans, 1980–1981* (Northbrook, Ill.: Who's Who Among Black Americans Publishing Co., 1981). Because of its geographical index, this reference work provides access to African Americans living in New Jersey.

9. Edward Clark identified African American writers in New England by con-

sulting members of the community. After using four African American literary biographies and one African American biographical directory, he telephoned "people working in offices of schools, colleges, universities, medical and technological schools" for information about current and past students and faculty. See Edward Clark, *Black Writers in New England: A Bibliography, with Biographical Notes, of Books by and About Afro-Americans Writers Associated with New England in the Collection of Afro-American Literature, Suffolk University, Museum of Afro-American History, Boston African American Historic National Site* (Boston: U.S. Department of the Interior, National Park Service, 1985); Patrick Kay Bidelman and Darlene Clark Hine consulted individuals in the community and local organizations as part of their investigation for the Black Women in the Middle West Project. The project sought to identify, collect, and preserve primary resource materials that would be used to write the history of African American women in Illinois and Indiana. See their *Black Women in the Middle West Project: A Comprehensive Resource Guide, Illinois and Indiana: Historical Essays, Oral Histories, Biographical Profiles, and Document Collections* (Indianapolis, Ind.: Indiana Historical Bureau, 1986).

10. Ceased publication in 1993.

11. Sibyl E. Moses, "The Identification and Bibliographic Control of African American Women Writers in New Jersey" (Ph.D. diss., University of Illinois, 1995).

Acknowledgments

A work of this kind required contacts and extended discussions with many people in various parts of New Jersey and other states. Because my travels throughout New Jersey were crucial for the accumulation of information about the authors, I wish to acknowledge the support of the New Jersey Historical Commission that provided the funding that made my initial travels and the publication of this work possible. My research was also funded, in part, by grants from the Graduate College at the University of Illinois at Urbana-Champaign and The Catholic University of America in Washington, D.C. I am also indebted to librarians and archivists throughout New Jersey, especially the staff of the New Jersey Historical Society, the Salem Country Historical Society, Rutgers University's Special Collections, and the Newark Public Library's New Jersey Collection.

My family, friends, and new acquaintances, both within and outside the academy, contributed in various ways to the success of this publication. My parents, Sibyl Chambliss Moses and John Edison Moses, instilled in me the importance of African American organizations and the role of their members as gatekeepers of our culture. My sister, Della Moses Walker, facilitated my networking with people throughout New Jersey, especially in the religious community. Glenderlyn Johnson, Grace Plater, Ophelia Pasley, Freddye Hill, Henrietta Parker, the Reverend Ernest Lyght, the late Maurice Hicks, the late James Brown, Giles Wright, Jean Harris, the Honorable Lawrence M. Lawson, Charles Payne, Edith Churchman, Sally Lane, and Rosemary Ellis all referred me to authors or to other people who were in turn helpful. I owe great debts of gratitude to every African American women writer in New Jersey, who often went out of their way to be helpful, sometimes traveled with me and constantly confirmed my conviction that it is important for New Jersey to know all of her writers. I especially thank Ameerah Ahmad, Daphne Benyard, Margery Wheeler Brown, the late Martha Hursey Brown, Georgetta M. Campbell, the late Lenora Dorin, E. Alma Flagg, Sally Page Hughes, Mary Jackson, Kristin Hunter Lattany, Eddiemae Livingston, Carrie McCray, the late Quadriyah Shakir, Ummil-Khair Zakiyyah Sharif, Patricia Nicely Simon, Helen Shaw, and Nancy Travis.

Very dear friends, Dr. Edwin J. Nichols, Harold Herman, professor emeritus, University of Maryland, and Akinsola A. Akiwowo, professor emeritus, Obafemi Awolowo University, provided an interest in and support for this project. Professor Donald W. Krummel and Professor Linda C. Smith, both of the University of Illinois, shared their knowledge of bibliography and the creation of reference tools, respectively, while Professor Chester

Fontenot shared his knowledge of African American literature and provided an opportunity for me to teach that subject. I am also grateful to my colleague, Professor Robert Mahony, and my research assistants at The Catholic University of America: Darren Jones, Tara L. Brazee, Sylvia Dye, Lisa Benjamin, and Jacqueline Johnson.

The presentation of photographs was made possible by the authors, numerous photographers, and a number of institutions: Moorland Spingarn Research Center, Howard University; Prints and Photographs Division, Library of Congress, Asbury Park Press Newspaper Archives, and The Albert and Shirley Small Special Collections Library, University of Virginia Library. Finally, *African American Women Writers in New Jersey* could not have been published without the unwavering support of New Jersey's African American communities.

African American Women Writers in New Jersey, 1836–2000

ABDUS-SAMAD, NI'MAT MUJAHID 1934–

Personal Former name Catherine Juanita Fortune Johnson. Born on 24 February 1934 in Wilmington, Delaware; first child of Cora Epps Hutchison Fortune (Tauheedah Mujahid) of Wilmington and Chester Mansfield Fortune, Jr. of Baltimore, Maryland; granddaughter (maternal) of Catherine Epps Hutchison of Wilmington and Albert David Hutchison of Chadds Ford, Pennsylvania; granddaughter (paternal) of Elizabeth Jane Howard Fortune of Accomack County, Virginia, and Chester Mansfield Fortune, Sr. of Baltimore; sisters: Carol Beverly Fortune, Constance Marie Fortune, Christine Elizabeth Fortune Wade, and Barbara Jean Fortune (Wajeehah Mujahid-Rashed); brothers: Chester Mansfield Fortune, III, Wesley Augustus Fortune, Sr., and Scott Leonard Fortune; husband: Kariem Abdulassmad (Leroy Joseph Johnson, divorced); child: Dawn Johnson. Education: Public School #21, Wilmington; Logan Demonstration School, Philadelphia, Pennsylvania; Jay Cooke Junior High School, Philadelphia; Simon Gratz High School, Philadelphia, 1948–1952; American University, Washington, D.C., 1961–1963; Antioch University, Philadelphia, B.A., human services and professional certification in elementary education, 1978, and M.A., administration, 1979; Temple University, Philadelphia, 45 credits toward Ph.D. in applied psychology, 1989. Religion: Al-Islam.
Residence in New Jersey Camden, 1971 to present.
Career File clerk, Gimbel Brothers, Philadelphia, 1952–1955; file clerk, Quartermaster Depot, Philadelphia and CIA, Langley, Virginia, 1955–1963; teacher, Sister Clara Muhammad School, Philadelphia; program director, Masters of Arts Program in Administration, Antioch University, Yellow Springs, Ohio; Beta House, Camden; instructor, Human Services Program, Camden County College, Blackwood, New Jersey, 1983–1998; owner, F-J Associates, Camden; 1982 to present.
Memberships Board of directors, Camden County YWCA (seven years); vice president, board of directors, Southwest Human Services Project of Philadelphia; Healthy Mothers/Healthy Babies Coalition of Camden County; secretary, board of trustees, Masjidullah, Philadelphia, 1983–1999; developing member, W. D. Mohammed Propagation Committee, Philadelphia.
Awards, Honors, Other Certificates Special Recognition Award from the board of trustees of Masjidullah, in recognition of dedication to community service and perseverance in spreading Al-Islam, December 1999.
Reflections
> "Among my memorable childhood experiences are: being part of the Junior Army at PS #21, where we sold stamps and bonds to help the war effort; the trauma of growing up in the big city of

1

Philadelphia after leaving the small-town atmosphere of Wilmington, Delaware (at that time); being the oldest child and helping to raise my brothers and sisters after the divorce of my parents; and graduating from high school and becoming responsible for my own life.

As an adult [my memorable experiences] are: my wedding day in Washington, D.C. and going on my honeymoon in New York and the birth of my only child, Dawn, on 8 July 1964. The most memorable experience of my adult years was my trip to Mecca, Saudi Arabia, in May 1993 to make the pilgrimage, or Hajj. The change in my life after that time is too immense to be detailed here and is only briefly covered in my book. I'm still living the change."

Publication

Abdus-Samad, Ni'mat. *From Dust to the Age of Full Strength: The Spiritual Journey of a Muslim Woman.* Pennsauken, N.J.: F-J Associates [1995]. [iv], 80.

Bio-Bibliographical Source

Abdus-Samad, Ni'mat Mujahid. "African American Women Writers in New Jersey Project: Biographical Questionnaire." Completed by Ni'mat Mujahid Abdus-Samad, 7 June 2001.

AHMAD, AMEERAH HASIN 1952–

Personal   Former name Valerie Hall. Born on 23 February 1952 in Jersey City, New Jersey; the youngest of four children of Mae Pearl Williams Hall (beautician and sewing operator) of Ocala, Florida, and Raymond Perceval Hall, II (World War II veteran, federal civil servant, and messenger) of Jersey City; granddaughter (maternal) of Minnie Fuller and James Williams of Florida; granddaughter (paternal) of Lottie Hall and Raymond P. Hall; sister: Brenda Hall (teacher); brothers: Raymond P. Hall III (attorney) and Vincent Hall (jazz drummer and pharmaceutical representative); married and divorced; children: Muslimah Ahmad, Kalimah Ahmad, Talib Ahmad, Musaddiq Ahmad, and Luqman Ahmad. Education: Public School #22, Jersey City; Lincoln High School, Jersey City, 1965–1969; Howard University, Washington, D.C., 1969; St. Peters College, Jersey City, 1982–1983; Sister Clara Muhammad School, Newark, New Jersey (teacher training and curriculum development courses). Religion: Al-Islam.

Residence in New Jersey   Jersey City, 1952 to present.

Career   Elementary teacher, Sister Clara Muhammad School, Newark, 1973–1984; workshop leader, Educational Arts Team, Department of Human Resources, Jersey City, 1986–1989; supervisory office clerk, U.S. Census Bureau, 1990; sound recorder and court aide, Superior Court of New Jersey, Newark, 1990 to present.

Memberships Board of directors and member, Muslim Community Arts Program, Jersey City.

Awards, Honors, Other Certificates Muslim Woman Achievement Award, for dedicated service to the Newark community, 1986; Paul Robeson Award, Community Awareness Series of the Jersey City Public Library, 1987; Outstanding Achievement as Author for the Anti-Drug Play, *Not Even Once,* coauthored with Sheila L. Harper, 1988.

Reflections

"I can recall my parents exposing the four of us to a well-rounded family life; in fact, the jazz and live music that was played in our very basement. I remember as a little girl the collection of poems my father wrote. This inspired me to write poetry at a very young age. My mother spoke of the racism that was and still is so prevalent. Even though I have chosen Al-Islam as my way of life, I am very grateful for their level of spirituality. This has influenced me to also seek Supreme guidance throughout my life."

Publications

Ahmad, Ameerah Hasin. *Muslim Children 1 to 10.* [Jersey City, N. J.]: The Author, 1983. 46, illus.

———. *New Dawn.* [Jersey City, N.J: Reflections Through Messages], 1986. 47 [1].

———. *Echoes & Visions; Reflections on a Life of Poetry.* N.p.: [Butterfly Reflections, 2000?]. 95, illus.

Bio-Bibliographical Source

Ahmad, Ameerah Hasin. "African American Women Writers in New Jersey Biographical Questionnaire." Completed by Ameerah Hasin Ahmad, September 1985.

ALI, ISLAH SAMIRAH BEYAH *SEE* BEYAH, ISLAH

AMOS, GLORIA LUCILLE WHITE 1921–

Personal Born on 19 June 1921 in New York, New York; daughter of Lucille Elsie Freeman White (homemaker) of Jamestown, Rhode Island, and Eugene White (Pullman porter) of New York; granddaughter (maternal) of Rosa Freeman of Warrington, North Carolina, and Henry Freeman of Peobus, Virginia; husband: Mason Roger Amos (window cleaner); children: Terrell Roger Amos, Barbara Ann Amos Whitaker, and Ken-

Gloria White Amos.
Photograph by Dennis Studios.

neth Anthony Amos. Education: Public School #90, New York, ca. 1926–1930; Public School #136, New York, 1930–1935; Harran High School, New York, 1935–1939; Ramapo College, Mahwah, New Jersey, 1989. Religion: Formerly Roman Catholic; now born-again Christian.

Residence in New Jersey   Englewood, 1966 to present.

Career   Clerk, membership department, Harlem YMCA, New York, 1940–1941; bookkeeper, A. J. Clark Real Estate Office, 1952–1969; Englewood Public Schools, Englewood, New Jersey, secretary, personnel office, maintenance department, and pupil service department; bookkeeper, business office, 1970–1994; secretary to principal, Janis E. Dismus Middle School.

Memberships   New Jersey Educational Association; Bergen County New Jersey Secretarial Association.

Awards, Honors, Other Certificates   Golden Poet's Award, Reno, Nevada, for poem "Separation"; resolution from Englewood Board of Education for novel, 1992; resolution from Englewood Board of Education for poetry; Outstanding Woman Role Model for 1993, New York Club of the National Association of Negro Business and Professional Women's Clubs, Inc.

Reflections

"In retrospect, Mrs. Gertrude McDoughal Ayers, the principal of Public School #90 and first black principal in the New York City Schools, influenced me when, during the assembly programs, she would lecture to the children that we should develop our talents and be the best at whatever we could do best.

Other inspirations for my writing were the receipt of awards for published poetry, the honor of being recognized by the Englewood Board of Education for my first published novel, and the receipt of outstanding praise from all whom have read the book. I was influenced by the words of Zora Neale Hurston. My thanks to Mrs. Poinsette, teacher; Mrs. Zap, psychologist; and Dr. Pruitt, my boss and principal; for their motivation and inspiration."

Publications

Amos, Gloria L. *Losing Yet Giving*. New York: Vantage Press, 1992. 261.

———. *Resurgence From the Abyss*. New York: Vantage Press, 1997. xiii, 261.

Bio-Bibliographical Source

Amos, Gloria L. "African American Women Writers in New Jersey: Biographical Questionnaire." Completed by Gloria L. Amos, January 1993.

BARAKA, AMINA 1942–

Personal Former name Sylvia Robinson Jones. Born on 5 December 1942 in Charlotte, North Carolina; the oldest child of Ruth Guest (garment worker) of Rock Hill, South Carolina, and James Clancy Robinson; granddaughter (maternal) of Leona Bacote and Patrick Bacote; sister: Sheila; brothers: Dwight, Johnny, Derek, and Charlie; husband: Imamu Amiri Baraka (writer, professor, and political activist); children: Vera Wilson, Wanda Wilson, Obalaji Malik Ali Baraka, Rasjua Alaziz Baraka, Amiri Sekou Baraka, Shani Isis Makeda Baraka, and Ahi Mwenga Baraka. Education: Robert Treat Elementary School; Morton Street School; Arts High School, 1961; Central Evening School (all located in Newark, New Jersey).

Amina Baraka.
Photograph by Lona Foote,
courtesy of the Lona Foote estate.

Residence in New Jersey Newark, 1943 to present.

Career Founding member of the Jazz Arts Society, a community organization of Newark artists, 1963–1966, Newark; original member of the "Spirit House Movers," a black theater group organized in 1967 by Amiri Baraka in Newark; performer, in the productions *Black Mass, Home on the Range,* and *Slave Ship,* written by Amiri Baraka; cofounder, with Amiri Baraka, Afrikan Free School, a community school for Afro-American children in Newark, 1968–1976; chairperson, Women's Division of the Committee for a Unified Newark, a citywide organization that led to the election of the first Black mayor of a large northeastern city; member, Central Committee of the Revolutionary Communist League, 1974–1978; organizer, African Women's Conference, which pulled together women from the United States, Africa, and the Caribbean, 1974; chairperson of committee that organized the Multi-national Women's Conference in New York, 1975; dancer (modern jazz) with Art Williams, Newark bass player.

Reflections

"Grandmother and grandfather were great storytellers. [I recall their] story about "Butterbean and Suzie" [when they performed as a] comedy team at the Apollo. In terms of journal writing, Amiri [influenced me]; [my writing evolved] in terms of understanding the power of writing, [that it was] more than folklore, [I] use writing for liberation."

Publications   *see also* Note on Baraka (after Bio-Bibliographical Sources, this entry)

Books

Jones, Sylvia. *Songs for the Masses.* N.p.: S. Jones, 1978. [38].

Baraka, Amiri, and Amina Baraka. *Confirmation, an Anthology of African American Women.* New York: Quill, 1983. 418.

Baraka, Imamu Amiri, and Amina Baraka. *The Music: Reflections on Jazz and Blues.* New York: Morrow, 1987. 332, illus.

Baraka, Amina, and Amiri Baraka. *5 Boptrees.* [Newark, N.J.: The Authors], 1992. 14.

Articles/Poetry/Other

Baraka, Amina. "For the Lady in Color." *Black Scholar* 12, no. 4 (July–August 1981): 54–55.

———. "Hip Songs (for Larry Neal)." *Black Scholar* 12, no. 4 (July–August 1981): 55.

———. "Looking for the Lyrics (for Jayne Cortez)." *Black Scholar* 12, no. 4 (July–August 1981): 54.

——— (Sylvia Jones). "Sometimie Women." *Black American Literature Forum* 16, no. 3 (fall 1982): 105.

——— (Sylvia Jones). "Sortin-Out." *Black American Literature Forum* 16, no. 3 (fall 1982): 106.

———. "Peoples Poet." *PoetryE* no. 9/10 (winter 1982–spring 1983): 105–106.

———. "Afroamerican Child." (A Documentation). *Stepping* (Anniversary Issue I) (1984): 13–15.

———. "Soweto Song." *Essence* 19 (February 1989):129.

Bio-Bibliographical Sources

Baraka, Amina. "Summary Resume." [Provided by author]. N.d. 1.

———. Interview by Sibyl E. Moses. Newark, N.J., December 1994.

Catala, Rafael, and James D. Anderson. *Index of American Periodical Verse: 1984.* Metuchen, N.J.: The Scarecrow Press, Inc., 1986.

Note

Two sources (Casper L. Jordan, *A Bibliographical Guide to African-American Writers,* Westport, Conn.: Greenwood, 1993, 16; and Rhonda Gilkin, *Black American Women in Literature: A Biography, 1976 through 1987,* Jefferson, N.C.: McFarland, 1989, 11) erroneously identified Amina Baraka as the author of the play, *What Was the Relationship of the Lone Ranger to the Means of Production? A Play in One Act.* New York: Anti-Imperialist Cultural Union, 1978. Amiri Baraka is the author.

BARTEL, CAROLE *SEE* HAYNES, OONA'O

BENYARD, DAPHNE HAYGOOD 1949–

Personal   Born on 24 February 1949 in Newark, New Jersey; second child of Esther Haygood (assistant teacher) of Newark; granddaughter (maternal) of Carrie Haygood and Littleton Haygood, both of Newark; sister: Jamilah Haygood; children: Zakiah Muhammad Benyard and Tahirah Latifa Benyard. Education: Morton St. School, Newark (grades K–1), 1954–1956; Newton St. School, Newark (grade 2), 1957–1958; St. Mary's School, Newark (grades 3–7), 1958–1963; Clinton Place Junior High School, Newark (grades 8–9), 1963–1964; South Side High School, Newark (grade 10), 1964–1965; Weequahic High School, Newark (grades 11–12), 1965–1967; Essex County College, Newark, A.S., social sciences, 1968–1970; Upsala College, East Orange, New Jersey, B.S., social science, Teachers Certificate, 1971–1973; Rutgers University, Newark, M.P.A., 1975–1978; New Jersey Institution of Technology, various courses, 1977–1986. Religion: Al-Islam.

Residence in New Jersey   Newark.

Career   Switchboard operator, Ford Motors, Newark, summer 1967; switchboard operator and clerk, Total Employment and Manpower (Team), Newark, 1967–1968; teacher/advisor, Essex County College, 1974–1976; personnel, Board of Education, Newark, summer 1975; assistant coordinator of mobile units, Department of Parks and Recreation, Newark, 1977; teacher, Board of Education, Newark, 1980–1981; senior comprehensive planner, Office of Planning and Grants, Newark, 1982–1985; teacher (poetry workshops), Essex House (female offenders community-based residency house), Newark, 1984–1985; teacher/advisor, Essex County College, Newark, 1985 to present.

Memberships   PTA; National Council of Negro Women, Newark Chapter; coordinator, Urban Voices, 1980 to present; Newark Alumni Inc.; Mind, Body, Soul Performers Collective.

Publications

  Books

Benyard, Daphne Haygood. *Poetry, Song and Limericks.* Newark, N.J.: Rudy Martin Corridon Press, 1984. 23 [1].

Benyard, Daphne Haygood, and Romelia Jones. *Two Women Poets in Residence.* Orange, N.J.: [The Authors], 1986. 30 leaves.

Benyard, Daphne Haygood. *In Touch.* Newark: Essex County College, 1988. 35.

Haygood-Benyard, Daphne. *The Doors Are Always Open.* East Orange: Daphne's Creations [1994]. 35.

Bio-Bibliographical Source

Benyard, Daphne Haygood. "African American Women Writers in New Jersey: Biographical Questionnaire." Completed by Daphne Haygood Benyard, December 1989.

BEYAH, ISLAH 1956–

Personal   Former name Denise Michelle Brown; complete name Islah Samirah Beyah Ali. Born on 23 May 1956 in Orange, New Jersey; eldest child of Diane Adrienne Brown Gregory (hairdresser) of Orange, and John Howard Pollard (electrician) of Newark, New Jersey; granddaughter (maternal) of Marion Lillian Preston Brown (deceased) of Orange and Ashton Brown (deceased) of Georgia; granddaughter (paternal) of Agnes Burwell Pollard of Bullocks, North Carolina, and Harvey J. Pollard (deceased) of Clarksville, Virginia; sisters: Lisa Nataldo Gregory Newsome, Aileen Louise Pollard, Danette Christine Pollard, Sabriyyah Karrieema Madyun (Pamela Jean Pollard), JoEllen Pollard, and Kim Lovella Pollard; brother: John Howard Pollard, Jr.; husbands: Rauf Sharrief Ali (social worker; divorced) and Qasim Karriem (divorced); children: Rashidah Gregory, Muhaimin Gregory, and Nuri Ali. Education: Oliver St. School (kindergarten), Newark, 1961; Summer Avenue School, New Jersey (grade 1), 1962; St. Michael's (grade 2), 1963; Blessed Sacrament School (grades 3–6), Newark, 1964–1968; Clinton Place Junior High School, Newark (grade 7), 1969; Harris School, Trenton, New Jersey (grade 7–GED), 1970–1971; Essex College of Business, Newark, 1974; Bloomfield College, Bloomfield, New Jersey, 1979; Essex County College, Newark, A.S., 1979–1980, 1985; Georgia State University, Atlanta, Georgia, B.S., social work, 2000. Religion: Al-Islam.

Residence in New Jersey   Orange, 1956–1958; Newark, 1958–1994.

Career   Clerk typist, New Jersey Division of Youth and Family Services, Newark, 1979–1980; secretary to Director of Cultural Affairs, Essex County Division of Parks, Recreation and Cultural Affairs, Newark, 1981; transportation secretary, Essex County Department of Planning and Economic Development, 1981–1983; planning secretary, Essex County Department Planning Division, 1983–1990; notary public of New Jersey, 1980 to present; proprietor, Distinctively Yours Apparel, 1991–1993; proprietor, Imani's Lemonde, 1993–1994; administrative assistant, Morehouse School of Medicine, Atlanta, 1994–1997; proprietor, Halsi Enterprises (Halsi Art Expressions & Halsi Handbags & Accessories), 1997 to present.

Memberships   Newark Writers Guild, 1986 to present; New Bones Writers Workshop, Harlem, New York, 17 April 1983; president, Sister to Sister Divine Sacred Women's Group, 1993 to present.

Awards, Honors, Other Certificates   Certificate, Women in Management, Essex County, 1981; certificate, Paraprofessionals of Essex County, Newark 1982.

Reflections

"My grandmother, Marion Preston Brown, was a familiar [*sic*] woman. She always instilled pride through her own accomplishment. She was a lover of beauty. She inspired in me a sense of support and security. She was comfortable like a warm full bosomed breast, although she didn't have one. Her love was unconditional and enduring and that's carrying with me now.

My life [and] the obstacles in my life, the rungs on the ladders I've had to climb, the pain that I endured, the triumphs, the children, the women in my life. God has always put a woman in my life to guide me since I was very very young. There have always been older women for some type of support system.

[Writers who influenced me include] Sonia Sanchez, [in her] poem "I'm a Talking about the Nation of Islam;" I loved the beat of the poem, the tempo. She made my heart beat, she made chills go up my spine when I read her poem. When I read Claude Brown's *Manchild in the Promise Land* I had to sneak and read it while my grandmother was at work. I remember reading it every night at grandmother's house. *The Autobiography of Malcolm X* influenced me a great deal; [I was encouraged] by his growth."

Publication

Beyah, Islah, and Jaleelah Karriem. *Love Period.* East Orange, N.J.: We Did It Publications, 1986. 43.

Bio-Bibliographical Sources

Beyah, Islah. "African American Women Writers in New Jersey: Bio-graphical Questionnaire." Completed by Islah Beyah, January 1989.

————. Letter to Sibyl E. Moses, 16 August 2001.

BIGGS, UNDRA ELISSA CLAY 1966–

Personal   Born on 18 February 1966 in Trenton, New Jersey; second child of Sarah Linda Clay and Charles Sylvester Clay; sister: Brenda Clay McLeon; husband: Alvin Ronald Biggs, Sr.; children: Miya Shantaz Jones-Biggs and Alvin Ronald Biggs, Jr. Education: Blessed Sacrament School, Trenton, ca. 1972–1980; Trenton Central High School, Trenton, ca. 1980–1984.

Residence in New Jersey   Trenton.

Career   Secretary, Treasury Department, State of New Jersey, Trenton, 1998 to present.

Memberships   Cofounder, Trenton Writers' Guild; Black Women in Publishing; Toastmasters International; volunteer, Angel's Wings.

Reflections

"My being a writer was never a decision. From the joy, completeness and purpose it gives to me, I know that is what God has created me to do. I was its, long before it became mine. As far back as I can remember I have been blessed with a passionate and fertile imagination. As a child I loved my dolls. When I played with them, in my soul, they were alive in a world that I created. I was also, and still am, a big daydreamer. And the daydreams were so good I remember wishing I could share them, as I [had] seen them, with others. Later in my teens I went through a phase of sketch drawing, and in high school I attempted to write my first novel. Therefore, the state of being imaginative and creative has always been a part of my life. But it wasn't until 1993 after some life changing events and the rebuilding of myself as an adult that the imagination and creativity manifested itself into a full-fledged fiction manuscript. God is the Being that I credit for being a writer!"

Publication

Biggs, Undra E. *When You Look At Me*. Riverdale, Md.: La Caille Nous Publishing Company, Inc., 2000. 238.

Bio-Bibliographical Source

Biggs, Undra Elissa Clay. "African American Women Writers in New Jersey: Biographical Questionnaire." Completed by Undra Elissa Clay Biggs, March 2001.

BLANKS, LOUISE SCOTT THOMPSON 1920–

Personal Born on 17 April 1920 in Smithville Township, Marlboro County, South Carolina; the eighth child of Louise Short Scott (housewife) of Marlboro County, South Carolina, and Eli Scott, Sr. (farmer) of Cheraw, South Carolina; granddaughter (maternal) of Lydia Malachi Short of Florida and Alex Short of Cheraw; granddaughter (paternal) of Dolly Scott of Trinidad, West Indies, and Tony Scott, Sr. of Cheraw; sisters: Lena Mae (deceased), Cora Lee (deceased), Shadie, and Daisy; brothers: Eli, Jr. (deceased), Bernard (deceased), and Benjamin; husband: George H. Blanks (operating engineer in construction); children: Rev. Mary L. Thompson, Frances M. Roberts, Cecelia M. Bonner, Gloria J. Ellis, Raymond Thompson (deceased), Edward, and Gary. Education: Linwood Public School, Pittsburgh, Pennsylvania, 1926–1930; Library Public School, Library, Pennsylvania, 1930–1933; David B. Oliver High School, Pittsburgh, 1933–1938. Religion: Baptist; First Union Baptist Church, Newtonville, New Jersey.

Residence in New Jersey Vineland, 1950–1966; Newtonville, 1966 to present.

Career Attendant, charge attendant, cottage supervisor, and later head cottage training supervisor, Vineland State School, Vineland, 1956–1982; accountant and notary public, Newtonville, 1976 to present.

Memberships Associate member, Atlantic Rural Development Coalition; American Society of Notaries, 1982 to present; treasurer of Pastors Aid, 1988–1989, Superintendent of Sunday School, 1988–1989, assistant superintendent of Sunday School, 1989, First Union Baptist Church, Newtonville.

Awards, Honors, Other Certificates Certificate of Merit, Better Traffic Committee of Pittsburgh (for traffic essay), 12 December 1935; Certified Head Cottage Training Supervisor, Vineland State School, 1963; Shelter Manager Certificate, Rutgers State University Extension Division, 1965; certificate, Supervision–Cottage Programs, State of New Jersey Department of Institutions and Agencies, 1965; certificate, National Tax Training School, Monsey, New York, 1975; Certificate of Appreciation for Support through Donations, Special Olympics of New Jersey, 1986–1987; certificate, National Society of Public Accountants, 1 August 1988; certificate, New Jersey Association of Public Accountants, 1989.

Reflections

"I have always been a great lover of nature. I was writing verses since I was ten years old. I had a profound interest in the Bible. God was my first inspiration. After [my sister] Lena learned of this gift, she always encouraged me. The oppression of the Black race and the love for all influenced me. My sister, Shadie Kollock, coauthored a book with Phillip Alegbe (*True Historical Facts about Africa.* New York: Carlton Press, 1961)."

Publication

Thompson, Louise Scott. *Between Earth and Sky.* [Seattle, Wash.: MLT Ma-Lot Publishers], 1982. 93.

Bio-Bibliographical Source

Blanks, Louise Scott Thompson. "African American Women Writers in New Jersey: Biographical Questionnaire." Completed by Louise Blanks, 1 March 1989.

BOOKER, SUE *SEE* THANDEKA

BROWN, DENISE MICHELE *SEE* BEYAH, ISLAH

BROWN, MARGERY WHEELER

Personal　Born in Durham, North Carolina; the youngest of three children of Margaret Hervey Wheeler (housewife) and John Leonidas Wheeler (teacher and business insurance salesman), both of Nicholasville, Kentucky; sister: Ruth Wheeler Lowe (deceased); brother: John Hervey Wheeler (deceased); husband: Richard Earle Brown (deceased); daughter: Janice Brown Carden. Education: Atlanta Public Schools (grades 1–6), Atlanta, Georgia; Atlanta University Preparatory School, Atlanta; Spelman College, Atlanta, B.A., 1932; Ohio State University, Art Studies, 1932–1934, 1935. Religion: Presbyterian.

Margery Wheeler Brown,
courtesy of Margery Wheeler Brown.

Residence in New Jersey Newark, 1946–1951; East Orange, 1951–1972; Orange, 1972 to present.

Career Art instructor, Hillside High School, Durham, 1934–1935; art instructor, Booker T. Washington High School, Atlanta, 1935–1937; art instructor, Spelman College, Atlanta, 1943–1946; art teacher, Newark Public School System, Newark, 1948–1974.

Awards, Honors, Other Certificates Phyllis Wheatley Literary Club Citation "Joy to Many Through Art," 1972; Proclamation, Books for Children and Young People, City of East Orange, New Jersey, 15 November 1982; Citation for Books, Newark Public Library, Newark.

Reflections

"I grew up in Atlanta, a college town, and an interesting, stimulating environment. To balance the effects of segregation and discrimination, Black parents made every effort to provide their children with cultural experiences and interests. Books and music were very much a part of our young lives. We were read to by our parents, taught to read by them, and later they read with us. Emphasis on Black leaders was ever present.

I am sure that this early preoccupation with books and authors created an interest in writing. My father wrote very well, although he never wrote for publication. My writing began easily, unplanned as I wrote observations of situations, vignettes of experiences, not for publication but as accounts of things I found interesting. The children's books simply evolved from this."

Publications

Books

Brown, Margery W. *That Ruby.* [Chicago: Reilly and Lee [1969]. 154.

———. *Animals Made by Me.* New York: G. P. Putnam [1970]. [32], illus.

———. *The Second Stone.* New York: G. P. Putnam [1974]. 124, illus.

———. *Yesterday I Climbed a Mountain.* New York: G. P. Putnam, 1976. [32], illus.

———. *No Jon, No Jon, No!* Boston: Houghton-Mifflin, 1981. 24.

———. *Afro-Bets Book of Colors: Meet the Color Family.* Illustrated by Culverson Blair. 1st ed. Orange, N.J.: Just Us Books, 1991. 1v. (unpaged), illus.

———. *Afro-Bets Book of Shapes.* Illustrations by Culverson Blair. 1st ed. Orange, N.J.: Just Us Books, 1991. 1v. (unpaged).

———. *Baby Jesus Like My Brother.* Illustrations by George Ford. 1st ed. East Orange, N.J.: Just Us Books, 1995. 1v. (unpaged).

Articles

Brown, Margery W. "Speaking of Pictures; Schoolma'am Pokes Gentle Fun at Scenes Every Teacher Knows." *Life Magazine* 37 (20 September 1954): 16–17.

———. "A Little Child Shall Lead Them." *School Arts Magazine* 56, no. 4 (December 1956): 29–30.

———. "Art Classes." *School Arts Magazine* 63, no. 10 (June 1964): 24–28.

———. "You See—This Is the Way It Is!" *School Arts Magazine* 68, no. 8 (April 1969): 30–33.

Illustrated Works

Allred, Gordon T. *Old Crackfoot.* An Astor Book. Illustrated by Margery Brown. New York: I. Obolensky [1965] 116.

———. *Dori, the Mallard.* An Astor Book. Illustrated by Margery Brown. New York: Astor-Honor, 1968. 116.

Stone, Elberta H. *I'm Glad I'm Me.* Illustrated by Margery W. Brown. New York: G. P. Putnam [1971]. [32].

Bio-Bibliographical Sources

Brown, Margery W. "African American Women Writers of New Jersey: Biographical Questionnaire." Completed by Margery W. Brown, summer 1987.

Commire, Anne, ed. *Something About the Author.* Detroit: Gale Research, 1973.

BROWN, MARTHA HURSEY 1924–1997

Personal Born on 20 October 1924 in Bridgeton, New Jersey; joined the ancestors on 17 January 1997. The oldest child of Nancy Christina Wesley Hursey (florist) of Bridgeton and James Wilmer Hursey (stadium custodian) of East New Market, Maryland; granddaughter (maternal) of Martha Wesley of Bridgeton and George Wesley of Salem County, New Jersey; granddaughter (paternal) of Margeret Hursey of Cambridge, Maryland, and Samuel Hursey of Salem, New Jersey; sisters: Christina Miles and Carole Ann Laster; brothers: James Hursey, Jr. and DeEdwin Hursey; husband: Saul T. Brown, Sr. (divorced); children: Sally T. Brown, Sherill T. Brown, and Saul T. Brown, Jr. Education: Bridgeton public schools, 1930–1938; Bridgeton High School, Bridgeton, 1938–1942; State Teachers College, Glassboro, New Jersey, B.A., education, 1946; Drexel University, Philadelphia, Pennsylvania, M.L.S.,

Martha Hursey Brown, courtesy of Sally Brown.

1966; Carnegie-Mellon University, Pittsburgh, Pennsylvania, M.A., history, 1970, and D.A., history, 1976. Religion: African Methodist Episcopal; Mt. Zion A.M.E. Church, Bridgeton.

Residence in New Jersey Bridgeton, 1920–1949 and 1955–1968.

Career Assistant director of public relations, Fisk University, 1947–1948; director of public relations, Tennessee State University, 1948–1949; news reporter, *Norfolk Journal and Guide*, 1949–1952; elementary teacher, Bridgeton Public School, Bridgeton 1955–1965; librarian, Bridgeton Public Schools, Bridgeton, 1966–1968; community relations administrative assistant, American Friends Service Committee; instructor, assistant professor and later associate professor of Afro-American and American women's history, Department of History, Central Michigan University, Mt. Pleasant, Michigan, 1972–1984; coordinator of women's studies, Central Michigan University, 1984; director of libraries and associate professor of history, Langston University, Langston, Oklahoma, 1984 to ca. 1989; associate professor, Old Dominion University, Norfolk, Virginia, 1990–1997.

Memberships   Lifetime member, Usher Board, 1959–1968, Mt. Zion A.M.E. Church, Bridgeton; affiliate member, Salter's Chapel, A.M.E. Church, Langston, 1984 to present; information officer and educational chairperson, 1961–1968, Bridgeton NAACP; founder and president, Women's Civic League, Bridgeton, 1963–1968; secretary, Women's Civic League, Bridgeton, 1964–1969; South Jersey Advisory Committee for Community Projects, American Friends Service Committee, 1965–1969; Advisory Committee, Civil Rights Commission (New Jersey), 1971–1972; Advisory Board, *Great Lakes Review, A Journal of Midwest Culture* (former coeditor), 1984–1985; coach, Langston University Bowl Team for Black History Competition at Cameron University, 1985–1986; American Historical Society; Association of Black Women Historians; Black Heritage Committee, Oklahoma Historical Society, 1984 to present; Executive Committee, Association of Black Women Historians, 1985 to present.

Awards, Honors, Other Certificates   NDEA Fellowship, Educational Media, 1967; TTT Fellowship, 1969; U.S. Office of Education, Fellowship (research), 1970; Ford Foundation Fellowship for Ethnic Studies, 1971; Honor Society, Phi Kappa Phi Graduate Chapter, 1972; Citation for Distinguished Service, Michigan Reformatory at Ionia Junior Chamber of Commerce, 1977; Michigan Council for the Humanities Grant (cultural series for inmates at the Ionia Reformatory, Ionia, Michigan), 1977–1978; Central Michigan University Creative Endeavors Award for Premier Display, 1978–1979; National Endowment for Humanities Grant, Summer Seminar. Research Project: "Attitudes Toward the Buffalo Soldier, 1867–1891," summer 1980; National Endowment for Humanities, Summer Seminar for College Teachers, Duke University. Project: Oral History Interviews on Changing Roles of Black Women in the Church, summer 1983.

Reflections

"I have always been very conscious of racial stereotypes and the resulting denial of opportunities. When I was a junior in high school, long before Blacks were admitted into professional sports, I greatly admired Black collegiate athletes. I decided then that I wanted to be a writer so I could let the world know about these outstanding young men. . . . Without question the greatest thing that ever happened to me was to be born to parents who were supportive of my ambitions and great believers in education. (All five of their children hold college degrees.)

A decided inspiration in my professional life was Thomas L. Dabney, a fellow news reporter, whom I met while working for the *Norfolk Journal and Guide* in the 1950s. To me, he personified the struggles of Blacks in the twentieth century. He had lost and never regained his public education job in 1929 because he had worked for equal salaries for Blacks. His life was a constant fight against injustice. Mr. Dabney had visited Russia, fought in France in World War II, and had interacted with persons like W.E.B. DuBois and Carter G. Woodson, the initiator of the Black History Week. He could relate numerous anecdotes concerning prominent Blacks who had lived from 1900 through the 1970s.

Publications

Book

Brown, Martha Hursey, Eugene Levy, and Roland M. Smith. *Faces of America*. New York: Harper and Row, Publishers, Inc., 1982. x, 726.

Articles

Brown, Martha Hursey. "A Listing of Non-Print Materials on Black Women." In *All the Women are White, All the Blacks are Men, but Some of Us Are Brave: Black Women's Studies,* edited by Gloria T. Hull, Patricia Bell Scott, and Barbara Smith, 307–326. Old Westbury, N.Y.: Feminist Press, 1982.

Brown, Martha Hursey. "Clothing." In *Dictionary of Afro-American Slavery,* edited by Randall M. Miller and John David Smith, 117–121. New York: Greenwood Press, 1988.

Bio-Bibliographical Sources

Brown, Martha Hursey. "African American Women Writers in New Jersey: Biographical Questionnaire." Completed by Martha Hursey Brown, spring 1987.

"Memorial Service of Dr. Martha H. Brown . . . January 30, 1997." Norfolk, Va.: New Mount Zion African Methodist Episcopal Church, 1997. [Obituary]

BROWN, VASHTI PROCTOR 1905–1995

Personal   Born on 9 October 1905 in Atlanta, Georgia; joined the ancestors in October, 1995, Montclair, New Jersey; the sixth child of Adelaide L. Davis Proctor (1870–1945) (musician, teacher) of Nashville, Tennessee, and Henry Hugh Proctor (1868–1933) (Congregational minister: First Congregational Church, Atlanta; Nazarene Congregational Church, Brooklyn, New York) of near Fayetteville, Tennessee; granddaughter (maternal) of Harriet Davis and Dock Davis, both of Nashville; granddaughter (paternal) of Hannah Weatherly and Richard Proctor; sisters: Muriel Proctor Holmes (deceased) and Lillian Proctor Falls; brothers: Roy Crazath Proc-

Vashti Proctor Brown, courtesy of Newark Public Library.

tor (deceased), Henry Proctor (deceased), and Richard Proctor (deceased); husband: John Alexander Brown (deceased) of New York, New York; Education: Fisk University, Nashville, B.A., 1927; Hunter College, New York. Religion: Unitarian Church; Unitarian Church of Montclair, Montclair.

Residence in New Jersey   Montclair, ca. 1957–1995.

Career   Teacher, reading, New York City and Brooklyn Public School Systems (elementary and junior high schools); reading consultant, New York City Board of Education's Junior High School Reading Project; clinical consultant, Manhattan Reading Center, New York.

Memberships   Fisk Alumni Club, New York.

Publications

Books

Brown, Vashti, and Jack Brown. *Proudly We Hail.* Illustrated by Don Miller. Boston: Houghton Mifflin, 1968. x, 118.

———. *Proudly We Hail; Teacher's Guide.* Boston: Houghton Mifflin, 1969. 30.

Brown, Vashti, Jack Brown, and Margaret Lalor. *Above the Crowd.* Illustrated by Don Miller. Boston: Houghton Mifflin, 1970. vii, 152.

———. *Out in Front.* Illustrated by Don Miller. Boston: Houghton Mifflin, 1971. vii, 150.

———. *Stronger Than the Rest. Houghton Mifflin Basic Education Program Series.* Illustrated by Don Miller. Boston: Houghton Mifflin, 1971. vii, 152.

Bio-Bibliographical Sources

Alumni Directory of Fisk University 1875–1930. Nashville, Tenn.: Fisk University, 1930.

Brown, Vashti Proctor. Interview by Sibyl E. Moses. Montclair, New Jersey, fall 1986.

Caldwell, A. B., ed. *History of the American Negro and His Institutions.* Georgia edition. Atlanta.: A. B. Caldwell Publishing Co., 1917.

Johns, Altona Trent. "Henry Hugh Proctor." *The Black Perspective in Music* 3, no.1 (spring 1975): 25–32.

U.S. Social Security Administration. Application for Social Security Account Number, completed by Vashti Proctor Brown, 9 September 1957.

BRYANT, IRENE MARTIN 1931–

Personal   Born on 10 April 1931 in Morristown, New Jersey; seventh child of Celeste Martin Martin (housewife) and Isaac Martin, Sr. (businessman), both of Jenkinsville, South Carolina; granddaughter (maternal) of Lannie Martin and Archie Martin, both of Jenkinsville; granddaughter (paternal) of Vera Martin and Peter Martin, both of Jenkinsville; sisters: Kate Martin Patterson, Venia Mae Martin, and Amy Martin Anderson; brothers: Jack Martin (deceased), T. D. Martin (deceased), Richard Delaine Martin, and Isaac Martin, Jr.; husband: William L. Bryant (recreation); children: Yolanda B. Joyner (teacher), Ingrid B. French (lawyer), Iris Bryant (deceased), and Michael Bryant (laborer). Education: Collinsville

Elementary School, Morristown (grades K–6); Alfred Vail Elementary School, Morristown (grades 7–9), 1943–1946; Morristown High School, Morristown, 1946–1949; Dover Business School, Dover, New Jersey, certified business courses. Religion: African Methodist Episcopal; Bethel A.M.E. Church, Morristown.

Residence in New Jersey   Morristown, 1931–1972; Mendham, 1973–1986.

Career   Secretary (various agencies), Morristown.

Memberships   NAACP, Morristown; Urban League, Morristown; musician (organized, directed, and played), Gospel Chorus, Bethel A.M.E. Church, Morristown, 1976.

Irene Martin Bryant.
Photograph by Olan Mills
Portrait Studio.

Reflections

"Whenever I've been asked to write about my childhood or adult experiences the one thing that comes to mind is the song "Ordinary People" (words by Danniebelle Hall). My life with my family was very modest, and all of my life I have been involved in church. My pastor, Rev. A. Lewis Williams encouraged me to have the book *Iris* published. When I decided to write about her because we thought she was one of God's "special children," I never dreamed of it being published, but Pastor Williams thought it should be shared by others and it was well received. I just think of myself as one of those "Ordinary People" that God used. I know that my book of *Iris* has helped many families and I am thankful that it had a purpose.

Publication

Bryant, Irene. *Iris.* New York: Carlton Press [1973]. 64.

Bio-Bibliographical Source

Bryant, Irene Martin. "African American Women Writers in New Jersey: Biographical Questionnaire." Completed by Irene Martin Bryant, February 1989.

Burnett, Gracie Diane 1960–

Personal   Born on 28 August 1960 in Camden, New Jersey; seventh child of Gracie Smith Burnett (nurse assistant) of Savannah, Georgia, and Prince Burnett of Macon, Georgia; granddaughter (maternal) of Louvenia Smith and Clayton Smith, both of Georgia; granddaughter (paternal) of Louvenia Burnett and Dock Burnett, both of Georgia; sisters: Cynthia M. Still, Patricia A. Kamara, Linda D. Vogues (deceased), and Vickie L. Burnett; brothers: Jerome M. Burnett, Larry M. Burnett, and Prince L. Burnett.

Education: Cooper's Poynt School, Camden, 1966–1971; Camden High School, Camden, 1974–1978; Rutgers University, Camden, B.A. Religion: Baptist.

Residence in New Jersey   Camden; Mt. Holly.

Reflections

"My writing in childhood [was stimulated by] . . . proverbs. The English of youngsters in southern New Jersey needed [more] imagery or artistry. The community [workers and Black cultural leaders] were not afraid to ask the school children [to write], and so I wrote for a couple of contests and newspapers."

Publication

Burnett, Gracie D. *Messages about Genuine Images.* New York: Vantage Press, 1986. 31.

Bio-Bibliographical Source

Burnett, Gracie D. "African American Women Writers in New Jersey: Biographical Questionnaire." Completed by Gracie D. Burnett [November 2001], 3.

BUTLER, ANNA LAND 1901–1987

Anna Land Butler,
courtesy of Joan Land Smith.

Personal   Born on 7 October 1901 in Philadelphia, Pennsylvania; joined the ancestors on 19 March 1987 in Atlantic City, New Jersey; daughter of Edith Frances Jones Land of Atlantic City and John Weaver Land, Sr. (d. 1945); sister: Edith Dempsey; brother: John Weaver Land, Jr.; husband: Floyd Butler (real estate salesman and manager); child: Maurice Alexander Hayes, Jr. (deceased). Education: Elementary schools, Atlantic City; Atlantic City High School, Atlantic City; Trenton State Teachers College, Trenton, New Jersey, 1922; Temple University, Philadelphia, 1953; Maryland State College, 1942–1945. Religion: Episcopal; St. Augustine's Episcopal Church, Atlantic City.

Residence in New Jersey   Atlantic City, 1902–1987.

Career   Teacher, Atlantic City Public Schools, 1922–1964 (taught many years at New Jersey Avenue Elementary School); newspaper correspondent, *Pittsburgh Courier,* Pennsylvania, 1936–1965; editor, *Responsibility,* official organ of the National Association of Negro Business and Professional Women's Clubs, Inc., 1955–1959; reporter, *Philadelphia Tribune,* 1965–1972; associate editor, *Eastern Area National Links Journal,* 1967–1970; head instructor and director, Morris Child Care Center, 1969–1972.

Memberships National Education Association; New Jersey Education Association; executive board and life member, Atlantic City Education Association, 1962–1964; Education Writers Association; Bermuda Writers Club, 1961; Trenton (alumni) Seashore Club; charter member, Phi Delta Kappa National Society, Iota Chapter; member, Planning Committee for Bal Masque, New Jersey Federation of Colored Women's Clubs; Theta Phi Lambda Sorority; Philadelphia Catholic Poetry Society, 1960–1966; charter member and board director, Philadelphia Cotillion Society; Heritage House; president, Atlantic City Study Center; Seaboard Council Heritage House; Northside Business and Professional Women's Club Inc.; Mu-Lit-So Sodality; Atlantic City Chapter Links Inc.; American Poetry Society, New York; vice president, Atlantic District Episcopal Churchwomen, Diocese of New Jersey; district chairman, Atlantic District New Jersey Episcopal Diocese; recording secretary and board member, St. Augustine Episcopal Church.

Awards, Honors, Other Certificates Creative Achievement Award, National Links, Inc., 1960; Veteran Teacher Award, New Jersey Organization of Teachers, 1961; Achievement Award, Northside Business and Professional Women, 1963; Legion of Honors Award, Chapel of Four Chaplains, 1963; Sach's Certificate of Recognition, 1963; Appreciation Award, National Links, Inc., 1964; Theta Phi Lambda Sorority Women's Showcase Award, Merit Award, 1964; National Association Sojourner Truth Award, 1966; Certificate of Merit, United Jaycees, 1967; Black Women's Community Service Award, Alpha Kappa Alpha, Theta Kappa Omega Chapter, 1970; Citation Creative Writing, New Orleans, 1972; Certificate of Award of Achievement, Outstanding Negro Woman, Imperial Daughters of Isis, 1972; Certificate of Appreciation, National Links, Inc., 1972; President's Service Award, Links, Inc. Atlantic City Chapter, 1973; Citation Religious Leadership, Women of Valor, Union of American Hebrew Congregations, Cultural Services, 1975; Eugene Wayman Jones, Cultural Civil Award, 1975.

Publications

Butler, Anna M. Land. *Album of Love Letters–Unsent.* New York: Margent Press, 1952. [xi, 13–63].

———. *Touchstone.* Wilmington, Del.: Delaware Poetry Center, 1961. 29.

———. *High Noon.* Charleston, Ill.: Prairie Press Books, 1971. 56.

Bio-Bibliographical Source

Butler, Anna M. Land. "Resume." [undated]. 3.

Social Security Death Index. "Anna Butler." Available: <http://www.ancestry.com> Accessed 7 June 2000.

Who's Who Among Black Americans, 1988. 5th ed. Lake Forest, Ill.: Educational Communications, Inc., 1988.

BUTLER, REBECCA BATTS 1910–2000

Rebecca Batts Butler,
courtesy of Trenton Photographers.

Personal   Born on 29 November 1910 in Norfolk, Virginia; joined the ancestors in 2000; second child of Gussie Vaughn Batts Overton (housewife and mother) of Norfolk and William Batts (saw mill operator) of Emporia, Virginia; stepfather: Andrew Overton; granddaughter (paternal) of Jesse Batts; husbands: Robert Butler (railroad troubleshooter; deceased) and Ellis Williams (personnel administrator); children: Roy Batts and Roland Batts (deceased). Education: John Woolcox Elementary School, Norfolk, 1917–1925; Booker T. Washington High School, Norfolk 1925–1929; Virginia State Normal School, Petersburg, Virginia, 1933; Glassboro State College, Glassboro, New Jersey, B.S., 1944; Temple University, Philadelphia, Pennsylvania, M.S., 1950; Temple University, Ed.D., 1965; Rutgers University, New Brunswick, New Jersey, 1950–1965. Religion: Baptist.

Residence in New Jersey   Cherry Hill.

Career   Teacher, Charlotte County, Virginia, 1930–1932, 1933–1934; elementary school teacher, Norfolk, 1936–1937; elementary school teacher, Camden, New Jersey; secondary English teacher, Camden; guidance counselor, Camden; supervisor guidance counselor, Camden; N.J. State Department; adult director and graduate instructor, Glassboro State College, 1969; adjunct professor, department administration, Glassboro State College, 1970.

Memberships   Member, board of directors, and chairperson, Camden County American Red Cross; member, board of directors, Camden County Visiting Nurses Association; president, Planned Parenthood, Greater Camden Area; vice president and research director, Association for Study of Afro-American Life and History; fannel and association member, United Way, Camden County; president, National Sorority Phi Delta Kappa, Eta Chapter; stewardess board, Chestnut Street U.A.M.E. Church; president, Negro Business and Professional Women, Camden; board of directors and national secretary, National Council for the Advancement of Citizenship; member, board of directors, American Association of Retired Persons; Defense Advisory Committee on Women in the Services; International Platform Association; national co-chairperson on aging, National Association of Negro Business and Professional Women's Clubs, Inc.; national coordinator of "Second Careers," National Sorority of Phi Delta Kappa,

Inc.; local organizer and board of directors, National Hook-up of Black Women, New Jersey; participating delegate, White House Conference on Aging, 1981; petitioner, Congressional Finance Committee on behalf of Social Security, 1981; lobbyist, Capital Hill effort to curtail costs of medical care, 1984.

Awards, Honors, Other Certificates Teacher of the Year Award, N.J. Organization of Teachers, 1953; Appreciation Award, Spanish Equivalency Teachers and Students of Camden, N.J., 1971; Community Service Award, Southern, N.J. Opportunities Industrialization Center (OIC), 1972; Service Award, Chestnut Street, U.A.M.E. Church, 1973; editor-in-chief, *The Krinnon: The Official Organ of the National Sorority of Phi Delta Kappa, Inc.,* 1973–1977; Outstanding Achievement, New Jersey Federation of Colored Women's Clubs, Inc., 1974; Service Award, Spanish Speaking Population of Camden, N.J., 1974; Thanks Award, Camden Adult Education Staff and Students, 1974; Commendation Award, N.J. State Department of Education, Division of Field Services, 1974; Meritorious Service Award, National Association of Negro Business and Professional Women's Clubs, Inc., 1975; Sojourner Truth Award, Camden and Vicinity Club of the Association Negro Business and Professional Women, 1976; Community Service Award, United Way of Camden County, 1976; Volunteer Service Award, Fannie J. Coppin Temple #57, 1976; Educational Achievement Award, N.J. State Improved Benevolent Protective Order of the Elks of the World, 1977; National Association of Negro Business and Professional Women's Clubs, Inc., 1977; Outstanding Alumni, Glassboro State College, 1978; Service Recognition, Association for Study of Afro-American Life and History, 1982; Humanitarian Award, General Conference of U.A.M.E. Churches, New Jersey; Certificate of Merit, Council for Advancement of Citizenship, 1983; editor-in-chief, *Perspectives* (annual magazine of the Eastern Region, The National Sorority of Phi Delta Kappa, Inc.), 1983–1986.

Reflections

"My most memorable childhood experience was sitting on my father's knee while he read to me from the Bible. I shall always remember his joy when he discovered that I could read the Bible and newspaper. He was a great debater and often participated in debates held at Shiloh Baptist Church, Norfolk, Virginia, where he was a deacon and superintendent of the Sunday School. He died when I was seven years old, but instilled in me the drive to achieve. My mother also taught basic values by which I live: honesty, cleanliness, the importance of earnings one way."

Publications

Butler, Rebecca Batts. *Profiles of Outstanding Blacks in South Jersey during the 1950's, 1960's, 1970's.* [Camden?]: Reynolds Publishers, Inc., 1980. 52, illus.

———. *Portraits of Black Role Models in the History of Southern New Jersey.* [Camden?]: Acme Craftsmen Publishers, 1985. 115, illus.

————. *Second Career Profiles: A Directory of Human Resources.* N.p.: BEGP Publishers, 1985. 109.

————. *Bronze Stars of the Delaware Valley.* Deptford, N.J.: CC Publishers, 2000. vii, 377.

Bio-Bibliographical Sources

Butler, Rebecca Batts. "African American Women Writers in New Jersey Project: Biographical Questionnaire." Completed by Rebecca Batts Butler, 18 October 1985.

————. "Resume." [undated]. 3.

BUTLER, SALLY CENTRAL 1925–

Sally Central Butler,
courtesy of Sally Central Butler.

Personal Born 15 June 1925 in Halifax County, Virginia; oldest child of Gladys Farmer Smith (housewife) of Vernon Hills (Halifax County), Virginia, and Albert Smith of Halifax County, Virginia; granddaughter (maternal) of Andrew Farmer; sister: Bessie Ransome; brother: Thomas Smith; husband: Booker Butler, Jr.; children: Jenell Sparks, Wayne Sparks, and Anekia Sistrunk. Education Woodstown High School, Woodstown, New Jersey. Religion: Baptist; Morning Star Baptist Church, Woodstown.

Residence in New Jersey Woodstown, 1940s; Salem; Carney's Point, 1970 to present.

Memberships President, Morning Star Baptist Church Missionary Circle, Woodstown.

Career Licensed practical nurse (private duty), New Jersey (36 years); licensed practical nurse, Memorial Hospital, Salem County, New Jersey.

Publications

Butler, Sally C. *Poems of Faith and Inspiration.* N.p., n.d. [11].

————. *Poems of Faith and Inspiration.* N.p. [after 1989]. [24].

————. *Poems of Faith and Inspiration.* [Carneys Point, N.J.: The Author], 1999? 14.

Bio-Bibliographical Sources

Butler, Sally C. Interview by Sibyl E. Moses. Carneys Point, New Jersey, September 2001.

————. Telephone conversation with Sibyl E. Moses, 19 April 2001.

CAMPBELL, BERTHA GEORGETTA MERRITT 1929–

Personal Born on 7 February 1929 in Clinton (Sampson County), North Carolina; oldest child of Sadie Herring Merritt (elementary school teacher) of Clinton and first-born daughter of the second family of William Edward Merritt (Baptist minister, elementary school principal, and newspaper editor) of Waycross, North Carolina; granddaughter (maternal) of Rosa Ella Herring and George B. Herring, both of North Carolina; granddaughter (paternal) of Harriet Merritt Ezzell (1842–1928) and Bill Marley Merritt, both of North Carolina; sister: Dr. Rena Ercelle Merritt Bancroft (junior college president); half sisters: Ernestine Merritt Lucas (teacher) and Pauline Merritt Solice (teacher; de-

Georgetta Merritt Campbell.
Photograph by Martin Kale.

ceased); half brother: Dr. William Edward Merritt (dentist); husband: Dr. Ulysses Campbell (dentist, divorced, deceased); child: Ulysses Edward Campbell. Education: Sampson County Training School (elementary and secondary school), Sampson County, North Carolina; Johnson C. Smith University, Charlotte, North Carolina, A.B., 1944–1947; North Carolina Central University, Durham, North Carolina, B.L.S., 1947–1948; Syracuse University (summers), Syracuse, New York, M.L.S., 1952–1956; Fairleigh Dickinson University, Rutherford, New Jersey, Ed.D., 1975–1978. Religion: African Methodist Episcopal.

Residence in New Jersey East Orange, Orange, and Montclair, 1956 to present.

Career Cataloger, University of Arkansas, Pine Bluff, Arkansas, 1948–1949; elementary school librarian, Public School System, Charlotte, 1949–1952; serials librarian, Texas Southern University, Houston, Texas, 1950; reference and government documents librarian, Morgan State University, Baltimore, Maryland, 1952–1957; children's librarian, West Orange Public Library, West Orange, New Jersey, 1957–1959; elementary school librarian, Bergen Street School, Newark, New Jersey, 1959–1960; assistant librarian, Bloomfield Senior High School, Bloomfield, New Jersey, 1960–1963; librarian, Bloomfield Senior High School, Bloomfield, 1964–1985; lecturer, Seton Hall University, South Orange, New Jersey, 1971–1975; adjunct faculty member, Caldwell College, Caldwell, New

23

Jersey; 1972–1975; media coordinator, West Orange Public Schools, West Orange, December 1985–1998.

Memberships American Library Association; New Jersey School Media Association (formerly on executive board), New Jersey Education Association; Bloomfield Education Association; American Society of Indexers; American Association of University Women, Bloomfield Chapter (formerly on executive board); Search and Screen Committee, Institute for Leadership Studies, Fairleigh Dickinson University; Media Workshop Committee, Seton Hall University; board of directors, Oakeside-Bloomfield Cultural Center. Former Memberships: League of Women Voters of Orange and East Orange; Town and Country Women, Inc.; Board of Directors, Leaguers, Inc., Newark; Board of Trustees, Community Council of the Oranges and Maplewood, New Jersey; supervisory board, Israel Memorial A.M.E. Church Credit Union; Essex County Dental Society Auxiliary; NAACP; Organization of Women for Legal Awareness; Urban League of Essex County; Delta Sigma Theta Sorority, Inc., Montclair Chapter; alumni associations of colleges attended; Montclair YWCA.

Reflections

> "My father was the most influential person in my life. When he died at age sixty-six (I was 11), his influence continued through my mother's continued speaking of him. Also, my brother and my sister-in-law's active interest in my welfare influenced me a great deal. My mother's family was quite involved too in educational endeavors. My mother's grandfather who had been a slave established the first school for Black people in Sampson County prior to the Civil War."

Publications

Book

Campbell, Georgetta Merritt. *Extant Collection of Early Black Newspapers: A Research Guide to the Black Press, 1880–1915 with an Index to the Boston Guardian, 1902–1904.* Troy, N.Y.: The Whitson Publishing Company, 1981. 401.

Article

Campbell, Georgetta M. "Library Orientation for College Freshmen." *Library Journal* 81, no. 10 (15 May 1956): 1224–1225.

Bio-Bibliographical Sources

Campbell, Georgetta Merritt. "African American Women Writers New Jersey: Biographical Questionnaire." Completed by Georgetta M. Campbell, winter 1989.

———. Conversations with Sibyl E. Moses. Newark and Montclair, New Jersey. Winter 1989, summer 1997, summer 1998.

———. "Resume." [undated]. 3.

CAMPBELL, GEORGETTA *SEE* CAMPBELL, BERTHA GEORGETTA MERRITT

CARMICHAEL, MARY ELIZABETH CORNISH 1935–

Personal   Born on 7 August 1935 in Port Norris, New Jersey; daughter of Lydia Mae Douglas Cornish (domestic and church pianist) of Virginia and John Edward Cornish, Sr. (seaman and chauffeur) of Maryland; granddaughter (maternal) of Lillian Douglas and Alexander Douglas, both of the eastern shore, Maryland; granddaughter (paternal) of Mary Cornish and Samuel Cornish, both of the western shore, Maryland; sisters: Rose, Cora, Gertrude, Renee, Maxine; brothers: John, Joseph, Samuel, George, Thelbert, Howard; married and divorced; children: Alan David Carmichael, Amy Sue Carmichael, and Anne Marie Carmichael. Education: Robbinstown School, Port Norris, New Jersey (grades K–2); Port Norris Elementary

Mary Cornish Carmichael, courtesy of Mary Cornish Carmichael.

School, Port Norris (grades 3–8); Millville High School, Millville, New Jersey, 1949–1952; Morgan State College, Baltimore, B.A., 1956; State University of Iowa, 1957; Glassboro State College, Glassboro, New Jersey (graduate studies in special education). Religion: United Methodist; John Wesley United Methodist Church.

Residence in New Jersey   Port Norris, 1935–1964; 1968 to present.

Career   Restaurant worker, Wildwood, New Jersey, and cannery worker during college; clerk/typist, office of the dean of women, Morgan State College, Baltimore; elementary, secondary and special education teacher in Port Norris, Vineland, Camden, Fairfield Township and Bridgeton, New Jersey, 1956 to present.

Memberships   Member and organist, men's chorus, John Wesley United Methodist Church; Commercial Township Board of Education; delegate to the NJSBA Assembly; chairperson and member, Commercial Township Zoning Board of Adjustments; Commercial Township Economic and Development Council; New Jersey Association of Black Educators; New Jersey Education Association.

Awards, Honors, Other Certificates   Community Service Award, Jack and Jill of America, Inc., Cumberland-Salem Chapter and Club #11, 1985.

Reflections

"My earliest memories of my mother included watching her make fantastic drawings to illustrate a story which she had read or created. By the time I entered kindergarten, I could read many of the stories in the old primer that was a prized possession. I always thought she was a genius because she also played an autoharp, a mandolin, a ukulele, a banjo, and the piano. My father was somewhat of a perfectionist. He was capable of doing many things that required skill and dexterity. He always encouraged us not to accept less than our best in all situations."

Publication

Carmichael, Mary Cornish. *Oh, Boy! Joy Roy!* New York: Vantage Press, 1984. 23.

Bio-Bibliographical Source

Carmichael, Mary E. C. "African American Women Writers in New Jersey Project: Biographical Questionnaire." Completed by Mary Carmichael, June 1989.

Clarke, Cheryl Lynn 1947–

*Cheryl Lynn Clarke,
courtesy of Cheryl Lynn Clarke.*

Personal   Born on 16 May 1947 in Washington, D.C.; daughter of Edna Mae Higgins Payne Clarke (District of Columbia government employee) of Marion, North Carolina, and James Sheridan Clarke (federal government employee) of Washington, D.C.; granddaughter (maternal) of Pearl Miller Higgins and William Higgins, both of North Carolina; granddaughter (paternal) of Bess Clarke and Sheridan Clarke, both of Washington, D.C.; sisters: Pearl Payne Cray Witherspoon, Breena Clarke Cooper, and Victoria Clarke Wood; brother: Charles T. Payne (deceased); life partner: Barbara J. Balliet, Ph.D. Education: St. Gabriel's Catholic School, Washington, D.C., 1954–1961; Immaculate Conception Academy, Washington, D.C., 1961–1965; Howard University, Washington, D.C., B.A., English, 1969; Rutgers University, New Brunswick, New Jersey, M.A., English, 1974; Rutgers University, New Brunswick, M.S.W., 1980; Rutgers University, New Brunswick, Ph.D., 2000.

Residence in New Jersey   New Brunswick, 1969–1986; Jersey City, 1986 to present.

Career   Teacher-counselor, Urban University Program, Rutgers University, New Brunswick, 1970–1974; lecturer, English Department,

Rutgers University, 1972–1974; coordinator of intake and assessment, Comprehensive Employment and Training Administration (CETA), Middlesex County, New Jersey, 1974–1978; staff development consultant (part-time), Alfonso Associates, Jersey City, New Jersey, 1979–1986; outreach worker (part-time), Community Outreach Program for Senior Adults, University of Medicine and Dentistry of New Jersey, Piscataway, New Jersey, 1980–1983; assistant coordinator of student activities, Office of Student Development and Campus Centers, Rutgers University, New Brunswick, 1980–1989; assistant dean for special populations and affiliated students, Office of Student Life, Rutgers University, New Brunswick, 1989–1992; director, Diverse Community Affairs and Lesbian-Gay Concerns, Rutgers University, New Brunswick, 1992 to present.

Memberships   Editor, Editorial Collective of *Conditions Magazine,* Brooklyn, New York, 1981–1990; board of directors, New York Women Against Rape, 1985–1988; founding member and fundraiser, New Jersey Women and AIDS Network, New Brunswick, 1987–1990; co-chairperson, board of directors , Center for Gay and Lesbian Studies, City University of New York Graduate Center, New York, 1990–1992; Board of Directors, Aestrea Lesbian Action Foundation, New York, 1997 to present.

Awards, Honors, Other Certificates   Nominated for 1994 Lambda Award for poetry, for *"Experimental Love."*

Reflections

"Black women writers of the late 20th century encouraged me to write by their exquisite examples. I majored in English, went to college during the Black Power/Black Arts Movements, and saw the power of poetry and other words used powerfully. In 1973, I came out as a lesbian and continued to write and read my poetry, carrying with me into feminist the assertiveness and boldness I learned during the Black Power era. I still use [and] believe in the power of words, writing, and writers (with the correct politics, that is). My sister, Breena Clarke, published a book entitled *River Cross My Heart* in 1999, and it was picked by the Oprah Book Club. A defining moment for me as a writer was when I self-published my first book of poems.

Publications

Books

Clarke, Cheryl. *Narratives: Poems in the Tradition of Black Women.* Drawings by Gaia. New Brunswick, N.J.: Sister Books, 1982. 51. Reprint, Latham, N.Y.: Kitchen Table—Women of Color Press, 1983, 1985, with the addition of "The Johnny Cake" and "Cantaloupe."

———. *Living as a Lesbian: Poetry.* Ithaca, N.Y.: Firebrand Books, 1986. 94.

———. *Humid Pitch: Narrative Poetry.* Ithaca, N.Y.: Firebrand Books, 1989. 129.

———. *Experimental Love: Poetry.* Ithaca, N.Y.: Firebrand Books, 1993. 84.

Poetry, Essays, and Literary Criticism

Clarke, Cheryl. "Lesbianism: An Act of Resistance." In *This Bridge Called My Back: Writings By Radical Women of Color,* edited by Cherrie Moraga and Gloria Anzaldua, n.p. Watertown, Mass.: Persephone Press, 1981. Reprint, Latham, N.Y.: Kitchen Table–Women of Color Press, 1984.

———. "The Failure to Transform: Homophobia in the Black Community." In *Home Girls: A Black Feminist Anthology,* edited by Barbara Smith, 190–201. Latham, N.Y.: Kitchen Table–Women of Color Press, 1983.

———. "Women of Summer." In *Home Girls: A Black Feminist Anthology,* edited by Barbara Smith, 222–246. Latham, N.Y.: Kitchen Table–Women of Color Press, 1983.

———. "Leavings." *Thirteenth Moon* 8, nos. 1 & 2 (1984): 133–141.

———. "IV." *Conditions* no. 11/12 (1985): 90.

———. "Kittatinny." *Conditions* (no. 11/12 (1985): 93.

———. "Living as a Lesbian at 35." *Conditions* no. 11/12 (1985): 91–92.

———. "Nothing." *Conditions* no. 11/12 (1985): 94.

———. "*Blue Heat* by Alexis De Veaux." *Conditions* no. 13 (1986): 154–158.

———. "gothic tourism." In *Tourist Attractions* (Top Stories, #25–26), edited by Anne Turyn and Brian Wallis, n.p. New York: Top Stories, 1987.

———. "If You Black Get Back." In *Ain't I a Woman,* edited by Illona Linthwaite, 5–6. London: Virago Press, 1987.

———. "The Space in Me Where Baldwin Lives." *Gay Community News* 15, no. 23 (20–26 December 1987): 8, 11.

——— (contributor). "1988: Some Thoughts from 15 Artists" by Gary Indiana. *The Village Voice* (19 January 1988): 95–96.

———. "Ann Petry and the Isolation of Being Other." *Belles Lettres: A Review of Books by Women* (fall 1989): n.p.

———. "Silence and Invisibility: Costly Metaphors." *Gay Community News* (19–25 February 1989): 7–8, 12.

———. "Bulletin." In *Bluestones and Salt Hay: An Anthology of Contemporary New Jersey Poets,* edited by Joel Lewis, 30–31. New Brunswick, N.J.: Rutgers University Press, 1990.

———. "Jazz Poem for Morristown, N.J. " In *Bluestones and Salt Hay: An Anthology of Contemporary New Jersey Poets,* edited by Joel Lewis, 29–30. New Brunswick, N.J.: Rutgers University Press, 1990.

———. "Knowing the Danger of Going There Anyway." In *Sojourner: The Women's Forum* (September 1990): 14–15.

———. "The Layoff." In *Bluestones and Salt Hay: An Anthology of Contemporary New Jersey Poets,* edited by Joel Lewis, 32–33. New Brunswick, N.J.: Rutgers University Press, 1990.

———. " 'Of Althea and Flaxie.' " In *Bluestones and Salt Hay: An Anthology of Contemporary New Jersey Poets,* edited by Joel Lewis, 27–28. New Brunswick, N.J.: Rutgers University Press, 1990.

———. ". . . She Still Wrote Out the Word Kotex on a Torn Piece of Paper Wrapped Up in a Dollar." In *Conversant Essays: Contemporary Poets and*

Poetry, edited by James McCorkle, 443–458. Detroit: Wayne State University Press, 1990.

———. "Cucumber." In *Serious Pleasure: Lesbian Erotic Stories and Poetry,* edited by Sheba Collective, 111–112. Pittsburgh, Pa.: Cleis Press, 1991.

———. "The Everyday Life of Black Lesbian Sexuality." In *InVersions: Writing by Dykes, Queers & Lesbians,* edited by Betsy Warland, 37–44. Vancouver: Press Gang Publishers, 1991.

———. "Great Expectations." In *Serious Pleasure: Lesbian Erotic Stories and Poetry,* edited by Sheba Collective, 69–70. Pittsburgh, Pa.: Cleis Press, 1991.

——— (contributor). " 'The Homoerotic Other,' Gay Voices, Black America: Essays from Twelve Black Gay and Lesbian Writers." *Advocate* (12 February 1991): 42.

———. "Living as a Lesbian Rambling." *Serious Pleasure: Lesbian Erotic Stories and Poetry,* edited by Sheba Collective, 171–173. Pittsburgh, Pa.: Cleis Press, 1991.

———. "Living as a Lesbian Underground." In *Serious Pleasure: Lesbian Erotic Stories and Poetry,* edited by Sheba Collective, 5–7. Pittsburgh, Pa.: Cleis Press, 1991.

———. " 'Making Face, Making Soul—Haciendo Caras: Creative and Critical Perspectives by women of Color' by Gloria Anzaldua." *Bridges: A Journal for Jewish Feminists and Our Friends* (spring 1991).

———. "Nothing." In *Serious Pleasure: Lesbian Erotic Stories and Poetry,* edited by Sheba Collective, 66–67. Pittsburgh, Pa.: Cleis Press, 1991.

———. "Saying the Least Said, Telling the Least Told: The Voices of Black Lesbian Writers." In *Piece of My Heart: A Lesbian Colour Anthology,* edited by Makeda Silvera, n.p. Toronto: Sister Vision, 1991. First published in *Lesbian and Gay Studies Newsletters,* Toronto, February 1990).

———. "Sexual Preference." In *Serious Pleasure: Lesbian Erotic Stories and Poetry,* edited by Sheba Collective, n.p. Pittsburgh, Pa.: Cleis Press, 1991.

———. "Vicki and Daphne." In *Serious Pleasure: Lesbian Erotic Stories and Poetry,* edited by Sheba Collective, 135–137. Pittsburgh, Pa.: Cleis Press, 1991.

———. "Sexual Preference." In *Serious Pleasure: Lesbian Erotic Stories and Poetry,* edited by Sheba Collective, 199. Pittsburgh, Pa.: Cleis Press, 1991.

———. "Greta Garbo." *Feminist Studies* 18, no. 3 (fall 1992): 627.

———. "Hurricane Season." In *The Word,* n.p. New York: St. Mark's Poetry Project, 1992.

———. "Rondeau." *Feminist Studies* 18, no. 3 (fall 1992): 625.

———. "The Turnstyle." *Feminist Studies* 18, no. 3 (fall 1992): 626.

———. "Living the Texts Out: Lesbians and the Use of Black Women's Traditions." In *Theorizing Black Feminisms: The Visionary Pragmatism of Black*

Women, edited by Stanlie M. James and Abena P. A. Busia, 214–227. London, New York: Routledge, 1993.

———. "Diaspora Legacy" and *The Marvelous Arithmetics of Distance: Poems 1987–1992* by Audre Lorde." *Women's Review of Books* 11, no. 12 (September 1994): 13–14.

———. "What is Found There: Notebooks on Poetry and Politics." *Belles Lettres: Review of Books by Women* (fall 1994): n.p.

———. "Out Outside the Classroom: The Co-Curricular Challenge." *Radical Teacher* (New York) (winter 1994): 23–25.

———. "The Loss of Lyric Space and the Critique of Traditions in Gwendolyn Brooks' *In the Mecca.*" *Kenyon Review* 17, no. 11 (winter 1995): 136–147.

———. "New Notes on Lesbianism." In *Frontline Feminism 1975–1995: Essays from Sojourner's First 20 Years,* edited by Karen Kahn, 10–13. San Francisco: Aunt Lute Books, 1995.

———. "Race, Homosocial Desire, and 'Mammon' in *Autobiography of an Ex-Colored Man.*" In *Professions of Desire: Lesbian and Gay Studies in Literature,* edited by George E. Haggerty and Bonnie Zimmerman, 84–97. New York: Modern Language Association of America, 1995.

"Cheryl Clarke in Sapphire's Precious' World: An Identity of One's Own." *Harvard Gay and Lesbian Review* (fall 1996).

Clarke, Cheryl. "A Slave's Sacred Supper." In *Cookin' with Honey: What Literature Lesbians Eat,* edited by Amy Scholder, 34–39. Ithaca, N.Y.: Firebrand Books, 1996.

Recordings

Clarke, Cheryl. *Narrative Poems in the Tradition of Black Women, Pacifica Tape Library, 1983; This Bridge Called My Back: Writings by Women of Color,* Los Angeles: Pacifica Tape Library, 1983.

———. "Hell Divin' Women." In *Tiny & Ruby: Hell Divin' Women* (video documentary), directed by Greta Schiller. New York: Jezebel Productions, 1988.

Bio-Bibliographical Sources

Clarke, Cheryl. "African American Women Writers in New Jersey: Biographical Questionnaire." Completed by Cheryl Clarke, June 2001.

Ferrara, Miranda H., ed. *The Writers Directory, 1996–1998.* Detroit: St. James Press, 1996.

Malinowski, Sharon, ed. *Black Writers: A Selection of Sketches from Contemporary Authors.* 2nd ed. Detroit: Gale Research, Inc., 1994.

———, ed. *Gay & Lesbian Literature.* Vol. 2. Detroit: St. John's Press, 1998.

Olendorf, Donna, ed. *Contemporary Authors: A Bio-Bibliographical Guide to Current Writers in Fiction, General Fiction, Poetry, Journalism, Drama, Motion Pictures, Television, and Other Fields.* Vol. 143. Detroit: Gale Research, Inc., 1994.

CLYBURN, EVELYN 1932–

Personal   Born on 26 December 1932 in
St. Louis, Missouri; husband: Carl Clyburn
(retired postal supervisor); children: Con-
rad and Sterling. Education: John Mar-
shall Elementary School, St. Louis;
Charles Sumner High School, St. Louis;
Stowe Teachers College, B.A., St.
Louis; Hunter College, New York, New
York; Fairleigh Dickinson University, Tea-
neck, New Jersey. Religion: Methodist.
Residence in New Jersey   Teaneck, 1964 to
present.
Career   Elementary school teacher, St.
Louis Public School System, St. Louis;
teacher, New York City Public Schools
Harlem District, New York; English teacher
(junior high and secondary schools),
Englewood Public School System, Engle-
wood, New Jersey.

Evelyn Clyburn,
courtesy of Evelyn Clyburn.

Reflections

"The love of poetry is a family tradition. I have enjoyed poetry all
of [my] life. [I] view poetry as the most basic means of vocal creative expression . . . [and] will long be remembered by [my]
long-suffering students as the teacher who required them to reg-
ularly recite poetry from memory. My mother and grandmother
both influenced my interest in poetry."

Publications

Clyburn, Evelyn. *Pictures, Popcorn, and Poems; A Collection of Poems by Eve
Clyburn.* Teaneck, N.J.: The Author, 1988. 24.
———. *US African-Americans.* Teaneck, N.J.: The Author, 1989. 16.
———. *Here is Woman; A Collection of Poems by Eve Clyburn.* Teaneck, N.J.:
The Author, 1990. 22.
———. *A Potpourri of Poetry.* Teaneck, N.J.: The Author, 1990. 19.

Bio-Bibliographical Sources

Clyburn, Evelyn. "African American Women Writers in New Jersey: Biographical Questionnaire." Completed by Evelyn Clyburn, March 1993.
———. "Biographical Notes." [Teaneck, N.J.: The Author, n.d.]. 1.

COLEMAN, CHRISENA ANNE 1963–

Personal   Born on 20 March 1963 in Hackensack, New Jersey; second
child of Dorothy Jean Chapman Coleman (teacher's aide) of East Orange,
New Jersey, and Wilbert Fredrick Coleman (lieutenant of detectives) of

Bronx, New York; granddaughter (maternal) of Anne Dora Banion Chapman and Samuel Chapman, both of Macon, Georgia; granddaughter (paternal) of Christabel Coleman Miller of Columbia, South Carolina, and John Miller of St. Petersburg, Florida; brother: Maurice Wilbert Coleman; children: Jordan Christopher Coleman and Justin David Coleman. Education: Fanny Hillers Elementary School, Hackensack, 1968–1974; Hackensack Middle School, Hackensack, 1974–1977; Hackensack High School, Hackensack, 1977–1981; Emerson College, Boston, Massachusetts, 1981–1982; Northeastern University, Boston, B.A., journalism, 1986. Religion: Baptist; Mt. Olive Baptist Church, Hackensack.

Residence in New Jersey Hackensack.

Career Family Literacy Program counselor, Hackensack Board of Education, Hackensack; journalist, *The Record,* Hackensack; journalist, *New York Daily News,* New York.

Memberships Former vice president, Garden State Association of Black Journalists; National Association of Black Journalists; Alpha Kappa Alpha Sorority, Inc.; former secretary, New York Press Club.

Awards Black History Honoree, NAACP, Passaic Chapter; Black Woman of Inspiration, Alpha Kappa Alpha, Bergen Chapter, 1992; Girl Scout Council of Bergen County Outstanding Achievement Award, March 1999; County of Bergen Certificate of Commendation for Fair Reporting, February 1993; Bergen County Parks Dept. Certificate of Appreciation, 1993; National Council of Negro Women Youth Incentive Award, May 1981.

Publications

Coleman, Chrisena. *Mama Knows Best: African-American Wives' Tales, Myths, and Remedies for Mothers and Mothers-to-Be.* New York: Simon & Schuster, 1997. 143, illus.

————. *Just Between Girlfriends: African-American Women Celebrate Friendship.* New York: Simon & Schuster, 1998. 206, illus.

Bio-Bibliographical Sources

"Chrisena Anne Coleman." *Biography Resource Center.* Detroit: Gale Group, 2001. Available:<http://www.galenet.com/servlet/BioRC> Accessed 19 September 2001.

Coleman, Chrisena Anne. "African American Women Writers: Biographical Questionnaire." Completed by Chrisena Anne Coleman, 3 October 2001.

COLLINS, ELSIE MCINTOSH 1922–

Personal Born on 25 April 1922 in Durham, North Carolina; oldest child of Ruth Lucille Richardson McIntosh (elementary school teacher) of Wilson's Mills, North Carolina, and Charlie McIntosh (laborer) of Laurenberg, North Carolina; granddaughter (maternal) of Allie Farmer Richardson and Emms Richardson, both of Wilson's Mills; sisters: Allie V. McIntosh Marshburn and Maggie Elizabeth McIntosh (deceased); children: Leslie

Jean Collins Ramsey and Kimberly Ruth Collins Myers. Education: Short Journey Elementary School, Short Journey, North Carolina, 1929–1935; Johnston County Training School, Smithfield, North Carolina, 1936–1940; Kittrell College, Kittrell, North Carolina, 1940–1942; Delaware State College, Dover, Delaware, B.A., secondary education, 1945; Columbia University, Teachers College, New York, New York, M.A., history and social studies, 1948–1952; The State of New Jersey, Department of Education, State Board of Examiners' classes at Rider University, Trenton, New Jersey, supervisory certification, 1974; The Union Institute, Cincinnati, Ohio, Ph.D., 1975–1977. Religion: Protestant, St. Paul United Methodist Church, Trenton.

Elsie McIntosh Collins.
Photograph by Paul R. Shelly.

Residence in New Jersey Trenton, 1964 to present.

Career Teacher (social studies and English), Booker T. Washington Junior High School and William Henry Comprehensive High School, Dover Special School District, Dover, Delaware, 1945–1960; teacher and supervisor, Vacation Bible School Summer Program, Abyssinian Baptist Church, Harlem, New York, summer 1953, 1954, 1955; teacher, Beth Jacob Jewish High School, Brooklyn, New York, 1961; teacher (core curriculum), Junior High School #5, Trenton, New Jersey, 1964–1968; cooperating teacher for Education and History Departments, Trenton State College, 1965–1968; participating teacher, Princeton University, summer 1965; teacher education demonstration teacher, Trenton State College, summer only, 1966–1970; master teacher/team leader, National Teacher Corps Project, Trenton Public Schools; assistant director, Career Opportunities Program, Trenton Public Schools, 1970–1971; curriculum specialist, Trenton Public Schools, 1975–1978; program planning specialist, Project Step-Up, Trenton, 1978–1979; curriculum specialist/instructor, Urban Education Program for Graduate Students, Trenton State College, Trenton, 1975–1990; assistant professor and later associate professor, Trenton State College, Trenton, 1971–1990; professor emerita, The College of New Jersey (formerly Trenton State College), Trenton, 1990 to present.

Memberships Alpha Kappa Alpha Sorority, Inc.; NAACP; Urban League of Greater Trenton; St. Paul United Methodist Church, Trenton, New Jersey: Chancel Chair and Soloist, 1964 to present; Council on Missions, 1979–1988, administrative board, 1980 to present; founder and chairperson, Community Education Advisory Council, Hamilton, New Jersey, 1977–1995; secretary, 1978–1982, and president, 1982–1994, board of directors, East Trenton Day Care Center, Trenton; founder and board of directors, St. Paul After School Drop-In Center for Elementary Children, 1980–1995; board of directors, Rescue Mission, Trenton, 1980 to present; Association of Interested Minorities in Hamilton, 1981 to present; representative to Trenton Ecumenical Area Ministry, United Methodist Church (Southern Jersey), 1982–1990; Phi Delta Kappa, Rider University Chapter, 1982–1990; trustee, John O. Wilson Neighborhood Service Center, Hamilton, New Jersey, 1982 to present; founder and board of directors, Young Scholars Institute, 1988 to present; Oral History Committee for the 250th celebration of the founding of Johnston County, North Carolina, 1746–1996; The Johnston County Heritage Commission, Smithfield, North Carolina, 1996 to present.

Awards, Honors, Other Certificates   Laurel Wreath Certificate of Appreciation, The Doctorate Association of New York Educators, 1980; Proclamation, Honorable John Rafferty, mayor, Hamilton, New Jersey, 1981; Community Service Award, Omicron Chapter, Chi Eta Phi Sorority, Inc., 1984; New Jersey Close-Up Commission, 1985; Presidential Citation in recognition of exemplary experiences that honor alma mater, Delaware State University, National Association for Equal Opportunity in Higher Education, Washington D.C., 1987; board or directors, Rescue Mission of Trenton, 1990; The Fai-Ho-Cho Club Annual Award, New Jersey General Assembly's Recognition, 1991; Certificate of Appreciation from the Honorable Darelyn Palmer, mayor of Trenton, 1992; Certificate of Appreciation, Trenton Ecumenical Area Ministry, 1993; Certificate of Appreciation, Union Hill A.M.E. Church, Wilson's Mills, North Carolina, 1997.

Reflections

"Being the first grandchild of the first daughter, I was truly the apple of my grandparents' eyes. I still draw happy mental pictures from periodic train rides with my grandmother from Wilson's Mills, N.C., to Durham, N.C., to visit my parents and sisters. It appears that my grandparents kept me with them in Wilson's Mills as much as my parents would allow. I also remember interesting chats with my grandmother as we walked through the woods or worked in her garden. The above episodes all occurred before I was five years old.

Two women became my mentors in Trenton and, therefore, orchestrated the events and situations that set the direction of my life. These women were Mrs. Bernice J. Munce, assistant superintendent of schools, and Mrs. Lottie Dinkins, chair of the English department, Trenton Central High School. Mrs. Dinkins was also the mother of New York City's mayor David Dinkins. Because of them, I became a member of a group of teachers to assist Dr. G. Leinwand, professor, New York University, to write special motivational materials for high school students. This project became known as "Problems of American Society." I did most of the research and writing for *Poverty and the Poor* and did the teacher's manual for *Problems of the Urban Poverty* and *The Negro in the City.*

These books and manuals were required usage in the junior schools and were subsequently used throughout the eastern United States.

The idea to write *Small Town Strutters* came from my cousin Ione Vinson, the same lady with whom I traveled daily to school when I was in elementary school. She knew so many stories about her childhood and the people and situations about Wilson's Mill that she thought would be an interesting book. So the two of us decided to write the book. She sent me to visit and talk with Dr. W. G. Wilson, M.D., because his grandfather founded the town. Many, many years later, 1997, after the death of my cousin, Ione Vinson, in 1993, and Dr. Wilson, in 1982, *Small Town Strutters* was published. The Ku Klux Klan became involved, so I withdrew from the project, but my idea never died."

Publications

Leinwand, Gerald. *Poverty and the Poor.* Assisted by Elsie Collins. New York: Washington Square Press [1968]. 158.

Collins, Elsie McIntosh. *Small Town Strutters; Life Stories from a North Carolina Lumber Mill Town.* Trenton, N.J.: Elsie M. Collins and Paul R. Shelly Publishers, 1997. 137, illus.

Bio-Bibliographical Source

Collins, Elsie M. "African American Women Writers in New Jersey: Biographical Questionnaire." Completed by Elsie M. Collins, 28 October 1999.

D

DARDEN, CAROLE *SEE* LLOYD, CAROLE DARDEN

DARDEN, NORMA JEAN

Norma Jean Darden.
Photograph by Chris Gulker,
courtesy of Los Angeles Public Library.

Personal Born in Newark, New Jersey; first child of Mamie Jean Sampson Darden (teacher, social worker, real estate developer and manager) of Camden, Alabama, and Walter Theodore "Bud" Darden (physician) of Wilson, North Carolina; granddaughter of Corine Johnson Sampson of Camden, Alabama, and William Sampson of Kentucky (maternal aunt and uncle); granddaughter (paternal) of Dianah Scarborough Darden (seamstress) and Charles Henry Darden (carpenter, first African American undertaker in North Carolina), both of Wilson, North Carolina; sister: Carole Darden Lloyd. Education: Nishuane School, Montclair, New Jersey; Hillside Junior High, Montclair; Oakwood School; Sarah Lawrence College, Bronxville, New York, B.A., drama; studied acting with Lee Strasberg and Wynn Handman; studied dance with Martha Graham (modern), Mia Slavinska (ballet), and Mary Jane Brown (tap); studied singing with Chapman Roberts; studied speech with Judy Magee and Shauna Kanter. Religion: Episcopal.

Residence in New Jersey Montclair.

Career Model, Wilhelmina Modeling Agency, New York, New York, 1969–1978, appearing in *Vogue, Harper's Bazaar, Mademoiselle, Seventeen, Glamour, Ladies' Home Journal, Esquire, New York Magazine, Life, Newsweek, The New York Times, New York Post,* and *Daily News;* actress (film), appearing in: *The Wiz, The Man Who Loved Women,* and *Cotton Club;* actress (theatre), appearing in Broadway and off-Broadway productions: *Weekend, The Shirt, Street Sounds, Underground, Nigger Nightmare, Les Femmes Noires, Uncle Tom's Cabin, Crucificado, Last Days of the British Honduras,* and *Rainlight;* actress (television), appearing in *Another World, The Doctors,* "Infinity Factory," "Midday Live," "Black Journal," and "Texas"; staff writer (fashion and beauty),

Essence magazine; fashion coordinator and publicity director, Jon Haggins, Inc.; president, Spoonbread Catering Company, New York.

Memberships Screen Actors' Guild; American Federation of Television and Radio Artists; Actors' Equity Association.

Awards, Honors, Other Certificates *Spoonbread and Strawberry Wine,* runner up Tasters Choice Award for Best Regional Cookbook, T. M. French Co., 1979

Publications

Book

Darden, Norma Jean, and Carole Darden. *Spoonbread and Strawberry Wine: Recipes and Reminiscences of a Family.* 1st ed. Line drawings by Doug Jamieson; wood engravings throughout text by Thomas Bewick. Garden City, N.Y.: Anchor Press, 1978. xi, 288. Reprint: New York: Fawcett Crest, 1978, 1980, and 1982; New York: Doubleday, 1994.

Article

Darden, Norma Jean. "How To Cook Like a Pro." *Essence* 16 (October 1985): 83–86.

Bio-Bibliographical Sources

Darden, Norma Jean. Letter to Sibyl E. Moses, 21 August 1985.

———. "Resume." (n.d.).

Darden, Norma Jean, and Carole Darden. *Spoonbread and Strawberry Wine: Recipes and Reminiscences of a Family.* 1st ed. Garden City, N.Y.: Anchor Press, 1978.

Lloyd, Carole Darden. "African American Women Writers in New Jersey Project: Biographical Questionnaire." Completed by Carole Darden Lloyd (sister), November 1996.

DAVIS-THOMPSON, ESTHER LOUISE 1954–

Personal Born on 28 May 1954 in Cape May Court House, New Jersey; child of Ruth Cordelia Davis Allen (secretary to high school principal) of Cape May, New Jersey; granddaughter (maternal) of Dorothy Virginia Turner Davis of Virginia; sisters: Carmen Viola Allen Smith, Vanita Lynn Allen Popper, and Josephine Lynette Allen; brother: James Arthur Allen, Jr.; husband: Arthur E. Thompson, Sr. children: Arthur, Jr., James, Shawn, Patrick, Amanda, Sarah, Colleen, Ryan, Ashley, and Alexander. Education: elementary and secondary education, Wildwood, New Jersey Public School System; Douglass College, New Brunswick, New Jersey, B.A., English and Early Childhood Education, 1976. Religion: Christian.

Residence in New Jersey Wildwood, 1954–1976; Camden, 1976 to present.

Career Director, after-school tutoring and summer activities programs, Camden Free Public Library, Camden; adjunct instructor, writing skills and child psychology, Camden County College, Camden; founder, Sisterhood Projects.

Reflections

"I had a woman-centered childhood. All around me the most beautiful Real Women swarmed and fussed and tended and cleaned and sewed and did hair and talked and laughed and cried and prayed and sang. And all of my adult life I have tried to figure out how they grew to be as wonderful as they were. Somehow these women took the essence of the raw experiences that life handed hem and spun it into enough golden rope to pull up the children. And my secret prayer has always been to be as Strong, as Proud, as Loving, Capable, Orderly, Calm, and Real and Resilient and Beautiful and Present and Powerful as they.

These exquisite women were my Queen examples. My examples of how to be and how not to be. These women took my hands and pulled me up to an awareness that if I couldn't do anything else in this life, I'd better just believe. Believe. Believe that God is really there/here. Believe that I am accountable, not only to God, but to every living soul who ever crosses my path of looks my way. Believe that there will always be a good meal. A clean, warm place to eat and talk and sleep. An honest way to make a living. A noble way to give out Love. A way back from trouble. A way for Good to happen. Refusing to believe for Good was the major sin. And so in writing. . . . I wish to express my gratitude to some of these Queens of Spirit: my mother Ruth, my aunt Althea Turner, my church mother Lottie Miller. And I wish to honor the spirits of those who have crossed over: my great-grandmother Mary Ruth Habersham, my grandmother Dorothy Virginia Turner Davis."

Publications

Davis-Thompson, Esther Louise. *MotherLove: Re-Inventing a Good and Blessed Future for Our Children.* Philadelphia, Pa.: Innisfree Press, 1999. 157, illus.

———. *Raising Up Queens: Loving Our Daughters Loud and Strong.* Philadelphia, Pa.: Innisfree Press, 2000. 153, illus.

Bio-Bibliographical Source

Davis-Thompson, Esther Louise. "African American Women Writers in New Jersey Project: Biographical Questionnaire." Completed by Esther Davis-Thompson, 19 September 2001.

DORIN, LENORA ALLEN 1912–1988

Personal   Born on 19 August 1912 in Mt. Olive, North Carolina; joined the ancestors ca. 17 May 1988; second child of Minnie Estella Kornegy Allen (housewife) and Fred Allen (farmer), both of Mt. Olive; granddaughter (maternal) of Matilda Kornegy and George Kornegy, both of Mt. Olive; granddaughter (paternal) of James Allen, of Mt. Olive; sisters: Maude

Allen and Lettie Allen; brothers: Charles Ennis Allen and Aneastus Allen; husband: Thomas E. Dorin, of Jacobtown, New Jersey. Education: Milton Elementary School, Mt. Olive and Dudley High School, Dudley, North Carolina; licensed practical nurse training, Allentown, New Jersey. Religion: African Methodist Episcopal; Union A.M.E. Church, Allentown. *Residence in New Jersey* Trenton, 1932–1935; Laurenceville, 1936–1946; Allentown, 1946–1988.

Career Farm work (picked beans), North Carolina; domestic work, Trenton; domestic work for Judge Warren Davis, Laurenceville, New Jersey; nurse for Dr. Walter Farmer, 1950–1957.

Lenora Allen Dorin.
Photograph by Trenton Photographers.

Memberships First Baptist Church, Trenton; Laymen's Organization, senior choir, Stewardess Board, and Christine Smith Missionary Society, Union A.M.E. Church, Allentown.

Awards, Honors, Other Certificates Service award, Laymen's Organization, Union A.M.E. Church, Allentown, New Jersey.

Reflections

"My father died young; and my mother insisted on responsibility—"do what you can do, even if only one bucket of beans."

Now where I got the idea to write the book. . . . The minister of the family [for whom I cared] first gave me the idea, so I pursued the idea. Then the youngest daughter said, "Mrs. Dorin I will give you the title for your book," she said, "My Adopted Family." So I went from there to my minister [of Union A.M.E. Church, Allentown] and he suggested that it would be good to try it and that was his idea, so from the three is where the whole idea started."

Publication

Dorin, Lenora. *My Adopted Family.* New York: Vantage Press, 1979. 33.

Bio-Bibliographical Sources

Dorin, Lenora. "African American Women Writers in New Jersey: Biographical Questionnaire." Completed by Lenora Dorin, August 1986.

———. Correspondence with Sibyl E. Moses. 17 September 1986.

———. Interview with Sibyl E. Moses. Allentown, New Jersey, August 1986.

Rhodes, Hazel. Correspondence with Sibyl E. Moses. 27 February 1989. Included undated copy of Lenora Dorin's death notice per Rhodes letter, published in "the local *Trentonian* newspaper a few days after her death on Tuesday, May 17, 1988."

DOWNING, THERESA BOWMAN 1946–

*Theresa Bowman Downing,
courtesy of Theresa Bowman Downing.*

Personal Born on 19 February in Hamilton Township, New Jersey; seventh child of Louira Wilcher Bowman (luncheonette owner) of Ellaville, Georgia, and John Bowman (foreman) of Wadesboro, North Carolina; granddaughter (maternal) of Miranda Terry Wilcher of Ellaville; granddaughter (paternal) of Virgil Bowman of Wadesboro, North Carolina; sisters: Alice Louise Pittman, Mary Gay, Christine White, Janie Smith, and Juanita Bowman Lambert; brother: Horace Bowman; husband: Daniel Downing; children: Erik Downing, Travis Downing, Jerry Gainer, and Shane Gainer. Education: Rowan Elementary School, Hamilton Township, 1951–1956; Junior High School #5, Trenton, New Jersey, 1956–1961; Trenton Senior High School, Trenton, 1961–1964; Montclair State College, Upper Montclair, New Jersey, B.A., science/biology, 1968; Montclair State College, Upper Montclair, M.A., Student Personnel Services, 1973.

Residence in New Jersey Trenton, 1956 to present.

Career Biology teacher, Steinhart High School, Hamilton Township, 1968–1971; graduate assistant, Educational Opportunity Fund and Housing, Montclair State College, Upper Montclair, 1971–1973; administrative assistant, Dean's Office, School of Educational and Community Services, Montclair State College, Upper Montclair, 1973–1979; assistant to the Dean for Academic Affairs, Mercer County Community College, Trenton, 1979–1980; assistant director of grants and coordinator of graduate off-campus programs, Trenton State College, Trenton, 1980–1983; senior program advisor, Thomas Edison State College, Trenton, 1983 to present; editor, *The LINK* (National Organization for Human Service Education), 1998 to present.

Memberships Mid-Atlantic Consortium for Human Services; National Association for Female Executives; National Association of University Women, Trenton Chapter; secretary, National Organization for Human Service Education, 1992–1997; Trenton Writers' Guild; Canal Banks Advisory Committee.

Publication

Downing, Theresa A. Bowman. *A Hard Head and Delayed Blessings: Poetry Reflecting the Life and Times of An African American Woman.* Trenton, New Jersey: The Author [1996]. 71, illus.

Bio-Bibliographical Source
Downing, Theresa Ann Bowman. "African American Women Writers in New Jersey: Biographical Questionnaire." Completed by Theresa Ann Bowman Downing, 20 September 2001.

DREWRY, CECELIA HODGES

Personal   Born in New York, New York; husband: Henry N. Drewry (divorced). Education: Hunter College, A.B., 1945; Columbia University, A.M., 1948; Shakespeare University of Birmingham, England, Certificate, 1949; Northwestern University, Ph.D., 1967; University of Ghana, Certificate, 1969.
Residence in New Jersey: Princeton.
Career   Instructor, Talladega College, Talladega, Alabama, 1945–1947; director of speech, Penthouse Dance and Drama Theatre, New York, 1948–1952; teacher, High School of Performing Arts, New York, 1952–1959; teacher, Princeton High School, Princeton, New Jersey, 1959–1961; associate professor, Rutgers University, New Brunswick, New Jersey, 1962–1970; visiting instructor, Teachers College, Columbia University, New York, 1968; visiting professor of English, Haverford College, Haverford, Pennsylvania, 1977; assistant dean and assistant professor, Princeton, New Jersey.
Memberships   American Association of University Women; trustee, Cedar Crest College, Allentown, Pennsylvania; Carnegie Foundation for Advancement of Teaching; NAACP; National Council of Negro Women; Princeton Association of Human Rights.
Awards, Honors, Other Certificates   Award for Excellence in Oral Interpretation of Literature, Northwestern University School of Speech; Alpha Psi Omega Honor Society; Danforth Association; honoree, Phi Delta Kappa.
Publication
Drewry, Henry N., and Cecelia H. Drewry. *Afro-American History: Past to Present.* New York: Scribner [1971]. xiii, 545.
Bio-Bibliographical Sources
Henderson, Ashyia N., and Shirelle Phelps, eds. *Who's Who Among African Americans.* 12th ed. Detroit: Gale Group, 1999.
Velazquez, Rita C., ed. *Directory of American Scholars. Vol. II (English, Speech, and Drama).* 9th ed. Detroit: Gale Group, 1999.

DUDLEY, FRANKIE W.

Personal   Born on 12 June [?] in Enfield, North Carolina; seventh child of Betty Harrison Wilkins (housewife) and Dayton Wilkins (planter), both of Enfield; granddaughter (maternal) of Nannie Harrison and Turner Harrison, both of Enfield; granddaughter (paternal) of Martha Wilkins and William Wilkins, both of Enfield; sisters: Christine Robertson and Sophia Jones; brothers: Roosevelt Wilkins (deceased), Jerry Wilkins, Nathaniel Wilkins (deceased), and Ivan Wilkins; husband: Benjamin R. Dudley (math supervisor and teacher); child: Brian C. Dudley. Education: Maude B. Hubbard School, Battleboro, North Carolina; Phillip High School and Swift Creek High School, Whitaker, North Carolina; Fayetteville State University, Fayetteville, North Carolina, B.A., 1954–1957; Temple University, Philadelphia, Pennsylvania, M.A.; Pacific University, California, research for doctorate, 1985–1993. Religion: Baptist, St. Matthews Baptist Church, Raleigh, North Carolina; previous membership: Parkway Baptist Church, Willingboro, New Jersey.

Residence in New Jersey   Willingboro, 1976–1998.

Career   Teacher and reading specialist.

Memberships   Alpha Kappa Alpha Sorority, Inc.; Sunday school teacher and chairperson of Christian Board of Education, Parkway Baptist Church, Willingboro.

Awards, Honors, Other Certificates   Recognition for helping children with essays, Philadelphia Bar Association's Young Lawyers Club, 1989; special recognition by principal, for dedicated service to children, 1985.

Reflections

"My college professor influenced me to write [during a] course in creative writing. [My decision to write was also influenced] by high school English teachers and by working with students in essay contests in the public school system of Philadelphia, Pennsylvania. These people are Dr. Wilt Temple and Hazel Logan, retired educator of Raleigh."

Publication

Dudley, Frankie W. *Poems and Short Stories for Young Children, A Focus on Creativity.* [n.p., 1997]. 87, illus.

Bio-Bibliographical Source

Dudley, Frankie E. "African American Women Writers in New Jersey: Biographical Questionnaire." Completed by Frankie E. Dudley, October 1999.

EDGE, SYLVIA CLARK 1936–

Personal Born on 14 December 1936 in Newark, New Jersey; daughter of Irma Powell Clark and Thomas Clark; sister: Marsha Clark Pickett; husband: Waldo O. Edge; child: Peter Thomas Edge. Education: Rutgers University, The State University, College of Nursing, B.S., 1954–1958; New York University, School of Education, M.A., 1961–1963.

Religion Episcopal.

Residence in New Jersey Newark; Montclair; Rockaway.

Career Staff Nurse, University Hospital, New York, New York, 1958–1959; staff nurse, Visiting Nurse Assistant of Newark, 1960–1961; instructor, Monmouth County Vocational Schools, summer 1963; consultant, Diploma School Nursing Education, NLU Special Program on Integration of Psychiatric-Mental Health, 1967–1969; instructor, St. Francis Hospital, School of Nursing, 1964–1967; instructor/associate professor, Middlesex County College, 1967 to present; instructor, Foreign Nurses, Alexian Brothers Hospital, 1972–1973; chairperson, Department of Nursing Education, Middlesex County College, Edison, New Jersey; dean, Middlesex County College, Division of Health Technologies, Edison.

Memberships Church school teacher, superintendent, church school, St. Philip's Episcopal Church, Newark, 1952–1970; block chairman, later secretary, Clinton Hill Area Rehabilitation Committee, 1959–1964; executive committee, Trinity Cathedral, Newark, 1967–1970; trustee, Oak Bluffs Trinity Episcopal Church, 1972 to present; National League for Nursing, 1974; American Nurses Association; bylaws committee, executive committee, psychiatric council, New Jersey State Nurses Association, 1974.

Awards, Honors, Other Certificates Appointed by governor to New Jersey Board of Nursing, 1982, and later elected to the position of secretary/treasurer; appointed to overall faculty of the Regents External Degrees in Nursing of the State of New York, 1983.

Publications

Books

Fielo, Sandra B., and Sylvia C. Edge. *Technical Nursing of the Adult: Medical, Surgical, and Psychiatric Approaches.* [New York]: Macmillan [1970]. xv, 588, illus.

———. *Technical Nursing of the Adult: Medical, Surgical, and Psychiatric Approaches.* 2nd ed. New York: Macmillan [1974]. xviii, 698, illus.

Southern Council on Collegiate Education for Nursing. *Choosing Pathways to Nursing Education.* Atlanta: Southern Council on Collegiate Education for Nursing in affiliation with the Southern Regional Education Board, 1992. 4.

Articles

Elliott, R., L. Johnson, S. Edge, E. Hoffman, and H. J. Bruhn. "An Analysis of Trends in the Legislation and Regulation of Nursing Practice." *Issues* 6, no. 4 (1985): 7–10.

———. "An Analysis of Trends in Nursing Education." *Issues* 7, no. 1 (1986): 6–8.

———. "An Analysis of Trends in the Role of the Licensed Practical Nurse." *Issues* 7, no. 2 (1986): 7–8.

———. "An Analysis of Trends in Society." *Issues* 7, no. 3 (1986): 4–8.

Edge, Sylvia. "State Positions on Titling and Licensure." N.p.: *NLN Publications* (December 1986): 129–159.

Bio-Bibliographical Sources:

Outstanding Educators of America, 1974. Washington, D.C.: Outstanding Educators of America, 1974.

Who's Who in American Nursing, 1984. Inaugural edition. Washington, D.C.: The Society of Nursing Professionals, 1984.

FAUSET, JESSIE REDMON 1882–1961

Personal Born on 27 April 1882 in Fredericksville, Camden County, New Jersey; joined the ancestors on 30 April 1961, in Philadelphia, Pennsylvania. The daughter of Anna Seamon Fauset and Redmon Fauset (minister); sisters: Carolina Susan Mabel, Mary Helen, Anna Bella, Beatrice Birdie, and Francis R.; brother: Ira Redmon; half-sister: Marian Fauset; half-brothers: Arthur Huff Fauset and Redmond Fauset; step-sisters: Emma Huff, Mae Huff; step-brother: Earl Huff; husband: Herbert Harris (businessman, married 1929). Education: Philadelphia High School for Girls, Philadelphia, 1900; Cornell University, Ithaca, New York, B.A., 1905; University of Pennsylvania, Philadelphia, M.A., 1919; Sorbonne, Paris, France, 1924–1925.

Religion African Methodist Episcopal.

Residence in New Jersey Fredericksville; Montclair, ca. 1939–1958.

*Jessie Redmon Fauset,
reprinted from* Opportunity:
The Journal of Negro Life, *12, no 1
(January 1934), by permission of the
National Urban League, New York,
New York, courtesy of the
Library of Congress.*

Career Teacher, Baltimore Public Schools, Baltimore, Maryland, 1905–1906; teacher (Latin and French), M Street High School (later Dunbar High School), Washington, D.C., 1906–1919; literary editor, *The Crisis*, 1919–1926; literary and managing editor, *The Brownies' Book*, 1920–1921; contributing editor, *The Crisis*, 1926–?; teacher, DeWitt Clinton High School, New York, 1927–1944; Visiting Professor of English, Hampton Institute, Hampton, Virginia, 1949–1950.

Memberships NAACP; Delta Sigma Theta Sorority, Inc.; College Women's Club, Montclair.

Awards, Honors, Other Certificates Honor graduate, Philadelphia High School for Girls, 1900; Phi Beta Kappa, Cornell University, 1905; delegate to Second Pan-African Congress, Delta Sigma Theta Sorority, Inc., London, 1921.

Reflections [from recorded interview by Marion L. Starkey]

"When I was a child I used to puzzle my head ruefully over the fact that in school we studied the lives of only great white people. I took it that there simply have been no great Negroes, and I was amazed when, as I grew older, I found that there were. It is a pity that Negro children should be permitted to suffer from that delusion at all. There should be a sort of "Plutarch's Lives' " of the Negro race. Some day, perhaps, I shall get around to writing it."

Publications

Books

Fauset, Jessie Redmon. *There is Confusion.* New York: Boni & Liveright, 1924. 297; London: Chapman & Hall, 1924.

———. *Plum Bun.* London: Elkin Mathews & Marrot, 1928. 381; New York: Stokes, 1929. 379.

———. *The Chinaberry Tree; A Novel of American Life.* New York: Stokes, 1931. 341; London: Elkin Mathews & Marrot, 1932.

———. *Comedy, American Style.* New York: Stokes, 1933. 327.

Short Stories

Fauset, Jessie Redmon. "Emmy." *Crisis* 5 (December 1912): 79–87; 5 (January 1913): 134–142.

———. "My House and a Glimpse of My Life Therein." *Crisis* 8 (July 1914): 143–145.

———. "There Was One Time, A Story of Spring." *Crisis* 13 (April 1917): 272–277; 14 (May 1917): 11–15.

———. "The Sleeper Wakes." *Crisis* 20 (August 1920): 168–173; 20 (September 1920): 226–229; 20 (October 1920): 267–274.

———. "When Christmas Comes." *Crisis* 25 (December 1922): 61–63.

———. "Double Trouble." *Crisis* 26 (August 1923): 155–159; 26 (September 1923): 205–209.

———. "Mary Elizabeth: A Story." *Crisis* (December 1919): 51–56.

———. "Merry Christmas to All: A Story." *Brownies' Book* (December 1920): 355–360.

———. "Ghosts and Kittens: A Story." *Brownies' Book* (February 1921): 46–51.

———. "Cordelia Goes on the War Path: A Story." *Brownies' Book* (May 1921): 148–154.

Poetry

Fauset, Jessie Redmon. "Rondeau." *Crisis* 3 (April 1912): 252; Pritchard, Myron T., and Mary White Ovington. *The Upward Path*, 120. New York: Harcourt Brace and Howe, 1920.

———. "Again It Is September." *Crisis* 14 (September 1917): 248.

———. "The Return." *Crisis* 27 (January 1919): 118; *Caroling Dusk: An Anthology of Verse by Negro Poets*, edited by Countee Cullen, 70. New York: Harper and Brothers, 1927.

———. "Mary Elizabeth." *Crisis* 19 (December 1919): 51–56.

———. "Oriflamme." *Crisis* 19 (January 1920): 128; *The Book of American Negro Poetry*, edited by James Weldon Johnson, n.p. New York: Harcourt, Brace and World, 1931.

———. "LaVie C'est La Vie." *Crisis* 24 (July 1922): 124; *Caroling Dusk: An Anthology of Verse by Negro Poets*, edited by Countee Cullen, 69. New York: Harper and Brothers, 1927; *The Book of American Negro Poetry*, edited by James Weldon Johnson, n.p. New York: Harcourt, Brace and World, 1931.

———. "Dilworth Road Revisited." *Crisis* 24 (August 1922): 167.

———. "Song for a Lost Comrade (to O.B.J.)." *Crisis* 25 (November 1922): 22.

———. "Rencontre." *Crisis* 27 ((January 1924): 122; *Caroling Dusk: An Anthology of Verse by Negro Poets,* edited by Countee Cullen, 70. New York: Harper and Brothers, 1927.

———. "Here's April!." *Crisis* 27 (April 1924): 277.

———. "Rain Fugue." *Crisis* 28 (August 1924): 155.

———. "Stars in Alabama." *Crisis* 35 (January 1928): 14.

———. " 'Courage!' He Said." *Crisis* 36 (November 1929): 378.

———. "Christmas Eve in France." *The Independent* (December 1917): 552.

———. "After School: A Poem." *Brownies' Book* (January 1920): 30.

———. "Dedication." *Brownies' Book* (January 1920): 32.

———. "At the Zoo: Verses." *Brownies' Book* (March 1920): 85–86.

———. "The Easter Idyl: A Poem." *Brownies' Book* (April 1920): 112–113.

———. "Douce Sourvenance." *Crisis* (May 1920): 42.

———. "Spring Songs: Verses." *Brownies' Book* (May 1920): 146–147.

———. "Two Christmas Songs: Verses." *Brownies' Book* (December 1920): 384.

Articles

Fauset, Jessie Redmon. "What to Read." *Crisis* (March 1912): 211–212.

———. "What to Read." *Crisis* (April 1912): 261–262.

———. "What to Read." *Crisis* (June 1912): 92–93.

———. "What to Read." *Crisis* (August 1912): 183.

———. "What to Read." *Crisis* (September 1912): 249–250.

———. "Some Books for Boys and Girls." *Crisis* (October 1912): 295–298.

———. "What to Read." *Crisis* (November 1912): 38.

———. "What to Read." *Crisis* (September 1913): 248.

———. "New Literature on the Negro." *Crisis* 20 (June 1920): 78–83.

———. "The Story of George Washington." *Brownies' Book* (February 1920): 64.

———. "Pastures New." *Crisis* (September 1920): 224–226.

———. "Three Books." *Crisis* (December 1920): 62–64.

———. "The Emancipator of Brazil." *Crisis* (March 1921): 208–209.

———. "Saint-George, Chevalier of France." *Crisis* (May 1921): 9–12.

———. "On the Bookshelf." *Crisis* (May 1921): 60–64.

———. "Nostalgia." *Crisis* (August 1921): 154–158.

———. "Impressions of the Second Pan-African Congress." *Crisis* 22 (November 1921): 12–18.

———. "What Europe Thought of the Pan African Congress." *Crisis* 22 (December 1921): 60–69.

———. "Looking Backward." *Crisis* (January 1922): 125–126.

———. "Sunday Afternoon." *Crisis* (February 1922): 162–164.

———. "No End of Books." *Crisis* (March 1922): 208–210.

———. "As to Books." *Crisis* (May 1922): 66–68.

———. "The Gift of Laughter" in *The New Negro,* edited by Alain Locke. New York: Boni, 1925.

———. "The Montessori Method—Its Possibilities." *Crisis* (July 1912): 136–138.

———. "Nationalism and Egypt." *Crisis* (April 1920): 310–316.

———. "Turkey Drumsticks. A Thanksgiving Story." *Brownies' Book* (November 1920): 342–346.

———. "Some Notes on Color." *The World Tomorrow* (March 1922): 76–77. Reprint: Herbert Aptheker, ed. *A Documentary History of the Negro People in the United States: 1910–1932.* Secaucus, N.J.: The Citadel Press, 1973: 354–358. "Negro View of the Color Problem" (condensed version). *Missionary Review* (June 1926): 442–443.

———. "The Symbolism of Bert Williams." *Crisis* (May 1922): 12–15.

———. "The Thirteenth Biennial of the N.A.C.W." *Crisis* (October 1922): 257–260.

Fauset, Jessie Redmon, and Alain Locke. "Notes on the New Books." *Crisis* (February 1923): 161–165.

———. "Out of the West." *Crisis* (November 1923): 11–18.

Fauset, Jessie Redmon. "The 'Y' Conference at Talladega." *Crisis* (September 1923): 213–215.

———. "Henry Ossawa Tanner." *Crisis* (April 1924): 255–258.

———. "New Books." *Crisis* (February 1924): 174–177.

———. "Dark Algiers The White." *Crisis* (April; May 1925): 155–159; 16–22.

———. "The Gift of Laughter" in *The New Negro,* edited by Alain Locke. New York: Boni, 1925. Reprint: New York: Atheneum, 1969: 161–167.

———. "The Enigma of Sorbonne." *Crisis* (March 1925): 216–219.

———. "This Way to the Flea Market." *Crisis* (February 1925): 161–163.

———. "Yarrow Revisited." *Crisis* (January 1925): 107–109.

———. "The Eucalyptus Tree: A Reverie of Rome, the Catacombs, Christianity, and the Moving Beauty of Italy." *Crisis* (January 1926): 116–117.

———. "The Negro in Art: How Shall He be Portrayed: A Symposium." *Crisis* (June 1926): 71.

———. "Our Book Shelf." *Crisis* (March 1926): 238–239.

———. "Rank Imposes Obligation." (Biographical essay on Martin Robinson Delany.) *Crisis* (November 1926): 9–13.

———. "In Talladega." *Crisis* (February 1928): 47–48.

[———]. "Wings for God's Chillun": The Story of Burghardt DuBois. *The World Tomorrow* (August 1929): 333–336. Published anonymously.

———. "Episodes in Tangier." *The Metropolitan: A Monthly Review* (January 1935): 8–9.

Translations

Fauset, Jessie Redmon, trans. "The Treasures of the Poor." *Crisis* (December 1917): 63–65.

————, trans. "The Return of the Bells. A Story." *Brownies' Book* (April 1920): 99–102.

————, trans. "Joseph and Mary Come to Bethlehem." Translated from Old French chanson. *Crisis* (December 1920): 72–73.

————, trans. "The Pool. A Poem. Amedee Brun." *Crisis* (September 1921): 205.

————, trans. "To a Foreign Maid." *Crisis* (February 1923): 158.

————, trans. "Kirongozi (Essays on Life in the Belgian Congo)." *Crisis* (March 1924): 208–209.

————, trans. "La Question des Noirs aux Etats-Unis," by Frank L. Schoell. *Crisis* (June 1924): 83–86.

————, trans. "The Sun in Brittany." *Crisis* (November 1927): 303.

Other Works

Fauset, Jessie. "Christmas Time." In *American Literature by Negro Authors,* edited by Herman Dreer, 255–263. New York: Macmillan, 1950.

————. "Color Struck." In *The Negro Caravan: Writings by American Negroes,* edited by Arthur P. Davis and Ulysses Lee, 189–196. New York: Citadel Press, 1941.

————. "Class." In *Cavalcade: Negro American Writing from 1760 to the Present,* edited by Arthur P. Davis and Saunders Redding, 354–358. Boston: Houghton Mifflin, 1971.

————. "Words! Words!" In *Caroling Dusk: An Anthology of Verse by Negro Poets,* edited by Countee Cullen, 65–66. New York: Harper and Brothers, 1927.

————. "Touche." In *Caroling Dusk: An Anthology of Verse by Negro Poets,* edited by Countee Cullen, 66–67. New York: Harper and Brothers, 1927.

————. "Noblesse Oblige." In *Caroling Dusk: An Anthology of Verse by Negro Poets,* edited by Countee Cullen, 67–68. New York: Harper and Brothers, 1927.

————. "Fragment." In *Caroling Dusk: An Anthology of Verse by Negro Poets,* edited by Countee Cullen, 70–71. New York: Harper and Brothers, 1927.

————. *The Book of American Negro Poetry,* edited by James Weldon Johnson. New York: Harcourt, Brace and World, 1931. "Dead Fires." In *Voices from the Harlem Renaissance,* edited by Nathan Huggins, 313. New York: Oxford University Press, 1976.

————. " 'Courage!' He Said." In *Double Blossoms,* edited by Edna Porter, 39–40. New York: Lewis Copeland Company, 1931.

————. "Erleuchtung." In *Afrika Singt: Eine Ausless Neuer Afro-Amerikanischer Lyrik,* edited by Anna Nussbaum, 126–127. Vienna: F.G. Speideische Verlagbuchhandlung, 1929.

————. "Oblivion." In *The Book of American Negro Poetry,* edited by James Weldon Johnson, n.p. New York: Harcourt, Brace and World, 1931.

————. "Christmas Eve in France." In *The Book of American Negro Poetry,* edited by James Weldon Johnson. New York: Harcourt, Brace and World, 1931.

———. "Batouala is Translated." *Crisis* (September 1922): 218–219.
———. "When Christmas Comes." *Crisis* (December 1922): 61–63.

Bio-Bibliographical Sources

Harris, Trudier, editor. *Afro-American Writers from the Harlem Renaissance to 1940.* Detroit: Gale Research Co., 1987.

Starkey, Marion L. "Jessie Fauset." [Interview]. *Southern Workman* 61 (May 1932): 220. As cited in Johnson, Abby Arthur, and Ronald Maberry Johns. *Propaganda and Aesthetics: The Literary Politics of Afro-American Magazines in the Twentieth Century,* 213. Amherst: The University of Massachusetts Press, 1979.

Logan, Rayford W., and Michael Winston, eds. *Dictionary of American Negro Biography.* New York: Norton, 1982.

Sylvander, Carolyn Wedin. *Jessie Redmon Fauset, Black American Writer.* Troy, N.Y.: The Whitston Publishing Company, 1981.

Wall, Cheryl A. "Jessie Redmon Fauset, 1882–1961" In *Past and Promise: Lives of New Jersey Women,* edited by Joan N. Burnstyn, 285–286. Metuchen, N.J.: Scarecrow Press, 1990.

Wall, Cheryl A. *Women of the Harlem Renaissance.* Bloomington: Indiana University Press, 1995.

FLAGG, E. ALMA WILLIAMS 1918–

E. Alma Flagg,
courtesy of E. Alma Flagg.

Personal Born on 16 September 1918 in City Point, Virginia; second child of Caroline Ethel Moody Williams (World War II munitions worker, clubwoman, and church woman) of Sumter, South Carolina, and Hannibal Greene Williams (sign painter and construction worker) of Wrightsboro, North Carolina; granddaughter (maternal) of Elizabeth Thompson Moody and Allen Moody; granddaughter (paternal) of Lucy Bowden Williams and Rev. Emanuel Williams; sister: Thelma W. Stephens Gillis; brothers: Rev. Dr. Hannibal Allen Williams, Samuel Donald Williams (deceased), and Harold Moody Williams (deceased); husband: Dr. J. Thomas Flagg (Professor Emeritus of Education, Montclair State College; deceased); children: Dr. Thomas Lyle Flagg and Mrs. Luisa Flagg Foley. Education: Public elementary school, Allentown, Pennsylvania, 1925; Chestnut St. School and Oliver St. School, Newark, New Jersey, 1926–1931; East Side High School, Newark,

1931–1935; Essex County Junior College, Newark, 1935–1937; Newark State College, B.S., 1937–1940; Montclair State College, Montclair, New Jersey, M.A., 1941–1943; Teachers College-Columbia University, New York, New York, Doctor of Education, 1955; Howard University, Washington, D.C., graduate studies, 1941–1943; Jersey City State College, Rutgers University, Newark; Syracuse University, Syracuse, New York. Honorary degree: Newark State College, Doctor of Letters, 1968. Religion: Presbyterian.

Residence in New Jersey   Newark, 1926 to present.

Career   Clerk, National Youth Administration, Newark, 1941–1943; elementary teacher, Washington, D.C., 1941–1943; grade teacher, 1943–1957; remedial reading teacher, Newark, 1957–1963; vice principal, 1963–1964; elementary school principal, Hawkins Street School, Newark, 1964–1967; director, assistant superintendent of schools in charge of curriculum, Newark Public Schools, Newark, 1967–1983; instructor, Virginia State College, Petersburg, Virginia; supervisor of student teachers (during retirement), adjunct instructor in English, Newark State College, Union, New Jersey, 1964; consultant, guest speaker in English, adjunct instructor, Rutgers University, Newark and New Brunswick; guest speaker in reading, Jersey City State College, Jersey City, New Jersey; guest speaker in reading, Montclair State College, Upper Montclair, New Jersey.

Memberships   Newark Preservation and Landmarks Committee; Newark Senior Citizen's Commission; life member and past president, Alpha Kappa Alpha Sorority, Inc.; Kappa Delta Pi; National Council of Teachers of English; National Council of Teachers of Mathematics; life member, National Council of Negro Women; life member, NAACP; Negro Business and Professional Women, North Jersey Unit; vice president, Newark Youth Art Exhibition; National Society for the Study of Education; American Association of University Women; Association for Supervision and Curriculum Development; National Alliance of Black School Educators; past president, League of Women Voters of Newark; Soroptimist International of Newark; National Council of Teachers of English; National Council of Teachers of Mathematics; YM-YWCA of Newark; vice president, Project Pride; Governor's Committee on Children's Services Planning, 1983–1987; Essex County Human Services Advisory Committee.

Awards, Honors, Other Certificates   North Jersey Unit, National Association of Negro Business Professional Women's Clubs, 1964; Newark Chapter, National Council of Negro Women, 1965; Newark Chapter, Zeta Phi Beta Sorority, 1965; Award for Distinguished Service to Education, Newark State College Alumni Association 1966; Citizenship Award, Weequahic Community Council, 1967; Woman of the Year, Alpha Kappa Alpha Sorority, 1968; East Side High School Alumni Roster of Superior Merit, 1969; Distinguished Service Award, Cosmopolitan Women's Club, 1970; First Hopewell Baptist Church, 1976; Aviation Advisory Council of New Jersey, 1977; Distinguished Service Award, Alpha Phi Alpha Fraternity, 1978; Community Service Award, Sigma Gamma Rho Sorority, 1979;

Delta Sigma Theta Sorority Award as a Pioneer in Education, 1980; Project Pride Award for Service, 1980 and 1981; Adam Clayton Powell Education Award, New Jersey Alliance of Black School Educators', 1981; Outstanding Contributions in Education Award, The Leaguers, Inc., 1982; resolutions by the New Jersey State Senate, the New Jersey State Assembly, Trustees of the Newark Free Public Library, Newark Municipal Council, Essex County Board of Chosen Freeholders, Newark Board of Education, Elizabeth Avenue, Weequahic Presbyterian Church, and the United Nations Association of Newark, 1983; establishment of the E. Alma Flagg Scholarship Fund, Inc. and awarded its first annual scholarship to Newark high school graduates, 1984; dedication of new elementary school on Third Street in Newark as E. Alma Flagg School, 1985; proclamation by the mayor of Newark establishing May 5, 1985, as E. Alma Flagg Day; resolution of commendation, Newark Municipal Council, 1985; Certificate of Appreciation, Essex County Executive, 1985; National Sojourner Truth Award, North Jersey Unit of the National Association of Negro Business and Professional Women's Clubs, 1985; certificate as outstanding graduate, East Side High School 75th Anniversary, 1986; Distinguished Alumna Award, Teachers College, Columbia University, 1986; Education Award, Essex County Civic Club, 1988.

Reflections

"My mother, who died in November 1987, had the greatest influence on my life. Raising five children by herself, she loved, supported, and encouraged me to do the best that I could do and to become the best that I could become. I am not satisfied that I have done that, but I am eternally grateful for her faith and support. I began writing poetry when I was in seventh grade at Chestnut Street School with Miss Anna Gerber as my teacher. As a child, I had poetry published in children's pages in newspapers, especially the Sunbeam Club in the *Newark Sunday Call.* Continuing to write in high school and college, I was Class Poet at East Side High School and a contributor to publications at Newark State College.

My teaching career in Newark began in 1943 and ended in 1983. . . . In 1964, with my appointment to Hawkins Street School, I became the first black principal of an integrated school in the city. In 1864, Mr. James M. Baxter was appointed to head The Colored School. My appointment carried the distinction of being made to the only black person ever appointed as a result of competitive written and oral examination. This is but a brief reference to a struggle which African American carried on for many years in their seeking fair treatment and merited promotions in the Newark School system."

Publications

Books

Flagg, E. Alma. *Lines and Colors: Twenty-One Poems.* Newark, N.J.: The Author, 1979. 22. Printed by Branford Press.

———. *Feelings, Lines, Colors.* Newark, N.J.: The Author, 1980. 36. Printed by Branford Press.

———. *Twenty More with Thought and Feeling.* Newark, N.J.: The Author, 1981. 20.

———. *Lines, Colors, and More . . .; A Commemorative Edition of the Poems of E. Alma Flagg.* Metuchen, N.J.: The Upland Press with the Kean University Foundation, 1998. 85.

Bio-Bibliographical Source

Flagg, E. Alma Williams. "African American Women Writers in New Jersey: Biographical Questionnaire." Completed by E. Alma Williams Flagg, winter 1989.

FLOURNOY, VALERIE ROSE 1952–

Personal   Born on 17 April 1952 in Camden, New Jersey; third child of Ivie Mae Buchanan Flournoy and Payton I. Flournoy, Sr. (chief of police, Palmyra; deceased); sisters: Celeste, Vanessa. Education: William Smith College, Geneva, New York, B.A., history, 1974; teacher's certificate, social studies (grades 7–12). Religion: Roman Catholic.

Residence in New Jersey   Palmyra.

Career   Clerk-typist, School and Library Services Division, Dell Publishing Company; assistant editor, Dial Books for Young Readers, New York City, 1977–1979; senior editor, Silhouette Books Division, Pocket Books, New York, 1979–1982; consulting editor, Second Chance at Love, The Berkley Publishing Group, New York, 1982–1983; editor-in-chief, Vis A Vis Publishing Company, Palmyra, 1985 to present.

Valerie Flournoy,
courtesy of Dial Books for Young Readers.

Memberships   Black Women in Publishing; Romance Writers of America.

Awards, Honors, Other Certificates   American Library Association Notable Book Award for *The Patchwork Quilt,* 1985; Christopher Award, The Christophers Inc., for *The Patchwork Quilt,* 1985; American Library Association/Social Responsibilities Round Table's Coretta Scott King Award for Illustrations, *The Patchwork Quilt,* 1985; Ezra Jack Keats' New Writer Award (first recipient), Ezra Jack Keats Foundation and The New York Public Library, 1986.

Publications
  Books
Flournoy, Valerie. *The Best Time of Day.* Illustrated by George Ford. Picture-
    back Series. New York: Random House, 1978. [32].
————. *The Twins Strike Back.* Illustrated by Diane deGroat. New York:
    Dial Press, 1980. [32]. Reprint, with illustrations by Melodye Rosales:
    Orange, N.J.: Just Us Books, 1994.
————. *The Patchwork Quilt.* Illustrated by Jerry Pinkney. New York: Dial
    Books for Young Readers, 1985. [32]. Reprint, London: Bodley Head,
    1985; [Washington, D.C.: National Library Service, 1987 (transcribing
    agency, National Braille Press [Boston], distributed by National Braille
    Press); Harmondsworth, U.K.: Puffin, 1987.
————. *Until Summer's End.* Garden City, N.J.: Doubleday, 1986. 186.
Flournoy, Valerie, and Vanessa Flournoy. *Celie and the Harvest Fiddler.* Paint-
    ings by James E. Ransome. New York: Tambourine Books, 1995. 1 vol.
    (unpaged).
————. *Tanya's Reunion.* Illustrated by Jerry Pinkney. New York: Dial
    Books for Young Readers, 1995. 1v. (unpaged).
Bio-Bibliographical Sources
Olendorf, Donna, ed. *Contemporary Authors: A Bio-Bibliographical Guide to
    Current Writers in Fiction, General Nonfiction, Poetry, Journalism, Drama,
    Motion Pictures, Television, and Other Fields.* Vol. 142. Detroit: Gale
    Research Inc., 1994.
Rollock, Barbara. *Black Authors & Illustrators of Children's Books: A Biograph-
    ical Dictionary.* 2nd ed. New York: Garland Publishing, 1992.
Who's Who Among African Americans. 12th ed. Detroit: Gale Group, 1999.
Winne, Judith W. "From Palmyra, Bright Tales of Black Experiences."
    Courier-Post, 5 December 1986, 10B.

FLOURNY, VANESSA 1952–

Personal   Born on 17 April 1952 in Camden County, New Jersey; daugh-
ter of Ivie Mae Buchanan Fournoy and Payton I. Flournoy, Sr. (chief of
police, Palmyra, N.J., deceased); sisters: Celeste and Valerie.
Residence in New Jersey   Palmyra
Publications
Payton, Vanessa. *All-American Girl.* First Love from Silhouette Series, no.
    38. New York: Silhouette Books, 1983. 187.
Flournoy, Valerie, and Vanessa Flournoy. *Celie and the Harvest Fiddler.* Paint-
    ings by James E. Ransome. New York: Tambourine Books, 1995. 1 vol.
    (unpaged).
Bio-Bibliographical Sources
Henderson, Ashyia N., and Shirelle Phelps. *Who's Who Among African Amer-
    icans.* 12th ed. Detroit: Gale Group, 1999.

Rollock, Barbara. *Black Authors & Illustrators of Children's Books: A Biographical Dictionary.* 2nd ed. New York: Garland Publishing, 1992.
Winne, Judith W. "From Palmyra, Bright Tales of Black Experiences." *Courier-Post,* 5 December 1986, 10B.

FREELAND, ANNABELLE ROBINSON 1934–

Personal   Born on 1 October 1934 in Glenwood, Georgia; second child of Vera Jackson Robinson (sharecropper) and Larfa "Buster" Robinson (sharecropper), both of Georgia; granddaughter (maternal) of Lizza New Jackson and George Jackson, both of Ailey, Georgia; granddaughter (paternal) of Nan Robinson and William Robinson of Glenwood; sisters: Fannie Mae Robinson Gleaton (deceased), Willie Maude Robinson Smith (deceased), Pearline Robinson Gleaton (deceased), Lillie Francis Robinson Williams, and Dorothy Pearl Robinson Solomon (deceased); brother: Franklin D. Robinson (deceased); husband: Lloyd Julius Freeland; children: Joseph Lafayette Wilson (deceased), Shonda Ann Wilson, and Lloid Toninetta Wilson Spaulding. Education: Glenwood Ele-

Annabelle Robinson Freeland, courtesy of Annabelle Robinson Freeland.

mentary School, Glenwood; Glenwood High School, Glenwood; Albany State College, Albany, Georgia, 1951–1954; Newark State College, Union, New Jersey, B.A., elementary education, 1970; Kean College, Union, New Jersey, M.A., interdisciplinary studies, 1978; New Brunswick Theological Seminary, New Brunswick, New Jersey, M.Div., 1988; Monrovia College, Monrovia, Liberia, D.D., 1988; United Theological Seminary, Dayton, Ohio, D. Min., 1997; further studies: Princeton Theological Seminary, Princeton, New Jersey; Interdenominational Seminary, Atlanta, Georgia. Religion: African Methodist Episcopal.
Residence in New Jersey   Long Branch, Red Bank, Tinton Falls, 1953 to present.
Career   Elementary teacher, Long Branch, New Jersey, 1970–1994; itinerant minister, African Methodist Episcopal Church (Englishtown, Ocean City, Trenton, and Fair Haven), 1976 to present; evangelist to Gonaives, Haiti, West Indies, 1987 to present; built Annabelle Freeland A.M.E. Church, Gonaives, 1989–1990; established Annabelle Freeland Christian School, Gonaives, 1990.

Memberships   Red Bank Greater Area Ministerial Group; West Side Ministerial Society, Red Bank, New Jersey.

Awards, Honors, Other Certificates   Teacher of the Month, Gregory School, Long Beach, New Jersey, September 1993; Pastor of the Year Award, Camden/Trenton District A.M.E. Church, 4 May 1994; Pastor of the Year Award, Grant Chapel A.M.E. Church, Trenton, 21 February 1995; Outstanding Leadership Award: Exemplary Role Model for Women in Ministry, Grant Chapel A.M.E. Church, Trenton, 19 April 1997; Certificate of Achievement, Church Women United, Trenton, April 1997; Outstanding Pastor, State of New Jersey General Assembly, April 1997; Certificate of Recognition of Untiring and Devoted Service, Quinn Chapel A.M.E. Church, Atlantic Highlands, New Jersey, January 1998; Outstanding Pastor, First Episcopal District, A.M.E. Church School, 23 October 1999; Annabelle Freeland A.M.E. Church, Gonaives, Haiti, named in her honor.

Reflections

"My second and third grade teacher, Mrs. Laura Bell Clinton, of Glenwood, Georgia, encouraged me to write the stories I used to tell and put the ideas on paper so that I might share with others. My children also encouraged me to write and to tell the story of my life as the daughter of sharecroppers and being born in a log cabin in the south."

Publication

Freeland, Annabelle. *Steps to Develop a Powerful Prayer Life: "In the Name of Jesus."* Brooklyn, New York: Word for Word Publishing Co., Inc. [1997]. xxi, 125.

Bio-Bibliographical Source

Freeland, Annabelle R. Telephone conversation with Sibyl E. Moses, 10 July 2001.

FULLILOVE, MINDY THOMPSON 1950–

Mindy Thompson Fullilove.
Photograph by Herb Way © 1994.

Personal   Born on 15 October 1950 in Irvington, New Jersey; oldest child of Margaret Ailene Brown Hunter Thompson (secretary) of Ohio and Ernest Leroy Thompson (labor organizer) of Maryland; granddaughter (maternal) of Minnie Brown and Don Brown; granddaughter (paternal) of Jennifer Thompson and Joshua Thompson; brother: Joshua Paul Thompson; husband: Michael Kaufman (married 1971, divorced 1983), Robert Elliott Fullilove III (married 1983); children: Kenneth Thompson Kaufman, Dina Tracy Shepard

Thompson Kaufman, and Molly Rose Thompson Kaufman. Education: Heywood, Oakwood, and Tremont Schools, Orange, New Jersey; Orange High School, Orange, diploma, 1967; Bryn Mawr College, Bryn Mawr, Pennsylvania, A.B., cum laude, history, 1971; Columbia University, New York, M.S., nutrition, 1974; Columbia University College of Physicians and Surgeons, New York, M.D., 1978. Religion: Unitarian Universalist.

Residence in New Jersey   Orange; Hoboken, 1990 to present.

Career   Lecturer, psychiatry, Albert Einstein College of Medicine, Bronx, New York, 1982–1983; assistant clinical professor in psychology, University of California at San Francisco School of Medicine, San Francisco, California, 1983–1990; assistant clinical professor, Dean's Office, University of California at San Francisco, San Francisco, 1986–1990; associate professor, clinical psychiatry and public health (sociomedical sciences), Columbia University, New York, 1990–2000; visiting associate professor, Graduate School of Public Health, University of Pittsburgh, Pittsburgh, Pennsylvania, 1998; professor, clinical psychiatry and public health, Columbia University, New York, 2000 to present; psychiatrist, New York State Psychiatric Institute, 1990 to present.

Memberships   American College of Psychiatrics; New York Academy of Medicine; American Psychiatric Association; American Public Health Association; president, Northern California Black Women Physicians, 1984–1986.

Awards, Honors, Other Certificates   Finalist, National Merit Scholarship, 1968; Edwin Gould Foundation for Children Scholarship, 1967–1971; Elizabeth Duane Gillespie Prize in American History, Bryn Mawr College, Bryn Mawr, 1970; Woodrow Wilson Fellowship, 1970; National Science Foundation Grant, 1973; Hannah E. Longshore Memorial Medical Scholarship, 1974; National Medical Fellowship, 1975; Sebrell Fellowship for Nutrition Research, American Medical Association, 1975; New York State Regents Physicians Shortage Area Scholarship, 1975–1978; Franklin C. McLean Award, 1978; National Medical Fellowship, 1978; Bernard J. Stern Award for Best Publication by New Author, AIMS, 1978; American Psychiatric Association-National Institute of Mental Health Minority Fellow, 1979–1982; Award for Drug Abuse Research, California Association of County Drug Program Administrators, 1989; Dana African-American Visiting Professor, Department of Psychiatry, University of Maryland at Baltimore, Baltimore, Maryland, 1994; National Acupuncture and Detoxification Association Annual Award, 1994; Osborne Medal, Osborne Foundation and Correctional Association, 1994; Best Doctors in New York, *New York Magazine,* 1996, 1998, 2000; "One of the Leading HIV Researchers in the United States," *Poz Magazine,* 1996; Outstanding Woman Scientist, Association of Women in Science, New York Metro Chapter, 1996; Maurice Faulk Fellow at the Center for Minority Health, University of Pittsburgh GSPH 1998–1999; honorary doctorate, Chatham College, 1999; Best Doctors in New York, *New York Magazine,* 2000.

Publications

Books

Thompson, Mindy. *The National Negro Labor Council: A History. American Institute for Marxist Studies Occasional Paper, no. 27.* New York: AIMS, n.d. 94.

Thompson, Ernest, and Mindy Thompson. *Homeboy Comes to Orange.* Newark: Bridgebuilder Press, 1976. 211.

Fullilove, Mindy Thompson. *The House of Joshua: Meditations on Family and Place.* Lincoln: University of Nebraska Press, 1999. 160, illus.

Articles

Fullilove, Mindy Thompson. "Metaphor and Pscyhe." *Black Psychiatrists of America Quarterly* 12 (1982): 12.

Fullilove, Mindy Thompson, and T. Reynolds. "Skin Color in the Development of Identity: A Biopsychosocial Model." *Journal of the National Medical Association* 76 (1984): 587–591.

———. "A Task-oriented Lunch Group." *Hospital and Community Psychiatry* 35 (1985): 1078.

Fullilove, Mindy Thompson, O. Pacheco, and C. Fourchard. "A Task-oriented Group in Day Hospital." *Journal of the National Medical Association* 7 (1985): 995–998.

Shea, S., and Mindy Thompson Fullilove. "Entry of Black and Other Minority Students into U.S. Medical Schools: A Historical Perspective and Recent Trends." *New England Journal of Medicine* 313 (1985): 933–940.

Fullilove, Mindy Thompson. "Family Therapy and Black Patients." *American Journal of Social Psychiatry* (winter 1986): 62–68.

Fullilove, Mindy Thompson, R. E. Fullilove, and K. Culler. "Black Education: A Psychiatric Perspective." *American Journal of Social Psychiatry* (winter 1986): 36–42.

———. "Intersecting Epidemics: Black Teen Crack and Sexually Transmitted Disease." *Journal of the American Medical Women's Association* 44 (1989): 146–147, 151–153.

Fullilove, Mindy Thompson, R. E. Fullilove, and E. Morales. "Psychoeducation: A Tool for AIDS Prevention in Minority Communities." *Journal of Psychotherapy and the Family* 6 (1989): 143–160.

Bowser, B. P., M. T. Fullilove, and R. E. Fullilove. "African American Youth and AIDS High Risk Behavior: The Social Context and Barriers to Prevention." *Youth and Society* 22 (1990): 54–66.

Fullilove, Mindy Thompson, R. E. Fullilove, K. Haynes, and S. Gross. "Black Women and AIDS Prevention: A View Towards Understanding the Gender Rules." *Journal Sex Research* 27 (1990): 47–64.

Fullilove, R. E., M. T. Fullilove, B. Bowser, and S. Gross. "Crack Users: The New AIDS Risk Group?" *Journal of Cancer Detection and Prevention* (January 1990): 363–368.

———. "Risk of Sexually Transmitted Disease Among Black Adolescent Crack Users in Oakland and San Francisco, CA." *Journal of the American Medical Association* 263 (1990): 851–855.

Gasch, H., D. M. Poulson, R. E. Fullilove, M. T. Fullilove. "Shaping AIDS Education and Prevention Programs for African Americans amidst Community Decline." *Journal of Negro Education* 60 (1991): 85–96.

Hargrave, R., M. T. Fullilove, and R. E. Fullilove. "Defining Mental Health Needs for Black Patients with AIDS in Alameda County." *Journal of the National Medical Association* 83 (1991): 801–804.

Wallace, R., and M. T. Fullilove. "AIDS Deaths in the Bronx 1983–1988: Spatiotemporal Analysis from a Sociogeographic Perspective." *Environmental Planning* 23 (1991): 1701–1723.

Catania, J. A., T. J. Coates, S. Kegeles, M. T. Fullilove, J. Peterson, B. Marin, D. Siegel, and S. Hulley. "Condom Use in Multi-ethnic Neighborhoods of San Francisco: The Population-based AMEN (AIDS in Multi-ethnic Neighborhoods Study." *American Journal of Public Health* 82, no. 2 (1992): 284–287.

Fullilove, Mindy Thompson, A. Lown, and R. E. Fullilove. "Crack 'Hos and Skeezers: Traumatic Experiences of Women Crack Users." *Journal of Sex Research* 29 (May 1992): 275–287.

Fullilove, Mindy Thompson, J. Wiley, R. E. Fullilove, E. Golden, J. Catania, J. Peterson, K. Garrett, D. Siegel, B. Marin, S. Kegeles, T. Coates, and S. Hulley. "Risk for AIDS in Multi-ethnic Neighborhoods of San Francisco: The Population-based AMEN Study." *Western Journal of Medicine* (1992): 32–40.

Morales, E., and M. T. Fullilove. " 'Many Are Called . . .': Participation by Minority Leaders in an AIDS Intervention in San Francisco. *Ethnicity and Disease* 21 (1992): 389–401.

Schwarcz, S. K., G. A. Bolan, M. T. Fullilove, J. McCright, R. Fullilove, R. Kohn, and R. Rolfs. "Crack Cocaine and the Exchange of Sex for Money or Drugs: Risk Factors for Gonorrhea Among Black Adolescents in San Francisco." *Sexually Transmitted Diseases* 19 (January–February 1992): 7–13.

Siegel, D., E. Golden, D. S. Schmid, A. E. Washington, J. G. Dobbins, S. Morse, M. T. Fullilove, W. C. Reeves, J. A. Catania, B. Marin, and S. B. Hulley. "Prevalence and Correlates of Herpes Simplex Infections: The Population-based AIDS in Multi-ethnic Neighborhoods Study." *Journal of the American Medical Association* 268 (1992): 1702–1708.

Catania, J. A., T. J. Coates, J. Petersen, M. Dolcini, S. Kegeles, D. Siegel, E. Golden, and M. T. Fullilove. "Changes in Condom Use Among Blacks, Hispanic, and White Heterosexuals in San Francisco: The AMEN Cohort Survey." *Journal of Sex Research* 30 (1993): 121–128.

Fullilove, Mindy Thompson, R. E. Fullilove, M. Smith, K. Winkler, C. Michael, P. Panzer, R. Wallace. "Violence, Trauma, and Posttraumatic Stress Disorder Among Women Drug Users." *Journal of Traumatic Stress* 6 (1993): 105–115.

Fullilove, Mindy Thompson, E. Golden, R. E. Fullilove, R. Lennon, D. Porterfield, S. Schwarcz, G. Bolan. "Crack Cocaine Use and High-risk Behaviors among Sexually-active Black Adolescents." *Journal of Adolescent Health* 14 (December 1993): 295–300.

Fullilove, Mindy Thompson, Rebecca Young, Paula Panzer, and Philip Muskin. "Psychosocial Issues in the Management of Patients with Tuberculosis." *Journal of Law, Medicine and Ethics* 21, no. 3–4 (fall–winter 1993): 324–331.

Washburn, A. M., R. E. Fullilove, M. T. Fullilove, P. A. Keenan, B. McGee, K. A. Morris, J. L. Sorensen, and W. W. Clark. "Acupuncture Heroin Detoxification: A Single-blind Clinical Trial." *Journal of Substance Abuse Treatment* 10 (1993): 345–351.

Catania, J. A., T. J. Coates, E. Golden, M. Dolcini, J. Petersen, S. Kegeles, D. Siegel, and M. T. Fullilove. "Correlates of Condom Use Among Black, Hispanic, and White Heterosexuals in San Francisco: The AMEN Longitudinal Survey. *AIDS Education and Prevention* 6 (1994): 12–26.

Loftus, Elizabeth, Sara Polonsky, and Mindy Thompson Fullilove. "Memories of Childhood Sexual Abuse: Remembering and Repressing." *Psychology of Women Quarterly* 18, no. 1 (March 1994): 67–84.

Siegel, D., S. A. Larsen, E. Golden, S. Morse, M. T. Fullilove, and A. E. Washington. "Prevalence, Incidence, and Correlates of Syphilis Seroactivity in Multi-ethnic San Francisco Neighborhoods. *Annals of Epidemiology* 4 (1994): 460–465.

Wallace, R., M. T. Fullilove, R. Fullilove, and P. Gould. "Will AIDS Be Contained within the U.S. Minority Urban Populations?" *Social Science and Medicine* 39 (1994): 1051–1062.

Wallace, R., D. Wallace, H. Andrews, R. Fullilove, and M. T. Fullilove. "The Spaciotemporal Sociographic Perspective: Understanding the Linkages of Central City and Suburbs." *Environmental and Planning* 27 (1995): 1085–1108.

Dolcini, M. Margaret, Joseph A. Catania, Kyung-Hee Choi, Mindy Thompson Fullilove, and Thomas J. Coates. "Cognitive and Emotional Assessments of Perceived Risk for HIV Among Unmarried Heterosexuals." *AIDS Education and Prevention* 8, no. 4 (August 1996): 294–307.

Eilenberg, Julia, Mindy Thompson Fullilove, Ron G. Goldman, and Lisa Mellman. "Quality and Use of Trauma Histories Obtained from Psychiatric Outpatients Through Mandated Inquiry." *Psychiatric Services* 47 (February 1996): 165–169.

Fullilove, Mindy Thompson. "Managing Change: Psychosocial Issues for Women." *Medscape* 1, no. 9 (1996). Available: <http://www.medscape.com/>. Accessed 12 July 2001.

———. "Psychiatric Implications of Displacement: Contributions from the Psychology of Place." *American Journal of Psychiatry* 153, no. 12 (December 1996): 1516–1523.

Schwartz, Anna, Julia Eilenberg, and Mindy Thompson Fullilove. "Gloria's Despair: Struggling Against the Odds." *American Journal of Psychiatry* 153, no. 10 (October 1996): 1334–1338.

Wallace, R., M. T. Fullilove, and A. J. Flisher. "AIDS, Violence, and Behavioral Coding: Information Theory, Risk Behavior, and Dynamic Process on Core-group Sociogeographic Networks." *Social Science and Medicine* 43 (1996): 339–352.

Fullilove, Mindy Thompson. " 'Biopsychosocial Model': Reply." *American Journal of Psychiatry* 154, no. 9 (September 1997): 1328–1329.

Fullilove, R. E., J. C. Edgoose, and M. T. Fullilove. "Chaos, Criticality and Public Health." *Journal of the National Medical Association* 89 (1997): 311–316.

Panzer, Paula G., and Mindy Thompson Fullilove. "Belinda's Puzzle: Assembling the Pieces of an Illness." *American Journal of Psychiatry* 154, no. 5 (May 1997): 677–680.

Fullilove, Mindy Thompson. "Promoting Social Cohesion to Improve Health." *Journal of the American Medical Women's Association* 53 (1998): 72–76.

Fullilove, Mindy Thompson, Veronique Heon, Walkiria Jimenez, Caroline Parsons, Lesley L. Green, and Robert E. Fullilove, III. "Injury and Anomie: Effects of Violence on an Inner-City Community." *American Journal of Public Health* 88, no. 6 (June 1998): 924–927.

Garcia-Soto, M., K. Haynes-Sanstad, R. E. Fullilove, and M. T. Fullilove. "The Peculiar Epidemic, Part I: Social Response to AIDS in Alameda County." *Environment & Planning* 30 (1998): 731–746.

Green, Lesley L., Mindy Thompson Fullilove, and Robert E. Fullilove. "Stories of Spiritual Awakening: The Nature of Spirituality in Recovery." *Journal of Substance Abuse Treatment* 15, no. 4 (July–August 1998): 325–331.

Watkins, B. X., R. E. Fullilove, and M. T. Fullilove. "Arms Against Illness: Crack Cocaine and U.S. Drug Policy." *Health and Human Rights* 2 (1998): 43–58.

Fullilove, M. T., and R. E. Fullilove. "Homosexuality and the African American Church: The Paradox of the 'Open Closet.' " *American Behavioral Scientist* 42 (1999): 1117–1129.

Fullilove, Mindy Thompson, and Robert E. Fullilove, III. "Stigma as an Obstacle to AIDS Action." *American Behavioral Scientist* 42, no. 7 (April 1999): 1117–1129.

Fullilove, M. T., L. L. Green, and R. E. Fullilove. "Building Momentum: An Ethnographic Study of Inner-city Redevelopment." *American Journal of Public Health* 89 (1999): 840–844.

Fullilove, Robert E., Mindy Thompson Fullilove, Mary E. Northbridge, Michael L. Ganz, Mary T. Bassett, Diane E. McClean, Angela A. Aidala, Donald H. Gemson, and Colin McCord. "Risk Factors for Excess Mortality in Harlem: Findings from the Harlem Household Survey." *American Journal of Preventive Medicine* 16, 3 supplement (April 1999): 22–28.

Watkins, B. X. and M. T. Fullilove. "Crack Cocaine and Harlem." Souls 1 (1999): 37–48.

Book Chapters

Fullilove, Mindy Thompson. "AIDS and Minority Communities: The Two Epidemics." In *Face to Face: A Guide to AIDS Counseling,* edited by James W. Dilley, Cheri Pies, and Michael Helquist, 230–240. San Francisco: University of California San Francisco AIDS Health Project, 1989.

Fullilove, Mindy Thompson, R. E. Fullilove, and E. Morales. "Psychoeducation: A Tool for AIDS Prevention in Minority Communities." In *Minorities and Family Therapy,* edited by George W. Saba, Betty M. Karra, and Kenneth V. Hardy, 143–160. New York: Haworth Press, 1990.

Stall, R., C. Frutchey, M. Fullilove, and P. Christen. "Lessons from San Francisco: Principles of Program Design." In *Ending the HIV Epidemic: Community Strategies in Disease Prevention and Health Promotion,* edited by Steven Petrow, Pat Franks, and Timothy R. Wolfred, 98–110. San Francisco: Network Publications, 1990.

Fullilove, Robert E., and Mindy Thompson Fullilove. "Black Men, Black Sexuality and AIDS." In *Black Male Adolescents: Parenting and Education in Community Context,* n.p. Lanham, Md.: University Press of America, 1991.

Wallace, R., M. T. Fullilove, and D. Wallace. "Family Systems and De-urbanization: Implications for Substance Abuse." In *Comprehensive Textbook of Substance Abuse,* edited J. Lowinson, et al., 944–955. Baltimore: Williams and Wilkins, 1992.

Lown, E. Anne, Karen Winkler, Robert E. Fullilove, and Mindy Thompson Fullilove. "Tossin' and Tweakin': Women's Consciousness in the Crack Culture." In *Psychological Perspectives: Women and AIDS,* edited by Corinne Squire, n.p. Gender and Psychology Series. London: Sage Publications, 1993.

Fullilove, Mindy Thompson. "Minority Women: Ecological Setting and Intercultural Dialogue." In *Psychological Aspects of Women's Health Care: The Interface between Psychiatry and Obstetrics and Gynecology,* edited by Nada L. Stotland and Donna E. Stewart, n.p. Washington, D.C.: American Psychiatric Press, Inc., 1993.

Fullilove, Mindy Thompson, and Robert E. Fullilove. "Understanding Sexual Behaviors and Drug Use Among African-Americans: A Case Study of Issues for Survey Research." In *Methodological Issues in AIDS Behavioral Research,* n.p. New York: Plenum Press, 1993.

Gasch, Helen, and Mindy Thompson Fullilove. "Working with Communities of Women at Risk: A Chronicle." In *Until the Cure: Caring For Women with HIV,* edited by Ann Kurth and Marsha Pravder, 183–199. New Haven, Conn.: Yale University Press, 1993. Reprint in *Women in Context: Toward a Feminist Reconstruction of Psychotherapy,* edited by M. P. Mirkin, n.p. New York: Guilford Press, 1994.

Fullilove, Mindy Thompson, and Robert E. Fullilove III. "Post-Traumatic Stress Disorder in Women Recovering From Substance Abuse." In *Anxiety Disorders in African Americans,* edited by Steven Friedman, n.p. New York: Springer Publishing Co, Inc., 1994.

Fullilove, R. E., W. Barksdale, M. T. Fullilove. "Teens Talk Sex: Can We Talk Back?" In *Sexual Cultures,* edited by Janice Irvine, 310–322. Philadelphia: Temple University Press, 1994.

Fullilove, R. E., and Mindy Thompson Fullilove. "Conducting Research in Ethnic Minority Communities: Considerations and Challenges." In *Drug Abuse Prevention with Multiethnic Youth,* edited by G. Botvin, S. Schinke, and M. Orlandi, 46–56. Thousand Oaks, Calif.: Sage Publications, 1995.

Perez, B., G. Kennedy, and M. T. Fullilove. "Childhood Sexual Abuse and AIDS: Issues and Interventions." In *Women at Risk: Issues in the Primary Prevention of AIDS,* edited by Ann O'Leary and Loretta Sweet Jemmott, 83–101. New York: Plenum Press, 1995.

Fullilove, Mindy Thompson. "Beyond Stereotypes: Stigma and the Counseling Process." In *The UCSF AIDS Health Project Guide to Counseling: Perspectives on Psychotherapy, Prevention, and Therapeutic Practice,* edited by James W. Dilley and Robert Marks, 209–224. San Francisco: Jossey-Bass Publishers, 1998.

Fullilove, Mindy Thompson. "AIDS and Social Context." In *AIDS-related Cancers and Their Treatment,* edited by Ellen G. Feigal, Robert J. Biggar, and Alexandra M. Levine, 371–385. New York: Marcel Dekker, Inc., 2000.

Bio-Bibliographical Sources

Fellows and Members of the American Psychiatric Association. *Biographical Directory, as of January, 1989.* Washington, D.C.: American Psychiatric Press, Inc., 1989.

Fullilove, Mindy Thompson. "African American Women Writers in New Jersey: Biographical Questionnaire." Completed by Mindy Thompson Fullilove, 26 January 2001.

———. *The House of Joshua: Meditations on Family and Place.* Lincoln: University of Nebraska Press, 1999. 160. illus.

———. "Resume." 8 June 2000. 15.

G

GAINES, KATHYRN ELIZABETH 1956–

Kathryn E. Gaines.
Photograph by Robert E. Gaines.

Personal Born on 25 July 1956 in Philadelphia, Pennsylvania; first child of Doris Priscilla Smith Gaines (librarian) of Camden, New Jersey, and Robert Gaines (Lieutenant of Tolls, Delaware River Port Authority) of Lawnside, New Jersey; granddaughter (maternal) of Hazel Frye Smith and James Still Smith; granddaughter (paternal) of Estella Gaines and Alfonso Gaines; brothers: Robert E. Gaines and Richard M. Gaines; child: Kimberly Christina Gaines. Education: Parkside Elementary School, Camden; Hatch Middle School, Camden; Camden High School, Camden, 1970–1974; Camden County College, Blackwood, New Jersey, A.A., 1974–1976; Glassboro (now Rowan) State College, B.A, 1976–1979. Religion: Methodist; Parkside Methodist Church, Camden; Jacobs A.M.E. Chapel, Mt. Laurel, New Jersey.

Residence in New Jersey Camden, 1956 to present.

Career Teacher, Hatch Middle School, 1974–1979; science teacher, Lawnside Middle School, Lawnside, New Jersey(grades 6–8), 1979–1980; teacher, basic skills, Linden School Adult Education Program, Linden, New Jersey, 1980–1981; teacher, basic skills, Sewell School, 1981–1982, Mantua; teacher, basic skills, Parkside Elementary School, 1982–1991; teacher, basic skills, Department of Corrections and Juvenile Services, 1991 to present.

Memberships NAACP; founder and acting president, Camden Chapter, National Hook-up of Black Women; New Jersey Education Association; Black Film Makers Guild.

Awards, Honors, Other Certificates Endorsed by Operation Push, Chicago, for poem "Color," 1990.

Reflections

"Coming of age in one of the oldest and largest Black families in the State of New Jersey is an experience in itself. The old-time stories that have been passed down through generation after generation, have stimulated me tremendously. I have been able to see through their lives, the pride, the pain and heartache, the struggles and the love that has kept them strong. [Other writers in my family] include [my great-great grandfather] Dr. James Still, author of *The Early Recollections and Life of Dr. James Still,* and [great-great uncle] William Still, author of *The Underground Railroad*. The reason that I chose the position of teaching as a career is because at an early stage in my life, I saw the need for basic skills teachers in the inner city of Camden. At an early age, I became aware of the lackadaisical attitudes that were permeating our school systems and I was determined to make a change for the betterment of our youth. It is for the above reason that I am now in my present teaching position at the Department of Corrections, Juvenile Services, Substance Abusers, between the ages of 14 and 18. The youths that end up in the correctional system are first known to be delinquent from school on a constant basis and everything begins to deescalate from there. I saw the need for change and decided to become part of the solution, and not part of the problem."

Publication

Gaines, Kathyrn E. *My Love, My Life, My Family STILL: A Collection of Poems.* Haddonfield, N.J.: Management Ventures International, 1989. [77], illus. Printed by Acme Craftsmen, Camden, N.J.

Bio-Bibliographical Source

Gaines, Kathyrn Elizabeth. "African American Women Writers in New Jersey: Biographical Questionnaire." Completed by Kathyrn Elizabeth Gaines, February 1993.

GILMORE-SCOTT, MONIQUE 1962–

Personal Born on 3 February 1962 in Newark, New Jersey; eldest child of Janeth Braye of Newark and Herman Gilmore of Thomson, Georgia; granddaughter (maternal) of Dorothy Williams of Savannah, Georgia, and Robert Edward Braye of Norfolk, Virginia; sister: Dr. Renee D. Gilmore; brother: Herman Joseph Gilmore; husband: Kenneth Scott (independent marketing agent); stepchildren: Jordan Joseph Scott; Aaron Joseph Scott; Ashley Jamece Scott. Education: Queen of Angels, Newark; Our Lady of All Souls, East Orange, New Jersey; Marylawn of the Oranges, South Orange, New Jersey, high school diploma, 1980; Rutgers University, New Brunswick, New Jersey, B.S., criminal law, 1985; University of Denver Law School, Denver, Colorado, 1985–1988. Religion: Christian.

*Monique Gilmore-Scott.
Photograph by Gail Espree,
courtesy of Glamour Photos.*

Residence in New Jersey   Newark; East Orange.
Career   Licensed vocational teacher, Mansfield Business College, Denver, 1985–1987; pharmaceutical representative, DuPont Pharmaceuticals, northern New Jersey; pharmaceutical representative, Boots Pharmaceutical, northern California; property manager, Greenbrier/Avalonbay, northern California; licensed vocational teacher, Property Management Training Institute, Hayward, California, 1995–1997.
Memberships   Delta Sigma Theta Sorority, Inc.
Awards, Honors, Other Certificates   Best Multicultural Romance Novel Award by *Affaire de Coeur Magazine* for *No Ordinary Love,* 1994; Best Multicultural Novel Award by *Romantic Times Magazine* for *The Grass Ain't Greener,* 1996; Career Achievement Award (nominee) by *Romantic Times Magazine,* 1996.
Publications
  Books
Gilmore, Monique. *No Ordinary Love.* New York: Pinnacle Books, 1994. 303.
———. *Hearts Afire.* New York: Pinnacle/Arabesque, 1995. 254.
———. *The Grass Ain't Greener.* New York: Kensington Publishing Corporation, 1996. 317; large print edition, Thorndike, Maine: G. K. Hall, 1999.
Gilmore-Scott, Monique. *Soul Deep.* New York: Kensington Publishing Corp., 1997. 251.
———. *Ties that Bind Way Down Deep: A New Kind of Novel.* First Writing Minds Fiction edition. Pleasanton, Calif.: Panache, 1998. 249.
———. *A Simple Guide to Football.* Pleasanton, Calif.: Writing Minds, 1999. ca. 100. Available: <http://www.Just4girlfriends.com> Accessed 28 April 2000.
Bio-Bibliographical Sources
Gilmore-Scott, Monique. "African American Women Writers in New Jersey: Biographical Questionnaire." Completed by Monique Gilmore-Scott, 2 June 2000.
———. Telephone interview by Sibyl E. Moses. 7 June 2000.
Writing Minds. "Monique Gilmore-Scott." Available: <http://www.writingminds.com/bio.htm> Accessed 28 April 2000.

GRANT, GWENDOLYN GOLDSBY

Residence in New Jersey   Newark.
Career   Advice columnist for *Essence* Magazine; psychologist, guest appearances on television shows: *Montel Williams, Good Morning America, Richard Bey, Sally Jesse Raphael, Ricky Lake, Oprah, The MacNeil/Lehrer News Hour, Black Entertainment TV, Geraldo, Regis and Kathy Lee, The Maury Povich Show, The Jerry Springer Show, Jenny Jones,* and CNN.
Memberships   Phi Delta Kappa Honor Society; Phi Kappa Phi Honor Society; Alpha Kappa Alpha Sorority, Inc.; life member, National Council of Negro Women; National Association of Black Journalists.

Awards, Honors, Other Certificates Bobby E. Wright Community Service Award by the Association of Black Psychologists.
Publication
Grant, Gwendolyn Goldsby. *The Best Kind of Loving: A Black Woman's Guide to Finding Intimacy*. New York: HarperCollins, 1995. x, 294.
Bio-Bibliographical Source
MediaRep Associates Speakers Bureau. "Dr. Gwendolyn Goldsby Grant ("The Energizer")." Available:<http://www.mediarcpspcakers.com/ Categories/ggrant.html> Accessed 23 May 2000.

GREENE, CAROLYN JETTER

Personal Born in Paulsboro, New Jersey; oldest of two children. Education: Rumson-Regional High School, Rumson, New Jersey; Douglass College (Rutgers University), New Brunswick, New Jersey (two years); Newark State College (now Kean College), Union, New Jersey, B.A., mathematics/education; Wayne State University, Detroit, Michigan, M.Ed., counseling; University of San Francisco, San Francisco, California, Ed.D., educational psychology/counseling psychology.
Residence in New Jersey Fair Haven.
Career Mathematics instructor, high school and college; counseling psychologist, college counseling center; consultant, business and education on career development, interpersonal relationships, diversity training, and so forth; licensed therapist, private practice; freelance writer.

Carolyn Jetter Greene, courtesy of Carolyn Jetter Greene.

Memberships American Association of Counseling and Development; Association of Black Psychologists; California Association of Counseling and Development; California Association of Marriage and Family Therapists; The ECL Reading Sassiety.
Awards, Honors, Other Certificates Woman of Excellence Award, Bay Area Jack and Jill of America, 1990; The H. B. McDaniel Award in Counseling, H. B. McDaniel Foundation, Stanford University School of Education, 1993; The Martin Luther King Award, San Francisco Bay Area Branch, NAACP, 2000.
Reflections
  "My life was influenced by many people, especially my parents, who taught and encouraged me to be anything I wanted to be.

They also told me to never let any male or any White person ever tell me what I could not do. In my high school years, I was influenced by two women, one White, Alna DeWinter, and one African-American, Mary Tate, who were mathematicians in a world in which both racism and sexism played a role in limiting access of African Americans and women to many occupations in the hard sciences. I mastered the subject very easily and became a devout scholar of geometry. Many considered this unusual for an African-American girl, but it was my passion.

I was always a voracious reader. I wrote short stories while in high school and took a creative writing course during my undergraduate years, and was told by my professors that I had a natural talent for "social satire"; however, I never did anything serious about developing this untapped talent until after I moved to California in the late 60s and was invited to attend a writing seminar in Pajaro Dunes with a group of African-American writers. I became fascinated with the possibilities and the opportunities and began dabbling with the written word. It was at this time that it occurred to me that the old adage, "The pen is mightier than the sword," is true, especially, when it comes to exposing social issues. This led to my publication of two books and several articles. Zora Neale Hurston, Ida Wells Barnett, and Maya Angelou have had the most influence on me as writers."

Publications

Books

Greene, Carolyn Jetter. *70 Soul Secrets of Sapphire*. Illustrated by Don C. Eaton. San Francisco, Calif.: Sapphire Publishing Company, 1973. [114].

―――. *Sapphire's Second Set of Soul Secrets*. Illustrated by Don C. Eaton. Hayward, California: Stone Fox Publications, 1977. [143]

Articles:

Greene, Carolyn J. "Bring It Down Front: Manufactured White Racism." *Essence* 6 (May 1975): 8.

―――. "Social Promotion in Education: Genocide for Black Youth." *Black Perspectives* 2, no. 6 (July 1985).

―――. "In America, When is a Black Man Not a Threat?" *San Jose Mercury News*, 20 April 1993.

―――. "May Your Christmases Not be White." *Oakland Tribune*, 17 December 1993. Reprint: *San Jose Mercury News*, 17 December 1993.

Bio-Bibliographic Source

Greene, Carolyn Jetter. "African American Women Writers in New Jersey: Biographical Questionnaire." Completed by Carolyn J. Greene, 25 April 2001.

GUYTON, DIANA BRENDA *SEE* KARRIEM, JALEELAH

HAILSTOCK, SHIRLEY T. 1948–

Personal Born on 12 June 1948 in Newberry, South Carolina; second child of
Hattie Belle Hailstock (deceased) and
Eugene Hailstock (deceased), both of
Newberry, South Carolina; granddaughter (maternal) of Rosie Belle Johnson;
granddaughter (paternal) of Sallie Far-
row Hailstock and Hillary Hailstock, both
of Vaughnville, South Carolina; children:
Ashleigh M. Coles and Christopher D.
Coles, III. Education: Washington Elementary School, Alexandria, Virginia
(kindergarten), 1953; Pierce Elementary
School, Washington, D.C. (grades 1–3),
1954–1956; Public School #75, Buffalo,
New York (grades 3–4), 1956–1957; Public School #31, Buffalo (grade 4), 1958;
Public School #75, Buffalo (grades 5–6),
1959–1960; Public School #87 (Clinton

*Shirley T. Hailstock,
courtesy of Shirley T. Hailstock*

Junior High School), Buffalo (grades 7–8); Buffalo East High School, Buf-
falo, 1962–1966; Howard University, Washington, D.C., B.S., chemistry,
1966–1971; Benjamin Franklin University, Washington, D.C., Associates
Degree, 1974–1977; Fairleigh Dickinson University, Teaneck, New Jersey,
M.B.A., chemical marketing, 1976–1977. Religion: Baptist.
Residence in New Jersey Englishtown, 1975–1986; Trenton, 1986–1994;
Plainsboro, 1994 to present.
Career Adjunct professor, accounting), Rutgers University, New
Brunswick, New Jersey; instructor, novel writing, Middlesex County Col-
lege; account payable department, Dynalectron, Washington, D.C.,
1967–1972; account payable department, International Group Plans,
Washington, D.C., 1972–1975; cost accounting, Johnson and Johnson,
New Brunswick, New Jersey, 1975–1979; systems accounts, Bristol-Myers
Squibb, Princeton, New Jersey, 1979–1995; systems analysis and sales
systems, Bracco Diagnostics, Princeton, 1995 to present.
Memberships Past president, New Jersey Romance Writers; member,
Romance Writers of America, 1989 to present (also held positions as
regional director, chairperson, publicity chairperson, and industry statistics
chairperson, RITA Contest); officer, Women Writers of Color.
Awards, Honors, Other Certificates Romance Writers of America, Golden
Heart (semifinalist), for *Ice Maiden,* 1990; Virginia Romance Writers, HOLT

Medallion (winner), for *Whispers of Love*, 1995; Utah Romance Writers, Heart of the West Award (third place), for *Whispers of Love*, 1996; Mystery/Suspense Writers, Kiss of Death Award (honorable mention), for *White Diamonds*, 1997; *Romantic Times Magazine*, Best Multicultural Romance of 1996 nomination, for *White Diamonds*, 1997; *Romantic Times Magazine* Career Achievement Award (winner), 1997; *Glamour Magazine*, "Fall in Love Again" List, for *Whispers of Love*, *White Diamonds*, and *Legacy*, 1997; Romancing the Web, Best Multicultural Romance Novel of 1997 (winner), for *Legacy*, 1998; Colorado Romance Writers, Colorado Writers Award of Excellence (finalist), for *Legacy*, 1998; Utah Romance Writers, Heart of The West Award (honorable mention), for *Legacy*, 1998; Waldenbooks, Bestselling Multicultural Romance Novel Award, for *Legacy*, 1998; Under the Covers Website, Reader Favorite Awards for 1997 (winner), for *Legacy*, 1998; *Romantic Times Magazine*, Best Christmas Anthology of 1998 (nomination), for *Winter Nights*, 1999; Florida Romance Writers, 100 Greatest Romances of the 20th Century List, for *Legacy*, 1999; Romance Writers of America, Artemis Award, for *Mirror Image*, 1999; First Coast Romance Writers, The Beacon (finalist), for *Opposites Attract*, 2000; Oklahoma Romance Writers, National Readers Choice Award (finalist), for *Opposites Attract*, 2000; Utah Romance Writers, Heart of the West Award, for *Clara's Promise*. Bay Area Poets Coalition, third place award, for "Immortality," 1985; Violetta Books, first place award, for "Immortality," 1987; *Psych It Magazine*, fourth place award, for "Memories," 1989. First African American director to sit on the board of the Romance Writers of America; first African American president of the New Jersey Romance Writers Chapter; first African American board member of the New Jersey Romance Writers of America; one of only two African American authors to have a book appear on the Top 100 Greatest Romances of the 20th Century List.

Reflections

"Mr. William D. Bennett comes first to mind as the person who had a profound influence in my life. He was my junior high school math teacher and my high school chemistry teacher. He never knew anything about my writing until after my first book was published, but he was my unofficial counselor/surrogate father in high school. Through the many discussions we had he made me believe I could do anything I wanted if I gave it my heart and worked at it. He also told me I should have a career to fall back on if something else didn't work out (like marriage). Indirectly, I've been influenced by various people who thought I couldn't reach my goal, that writing was a dream and no one would want to read anything I wrote. With an 'I'll show you' attitude I went on to work at my dream instead of listening to their negativism. It gives me enormous satisfaction to quietly smile in their presence without being too smug or saying 'see.' Today the people who tend to still influence me are the wonderful writers I love to read."

Publications
Books
Hailstock, Shirley. *Whispers of Love*. New York: Windsor Publishing Corp., 1994. 411.

———. *Clara's Promise*. New York: Kensington Publishing Corp., 1995. 409.

———. *White Diamonds*. New York: Arabesque Books, 1996. 408.

———. *Legacy*. New York: Kensington Publishing Corp., 1997. 295.

———. *Mirror Image*. New York: Kensington Publishing Corp., 1998. 283.

Ray, Francis, Shirley Hailstock, and Donna Hill. *Winter Nights*. New York: Kensington Books, 1998. 290.

Hailstock, Shirley. *Opposites Attract*. New York: BET Publications, 1999. 293.

———. *More than Gold; Holiday Cheer*. Washington, D.C.: BET Publications, 2000. 320.

Novellas in Anthologies
———. "Engagement." In *I Do!*, by Robyn Amos, Gwynne Forster, and Shirley Hailstock, n.p. New York: Kensington Publishing Corp., 1998. 314.

———. "Kwanzaa Angel." In *Winter Nights*, by Francis Ray, Shirley Hailstock, and Donna Hill, n.p. New York: Kensington Books, 1998. 290.

———. "An Estate of Marriage." In *Island Magic: Four Novellas*, by Rochelle Alers, Shirley Hailstock, Marcia King-Gamble, and Felícia Mason, n.p. New York: St. Martin's Paperbacks, 2000. 312.

Poems
Hailstock, Shirley. "Immortality." *Bay Area Poet's Coalition*, 7 (1985): 65.

———. "Lineage Portrait." *Mind in Motion* (winter 1985): n.p.

———. "Memories." *Psych It Magazine*, n.p., 1985.

———. "Breaking Point." *Parnassus Literary Journal*, 10 (summer 1986): 33.

———. "Immortality." *Eve's Legacy* 3 (1986–1987).

———. "Immortality." N.p.: Violetta Books, 1987.

———. "By the Fire Santa Sat." N.p.: Rising Star Press, 1987.

———. "Memories." *New Voices Literary Journal* (1989): n.p.

———. "Hanging Trees." *The Shooting Star Review* (summer 1989): n.p.

Bio-Bibliographical Sources
Hailstock, Shirley. "African American Women Writers in New Jersey: Biographical Questionnaire." Completed by Shirley Hailstock, 12 May 2000.

———. Letter to Sibyl E. Moses, 2 August 2000.

"Shirley Hailstock Bio." Available: <http://www.geocities.com/Paris/Bistro/6812/bio.html> Accessed 13 September 1999.

HALL, VALERIE *SEE* AHMAD, AMEERAH

HAYES, LEOLA GRANT 1924–2000

Leola Grant Hayes,
courtesy of Spurgeon S. Hayes.

Personal Born on 29 March 1924 in Rocky Mount, North Carolina; joined the ancestors on 18 February 2000. The third child of Minnie Brown Grant and General Ulysses Grant, both of North Carolina; sister: Elsie M. Grant Rogers; brothers: John D. Grant (deceased) and Claude Grant (deceased); husband: Spurgeon S. Hayes. Education: Winston Salem State University, Winston Salem, North Carolina, B.S., elementary education; New York City University, New York, New York, M.S., elementary education, and M.S., supervision and guidance; City University of New York, New York, M.S., special education; New York University, New York, Ed.D., special education. Religion: Baptist; Shiloh Baptist Church, New Rochelle, New York.

Residence in New Jersey Leonia, ca.1964–2000.

Career Teacher, New York Institute for the Blind, New York; teacher and supervisor, Passaic and Bergen County Public School system; special education supervisor, Fair Lawn Public School System, Fair Lawn, New Jersey; professor, special education and counseling, William Paterson College, Wayne, New Jersey.

Memberships American Association of Mental Deficiency; Council of Exceptional Children; National Education Association; New Jersey Education Association; Association of Higher Education; William Paterson University Faculty Association; Association for Children with Learning Disabilities; Association for Brain Injured Children; Alpha Kappa Alpha Sorority, Inc.

Awards, Honors, Other Certificates Hannah C. Solomon Award, Fair Lawn Jewish Women's Organization, 1959; Education Award (Special Education), Business and Professional Women in Bergen County, 1960; nominee, Joseph P. Kennedy Foundation Award, 1964.

Publications

  Books

Hayes, Leona. *Come and Get It: Reading for Information Through Recipes.* New York: Exposition Press, 1976. 57, illus.

————. *I Can Help the Teacher: A Program for Training the Nonacademic Teacher Aide.* Hicksville, N.Y.: Exposition Press, 1977. 71, illus.

————, comp. *Occupational and Vocational Interest for the Exceptional Individual.* Washington, D.C.: University Press of America, 1977. 97, illus.

————. *A Fountain of Language Development for Early Childhood Education and the Special Child, Too.* New York: Vantage Press, 1991. xvii, 140, illus.

Articles

Hayes, Leona. "Reading by Item Analysis." *Pointer* 21, no. 2 (winter 1976): 25–26.

————. "Your Child is Retarded." *Pointer:* 21, no. 2 (winter 1976): 64–69.

Bio-Bibliographical Sources

Hayes, Leola Grant. "African American Women Writers in New Jersey: Biographical Questionnaire." Completed by Leola G. Hayes [undated].

"In Loving Memory of Dr. Leola Grant Hayes . . ." [obituary] Paterson, New Jersey: Gilmore Memorial Tabernacle, 2000. [4].

HAYNES, OONA'O

Personal   Former name Carole Bartel. Born on 13 May; husband: Reginald Anthony Haynes; children: Alethia and Kianya.

Residence in New Jersey   East Orange, ca. 1967 to present.

Career   Public relations director, The Hope Factory, East Orange, 1967–1969; public relations manager, Albert Merrill School, New York, New York, 1970–1972; managing editor, *Essex Forum Newspaper,* East Orange, 1972–1977; assistant editor and staff writer, Congress of Racial Equality, New York, 1975–1977; public relations consultant, Bruno Associates, Bloomfield, New Jersey, 1979–1984; assistant editor, *Amsterdam News,* New York, 1984–1985; president and CEO, Photo Typesetting Plus, East Orange, 1985–1990; writer, producer, and performer (one-woman shows, poetry dramatizations): WLIB Radio (Gary Bird Show), 1970s, Rahway State Prison, 1979–1981, Trenton State Prison, 1982–1983, Jamesburg Reformatory, and Whole Theatre; Scotts Manor, 1985; WBGO Radio, 1986–1990; Focus on New Jersey with Kae Thompson Payne TV 3, 1987, Newark; National Black Publisher's Association, 1987; Channel 48, "Death and Destruction . . . Crack," 1988; National Black Caucus, 1989; Woman to Woman, Suburban Cable 3, 1990; Channel 13, Newark, "You Have Not Been a Pleasant Experience . . . Good Brother," 1990; Montclair Public Library; East Orange Public Library; Montclair Museum, 1990; Essex County College, 1990; University of Medicine & Dentistry, 1990; Jersey City State College, 1986; The Hope Factory; WSOU Radio, Seton Hall University, 1990; National Association of Black Elected Officials, New York Cable, 1991; WNJR Radio, 1992 National Federation of Colored Women's Clubs, "Mother Hale," 1992; Bethany Baptist Church, 1991

Publications
  Book
Haynes, [Carole Bartel] Oona'o. *I Call Him Reggie; They Call Him #59746.*
  [Newark, N.J.]: Citizen's Defense Committee, 1979. 60.
  Articles
Bartel, Carole. "Death of Young Danny." *Core Magazine* (winter 1975):
  23–24.
———. "The Sexism Sickness/ The Racism Killer." *Core Magazine* (winter
  1975): 17–18.
Bartell [sic], Carole. "What is the Black Role in the Bicentennial?" *Core
  Magazine* Bicentennial Issue (1976): 6.
Bartel, Carole. "History Repeats Itself." *Core Magazine* (March 1976):
  15–17.
———. "Hunger . . . Future of the World?" *Core Magazine* (March 1976):
  28–29.
Bio-Bibliographical Sources
Haynes, [Carole Bartel] Oona'o. *I Call Him Reggie; They Call Him #59746.*
  [Newark, N.J.]: Citizen's Defense Committee, 1979.
Haynes, Oona'o. "Employment Resume." Provided by the author [1993].
  1.
———. "Performance Resume." Provided by the author [1991]. 1.

HENDLEY, ESSIE LEE KIRKLAND

Personal   Born on 12 February in Valdosta, Georgia; ninth child of Linia
Castilla Showers Kirkland (housewife) of Eastman, Georgia, and Rev. Dr.
John Allyne Kirkland, D.D. (minister and professor of theology) of Cam-
den, South Carolina; brothers: William Earle Holmes Kirkland (deceased);
Isaac David Shivers Kirkland (deceased); Rev. Robert Benjamin Kirkland (deceased); John Allyne Kirkland, Jr.; sisters: Rachel Jewell Kirkland
Jenkins, Amy Elizabeth Kirkland Thomas, Linia Castilla Kirkland (deceased),
and Ethelene Victoria Kirkland Drayton (deceased); husband: Barney M.
Hendley; children: Elleanor Jean Hendley (reporter and TV producer)
and Marsha Dianne Hendley Hill (consumer fraud investigator). Education: Baxley, Georgia Public Schools, 1931–1932; Cuyler Junior High,
Savannah, Georgia, 1932–1939; Alfred E. Beach High School, Savannah,
1939–1943; Savannah State College, Savannah, B.S., social studies, 1944–
1950; Seton Hall University, Newark, New Jersey, credits for elementary
education, 1953–1954; Jersey City State College, Jersey City, New Jersey,
1954–1955; Kean College, Union, New Jersey, M.A., early childhood education, 1974. Religion: Presbyterian; Bethel Presbyterian Church, Plainfield, New Jersey.
Residence in New Jersey   Jersey City, 1953–1962; Plainfield, 1962 to present.
Career   Teacher, Georgia Public School System, 1950–1953; teacher (elementary), Jersey City Public Schools, Jersey City, 1953–1961; teacher, Edi-

son Township Public Schools (Stelton School and Oak Tree School), Edison, New Jersey 1962–1978.

Memberships   Former president, National Association of University Women; life member, National Council of Negro Women; Phi Delta Kappa National Sorority; American Association of University Women; advisory committee, Plainfield Public Library Project Outreach; former board member, YWCA; Board of Governors, Foundation Development Committee, Muhlenberg Regional Medical Center, Plainfield; Chairperson, Wheel Chair Drive and Lifeline Support System, Muhlenberg Regional Medical Center, Plainfield.

Awards, Honors, Other Certificates   Honored by Board of Governors for Wheel Chair Drive and Lifeline Support System, Muhlenberg Regional Medical Center, Plainfield,; Woman of the Year, National Association University Women, Plainfield/New Brunswick Branch, 1985; chairperson, fashion show, Phi Delta Kappa Sorority, 1975; first Black and two-time delegate, national convention, New Jersey Educational Association; Outstanding Woman in Journalism, National Association of University Women; featured in Bamberger's Art Gallery for "Women of Achievement"; Achievement in the Field of Education Award, National Sorority of Phi Delta Kappa; Outstanding Educator Award, National Council of Negro Women.

Reflections

"My childhood was a happy one with devoted and supportive parents who encouraged me to seek whatever ambition I desired. My father was a professor and minister, along with serving as the secretary of the Georgia Baptist Association. He was the author of many articles for the Association's publication. He always encouraged us to express ourselves fluently. In later years he lost his eyesight and it was at this time each child was given an assignment to write for him as he dictated. I was always happy to write because the words and phrases he used, helped to enlarge my vocabulary. I was so thrilled at this assignment that I began writing for myself. My mother was always in the background encouraging me. My father and mother both guided me constructively, to exercise any talent I had. They realized that I was a creative person with a wide range of talents so they encouraged me to explore all of them. I was inspired to sing because I showed promise in that area. I sang in churches, at receptions, invited as guest of clubs, guest soloist for the USO, etc. . . . My writing talent became better known when I wrote for the college newspaper and later wrote and published a play, *A Creative: Name Board,* and ultimately authored a book entitled *So You Want to be a Teacher.* I now write for the church newsletter and am in the process of writing two more books. My parents were my beginning supporters during my early years, as well as my teachers. Through my adolescence and teen-hood my older brothers and sisters encouraged me."

Publication

Hendley, Essie Lee Kirkland. *So You Want To Be A Teacher.* New York: Carlton Press [1974]. 46.

Bio-Bibliographical Sources

Hendley, Essie Lee Kirkland. "African American Women Writers in New Jersey: Biographical Questionnaire." Completed by Essie Lee Kirkland Hendley, 11 November 1986.

―――. "Resume." [N.d.; ca. 11 November 1986]. 3.

HINTON, MAURITA MILES 1927–

Personal Born on 13 February 1927 in Orange, New Jersey; seventh child of Mary Blanche Cottman Miles (school teacher and minister's wife) of Pocomoke City, Maryland, and William Alfred Thomas Miles (Methodist minister) of Hopewell, Maryland; granddaughter (maternal) of Harriet Cottman and Edward Cottman, both of Pocomoke City; granddaughter (paternal) of Sabra Johnson Miles and William Alfred Thomas, both of Hopewell; brothers: Brice (deceased), Homer (deceased), and Thomas; sisters: Esther (deceased), Blanche, and Bessie (deceased); husband: David Henry Hinton (Tuskegee Airman, 30-year U.S. Air Force retiree, deceased). Education: Laurel, Delaware, 1933–1935; Ridgely, Maryland, 1935–1940; Wittman, Maryland, 1941–1942; Trenton, New Jersey, 1942; Trenton Central High School, Trenton, 1942–1945; Trenton State College, Trenton, 1945–1946; Storer College, Harper's Ferry, West Virginia, B.A., 1946–1949; Hampton University, Hampton, Virginia, M.A., 1949–1952; Syracuse University, Syracuse, New York, Ph.D., 1969–1972. Religion: United Methodist.

Residence in New Jersey Orange, 1927–1928; Trenton, 1942–1946, 1954–1964, Lawnside, 1946–1947; Ewing, 1964 to present.

Career Public school teacher, Bradenton, Florida, 1949–1954; public school teacher, Trenton, 1954–1968; team leader, National Teachers Corps, Temple University, Philadelphia, Pennsylvania, 1968–1969; research assistant/associate, coteacher, Syracuse University, Syracuse, 1969–1972; professor of education administration, California State University, Sacramento, California, 1972–1978.

Memberships Life member, Pi Lambda Theta Honor and Professional Society; life member, National Association of University Women; life member, National Association for the Advancement of Colored People; life member, Phi Delta Kappa International Educational Fraternity; League of Women Voters. United Methodist Church: lay delegate from Cadwalader-Asbury United Methodist Church to the Southern New Jersey Annual Conference, 1980–1984; chairperson, Pastor Parish Relations Committee, 1980–1984; administrative board of Cadwalader-Asbury United Methodist Church, 1984; president, United Methodist Women of Cadwalader-Asbury United Methodist Church, 1984–1986; certified lay speaker, United Methodist

Church, 1980 to present; chairperson, Church Extension for the 363 churches in Southern New Jersey Conference, 1981; Southern New Jersey Conference Delegate to North East Jurisdiction Convocation for Laity, 1983–1985; chairperson, Southern New Jersey Black Methodists for Church Renewal, 1982 and 1986; Multiethnic Center for Ministry; Southern New Jersey Conference Nominations Committee; Planning Committee, North East Jurisdiction Convocation for Laity; vice president, North West District United Methodist Women.

Awards, Honors, Other Certificates NDEA Fellowship, 1969–1972; Woman of the Year by National Association of University Women, 1971.

Reflections

> "My experience as a preacher's daughter with my parents and six siblings was my primary learning experience. My writing experiences began early when I was required to write essays and short stories for my Literature and English classes. I did well and usually received good grades. When I reached college I had more papers to write and once I owned a typewriter, was often paid to write papers for other students. I completed writing a master's thesis and doctoral dissertation, and finally my life story."

Publication

Hinton, Maurita Miles. *Preacher's Daughter.* Chapel Hill, North Carolina: Professional Press, 1999. xviii, 168.

Bio-Bibliographical Sources

Hinton, Maurita Miles. "African American Women Writers in New Jersey: Biographical Questionnaire." Completed by Maurita Miles Hinton, February 2000.

———. Correspondence with Sibyl E. Moses [March 2000].

HOLLEY, MARY ROSE 1949–

Personal Born on 7 June 1949 in Windsor, North Carolina; third child of Ruth Armetia Holley (housewife) and Cecil William Holley (factory worker and farmer), both of Merry Hill, North Carolina; granddaughter (maternal) of Mary Susan Cobb and Isariel Pearl Cobb, both of Merry Hill; granddaughter (paternal) of Mamia Holley and Lee Holley, both of Merry Hill; sister: Celes; brothers: Cecil Holley, Jr., Carl Holley, Kenneth Holley, and Gregory Holley. Education: Cherry Elementary School, Merry Hill, 1956–1957; Amanda Smith Cherry Elementary School, Harrellsville, North Carolina, 1957–1963; Calvin Scott Brown High School, Winton, North Carolina, 1963–1967; Saint Augustine's College, Raleigh, North Carolina, B.A., sociology, 1967–1971; Fisk University, Nashville, Tennessee, M.A., sociology, 1971–1973; University of North Texas, Denton, Texas, Ph.D., sociology, 1973–1978. Religion: Baptist.

Residence in New Jersey Montclair 1982 to present.

Career   Research assistant and teaching fellow, University of North Texas-Denton, Texas, 1973–1978; associate professor (sociology), St. Augustine's College, Raleigh, North Carolina, 1978–1982; Fulbright Visiting Professor, National University of Lesotho, Lesotho, Southern Africa, 1988–1989; assistant professor (sociology), 1982–2000, faculty special assistant to provost/vice president for Academic Affairs, 1990–1993; and associate professor (sociology), 2000 to present, Montclair State University, Montclair, New Jersey.

Memberships   Senior class president, Saint Augustine's College, 1970–1971; board member, Society on Aging of New Jersey; chairperson, Senior Citizens Advisory Committee, Montclair, 1992–1996; DuBois-Johnson Frazier Award Committee, 1996–1999; board member, Essex County Mental Health Advisory Board, 1997–1999; Association of Black Sociologists, 1997–2000; Fulbright Association.

Awards, Honors, Other Certificates   Participant, Phelps-Stokes Fund West African Heritage Seminar to the Ivory Coast, Burkina Faso, and Sierra Leone, 1979; National Science Foundation Conference Award for participation in the "Conference on Educating Computing for Minority Institutions," A&T State University, Greensboro, North Carolina, 1980; National Endowment for the Humanities Conference Award to attend "The Comparative Study of Slavery" seminar, Department of Sociology, Harvard University, Cambridge, Massachusetts, 1981; New Jersey State Action Coalition Award to assist the National Council of Negro Women to address teenage pregnancy, 1986; Fulbright Award, National University of Lesotho, Lesotho, Southern Africa, August 1988–June 1989; summer fellow, Center for Technological Studies, New Jersey Institute of Technology, 1990; Grotta Foundation of New Jersey Grant for the project: "Issues of Social Change: An Intergenerational Project," 1999.

Reflections

"Since I lived in a rural area in North Carolina, my early childhood consisted of school and related activities: Sunday school, church, 4-H club, and track. I excelled academically throughout my primary, secondary, college, and graduate education. For example, I was the salutatorian of my eighth grade class. I graduated with honors from high school and college and was the first African-American female to complete a doctorate in sociology from the University of North Texas-Denton in 1978.

I had an aunt, Maude Thompson, who taught at the college level and several cousins were teachers. They encouraged me to think about teaching as an occupation. During my senior year of college I enrolled in a reading course taught by Dr. Jacquelyne J. Jackson of Duke University. She shared with the class some of her ongoing research in the area of aging. Her academic enthusiasm encouraged me to think about exploring sociology of aging, which I did as my substantive area in sociology. Dr. Jackson made substantial contributions to ethnogerontology, the study of people of color during the aging process. Her research and writings are in this area."

Publications

Books

Elder, Kenneth, Mary R. Holley, and Hiram Friedsam. *Needs of Elderly Texans.* Denton, Tex.: Center for Studies in Aging, The School of Community Services, North Texas State University, 1975. 258 leaves.

Holley, Mary R. *Social Policies for Social Problems Approaching the 21st Century.* Dubuque, Iowa: Kendall/Hunt Publishing Company, 1999. vi, 95.

Articles, Book Chapters, Reviews

Holley, Mary R. "Clara McBride Hale," "Jennifer Holiday," "Charlayne Hunter-Gault," "Gertrude Elisa Johnson-Ayer McDougald," and "Nina Simone." In *Notable Black Women,* edited by Jessie Carney Smith, n.p. Detroit: Gale Research Inc., 1992.

———. "Components of Life Satisfaction of Older Texans: A Multidimensional Model," *Black Aging* III (April and June 1978): 113–121.

———. "Elderly Women in Developing Societies: An Examination of the Social Exchange Model." In *Aging in Developing Societies: A Reader in Third World Gerontology,* edited by John H. Morgan, n.p. Bristol, Ind.: Wyndham Hall Press, 1984.

———. Review of *All Is Never Said: The Narrative of Odette Harper Hines,* by Judith Rollins. *Gender and Society* 12 (2 April 1998): 237–238.

———. Discrimination: Direct Institutionalized." In *Racial and Ethnic Relations in America,* vol.1, edited by Carl L. Bankston III, et al., 309. Pasadena, Calif.: Salem Press, 2000.

———. "White 'Race.' " In *Racial and Ethnic Relations in America,* vol. 3, edited by Carl L. Bankston III, et al., 1044–1045. Pasadena, Calif.: Salem Press, 2000.

Bio-Bibliographical Sources

Holly, Mary Rose. "African American Women Writers in New Jersey: Biographical Questionnaire." Completed by Mary R. Holley, 19 June 2000.

Holley, Mary Rose. "Vitae of Mary R. Holley." 2000. 6.

HOLMES, LINDA JANET 1949–

Personal Born on 16 April 1949 in Newark, New Jersey; oldest child of Ann L. Howard Holmes (home economics teacher) of Lexington, Kentucky, and Robert Otis Holmes (optician) of Edgefield, South Carolina; granddaughter (maternal) of Mary Howard and Walter Howard, both of Lexington (Fayette County); sister: Mary Ann Holmes Cool; child: Ghana Smith. Education: Washington School, East Orange, New Jersey, 1954–1961; Vernon L. Davey Junior High School, East Orange, 1961–1963; East Orange High School, East Orange, 1963–1967; Douglass College, New Brunswick, New Jersey, B.A., journalism, 1967–1971; Rutgers

Linda Janet Holmes.
Photograph by Steven Riker,
courtesy of MotoPhoto and
Portrait Studio.

University, Newark, New Jersey, M.P.A., 1976–1978; Columbia University, New York, New York, graduate studies in socio-medical sciences, 1990–1994. Religion: Baptist; New Hope Baptist Church, Newark; previous memberships, Thirteenth Avenue Presbyterian Church, Newark, and Elmwood Presbyterian Church, East Orange.

Residence in New Jersey   East Orange, 1949 to present.

Career   Reporter/correspondent (various media: *The Daily News,* Dar-es-Salaam, Tanzania; *The Bergen Record,* Hackensack, New Jersey; *The Home News,* North Brunswick; *WLIB-AM,* New York; *Community News Service,* New York), 1972–1974; assistant professor, School of Health Related Professions, University of Medicine and Dentistry of New Jersey, 1978–1986; project specialist, Commissioner's Office, Department of Health, HealthStart, 1986–1988; research scientist, New Jersey Department of Health, 1988–1990; graduate research assistant, Harlem Hospital Prevention Center, 1990–1991; research scientist, New Jersey Department of Health, Family Health Services, 1991–1997; executive director, Office of Minority Health, New Jersey Department of Health and Senior Services, 1997 to present.

Memberships   American Public Health Association, 1977 to present; Black Women's Health Project, 1981 to present; trustee, Essex County Planned Parenthood Board, 1984–1988; board of directors, National Women's Health Network, 1992–1996; board of trustees, New Jersey Women and AIDS Network, 1995–1997.

Awards, Honors, Other Certificates   The American Publishers Award, 1968–1971; Mabel Smith Douglass Award, Douglass College, Rutgers University, 1976; Public Health Fellow, Department of Health, Education and Welfare, 1976; principal investigator, "Birth Room Demonstration Project," Hunterdon Health Fund, 1978–1979; Independent Fellowship, National Endowment for the Humanities, "Oral History Project on Southern Black Midwives," 1981–1982; chairperson, "Spelman Working Meeting to Promote Research on Midwifery," United Methodist Church, Women's Division Grant, 1984; coordinator, "Project to Improve Health Care for Indigent Women and Children in New Jersey," Ford Foundation Grant, New Jersey Department of Health, 1987–1990; President's Fellow, Columbia University, 1990; Julia Baxter Bates Award, Douglass College, Rutgers University, 1993; instructor, Auburn University; visiting scholar, The Calhoun School, Lowndes County, Alabama, 1997.

Reflections

"I first experienced the joy and the reward of writing in the third grade. Struggling to nearly midnight to finish a poem, my dad literally came to the rescue in the middle of the night with assistance and support. My third grade teacher, the only Black teacher in the school, shared the poem with the school principal, and I was invited to read this poem to a nighttime meeting of the school PTA. I noticed that I was the only child present.

My next memory was a wonderfully energetic sixth grade teacher who wrote in my graduating autograph book words that celebrated my creativity. From there, most of my writing poured into the junior high school and high school newspapers, with my final achievement being editor of the high school newspaper.

As a college journalism major, I spent a summer working as an intern at the *Newark Evening News,* not long before its demise. When Livingston College opened at Rutgers University, I met the teacher who published my very first short story, a highly politicized "Chicken Licken," which appeared in Toni Cade's (Bambara) *Tales for Black Folks.* More than anyone else, Toni was a life-long inspiration, guiding me and giving me the courage to express my writing spirit."

Publications

Books

Holmes, Linda Janet, and Margaret Charles Smith. *Listen To Me Good: The Life Story of an Alabama Midwife.* Columbus: Ohio State University Press, 1996. xvii, 178, illus.

————. *Morning Star Arising: The Calhoun School and Its Vision.* Lotohatchee, Ala.: The Calhoun School, February 2000. 32.

Articles and Book Chapters

Holmes, Linda Janet. "Consumerism, Pregnancy, and Childbirth." In *Principles and Practice of Obstetrics and Perinatalogy,* edited by Leslie Iffy and Harold A. Kaminetzky, 1813–1819. New York: John Wiley & Sons, Inc. 1981.

————. "Alabama Granny Midwife." *Journal of the Medical Society of New Jersey* 81, no. 5 (May 1984): 389–391.

————. "Louvenia Taylor Benjamin, Southern Lay Midwife: An Interview." *Sage* 2, no. 2 (fall 1985): 51–54.

————. "African American Midwives in the South." In *The American Way of Birth,* edited by Pamela S. Eakins, 273–291. Philadelphia: Temple University Press, 1986.

————. "The Insurance Crisis." *Ms. Magazine* 15, no. 12 (June 1987): 74.

————. "The Life of Lena Edwards." *New Jersey Medicine* 85, no. 5 (May 1988): 431–435.

————. "Thank You Jesus to Myself: The Life of a Traditional Black Midwife."[Interview with Mattie Hereford]. In *The Black Women's Health*

Book: Speaking For Ourselves, edited by Evelyn C. White, 98–106. Seattle, Wash.: Seal Press, 1990, 1994.

———. "Black Midwives, Southern." In *Encyclopedia of Childbearing: Critical Perspectives,* edited by Barbara Katz Rothman, 258–260. New York: Henry Holt and Company, 1993.

———. "An Interview with Molly Joel Coye, Public Health Commissioner." *New Jersey Medicine* 85, no. 6 (February 1995): 513–515.

Holmes, Linda Janet, L. Ziskin, K. O'Dowd, and R. Martin. "Medical Partnerships with Community-Based Organizations in Violence Prevention: A Public Health Approach." *New Jersey Medicine* 92, no. 2 (February 1995): 96–98.

Bio-Bibliographical Sources

Holmes, Linda Janet. "African American Women Writers in New Jersey: Biographical Questionnaire." Completed by Linda Holmes, 8 May 2001.

———. "Resume." N.d., 7.

HOOKS, HELEN SHAW *SEE* SHAW, HELEN

HOWELL, CHRISTINE MOORE **1898–1972**

Christine Moore Howell,
courtesy of Donald P. Moore.

Personal Born on 19 March 1898 in Princeton, New Jersey. Joined the ancestors 13 December 1972 in New Brunswick, New Jersey. The daughter of Mary Adelaide Williams Moore (housewife, 1873–1931) and William Moore (businessman, 1863–1920), both of Hillsboro, North Carolina; sister: Bessie Moore (1896–1922); brothers: Arthur C. Moore (1893–1974) and Willie Moore (1901–1919); husband: Edward Gaylord Howell, M.D (1898–1971). Education: Princeton High School, Princeton; De Laurenberg's, Princeton (diploma), 1919; Warren's Institute, Pittsburgh, Pennsylvania; Knock's School of Beauty Culture, Philadelphia, Pennsylvania; Nestle's, New York; Sidonia Institute, Paris, France; special laboratory training under chemist Louis DuBois, New Brunswick. Religion: Baptist; The Ebenezer Baptist Church, New Brunswick.

Residence in New Jersey Princeton; New Brunswick.

Career Owner, Christine Cosmetics, Inc., Princeton, New Jersey; owner and cosmetologist, Christine's Beauty Salon, Princeton; owner/manufacturer, Christine Moore Corporation (laboratory), Princeton; appointed, board member, New Jersey State Board of Beauty Culture Control, 1935–1941 and 1945–1949 (elected chairperson for three terms).

Memberships New Brunswick Urban League; NAACP; Central Jersey Links; Princeton Group Arts, Inc.; Archousa of Sigma Pi Phi Fraternity, Inc.

Publication

Howell, Christine Moore. *Beauty Culture and Care of the Hair.* New Brunswick, N.J.: Hill Publishing Company, 1936. iii–xv, 123, illus.

Bio-Bibliographical Sources

"Beauty Salon for Social Register." *Ebony* 4 (May 1949): 31–32.

Howell, Christine Moore. "African American Women Writers in New Jersey: Biographical Questionnaire." Completed by Donald Moore (Christine Moore Howell's nephew), Princeton, New Jersey, January 2001.

Who's Who in Colored America 7th ed. Supplement. Yonkers-on-Hudson, N.Y.: Christian E. Burckel and Associates [1950]. 274.

HUDSON, CHERYL AUVAL WILLIS 1948–

Personal Born on 7 April 1948 in Portsmouth, Virginia; child of Lillian Beatrice Watson Willis (elementary and high school teacher) of Charlottesville, Virginia, and Hayes Elijah Willis, III (businessman and insurance salesman) of Richmond, Virginia; granddaughter (maternal) of Viola Carter Watson and Louis Caroll Watson, both of Charlottesville; brothers: Hayes Willis (deceased), Roderick Willis, and Orion Willis; husband: Wade Hudson; children: Katura J. Hudson and Stephan J. Hudson. Education: Mount Hermon Elementary School, Portsmouth, 1954–1960; S. H. Clarke Junior High School, Portsmouth, 1960–1962; I. C. Norcom Senior High

*Cheryl Willis Hudson,
courtesy of Just Us Books.*

School, Portsmouth, 1962–1966; Oberlin College, Oberlin, Ohio, B.A., 1966–1970; further studies: Radcliffe College, Cambridge, Massachusetts; Northeastern University, Boston, Massachusetts; Parsons School of Design, New York, New York. Religion: Baptist; Imani Baptist Church, East Orange, New Jersey.

Residence in New Jersey East Orange, 1973 to present.

Career Art editor, Houghton Mifflin Company; design manager, School Textbook Division, Macmillan Publishing Company, New York; art director, Arete Publishing Company, Princeton, New Jersey, 1979–1982; cofounder, vice president, and editorial director, Just Us Books, Inc., East Orange, 1988 to present.

Memberships   Children's Book Council, New York; advisory board, Small Press Center, Inc., New York; advisory board, Langston Hughes Library, Children's Defense Fund, Clinton, Tennessee, 2000 to present; advisor, Read-Up! Book Club, East Orange.

Awards, Honors, Other Certificates   Blackboard Award, American Booksellers Association; Multicultural Book Award, Multicultural Publishing and Education Council, 1992–1995; Ben Franklin Award, Publisher's Marketing Association, 1993; Stephen Crane Book Award, Newark Public Library, 2001.

Reflections

"Parents and older brother Hayes were greatest influence on [my] interest in books and literacy."

Publications

Hudson, Cheryl Willis. *Afro-Bets ABC Book.* Orange, N.J.: Just Us Books, 1987. [24], illus.

Hudson, Cheryl Willis, and Bernette G. Ford. *Bright Eyes, Brown Skin.* Illustrated by George Ford. Orange, N.J.: Just Us Books, 1990. 1 vol. (unpaged).

———. *Good Morning, Baby.* Illustrated by George Ford. New York: Scholastic, 1992. 1 vol. (unpaged).

———. *Good Night Baby.* Illustrated by George Ford. New York: Scholastic, 1992. 1 vol. (unpaged).

———. *Animal Sounds for Baby.* Illustrated by George Ford. New York: Scholastic, 1995. [10].

———, comp. *Hold Christmas in Your Heart: African-American Songs, Poems, and Stories for the Holidays.* New York: Scholastic, 1995. 32, illus.

———. *Let's Count Baby.* Illustrated by George Ford. New York: Scholastic, 1995. [10].

Hudson, Wade, and Cheryl Hudson, comps. *How Sweet the Sound: African-American Songs for Children.* Illustrated by Floyd Cooper. New York: Scholastic, 1995. 48.

Hudson, Cheryl Willis, and Wade Hudson, comps. *Kids' Book of Wisdom: Quotes from the African American Tradition.* East Orange, N.J.: Just Us Books, 1996. 62.

Hudson, Cheryl Willis, adapt. *Many Colors of Mother Goose.* Illustrated by Ken Brown, Mark Corcoran, and Cathy Johnson. East Orange, N.J.: Just Us Books, 1997. 1 vol. (unpaged).

Hudson, Wade, and Cheryl Willis Hudson, comps. In Praise of Our Fathers and Our Mothers: A Black Family Treasury by Outstanding Authors and Artists. East Orange, N.J.: Just Us Books, 1997. 131, illus.

Hudson, Cheryl Willis. Glo Goes Shopping. Illustrated by Cathy Johnson. East Orange, N.J.: Just Us Books, 1999. 1 vol. (unpaged).

Bio-Bibliographical Source
Hudson, Cheryl. "African American Women Writers in New Jersey: Bio-graphical Questionnaire." Completed by Cheryl Hudson, 19 April 2001.

HUGHES, SALLY PAGE

Personal Born on 24 May in Elizabeth, New Jersey; second child of Irene Miller Page (housewife) and Jeff Page (laborer), both of Columbia, South Carolina; granddaughter (maternal) of Darkess Miller; granddaughter (paternal) of Easter Page and William Page; sister: Ruth Page; brothers: Patrick Page (deceased), Jefferson Page (deceased), and William Page (deceased); husband: Edward Hughes (married 1954, licensed practical nurse, deceased); child: Edward J. Hughes. Education: Benjamin Franklin Elementary School #13, Elizabeth, 1934–1935; George Washington Elementary School #1, Elizabeth, 1935–1940; Grover Cleveland Junior High School, Elizabeth, 1941–1944; Battin High School, Elizabeth, 1944–1947; Upsala College, East Orange, New Jersey (night classes, 102 credits), 1969–1975; Kean

Sally Page Hughes, courtesy of Sally Page Hughes.

College (formerly Newark State College), Union, New Jersey (night classes), 1962–1969; Urban Education Corps. Teacher Training Program (2nd Grade), Upsala College, East Orange, 1969–1971. Religion: Protestant; ordained Evangelist; Shiloh Baptist Church, Elizabeth.

Residence in New Jersey Elizabeth, from birth until 1954, 1962 to present; Plainfield, 1954–1962.

Career Merrow machine operator in romper factory; secretary/stenographer, Visiting Nurse Association, Plainfield, 1955–1960; secretary/stenographer, Kean College, Union, New Jersey, 1962–1969; secretary to editor and editorial writer, *The Daily Journal,* Elizabeth, 1971–1975; principal clerk, Schering-Plough Corporation, Union, 1974–1975, 1976–1980; unit secretary, Training Unit, Elizabeth Multi-Service Center (CETA), Elizabeth, 1980–1982; administrative secretary, Board of Education, Elizabeth, 1982 to present.

Memberships Elizabeth Education Association; New Jersey Education Association; National Education Association; NAACP; Sunday School teacher, choir member, and missionary board member, Shiloh Baptist Church.

Awards, Honors, Other Certificates   Professional Woman of the Year, Union County Club, National Association of Negro Business & Professional Women's Clubs, Inc., 1991; Talent Spotlight featured poet, TKR Cable Company, Channel 12, Elizabeth; featured poet, Dr. Albert J. Lewis's CTN-Gospel Hour Musical TV Station, August 1991; selected for inclusion in MARQUIS *Who's Who in the East,* 24th ed. Songs: "Where Shall I Be" (originally composed by William Page) and "On the Winning Side" (on country singer Kate Miller's *Hallelujah* album, Rainbow Records, 1992).

Reflections

"My father played piano; my mother was a singer. She sang in the church choir, community chorale, and in the community. She won a prize singing Schubert's *Ave Maria.* She sang lots of classical songs and spiritual and also recited poetry. Growing up we had several books in our library of African-American poets. My mother was my role model. I grew up in a family that loved singing. When I left high school, I wanted to be a pop singer, but my family said it wasn't practical. Although I had the skills in business education, employment in an office was not open to coloreds. [I] went to college to change [my] career but left college in senior year due to illness and never returned.

As I got older, I got the desire to write. In college, received good marks on written reports. I longed to write a book one day. My late brother, William Page, passed away in December 1989. I sat down one day to express my feelings and my loss and wrote three poems to his memory. Later, encouraged by friends who had seen my work, I began sending my poems to publishers. This is how I began writing poetry. My brother William Page composed a spiritual called "Where Shall I Be." My late brother Jefferson Page also wrote songs and poetry."

Publications

Hughes, Sally Page. *New Beginnings.* Whitehall, Pa.: Anderie Poetry Press, 1991.

———. *Inspiration: Poems.* [Cranford, N.J.]: Rose Shell Press [1993]. [iii] 26 [3], illus.

———. *E'Port: A Poetic Memoir.* St. John, Kan.: Chiron Review Press, 2000. 44, illus.

Bio-Bibliographical Sources

Hughes, Sally Page. "African American Women Writers in New Jersey: Biographical Questionnaire." Completed by Sally Pages Hughes, 3 February 1993.

———. Interview by Sibyl E. Moses. Elizabeth, New Jersey, February 1993.

Polk, Jennifer. "Elizabeth Poet's Songs Heard on Gospel Album." *The Star Ledger,* 12 July 1992.

Thomas, James. "An End and a Beginning: Brother's Death Brings Out Elizabeth Woman's Poetry." *The Star Ledger,* 24 December 1992.

HUNTER-LATTANY, KRISTIN ELAINE EGGLESTON 1931–

Personal Born on 12 September 1931 in Philadelphia, Pennsylvania; only child of Mabel Lucretia Manigault Eggleston (pharmacist and teacher) and George Lorenzo Eggleston (elementary school principal and U.S. Army Officer) of Washington, D.C.; granddaughter (maternal) of Lena Anderson Manigault of Oxford, Pennsylvania, and Benjamin Manigault of Charleston, South Carolina; granddaughter (paternal) of Gillie Tyree Eggleston Burgess of Spottsylvania County, Virginia, and Charles Terrell Eggleston; husbands: Joseph Hunter (1952–1962, divorced) and John I. Lattany, Sr. (1968 to present). Education: Charles Sumner School, Camden, New

Kristin Hunter-Lattany.
Photograph by John I. Lattany.

Jersey; Magnolia Public School, Magnolia, New Jersey; Haddon Heights High School, Haddon Heights, New Jersey, 1947; University of Pennsylvania, Philadelphia, 1947–1951, B.S., education, 1951.

Residence in New Jersey Camden, 1931–1941, 1971–1983; Atlantic City, summers 1959 and 1963; Cape May, 1970–1971; Magnolia, 1941–1952, 1983 to present.

Career Columnist and feature writer, Pittsburgh Courier, 1946–1952; teacher, Camden, 1952; copywriter, Lavenson Bureau of Advertising, Philadelphia, 1952–1959; copywriter, Werman and Schorr, Inc., Philadelphia, 1962–1963; research assistant, School of Social Work, University of Pennsylvania, 1961–1962; information officer, City of Philadelphia, 1963–1964, 1965–1966; director of health services, Temple University, Philadelphia, 1971–1972; director, Walt Whitman Poetry Center, Camden, 1978–1979; writer-in-residence, Emory University, Atlanta, Georgia, 1979; lecturer in Creative Writing, 1972–1979, adjunct professor of English, 1981–1983; senior lecturer in English, University of Pennsylvania, 1983 to present.

Memberships Member, Advisory Board, University of Pennsylvania *Gazette*, 1974–1976; advisor, Friends of the Free Library of Philadelphia, 1977 to present; panelist, Literature, Pennsylvania State Council on the Arts, 1981; panelist, Artists in Education, Pennsylvania State Council on the Arts, 1986–1988; chairperson, Fiction Board, *Shooting Star Review*, 1989 to present. Other Professional Memberships: Authors Guild; founder and president, MACAW Writers Cooperative; Modern Language Association; National Council of Teachers of English; P.E.N.; Alpha Kappa Alpha Sorority, Inc.

Awards, Honors, Other Certificates   Fund for the Republic First Prize—TV Documentary, 1955; John Hay Whitney Fellowship, 1959–1960; Philadelphia Athenaeum Literary Award, 1964; Bernard DeVoto Fellowship, Bread Loaf Writers Conference, Middlebury College, 1965; National Council on Interracial Books for Children Award, 1968; Sigma Delta Chi Best Magazine Reporting of the Year Award, 1968; National Conference of Christians and Jews Brotherhood Award, 1969; University of Wisconsin Cheshire Cat Seal, 1971; Silver Slate-Pencil Award and Dolle Mina Prize (The Netherlands), both in 1973; *Chicago Tribune Book World* Prize, 1973; Christopher Award, 1974; Drexel University Children's Literature Award, 1981; New Jersey State Council on the Arts Prose Fellowship, 1981–1982 and 1985–1986; Coretta Scott King Award Honor Book for *Lou in the Limelight,* 1982; Pennsylvania State Council on the Arts Literature Fellowship, 1983–1984.

Publications

  Books

Hunter, Kristin. *God Bless the Child.* New York: Scribner, 1964. 307. Reprint, London: Muller, 1965; as *Ein Mädchen Namens Rosie,* Frankfurt: Büchergilde Gutenberg, 1968; New York: Bantam Book, 1970; as *Rosaly Flemings,* Bergisch Gladbach, Germany: G. H. Lübbe, 1984; Washington, D.C.: Howard University, 1986.

———. *The Landlord.* New York: Scribner [1966]. 338. Reprint, New York: Avon, 1969, 1971; London: Pan Book, 1970; as *Das Haus in der Poplar Street,* Cologne, Germany: Kiepenheuer and Witsch, 1966, 1970; as *De Huisbaas,* Antwerp: Leopold's Gravenhage, 1972; as *Das Haus in der Poplar Street,* Bergisch Gladbach, Germany: G. H. Lübbe, 1972; film adaptation: *The Landlord,* United Artists, 1970.

———. *The Soul Brothers and Sister Lou.* New York: Scribner, 1968. 248. Reprint, New York: Avon, 1969; London: MacDonald, 1971; as *Det Kallas Soul* [Stockholm]: Saga, 1971; as *De Soul Brothers en Sister Lou,* Antwerp: Leopold's Gravenhage, 1972; as *Lieder Haben Keine Farbe,* Stuttgart, Germany: Franckh'sche Verlagshandlung, 1974; London: Women's Press, 1987; Oxford: Heinemann Educational, 1988; London: Livewire, 1993.

———. *Boss Cat.* New York: Scribner [1971]. Illustrated by Harold Franklin. Reprint, New York: Avon Books, 1975. 58.

———. *The Pool Table War.* Boston: Houghton Mifflin, 1972. 35.

———. *Uncle Daniel and the Raccoon.* Boston: Houghton, 1972. 34.

———. *Guests in the Promised Land* [short story collection]. New York: Scribner, 1973. 133. Reprint, New York: Avon, 1976; as *Das Land der Verheissung,* Baden-Baden, Germany: Signal Verlag, 1977.

———. *The Survivors.* New York: Scribner, 1975. 308. Reprint as *Wer Überleben Will,* Baden-Baden, Germany: Signal Verlag, 1977.

———. *The Lakestown Rebellion.* New York: Scribner, 1978. 314.

———. *Lou in the Limelight.* New York: Scribner, 1981. 296.

Lattany, Kristin Hunter. *Kinfolks.* New York: Ballantine Books, 1996. 276. Reprint, New York: Ballantine Books, 2000.

Lattany, Kristin. *Do Unto Others.* 1st ed. New York: One World, 2000. 265.

Short Stories and Poems

Hunter, Kristin. "Graven Images." *The Nation,* 1957.

———. "Africa Speaks to the West." Poster (*Poetry on the Buses*). Pittsburgh, Pa.: Carnegie-Mellon University, 1976.

———. "To Walk in Beauty." *Sub-Deb Scoop,* 1953: n.p.

———. "Supersonic." *Mandala,* 1956: n.p.

———. "There Was a Little Girl." *Rogue,* 1959: n.p.

———. "An Interesting Social Study." In *The Best Short Stories by Negro Writers,* edited by Langston Hughes, n.p. Boston: Little Brown, 1967.

———. "Debut." *Negro Digest,* June 1968: n.p.

———. "Honor Among Thieves." *Essence* (April 1971): 34–35.

———. "How I Got in the Grocery Business." *Black World* (June 1972): 58–64.

———. "The Tenant." *The Pennsylvania Gazette* (Philadelphia), 1972, n.p.

———. "Come Out of that Corner." *Seventeen* (October 1974), n.p.

———. "Bleeding Berries." *Callaloo* 6, no. 2 (1979): 25–35.

———. "The Jewel in the Lotus." *Quilt* 1, 198?: n.p.

———. "Bleeding Heart." *Hambone* (Santa Cruz, California) 1983.

———. "Perennial Daisy. *Nightsun* (Frostburg, Maryland), 1984.

———. "Brown Gardenias." *Shooting Star Review* (Pittsburgh, Penn.) (fall 1987).

———. "Love, African Style." *Shooting Star Review* (winter 1988): 14.

Anthologies

Hunter, Kristin. An Interesting Social Study." In *The Differing Eye; An Introduction to Literature.* Compiled by William C. Dotson, 103–110. Glencoe Press: Beverly Hills, Calif., 1970.

———. "Debut." In *Black American Literature: Fiction,* edited by Darwin T. Turner, 131–139. Columbus, Ohio: C. E. Merrill Pub. Co., 1969.

———. "Debut." In *The Norton Introduction to Literature: Fiction,* edited by Jerome Beaty, 267–273. New York: W.W. Norton, 1973.

———. "Debut." In *Women & Men & Men & Women,* edited by William Smart, 8–14. New York: St. Martin's, 1975.

———. "Debut." In *Adolescence in Literature,* edited by Thomas West Gregory, 160–166. New York: Longman, 1978.

Articles

Hunter, Kristin. "Report from South Street." *Philadelphia Magazine* 58, no. 8 (August 1967): 93–100.

———. "Pray for Barbara's Baby." *Philadelphia Magazine* 59, no. 8 (August 1968): 48–105.

———. "The Devil in Bucks County." *Philadelphia Magazine* 61, no. 1 (January 1970): 49–54.

———. "Better Dark than Black." *Philadelphia Magazine* 62, no. 9 (September 1970): 75–136.

———. "Soul City North." *Philadelphia Magazine* 63, no. 5 (May 1972): 100–162.

————. "A Biblical Answer to the Book-Banners" *Catholic Library World,* September, 1981.

————. "Reconstruction of Stereotypes" *The National Leader*, September 23, 1982.

————. "Why Buckwheat Was Shot" *Melus* 2, no. 3 (fall 1984): 79–85.

Bio-Bibliographical Sources

Hunter, Kristin. [Résumé] Writer, Lecturer. [undated] 1p.

Lattany, Kristin Hunter. "African American Women Writers in New Jersey: Biographical Questionnaire." Completed by Kristin Hunter Lattany, 14 August 1985.

————. Correspondence to Sibyl E. Moses, 14 August 1985.

JACKSON, MARY JANE RAY 1924–

Personal Born on 2 September 1924 in Wayne County, North Carolina; fourth child of Mamie Hobbs Ray (housewife) and Lawrence Ray (farmer), both of Wayne County; granddaughter (maternal) of Adelia Ray and Paul Ray, both of Wayne County; sister: Margaret Ray Coley; brothers: Nathaniel Ray and Clinton Ray (deceased); husband: Stephen H. Jackson, Jr.; child: Vincent L Cooper. Education: Faro Elementary School, Faro, North Carolina; Fremont High School, Fremont, North Carolina, 1937–1941. Religion: Baptist; Friendship Baptist Church, Trenton, New Jersey.

Mary Ray Jackson.
Photograph by Stephen H. Jackson, Jr.

Residence in New Jersey Trenton, 1949 to present.

Career Coil feeder operator, Westinghouse, Trenton; punch press operator, General Motors, Ewing, New Jersey.

Memberships Recording secretary, Local #443, United Electrical Workers, Westinghouse (first Black union officer elected), early 1940s; former chairperson, Public Relations Committee, Friendship Baptist Church, Trenton; Trenton Chapter, Congress of Racial Equality, mid 1950s; board of directors, Southern Christian Leadership Conference, Trenton (under Mrs. Edith Savage); lifetime membership, chairperson, NAACP (under Arthur Shack), 1968; Trenton office manager, Robert Kennedy's 1968 presidential campaign; member, Young Democrats of Mercer County, New Jersey; cochairperson, Young Democrats Voters Registration Drive, Mercer County, 1969; former membership chairperson, New Democratic Coalition, Trenton; active volunteer, mayoral election campaigns of the Hon. Arthur J. Holland, 1970 and 1974; active volunteer, campaign of Anthony P. Carabelli for East Ward Councilman; board member and board secretary, Public Service Coordinating Agencies, a Model Cities Program, under the direction of Nathaniel Cobb, 1972; Executive Committee, Democrats of Mercer County; Relief Committee in the big flood of 1971, served with Eugene McQuaid; Red Cross volunteer, flood of 1971; member, Mayor's Advisory Committee on Community Relations; Women's Division of the Democratic Party of Mercer County; board of directors, East Trenton Center (sponsored by the United Presbytery), Trenton; Arthur J. Holland Booster Club; Anthony P. Carabelli Booster Club; Citizens Coalition of Mercer County for School Board Elections; Local #731, United Auto

Workers, General Motors, Ewing; committee person, East Ward District #3, 1968–1996; volunteer, voters registration drive in Mercer Country; helped prepare for Trenton appearance of presidential candidate Governor Jimmy Carter on his historic Whistlestop Train campaign; Steering Committee of "51.3% Women for Jimmy Carter"; vice chairperson and membership chair, Trenton Democratic Club, Trenton.

Awards, Honors, Other Certificates   Certificate for Outstanding Work, Southern Christian Leadership Conference, Trenton; recruiter for Resurrection City, Washington, D.C.; fund raiser and volunteer, historic Poor People's March through Trenton; volunteer, Jail without Bail, along with the Rev. Ralph Abernathy, serving term of five days in jail; NAACP Award for contributions to membership campaign, 1968 and 1983; North Ward Democratic Club Award, 1983; Neighborhood Housing Services Award, 1986; Bronzettes Inc. Award, 1988.

Reflections

"My cousin Lettie Cruse started me reading at a very young age and got me into plays in church, Salisbury A.M.E. Church in Faro, North Carolina. I still do lots of reading. My friend, Lelia Wishart, the coauthor of the book, used to eat at my house and I [would eat] at her house, so she thought we should do the book."

Publication

Jackson, Mary, and Lelia Wishart. *The Integrated Cookbook; or, The Soul of Good Cooking*. Chicago, Ill.: Johnson Publishing Co., 1971. 135, illus.

Bio-Bibliographical Source

Jackson, Mary R. "African American Women Writers in New Jersey: Biographical Questionnaire." Completed by Mary R. Jackson, August 1999.

Norma Lynn Jarrett.
Photograph by Randy B. Carodine.

JARRETT, NORMA LYNN 1965–

Personal   Born on 13 August 1965 in Neptune, New Jersey; daughter of Ethel Page Jarrett (deceased) of Rockfish, Virginia, and Norman David Jarrett (electrical engineer) of Reidsville, North Carolina; granddaughter (maternal) of Annie and Sam Page; granddaughter (paternal) of Carrie Jones Jarrett and Norman Jarrett, Sr., both of Reidsville, North Carolina; sister: Paulette Jones; brother: Stephen Jarrett. Education: Green Grove Elementary, Neptune, New Jersey, 1970–1975; Ocean Grove Middle School, Ocean Grove, New Jersey, 1975–1977; Neptune Junior High School, Neptune, 1977–1980; Neptune Senior High School, Neptune, 1980–1983; North Carolina Agricultural and Technical State University, Greensboro, North Carolina, B.S. (Industrial Technology), 1987; Center for Advanced Legal Studies, Houston, Texas, paralegal certificate, 1992; Thurgood Marshall School of Law, Houston, J.D., 1999. Religion: Christian, Lakewood Church, Houston, previous membership: The Church Without Walls.

Residence in New Jersey   Neptune, 1965–1983.

Career   Production Scheduler, General Motors, Lockport, New York, 1988–1990; contracts analyst, Groth Corporation, Houston, 1991–1993; legal searcher, Shell Oil, Houston, 1994–1995; placement consultant, Quintessence Corporate Staffing, Houston, 1995–1996; legal coder, IKON Digital Solutions, Houston, 1996–1997; judicial law clerk, Harris County, 151st Civil District Courts, Houston, 1996–1997; owner, E-Page Publishing, Houston, 1999 to present.

Awards, Honors, Other Certificates   *Who's Who Among American Colleges and Universities;* Best Contemporary Christian Fiction, Sister Circle Book Club, Dallas, Texas; Outstanding Young African-American Leader of Houston, Interfaith Ministries, Houston.

Reflections

"I spent a lot of time when I was a child reading and writing. I was always an introvert. While most kids were running in the street, I remember spending many hours in my room doing anything creative. I liked to write, make up stories, and draw. I know my creativity came from my mother. She liked to draw. I remember writing poems but never really doing anything with them. English was one of my favorite subjects. As a teenager, I remember reading books by Judy Blume. Later, I remember reading books that were more advanced for my age. One in particular that stood out was *Evergreen.*

I like to write about things that appeal to most young women. I am also an emotional person who likes to write about real pain, healing, love, and other feelings people can relate to. I lost my mother right after I graduated from college. That left a major void in my life. Consequently, my relationship with God intensified. God has a big influence on my writing as well. My first novel ties many themes of my life together. It is a novel about women, all at different places. It celebrates friendship. That is important to me. I was blessed to have many good friends in my life. It celebrates the importance of family and healing from the past. My mother's death had a big influence on my family. She held it together. When I wrote my first novel, I was simply writing about a group of women, but soon, many themes began to surface.

As far as particular authors, there were several that had an impact on my life. The very first one was Terri McMillan. I distinctly remember meeting her in Houston at a small library. When she finished speaking she said "anybody can do this." She wrote about "Black women in a professional light." She made us know her characters with such humor and realness. She opened the door for writers like us. The second influence was Maya Angelou. She came to Houston to speak, and I met her on the way out. She talked about our people having "grace." She is the epitome of that characteristic. I also love Benilde Little, who also introduced us to Black professional women who dealt with love, independence, and career issues. There are others, but these individuals prompted me to "put pen to paper."

As my life continues to transform, I look to more spiritual influences to enhance my fiction. I wish to write about women we can relate to but with a positive message. I want to continue to build strong male characters and give people hope. I know that many women deal with depression and never heal from the past. I want people to read my work and say, 'wow, I thought I was the only one that felt that way.' I want to expose the problem, but I also want to walk them through the solution. I also want to introduce readers to God through lovable, humorous, realistic characters. I want non-Christians to read the book and open their hearts to God. However, I still want them to be entertained and not threatened. I want Christians to read my work and be renewed, refreshed, uplifted and entertained as well. Everyday, I gain insight and inspiration through friends, family, experiences, and "The Holy Spirit."

Publications

Jarrett, Norma Lynn. *Coffee Table Quotes for the Contemporary Christian*. Houston, Tex.: The Author, 1998. 70.

———. *Sunday Brunch*. Houston: E-Page Publishing, 1999. 223.

Bio-Bibliographical Source

Jarrett, Norma Lynn. "African American Women Writers in New Jersey: Biographical Questionnaire." Completed by Norma Lynn Jarrett, 28 August 2001.

JOHNSON, ALICE PERRY 1932–

Personal   Born on 5 September 1932 in Newark, New Jersey; third daughter of Goldie Cheatham Perry (housewife) of Richmond, Virginia, and William Perry (railroad worker) of Macon, Georgia; sisters: Hazel Perry Holder (deceased) and Hattie Perry Hays; husband: C. Archibald Johnson, M.D. (physician); children: Lawrence Johnson, Wayne Johnson, and Patricia Johnson. Education: Lincoln Elementary School, East Orange, New Jersey; East Orange High School, East Orange, 1946–1950. Religion: Episcopal.

Residence in New Jersey   Newark; East Orange.

Career Owner and designer, APJ Omodele Dolls, Inc.; employee, U.S. Government, Washington, D.C., designed and built housing units for lease to embassies, organizations, and also low cost rentals for U.S. Government in Liberia, West Africa; U.S. Government, Thailand.

Memberships Zonta International, Liberian Chapter; International Women's Club (Liberia); Women's Auxiliary of Liberian Medical and Dental Association; cofounder, Montana Morton Scholarship Foundation (Liberia), 1984–1990; American Bridge Association; American Contract Bridge League.

Alice Perry Johnson,
courtesy of Alice Perry Johnson.

Awards, Honors, Other Certificates Panel discussion, TV appearances, Liberia, West Africa; Mother of the Year, awarded by Liberian Church; Liberian Government Representative to Sierra Leone to review books for African Students; Liberian Education and Culture Organization Award (LECO) for contributions to education and the arts in Liberia.

Reflections

"[The] death of my mother when I was two years old had a devastating effect on my early years. A friend of a foster parent, William Hunter Maxwell, a published writer in East Orange, influenced my need to write and introduced me to the other arts, painting and music. In Liberia, Bai T. Moore encouraged me greatly to continue writing. He was one of Liberia's greatest authors.

Publications

Books

Johnson, Alice Perry. *One Step Ahead: Poetry and Prose.* [Monrovia, Liberia: Printed by Liberian Publishing, 1972]. 112, illus.

———. *Africa Is a Woman: Verse and Prose.* [Monrovia, Liberia]. 1976. vii, 71, illus.

Poems

Johnson, Alice Perry. "The Beginning of a Kpelle Woman." In *Daughters of Africa: An International Anthology of Words and Writings by Women of African Descent from the Ancient Egyptian to the Present,* edited by Margaret Busby, 414. New York: Ballantine Books, 1992.

Bio-Bibliographical Sources

Johnson, Alice Perry. "African American Women Writers in New Jersey: Biographical Questionnaire." Completed by Alice Perry Johnson, fall 1996.

———. Email correspondence with Sibyl E. Moses, 7 July 2001.

JOHNSON, CATHERINE JUANITA FORTUNE *SEE* ABDUS-SAMAD, NI'MAT

JOHNSON, BIRDIE (BYERTE) WILSON

Birdie (Byerte) Wilson Johnson.
Photograph by Dennis Sawyer.

Personal Daughter of Margaret Donaldson Wilson and Isadore Frederick Wilson, Sr. (minister); husband: Ed Johnson; children: Durwin Frederick, James Edward, and Margaret Patricia. Education: Miller University, Music D. (honorary); Bloomfield College, Bloomfield, New Jersey, B.A.; Princeton Theological Seminary, Princeton, New Jersey, M.A. (Christian education); Kean College/Westminster Choir College, M.A.; Drew University, Madison, New Jersey, M.Ph., 1996; Drew University, Madison, Ph.D., 1998. Religion: United Methodist; St. Mark's United Methodist Church, Montclair, New Jersey.
Residence in New Jersey Montclair.
Career Choral director, music department, Bloomfield, 1977–1995; television production consultant, National Broadcasting Co., New York, New York, 1984–1986; assistant registrar, Bloomfield College, Bloomfield, 1988–1993; music director, Third Westminster Presbyterian Church, Elizabeth, New Jersey, 1990–1999; dean, Westminster Institute of Music for Children, 1995–1999; teaching Assistant Professor, Drew University, 1995 to present; director, Baroque Chorale of North Jersey; director, Fine and Performing Arts and Music, Jamas Children's University, East Orange.
Memberships North Jersey Alumnae Chapter, Delta Sigma Theta Sorority, Inc.; Presbyterian Association of Musicians; Arts in Education; New Jersey Performing Arts Center; Youth Orchestra Festival Committee; American Choral Directors Association; American Guild of Organists; Paul Robeson Guild of the National Association of Negro Musicians.
Awards, Honors, Other Certificates Distinguished Alumna, Master of Arts in Liberal Studies program, Kean College, 1991.
Publications
Johnson, Birdie Wilson. *Succeed My People! The Story of Charles Albert Tindley: African–American Pastor, Theologian, Hymn–Writer.* [Newark, N.J.: Preston Publications Co., 1992]. Printed by Brentwood Christian Press, Columbus, Ga. 48, illus.
———. *Leadership, Struggles, and Challenges of Hortense Ridley Tate: A Twentieth Century African–American Woman's Legacy to Methodism and Community Service.* Newark, N.J.: The Shepherd's Library, 1999. 32, illus.

Bio-Bibliographical Sources

Johnson, Birdie Wilson. *Succeed My People! The Story of Charles Albert Tindley: African–American Pastor, Theologian, Hymn-Writer.* [Newark, N.J.: Preston Publications Co., 1992]

Johnson, Byerte W. "Resume." [ca. 12 June 2000], 3.

JONES, SYLVIA ROBINSON SEE BARAKA, AMINA

K

Jaleelah Karriem.
Photograph by Fredrica Willmont.

KARRIEM, JALEELAH 1947–

Personal Former name Diana Brenda Guyton; complete name Jaleelah Karriem Abdul-Ghaffar. Born on 11 June 1947 in Newark, New Jersey; first child of Shirley Delina Drake Guyton Stewart (factory assembler) and Arnold Guyton (municipal civil servant), both of Newark; raised by stepmother, Fannie Mae Sessoms Watson; granddaughter (maternal) of Amy Elizabeth Randolph Drake of Clinton, New Jersey, and Orange Drake of Newark; granddaughter (paternal) of Theresa Olivia Simmons Guyton, of Savannah, Georgia, and William Guyton, Sr. of Dublin, Georgia; sisters: Wakil Murrawakkil Abdul-Ghaffar (former name Renee Lamont Dozier, deceased) and Latifah Rasheedah Abdul-Ghaffar Muhammad (former name Marcella Ann Guyton); husband: Omar Subhaan (artist; divorced); child: Rahjan Karriem Abdul-Ghaffar. Education: Waverly Avenue Grammar School, Newark, 1952–1959; Clinton Place Junior High School, Newark, 1959–1962; Weequahic High School, Newark, 1962–1964; diploma, Central Evening High School, 1965; Essex College of Business, secretarial degree, 1967; further studies: Afrikan Poetry Theater Workshop, Jamaica, Queens, New York, 1986; Urban Voices Poetry Workshop, Newark, 1986; Essex County College, ongoing course work, 1986 to present. Religion: Al-Islam.

Residence in New Jersey Newark, 1947–1984; East Orange, 1984 to present.

Career Senior concessions attendant, National Movie Theater, Newark, 1962–1965; factory assembler, Western Electric, 1965–1967; secretary to the director, Joint Apprenticeship Program, Newark, 1967; assistant manager, Shabazz Sundries, Newark, 1967–1968; secretary to director of dental department, Public Employment Program, Newark Health Department, Newark, 1971–1972; secretary to director of custodial services, Newark Board of Education, Newark, 1972–1973; senior clerk transcriber, Essex County Probation Department, Newark, 1973 to present; volunteer, WBGO/Jazz, Newark, 1986 to present.

Memberships A.A. Universal Arabic Association, Inc., Elm, New Jersey, 1967–1977; Islamic Center of East Orange, New Jersey (affiliation); Islamic Cultural Center, Newark; Newark Writer's Guild, Newark, 1986 to present; founding member, Newark Writers Collective, Newark; member and past president, TRIAGE, a poetry performance troupe; registered poet with Poets and Writers, Inc., New York and the Woodson Foundation, Newark.

Awards, Honors, Other Certificates   Golden Poets Award, World of Poetry, California, 1988; National Arts Week award for outstanding contributions in the field of poetry, East Orange Major's Office of Arts and Cultural Affairs, 1988.

Reflections

"Islah Beyah encouraged me to submit my first collection of six poems to the Newark Public Library's Annual Poetry Search. Taking her advice resulted in my first publication of my earliest work. The women in my family developed character, ambition, strength, personality and a sense of pride, dignity, humor; two girl friends started the pen to move. One supported the idea that 'poetry was always in me, so write what you think down.' [Strong influences on my life include] my best friend, Daalmah Talley; my sister Latifa Muhammad for cheering me on; Fannie Mae, beloved stepmother deceased; [and] Theresa Olivia Guyton, paternal grandmother, deceased."

>Love is
>Just what it is
>LOVE
>Period
>Different for me
>Another different for you
>Distinctly different together
>>Jaleelah Karriem
>>17 January 1987

Publication

Beyah, Islah, and Jaleelah Karriem. *Love Period: Expressions of Love's Twist and Challenges.* East Orange, N. J.: We Did It Publications, 1986. [43].

Bio-Bibliographical Sources

Karriem, Jaleelah. "African American Women Writers in New Jersey: Biographical Questionnaire." Completed by Jaleelah Karriem, 17 January 1987.

———. Interview by Sibyl E. Moses. Newark, New Jersey, 17 January 1987.

———. Letter to Sibyl E. Moses, 31 March 1989.

KEARSE, AMALYA LYLE 1937–

Personal   Born on 11 June 1937 in Vauxhall, New Jersey; oldest child of Myra Lyle Smith Kearse (physician) of Lynchburg, Virginia, and Robert Freeman Kearse (postmaster); granddaughter (maternal) of Clara Roberta Alexander Smith (schoolteacher) and Theodore Parker Smith (schoolteacher), both of Lynchburg; great-granddaughter of Amalie Terry Alexander and Royal Alexander; brother: Robert Alexander Kearse. Education: Wellesley College, B.A., 1955–1959; University of Michigan, Ann Arbor, J.D., cum laude, 1959–1962.

Residence in New Jersey   Vauxhall.

Career   Research assistant to Professor John W. Reed, University of Michigan Law School, 1960–1962; research assistant to Professor Alan N. Polasky, University of Michigan Law School, 1961–1962; associate, Hughes, Hubbard & Reed, New York, 1962–1969; partner, Hughes, Hubbard, and Reed, New York, 1969–1979; judge, U.S. Court of Appeals for the Second Circuit, 1979–present. Nominated for appointment by President Carter on 2 May 1979; confirmed by the Senate. Admitted to New York State Bar, 1963; admitted to U.S. Supreme Court, 1967.

Memberships   Association of the Bar of the City of New York, Young Lawyers Committee, 1964–1969 (chairperson, 1967–1969); lecturer, evidence, New York University Law School, 1968–1969; Committee on Civil Rights, 1969–1970; Committee on Judicial Selection and Tenure, 1970–1971; Lawyer's Committee for Civil Rights Under Law, Executive Committee, 1970–1979; Committee on State Courts of Superior Jurisdiction, 1971–1972; director, Legal Aid Society, 1973–1977; American Contract Bridge League National Laws Commission, 1975 to present; Committee of the Judiciary, 1976–1979; trustee, New York City YWCA, 1976–1979; President's Committee on Selection of Federal Judicial Officers, 1977–1978; board of directors, NAACP Legal Defense and Endowment Fund, 1977–1979; American Law Institute, 1977 to present; American Bar Association, Litigation Section (council member), 1978–1979, Antitrust Section, 1978–1979, National Urban League, 1978–1979; fellow, American College of Trial Lawyers, 1979 to present; chairperson, C. Bainbridge Smith Scholarship Committee, 1979 to present; Judicial Administration Division, 1980 to present.

Awards, Honors, Other Certificates   National Women's Pairs Bridge Champion, 1971, 1972, World Division, 1986; National Women's Teams Bridge Champion, 1987, 1990, 1991; Bridge Personality of the Year, International Bridge Press Association, 1980; Outstanding Achievement Award, University of Michigan, 1982; Golden Plate Award, American Academy of Achievement, 1984; Order of the Coif; Jason L. Honigman Award, Outstanding Contribution to Law Review Editorial Board, University of Michigan.

Publications

  Books

American Bridge Contract Bridge League. *The Official Encyclopedia of Bridge.* Authorized by the American Contract Bridge League and prepared with the assistance of its staff, Richard L. Frey, editor in chief, Alan F. Truscott, executive editor, Amalya L. Kearse, editor. 3rd ed. Rev. and expanded. New York: Crown Publishers, 1976. 858, illus. Rev. ed., London: Ernest Benn, 1977.

Kearse, Amalya. *Bridge at Your Fingertips.* New York: A & W Visual Library, 1979. 320, illus.

———. *Bridge Conventions Complete.* New York: Hart Publishing Company [1975]. 624. Reprint, New York: Hart Publishing Company, 1976; revised and expanded, London: A and C. Black, 1977; revised and expanded, Louisville, Ky.: Devyn Press, 1984, 1990.

Translations

Le Dentu, Jose. *Championship Bridge.* Translated from the French and edited by Alan Truscott and Amalya Kearse. London: A. and C. Black, 1975. xi, 308.

———. *Bridge Analysis.* Translated from French and edited by Amalya Kearse. New York: Hart Publishing Co., 1978. 287, illus. Reprint, London: Hale, 1979.

Bio-Bibliographical Sources

Dornette, W. Stuart, and Robert R. Cross. *Federal Judiciary Almanac.* New York: John Wiley and Sons, 1986.

Lloyd, Esther Vincent. "Myra Lyle Smith Kearse, 1899–1982." In *Past and Promise: Lives of New Jersey Women,* n.p. Syracuse, New York: Syracuse University Press, 1997.

1999 Winter Judicial Staff Directory. Alexandria, Va.: CQ Directories, 1999.

Phelps, Shirelle, ed., *Contemporary Black Biography: Profiles from the International Black Community.* Vol. 12. Detroit: Gale Research, 1996.

Who's Who in America, 1997. Vol. 1, A–K. 51st ed. New Providence, N.J.: Marquis Who's Who, 1996.

KENYATTA, JANICE GREEN 1953–

Personal Born on 8 August 1953 in Newark, New Jersey; middle child of Marion Rayford Green (deceased) of Newark and Thomas Green (longshoreman) of Sanford, North Carolina; granddaughter (maternal) of Anna Mae Buchannan of Charlotte, North Carolina, and James E. Rayford of New Orleans, Louisiana; granddaughter (paternal) of Patience Cunningham and Thomas Green, both of Blythewood, South Carolina; sisters: Angela Green and Atonia Green; brother: Thomas Green, Jr.; husband: Kamau T. wa-Kenyatta (professor, lecturer, author, and entrepreneur); children: Aliya Shani Kenyatta and Ayanna Kai Kenyatta. Education: South 10th St. School, Newark, 1959; 15th Ave. School, Newark, 1960–1963; South 17th Street School, Newark, 1963–1967; Essex County Vocational and Technical High School, Newark, 1967–1970; Essex County College, Newark, A.S. secretarial science, 1970–1972; Montclair State University, Montclair, New Jersey, B.A., 1972–1975; Montclair State University, Montclair, M.A., business and secretarial education, 1975–1977.

Residence in New Jersey Newark, 1953–1969; Orange, 1969–1976, 1981–1987; Piscataway, 1976–1981; Princeton, 1987–1991; Somerset, 1991 to present.

Career   Business teacher, Essex County Vocational and Technical High School, Newark, 1976 to present.

Awards, Honors, Other Certificates   Alpha Epsilon Beta Honor Society, 1972; Who's Who Among Students in American Junior Colleges, 1972; Graduate Assistant Fellowship, Montclair State University, 1975; Delta Pi Epsilon Honorary Graduate Fraternity, 1976; contestant and Outstanding Interview Award, Mrs. New Jersey, USA Pageant, 1992; Who's Who Among America's Teachers, 1996; Governor's Teacher Recognition Award, 2000.

Reflections

"Two professors at Essex County College had a profound influence on my life, Professor Carolyn Norwood and Professor June Bailey. My mother, however, had the most influence overall. She taught me that if you wanted something bad enough and you set your mind to it, you will achieve it. She was also my backbone and supported wholeheartedly anything I set out to do.

Since I was a small child, I have always been an avid reader. I would always prefer to stay in the house and read a book instead of going outside to play with my brother and sisters and the other children. I found that reading opened up a new world for me, and I learned an awful lot from reading. Reading also helped to expand my vocabulary. This is why I have adopted the phrase, 'The more you learn, the less you fear.'

When I was 15 years old, I decided then that I wanted to write a novel. I did start it, but didn't get too far due to other distractions. The writer that influenced me the most and sparked my interest in writing at an early age was James Baldwin. I read every one of his books. Some of them I even read twice. Motivational writers such as Les Brown and Dennis Kimbro have also had a great impact on me and inspired me to write."

Publication

Kenyatta, Kamau, and Janice Kenyatta. *Black Folk's Hair, Secrets, Shame, and Liberation.* [Somerset, N.J.]: Songhai Publications, 1996. 118, illus.

Bio-Bibliographical Source

Kenyatta, Janice. "African American Women Writers in New Jersey: Biographical Questionnaire." Completed by Janice Kenyatta, 5 May 2000.

KHAN, LUREY 1927–

Personal   Born 11 November 1927 in Camden, New Jersey; fourth child of Mabel Emmaretta Smith Khan of Medford, New Jersey, and Fazil Ameir Khan of Northwest Frontier Province, India (now Pakistan); granddaughter (maternal) of Emmaretta Still Smith of Medford, and Jacob Smith of Virginia; granddaughter (paternal) of Amier Khan of Northwest Frontier Province, India, and his wife of Punjab Province, India; sisters: Nurjahan

Hamilton, Lorraine Khan-Broy, and Betty Khan; brother: Anthony Khan; husband: John Lewis Thomas (deceased); child: Emily Margaret Thomas. Education: Lafayette School, Boston, Massachusetts, 1930s; Hyde School, Boston, Massachusetts, 1933–1941 (racially segregated schools), Roxbury, Massachusetts; Girls High School, Boston (College Prep Magnet High School), 1941–1945; Boston College, Boston, 1945–1946, 1963–1965; Harvard University, Cambridge, Massachusetts, 1966; New England Hospital for Women and Children, Laboratory Technology Training Program, 1953–1954. Religion: Roman Catholic.

Residence in New Jersey Camden.

Career Laboratory technologist and chemist in Boston area hospitals, research laboratories, and industry, 1954–1992: medical technician, New England Hospital, Boston, 1954–1958; Children's Hospital, Boston, 1958–1961; research assistant, Harvard Medical School, Boston, 1961–1966; bacteriologist, H. P. Hood & Co., Inc., Charlestown, Massachusetts, 1966–1968; brewing chemist, Carling Brewing Co., Natick, Massachusetts, 1968–1972; research assistant, Harvard Medical School, Boston, 1972–1977; administrator, Sears Roebuck & Co., Boston, 1978–1980; medical technologist, Smithkline Beecham Co., Waltham, Massachusetts, 1981–1992.

Lurey Khan,
courtesy of Lurey Khan.

Memberships Author's Guild Inc.; Author's League, New York, 1975 to present.

Awards, Honors, Other Certificates Honors in the summer advanced writing program, Harvard University, Cambridge, 1966; Mary Roberts Rinehart Foundation Grant in Creative Writing (New York), 1978; Mary Lizzie Saunders Clapp Scholarship, Schlesinger Library on the History of Women, Radcliffe College, Cambridge 1985; Urbanarts, honorable mention in prose, Massachusetts Council of the Arts and Humanities, 1987.

Reflections

"My mother, the late Mabel Smith Khan of Medford, New Jersey, transferred to all her children the legacy of the Still Family, free blacks in New Jersey, 1805. She made me proud to be an African-American, and I wanted to take the family history to a larger world. I saw in my forebearers a touch of greatness that inspired me to live up to their love of family and hard work. Yet it was not my mother who led me into writing as a career. After working in technology and science in the Greater Boston area for many years, I enrolled in the Advanced Writing Program in 1966 at the Harvard Summer School. My professor, in this select, small class recognized in me what he called a 'gift' in novel writing, which I worked hard to develop into a marketable skill.

One Day Levin . . . He Be Free; William Still and the Underground is the story of the Still family from Indian Mills and Medford, New Jersey, and William Still's life as an antislavery agent in Philadelphia. William Still is my great-grandfather."

Publications

Book

Khan, Lurey. *One Day Levin . . . He Be Free; William Still and the Underground Railroad*. New York: E. P. Dutton, 1972. 231.

Articles

Khan, Lurey. "An American Pursues Her Pakistani Past." *Asia: The Journal of the Asian Society* 12, no. 6 (10 March 1980): 34–39.

———. "Caught in the Web of Traffic and Parking." *South End News* 14, no. 22 (14–20 July 1983): 6.

———. "Mrs. Margity's Cat." *South End News* 14, no. 23 (11–17 August 1983): 6, 14.

Bio-Bibliographical Sources

Khan, Lurey. "African American Women Writers in New Jersey: Biographical Questionnaire." Completed by Lurey Khan, 14 January 2000.

———. "Literary Resume." [undated] 2.

———. Telephone conversation with Sibyl E. Moses, 14 December 1999.

KOFIE, NANCY *SEE* TRAVIS, NANCY ELIZABETH

LAYNE, PATRICIA

Personal   Sister: Carole Willis. Education: University of Arizona, B.A.; Rutgers University; New York University, New York, M.A., 1969.
Residence in New Jersey   Montclair.
Career   Teacher, Los Angeles, California, and Washington, D.C. public school systems; head teacher, Head Start Program, Montclair Public School System, Montclair.
Publication
Layne, Patricia. *Peter, the Peculiar Guinea Pig.* New York: Vantage Press, 1976.
Bio-Bibliographical Sources
Layne, Patricia. *Peter, the Peculiar Guinea Pig.* New York: Vantage Press, 1976.
Lyght, Ernest S. Letter to Sibyl E. Moses, 8 September 1986 and 7 October 1986.

LATTANY, KRISTIN HUNTER *SEE* HUNTER-LATTANY, KRISTIN ELAINE EGGLESTON

LAWS, DORIS MAE *SEE* SHARIF, UMMIL-KHAIR ZAKIYYAH

LEE, HELEN CORINNE JACKSON
1908–1997

Personal   Born on 23 July 1908 in Richmond, Virginia; joined the ancestors on 3 December 1997 in Trenton, New Jersey. The fifth of seven children born to Nannie Jessaline Brisby Jackson (school teacher and housewife) of New Kent County, Virginia, and Charles Neason Jackson (building superintendent) of Richmond; granddaughter (maternal) of Ann Cumber Brisby and William Henry Brisby (1831–1916), member of the Virginia House of Delegates (1869–1871), both of New Kent County; granddaughter (paternal) of Elizabeth Jackson; sisters: Geraldine Jackson, Marjory J. Andrews, and Theresa Jackson; brothers:

Helen Jackson Lee.
Photograph by Mindillo,
courtesy of Barbara N. Lee.

Charles, Harold, and Miles; husband: Robert Edward Lee (pharmacist, deceased); children: Barbara Nan Lee and Robert Edward Lee, Jr. Education: Van de Vyver Academy, Richmond (grades K–3); Hartshon Day School, Richmond (grades 4–6); Virginia Randolph Training School, Glen Allen, Virginia (grades 7–8); Virginia State Preparatory School, Petersburg, Virginia (grades 9–12); Virginia State College, Petersburg, 1926–1930, B.A. (English and French); Rider College, Trenton, 1943–1945. Religion: Roman Catholic; Our Lady of the Divine Shepherd Church, Trenton.

Residence in New Jersey Trenton, 1940–1997.

Career Teacher, Fauquier Training School, Goochland County, Virginia, 1930–1932; newspaper reporter, *Philadelphia Tribune*, 1935, *Philadelphia Independent*, 1937–1938, *Pittsburgh Courier*, 1938–1940, Philadelphia edition of the *Chicago Defender*, 1936–1937, Trenton correspondent, New Jersey edition of the *Afro-American*, 1942–1955; clerk typist, New Jersey Unemployment Compensation Commission, Trenton, 1942–1947; senior clerk stenographer, New Jersey Department of Human Services (formerly New Jersey Department of Institutions and Agencies), Trenton, 1947–1962; secretary to the Fire Marshall, New Jersey Department of Human Services, Trenton, 1962–1965; assistant supervisor of the Stenographic Pool, New Jersey Department of Human Services, Trenton, 1965–1967; public information assistant, Trenton, 1967–1971; social worker, Trenton, 1971–1973.

Memberships Alpha Kappa Alpha Sorority, Inc.; charter member (1952), historian, Alpha Kappa Alpha Sorority, Epsilon Upsilon Omega Chapter; New Jersey Historical Society; Friends of the Cadwalader Branch of Trenton Public Library; Trenton Museum Society; Board of Directors, YWCA Trenton, 1974–1980; organized and directed children's theater for more than one hundred children, Blessed Martin Children's Theater, at Our Lady of the Divine Shepherd Church, Trenton, 1941–1948,; NAACP, Trenton Branch; Mt. Carmel Guild; Our Lady of Divine Shepherd Catholic Church, Women's Organization, Secretary of Altar Rosary Society.

Awards, Honors, Other Certificates Meta A. Griffith Service Award, Zonta Club of Trenton, 1986; Award for Outstanding Service, Bronzettes, Inc., 1978/1979; Precious Pearl Award for Outstanding and Dedicated Service to the Community, Alpha Kappa Alpha Sorority, 1975; honor upon publication of autobiography and in appreciation for dedicated years of creative service to sorority and community, Alpha Kappa Alpha Sorority, Epsilon Upsilon Omega Chapter, Founder's Day Luncheon, 25 February 1978; Saluted by the Top Ladies of Distinction, Inc., 5 May 1979; Community Service Award, Metro Civic League, 1978; proclamation "Helen Jackson Lee Day," by Mayor Maynard Jackson, proclamation, Atlanta, Georgia, 19 Judy 1980; honored for dedication and service to the community and especially to our public school students, County of Mercer, New Jersey, Board of Chosen Freeholders, 20 March 1986; award for contributions to the history of New Jersey, New Jersey Legislature, 1994.

Reflections

"My mother used to write poetry, and told us [that] writing is a disease that you're afflicted with—that you are compelled to do. Don't do it because you want to—but have to. Mother used to read a story every night waiting for father to return home. She told children all the time [that] 'You must read a lot—reading stimulates the mind.' "

Publication

Lee, Helen. *Nigger in the Window.* Garden City, N.Y.: Doubleday and Company, Inc., 1978. 239.

Bio-Bibliographical Sources

Jackson, Luther Porter. *Negro Office–Holders in Virginia 1865–1895.* Norfolk, Va.: Guide Quality Press, 1945. 6.

Lee, Helen Jackson. Interview with Sibyl E. Moses, Trenton, New Jersey, 21 January 1987.

"Mass of Christian Burial for Helen Jackson Lee, 1908–1997." Trenton, N.J.: Our Lady of the Divine Shepherd Church, 1997. [obituary].

LEE, JARENA **1783–?**

Personal Born on 11 February 1783 in Cape May (Cape May County), New Jersey. Joined the ancestors after 1836, date unknown. Lived beyond the age of fifty. Children: two, one of whom was a son (names not known); husband: Joseph Lee (pastor, Snow Hill, New Jersey). Religion: African Methodist Episcopal.

Residence in New Jersey Cape May County, 1783-ca. 1790; Snow Hill (Lawnside), ca. 1811-ca. 1817.

Career Servant maid, family of Mr. Sharp, 1790-? (ca. sixty miles from Cape May); preacher, African Methodist Episcopal Church, 1807 until after 1836. Recognized that she was called to preach by Bishop Richard Allen, ca. 1815. Preaching engagements in New Jersey (Trenton, Princeton, Burlington, Salem, and Snow Hill), Delaware, and Pennsylvania.

Memberships Free African Society.

Jarena Lee, courtesy of the Library of Congress.

Publications

Lee, Jarena. *The Life and Religious Experience of Jarena Lee, a Coloured Lady, Giving an Account of Her Call to Preach the Gospel.* Philadelphia: The Author, 1836. 24.

————. *Religious Experience and Journal of Mrs. Jarena Lee, Giving an Account of Her Call to Preach the Gospel.* Rev. and corrected from the original manuscript, written by herself. Philadelphia: Published for the author, 1849. 97, illus. (port.).

Bio-Bibliographical Sources

Lee, Jarena. *Religious Experience and Journal of Mrs. Jarena Lee, Giving an Account of Her Call to Preach the Gospel.* Rev. and corrected from the original manuscript, written by herself. Philadelphia: Published for the author, 1849. 97, illus. (port.).

Loewenberg, Bert James, and Ruth Bogin, eds. *Black Women in Nineteenth-Century American Life: Their Words, Their Thoughts, Their Feelings.* University Park: The Pennsylvania State University Press, 1976.

LINDSEY, HELEN MARIE TUDOS LEE 1897–1987

Personal   Born on 24 August 1897 in Bridgeton, New Jersey; joined the ancestors in July 1987; husband: Leemond S. Lindsey; child: Mabel L. Wilson. Education: Elementary schools in Bridgeton; Bridgeton High School, Bridgeton; Trenton Normal School, Trenton, New Jersey; University of Pennsylvania; Temple University, Philadelphia, Pennsylvania; Glassboro State College, Glassboro, New Jersey; Rutgers University. Religion: African Methodist Episcopal; Mt. Pisgah A.M.E. Church, Salem, New Jersey.

Residence in New Jersey   Bridgeton; Salem.

Career   Teacher, Lincoln School, Trenton; teacher, No. 9 School, Swainton, New Jersey; teacher, Salem City School System, Salem (for forty years).

Memberships   Elks; original member, New Jersey Organization of Teachers; life member, New Jersey Congress of Parents and Teachers.

Awards, Honors, Other Certificates   Teacher of the Year, New Jersey Organization of Teachers; "Key to the City," City of Salem.

Publication

Lindsey, Helen L. *The Little African Book: A Story of Feta and Her Family.* New York: Carlton Press, 1972. 48, illus.

Bio-Bibliographical Sources

Butler, Rebecca Batts. *Profiles of Outstanding Blacks in South Jersey During the 1950's, 1960's, 1970's.* [Cherry Hill, N.J.]: Reynolds Publishers, Inc. [1980].

Lindsey, Helen L. *The Little African Book: A Story of Feta and Her Family.* New York: Carlton Press, 1972.

Social Security Death Index. "Helen Lindsey." Available: <http://www.ancestry.com> Accessed 28 June 2000.

Wilson, Mabel Lindsey. Interview with Sibyl E. Moses, Bridgeton, New Jersey, 12 April 1985.

LITTLE, BENILDE ELEASE 1958–

Personal   Born in 1958 in Newark, New Jersey; daughter of Clara Little (nurse's aide) and Matthew Little (General Motors employee; civic leader); husband: Clifford Virgin, III (stockbroker); daughter: Baldwin. Education: Howard University, Washington, D.C., B.A., journalism, 1981; further studies: Northwestern University, Evanston, Illinois, broadcast journalism, 1982.

Residence in New Jersey   Newark; South Orange.

Career   Reporter, *The Star Ledger,* 1982–1985; reporter, *People Magazine,* 1985–1989; senior editor, *Essence Magazine,* 1989–1991.

Awards, Honors, Other Certificates   Go On Girl Book Club, National Best New Author, 1996; NAACP Image Award (finalist), 1996.

Publications

Books

Little, Benilde. *Good Hair: A Novel.* New York: Simon & Schuster, 1996. 237. Reprint, New York: Scribner, 1997.

———. *The Itch: A Novel.* New York: Simon & Schuster, 1998. 216. Reprint, New York: Scribner Paperback Fiction, 1999.

Articles

Little, Benilde. "Brooklyn's Baby Mogul, Spike Lee, Finds the Freedom He's Gotta Have." *People Weekly* 26 (13 October 1986): 67.

———. "Mariel Hemingway and Husband Stephen Crisman Do It Their Way at a Café Called Sam's." *People Weekly* 25 (21 April 1986): 71–72.

Small, Michael, and Benilde Little. "In Need of an Angel (II)." *People Weekly* 27 (27 April 1987): 94–95.

Little, Benilde. "Restaurant Queen Trixie Traded A Future On Wall Street for a Place in Hell's Kitsch-In." *People Weekly* 30 (17 October 1988): 125–127.

———. "Derrick Bell: Harvard's Conscience." *Essence* 21 (November 1990): 44.

———. "Janet Hubert." *Essence* 21 (December 1990): 33.

———. "Randy Crawford: Jazzy Rhythm 'N' Blues." *Essence* 21 (August 1990): 48.

———. "Robert Johnson: The Eyes Behind BET." *Essence* 21 (November 1990): 48.

———. "TV's Bill Cosby in Ghost Dad, The Movie (Interview)." *Essence* 21 (June 1990): 38.

———. "Dating Blind." *Essence* 22 (October 1991): 64–66.

———. "George C. Wolfe: On Our Beauty and Complexity." *Essence* 21 (February 1991): 35.

———. "John Singleton." *Essence* 22 (September 1991): 43.

———. "Jon Lucien: After A 15-Year Lull, He's Back and Even More Soulful." *Essence* 22 (October 1991): 42.

———. "Just Gladys." *Essence* 22 (October 1991): 52–54+.

———. "Oleta Adams: After Nearly 20 Years, She's Hit." *Essence* 22 (June 1991): 34.

———. "Bill T. Jones: A Meaningful Life." *Essence* 22 (January 1992): 36.

———. "Giancarlo Esposito: After More Than 20 Years, He's Finally Getting Some Multidimensional Roles That Help Him Flex His Talent." *Essence* 23 (December 1992): 36.

———. "Eco-Fashion." *Essence* 25 (August 1994): 20.

———. "Benilde Little on Social-Class Divisions." *Essence* 27 (September 1996): 104.

———. "Good Hair." *Essence* 27 (September 1996): 104+

———. "How Can You Bring Spirituality into Your Life? (Interview with Gloria Wade-Gayles and Renita Weems)." *Essence* 27 (July 1996): 54.

———. "Wheel Fun!" *Essence* 24 (August 1996): 24+.

———. "How Can We Encourage Our Children to Stay in College? (Interview with Johnnetta Cole and Ruth Simmons)." *Essence* 28 (May 1997): 104+.

Bio-Bibliographical Sources:

"Benilde Little." *Contemporary Black Biography: Profiles from the International Black Community.* Vol. 21. Farmington Hills, Mich.: The Gale Group, 1999.

Who's Who Among African Americans. 11th ed. Detroit: Gale Research, 1998.

LIVINGSTON, EDDIEMAE **1919–**

Eddiemae Livingston.
Photograph by Herbert D. Glenn.

Personal Born on 13 July 1919 in Newberry (Newberry County), South Carolina; ninth of eleven children of Mamie Hodges Livingston (housewife) of Whitmire, South Carolina, and Edward Livingston (sharecropper/farmer); granddaughter (maternal) of Mary and Henry Hodges, both of South Carolina; sisters: Celia L. Cousins, Esther L. Ford, Sarah L. Boyd (deceased), Myrtle Livingston Wicks (deceased), Fayetta L. Scott (deceased), and Mariah L. Walton (deceased); brothers: Jefferson Livingston (deceased) and Harold Livingston (deceased). Education: Drayton Street School, Newberry (grades 1–7), 1927–1934; Drayton Street High School, Newberry (grades 8–11), 1934–1938; Benedict College, Columbia, South Carolina, B.S. (mathematics), cum laude, 1942. Religion: Baptist; Hopewell Baptist Church, Newark, New Jersey.

Residence in New Jersey   Newark, 1942 to present.

Career   Federal civil servant (providing family allowances to soldiers' families), Office of Dependency Benefits, Washington, D.C., September 1942–November 1942; federal civil servant, Office of Dependency Benefits, Newark, 1942–January 1947; city civil servant, Bureau of Child Hygiene, City of Newark Division of Health, Newark, September 1947–1963; Chest Disease Bureau, City of Newark Division of Health, Newark, 1963–1973; City of Newark Division of Welfare, Newark, 1973–1982; City of Newark, Municipal Council, July 1982–1999.

Memberships   Life membership, Golden Heritage Club, NAACP; financial secretary, Hopewell Baptist Church, Newark, 1976 to present; recording secretary, North Jersey Duplicate Bridge Club; treasurer, Eastern Section of American Bridge Association, 1967–1982; recording secretary, New Jersey Bridge Unit; Iota Phi Lambda Sorority.

Awards, Honors, Other Certificates   Hailed by members of the Newark community as the "Poet Laureate of the City of Newark"; selected to write poem for the 1 July 1974 inaugural celebration of Newark mayor, Kenneth A. Gibson; high school valedictorian, award for best grades in English; "pin," Stenotype Institute, New York, New York.

Reflections

> "No single person [had an impact] on my life. The *group* that made the greatest impact was the NAACP. They saved my job [in] Washington, D.C. That employment was to become the stepping-stone to all of my future employment. Because of discriminatory practices in 1942, the Federal government attempted to thwart my transfer to Newark, New Jersey. Since I had given up the school to which I had been assigned to teach, when I went to work a month before with the Federal government; I would have been unemployed. Hence, my support now of the NAACP [by] Life Membership and Golden Heritage Membership."

Publication

Livingston, Eddiemae. *Bridge Reflections in Rhyme*. Newark, N.J.: The Author, 1983. 22.

Bio-Bibliographical Source

Livingston, Eddiemae. Interview by Sibyl E. Moses, Newark, New Jersey, Fall 1990.

Lloyd, Carole Darden 1944–

Personal   Born on 21 May 1944 in Newark, New Jersey; second child of Mamie Jean Sampson Darden (teacher, social worker, real estate developer, and manager) of Camden, Alabama, and Walter Theodore "Bud" Darden (physician) of Wilson, North Carolina; granddaughter (maternal aunt and uncle) of Corine Johnson Sampson of Camden and William Sampson of Kentucky; granddaughter (paternal) of Dianah Scarborough Darden (seam-

Carole Darden Lloyd.
Photograph by Chris Gulker,
courtesy of Los Angeles Public Library.

stress) and Charles Henry Darden (carpenter, first African American undertaker in North Carolina), both of Wilson; sister: Norma Jean Darden; husband: Edward G. Lloyd (chief financial officer); child: Jason Lloyd. Education: Nishuane School, Montclair, New Jersey; Hillside Junior High, Montclair; Oakwood School, 1959–1962; Sarah Lawrence College, Bronxville, New York, B.A., 1962–1966; Fordham School of Social Work, New York, New York, M.S.W., 1968–1971. Religion: Baptist; Abyssinian Baptist Church, Harlem, New York.

Residence in New Jersey   Montclair.

Career   Social work administrator, Wiltwyck School for Boys, Esopus, New York.

Memberships   Board of directors, Community Access, Inc.

Awards, Honors, Other Certificates   Runner-up, Tasters Choice Award, for *Spoonbread and Strawberry Wine*, 1979; Mother of the Year Award, Metropolitan Chapter, Jack and Jill, for work with teen group; Outstanding Achievement in the Arts, National Association of Business and Professional Women's Club, 1980.

Publication

Darden, Norma Jean, and Carole Darden. *Spoonbread and Strawberry Wine: Recipes and Reminiscences of a Family.* Line drawings by Doug Jamieson [wood engravings throughout text by Thomas Bewick]. 1st ed. Garden City, N.Y.: Anchor Press, 1978. xi, 288. Reprint, New York: Fawcett Crest, 1978, 1980, 1982; New York: Doubleday, 1994.

Bio-Bibliographical Sources

Darden, Norma Jean, and Carole Darden. *Spoonbread and Strawberry Wine: Recipes and Reminiscences of a Family.* Garden City, N.Y.: Anchor Press, 1978.

Lloyd, Carole Darden. "African American Women Writers in New Jersey: Biographical Questionnaire." Completed by Carole Darden Lloyd, November 1996.

LOWERY, PAULINE MASON

Personal   Born in Newark, New Jersey.

Residence in New Jersey   Newark.

Publication

Lowery, Pauline. *Poems of Life.* [Newark, N.J.]: The Author, 1980. 16.

MATHIS, SHARON YVONNE BELL
1937–

Sharon Bell Mathis.
Photograph by Marcia Cynthia Bell.

Personal Born on 26 February 1937 in Atlantic City, New Jersey; daughter of Alice Mary Frazier Bell (1916–1983; writer and artist) of Atlantic City and John Willie Bell of New Orleans, Louisiana; granddaughter (maternal) of Mary Frazier of Eastern Shore, Maryland, and Richard H. Frazier of Richmond, Virginia; sisters: Patrellis Bell Booth (deceased) and Marcia Cynthia Bell; brother: John W. Bell, Jr.; husband: Leroy Franklin Mathis (deceased); children: Sherie M. Mathis-Diggs, Stacy T. Mathis-Collins, and Stephanie A. Mathis-Hamilton. Education: Public School #70, Brooklyn, New York; Holy Rosary Elementary School, Brooklyn; St. Michael's Academy, New York (grades 9–12), 1950–1954; Morgan State College, Baltimore, Maryland, B.A., sociology, 1954–1958; The Catholic University of America, Washington, D.C., M.S.L.S, 1974. Religion: Roman Catholic; attends Ebenezer African Methodist Episcopal Church, Fort Washington, Maryland.

Residence in New Jersey Atlantic City.

Career Interviewer, Children's Hospital of D.C., 1958–1959; teacher, Holy Redeemer Elementary School, Washington, D.C., 1959–1965; teacher, District of Columbia Public Schools, Washington, D.C., 1965–1975: special education teacher, Bertie Backus Junior High School, 1965–1966; teacher, Charles Hart Junior High School, 1966–1972; teacher, Stuart Junior High School, 1972–1975; writer-in-charge, Children's Literature Division, D.C. Black Writers Workshop; writer-in-residence, Howard University, Washington, D.C., 1972–1973; librarian, District of Columbia Public Schools, Washington, D.C., 1975–1995: librarian, Benning Elementary School, 1975–1976, Wasington, D.C.; library media specialist, Friendship Education Center (now Patricia Roberts Harris Educational Center).

Memberships Board of advisors, Lawyers Commission of District of Columbia Commission on the Arts, 1972–1973; Black Women's Community Development Foundation, 1973–1974; American Library Association; The Author's Guild.

Awards, Honors, Other Certificates Benjamin F. Jackson Prize in Sociology, Morgan State College; Eliza Jane Cummings Medal in Sociology, Morgan State College; Emmanuel Chambers Memorial Scholarship, Sociology,

Morgan State College; nominated by National Conference Christians and Jews for Books for Brotherhood List, 1970; Council on Interracial Books for Children for *Sidewalk Story;* one of the Child Study Association of America's Children's Books of the Year, 1971, for *Sidewalk Story;* one of the Outstanding Books of Year, *New York Times,* 1972; Coretta Scott King Award, 1974, for *Ray Charles;* one of ALA's Best Young Adult Books of the Year, 1974, for *Listen for the Fig Tree;* Newbery Honor Book, 1976, for *The Hundred Penny Box;* District of Columbia Association of School Librarians Award, 1976; Arts and Humanities Award, Archdiocese of Washington, D.C., 1978; Arts and Letters Award, Delta Sigma Theta Sorority, 1985; Outstanding Writer Award, Writing-to-Read Program, District of Columbia Public Schools, 1986; Ten Top Youth Sports Books, *Booklist Magazine,* September 1998, for *Running Girl: The Diary of Ebonee Rose.*

Reflections

"My mother, Alice, had a best friend living next door to her on Virginia Avenue. The child's name was Bertha Reed, child of Dewey and Isabel Reed. The two of them pledged that they would be godmothers to one another's children. Bertha Reed Lee McDonald never had a child and stood by her pledge when her friend's first child was born. She was a real godmother who sent gifts constantly but, most of all, she saw that I attended Morgan State University (my godmother was a public school teacher in Baltimore, Maryland). I was spoiled rotten by this master teacher who enjoyed creative writing and encouraged me while I spent summers (1951–1954) in her home. Upon graduation from St Michael's, I moved permanently into her home and stayed until I married Leroy Franklin Mathis on July 11, 1957. My godmother was a graduate of Coppin State College and Morgan State.

My mother married my father shortly after graduating from Atlantic City High School and never attended college, but she greatly influenced me to be a writer, because she was an extraordinary poet who loved to read as well as draw. Alice Frazier Bell published a poem, "Memories," in *The Negro History Bulletin* which she wrote at seventeen. She also published in *Ebony JR!.* In her high school yearbook, she mentioned that she wished to be a writer. Another dream was that she would be able to train to be a registered nurse. Additionally, she was an avid reader who filled our home with the books written by African American writers. I was familiar with the work of Richard Wright, Frank Yerby, Langston Hughes, Frederick Douglass, Ann Petry, Zora Neale Hurston, and others. All of my siblings—and my father (91 years of age on 13 September 2001) were and are avid readers."

Publications

Books

Mathis, Sharon Bell. *Brooklyn Story.* Illustrated by Charles Bible. *A Challenger Book. Black Series.* 1st ed. New York: Hill and Wang [1970]. 56.
———. *Sidewalk Story.* Illustrated by Leo Carty. [1st ed.]. New York: Viking

Press, 1971. 71Reprint, New York: Camelot Books, 1973; New York: Kestrel, 1986; New York: Puffin Books, 1986.

———. *The Hundred Penny Box*. Illustrated by Leo and Diane Dillon. New York: Viking Press, 1972. 47. Reprint, New York: Viking Press, 1975; ; New York: Random House, 1977, 1979; N.p.: Newberry, 1977; N.p.: American School, 1979; New York: Puffin Books, 1986; New York: Scholastic, 1989. Video recording: Los Angeles: Churchill Films, 1979; New York: Random House Video, 1986. Motion picture: 1979 by Churchill Films, Los Angeles. Italian edition: *La Scatola dei Centro Penny*, translated by Angela Ragusa. Milan: Mondadori, 1997.

Mathis, Sharon Bell. *Listen for the Fig Tree*. [1ˢᵗ ed.]. New York: Viking Press, 1972. 175. Reprint New York: Avon Books, 1975; New York: Puffin, 1990.

———. *Teacup Full of Roses*. New York: Viking Press, 1972. 125. Reprint, New York: Avon, 1972; large print edition, Boston: G. K. Hall, 1973; New York: Viking, 1977; New York: Puffin, 1986, 1987.

———. *Ray Charles*. Illustrated by George Ford. A Crowell Biography. New York: Crowell [1973]. 31. Reprint, New York: Lee and Low, 2001.

———. *Cartwheels*. *Sprint Books*. New York: Scholastic Book Services, 1997. 96, illus.

———. *Red Dog, Blue Fly: Football Poems*. Pictures by Jan Gilchrist Spivey. New York: Viking Press, 1991. [29].

———. *Running Girl: The Diary of Ebonee Rose*. 1ˢᵗ ed. San Diego: Harcourt Brace, 1997. 60.

Articles, Short Stories, and Poetry

Mathis, Sharon Bell. "Ladies Magazine." In *Night Comes Softly Black Like Me: An Anthology of Black Female Voices*, edited by Nikki Giovanni, n.p. [Newark, N.J.: Printed by Medic Press, 1970].

———. "R.S.V.P." In *Night Comes Softly Black Like Me: An Anthology of Black Female Voices*, edited by Nikki Giovanni, n.p. [Newark, N.J.: Printed by Medic Press, 1970].

———. "Arthur." *Essence* 2, no. 11 (March 1972): 50–51.

———. "My Mother Was Beautiful in the Warmth of Spring." *Negro History Bulletin* 35, no. 3 (March 1972): 67.

———. "Ernie Father." *Black World* 22, no. 8 (June 1973): 57–59.

———. "True/False Messages for the Black Child: Racism in Children's Literature." *Black Books Bulletin* 2, nos. 3 and 4 (winter 1974): 12–19.

———. "Ten Pennies and Green Mold: Address." *Horn Book* 52 (August 1976): 433–437.

———. "Godmother." In *Join In: Multiethnic Short Stories by Outstanding Writers for Young Adults*, edited by Donald R. Gallo, 173–199. New York: Delacorte Press, 1993.

Bio-Bibliographical Sources

Lystad, Mary. "Sharon Bell Mathis." In *Twentieth-Century Young Adult Writers*, edited by Laura Standley Berger, 426–427. Detroit: St. James Press, 1994.

Mathis, Sharon Bell. "African American Women Writers in New Jersey: Biographical Questionnaire." Completed by Sharon Bell Mathis, 26 May 2001.

————. Letter to Sibyl E. Moses, 23 October 1986.

McCRAY, CARRIE ALLEN 1913–

Carrie Allen McCray,
courtesy of Driggers Photography.

Personal Born on 4 October 1913 in Lynchburg, Virginia; ninth child of Mary Rice Hayes Allen (teacher) of Harrisburg, Virginia, and William Patterson Allen (lawyer) of Danville, Virginia; granddaughter (maternal) of Harriet Jones and John R. Jones, both of Harrisonburg; granddaughter (paternal) of Lucretia Allen and Henry Allen, both of North Carolina; brothers: Willis Hayes (died in infancy), Gregory Hayes (deceased), Will Elbert Hayes (deceased), and Hunter Hayes; sisters: Minnie Hayes (deceased), Malinda Hayes (deceased), Rosemary Allen Jones, and Dolly Allen Nesbitt; husbands: Scott Young (post office worker and owner of mobile library) and John Henry McCray (journalist and political rights activist in South Carolina; in the 1940s, John Henry McCray founded the Progressive Democrats, a Black party, which protested political exclusion. His party was credited for defeating Strom Thurman in his first run for office); child: Winfield Scott Young. Education: Virginia Seminary Elementary, Lynchburg, Virginia (grade 1), 1918–1919; Spaulding Elementary School, Montclair, New Jersey; Hillside School, Montclair, 1920–1928; Montclair High School, Montclair, 1928–1931; Talladega College, Talladega, Alabama, 1931–1935, A.B., sociology, 1935; New York University, New York, New York, School of Social Work, M.S.W., 1955. Religion: Baptist; Second Calvary Baptist Church, Columbia, South Carolina.

Residence in New Jersey Montclair, 1920–1943, 1955–1957; Asbury Park, 1943–1945.

Career W.P.A. Project-Negro History (New Jersey), 1936–1938; social worker, Katy Ferguson House, New York, 1938–1941; social worker, Children's Aid Society, Detroit, Michigan, 1943–1945; director of Community Center, Asbury Park, New Jersey; social worker, Five Points House, New York; social worker (positions held: caseworker, supervisor, director of health and psychiatric services, assistant director of the agency), Sheltering Arms Children's Service, New York, 1952–1965; associate professor of social work and sociology, Talladega College, Talledega, 1965–1979.

Memberships NAACP; Alpha Kappa Alpha Sorority, Inc.; South Carolina Writers Workshop; Board of Governors of the South Carolina Academy of Authors.

Awards, Honors, Other Certificates Teacher of the Year U.N.C.F. Award, 1976; one of the founders and first board members of the South Carolina Academy of Authors (their Carrie Allen McCray Literary Award is named in her honor).

Reflections

"Four major influences in my life were my mother, Mary Allen; Hortense Tate, YWCA girl reserve action when growing up; Louise Love, a social worker; and Anne Spencer, the Harlem Renaissance and poet. My mother, who bought me books of the Harlem Renaissance poets and Anne Spencer the poet were my greatest influences in relation to writing. One of my most memorable experiences was in the sixties helping to organize grass roots organizations in Talladega, Alabama, first Pullim Street Center, then Community Life Institute. Both organizations were fighting for equal rights in the schools, politically, employment, and better services in the Black Community (1960s).

Another memorable experience was working on the WPA Negro History Project and spending hours in the Schomburg Library in New York doing research (1935 or later); and the third most memorable experience was going to the University of Edinburgh in Scotland to present a research paper, "The Impact of Segregation on Child Development" before the World Federation of Mental Health [in 1960]. And always for a mother it has to be the birth of her child [in 1941]. The publication of *Freedom's Child* and the positive response it has received throughout the country. [Finally] reaching the age of 85 and still writing. What a blessing!"

Publications

Books

McCray, Carrie Allen. *Piece of Time*. Crimson Edge Chapbook. Goshen, Conn.: Chicory Blue Press, 1996. Reprint, in *The Crimson Edge, Older Women Writing*, edited by Sondra Zeidenstein, n.p. Goshen, Conn.: Chicory Blue Press, 1996.

————. *Freedom's Child: The Life of a Confederate General's Black Daughter.* Chapel Hill, N.C.: Algonquin Books, 1998. Paperback issue, New York: Penguin Books, 1998.

Short Stories, Single Poems, and Other Writings

McCray, Carrie. "Adjö means Goodbye." In *Beyond the Angry Black*, edited by John A. Williams, n.p. New York: Cooper Square Publishers, 1966. Reprint, in *Reading Literature*, n.p. Evanston, Ill.: McDougal and Little, 1989.

————. "The Black Woman and Family Roles." In *The Black Woman*, edited by LaFrances Rogers-Rose, n.p. Beverly Hills, Calif.: Sage Publications, 1980.

―――. "Nobody Wrote a Poem." In *Moving Beyond Words,* edited by Gloria Steinem, n.p. New York: Simon and Schuster, 1994.

―――. "Hats", *Ms Magazine,* September/October 1995, n.p.

―――. Selected Poems. In *The River Styx* 49, edited by Richard Newman, n.p. St. Louis, Miss.: Multicultural Literary Explorers, 1997.

Bio-Bibliographical Source

McCray, Carrie Allen. "African American Women Writers in New Jersey: Biographical Questionnaire." Completed by Carrie Allen McCray, 29 September 1999.

McGriff, Hope Taylor *see* Taylor, Hope

McKay, Lenora Sylvia Walker 1917–1994

Lenora Walker McKay.
Photograph by Russ DeSantis,
courtesy of Asbury Park Press.

Personal   Born on 31 May 1917 in Neptune, New Jersey; joined the ancestors in September 1994. The third child of Rosa Hanna Greene Walker (teacher) of Culpepper, Virginia, and Charles John Henry Walker (minister, Shiloh Baptist Church, Manasquan, New Jersey, and Bethany Baptist Church, Farmingdale, New Jersey) of Orange, Virginia; granddaughter (paternal) of Sylvia Jackson Walker of Virginia and Andrew Walker; sisters: Griselda Olitzka Walker Clarke and Quthella Reba Walker Oates; brother: Charles Thomas Walker, Jr.; husband: Francis Morris McKay, Sr. (federal Civil Service worker, retired), married in 1947; child: Francis M. McKay, Jr., M.D. Education: Ridge Avenue Elementary School, Neptune, New Jersey, 1930; Neptune High School, Neptune 1934; Monmouth Junior College (now Monmouth College), Monmouth, New Jersey; Virginia State College, Petersburg, Virginia, B.A., education in social science, 1938. Religion: Baptist; United Fellowship Baptist Church, Asbury Park, New Jersey.

Residence in New Jersey   Neptune, 1917–1994.

Career   Writer for high school and college newspapers; secondary school social studies teacher, Lancaster, South Carolina, 1939–1940; parent education teacher, WPA, Neptune and Asbury Park, 1940–1941; social worker, Monmouth, County Board of Social Services, Neptune, 1942; administrative supervisor, Monmouth County Board of Social Services, Neptune.

Memberships Advisory board, NAACP, Asbury Park/Neptune Branch; founder and first president, Monmouth County Business and Professional Women's Council, 1950 to 1980s; board of trustees, Westside Community Center; Citizens' Advisory Panel for Community Development, Neptune; Youth Civic League; Neptune Civic League; Neptune Community Organization; Neptune Neighborhood Council; New Jersey Black Issues Convention; Mt. Pisgah Baptist Temple, Social Action Committee; United Fellowship Baptist Church, Social Action Committee and Pulpit Committee.

Awards, Honors, Other Certificates Top graduate, Ridge Avenue Elementary School, Neptune; Special award, Monmouth County Business and Professional Women's Council; Rotary Club Award (community affairs); Lion's Club Award (community action); scored highest mark ever recorded on entrance examination for Monmouth Junior College.

Reflections

"First book, the bicentennial tribute [came about as the result of a] Black judge [approaching me and saying that] every ethnic group was making [a] contribution, and that the Black perspective was needed, and asked me to do it; that was Judge Phillip Gumbs, Aberdeen Township. Second book—[I] became interested in writing and discussing the 1960s and changes that came about in family life. This motivated me to record traditions in the Black family. Parents stimulated [my] interest in writing. Minister wrote sermons. Father taught Hebrew and was a linguist. I received a $10 gold piece from Ridge High School as the top graduate in the class. Later received a journalism pin in high school, and I wrote for the school paper in high school and in college. My son writes for the *Journal of the American Medical Association.*"

Publications

McKay, Lenora Walker. *The Blacks of Monmouth County: A Bicentennial Tribute.* 1st ed. [Neptune, N.J.]: The Author, 1976. 137.

———. *Mama and Papa.* [Neptune]: The Author, 1984. 166, illus.

Bio-Bibliographical Source

McKay, Lenora Walker. Interview by Sibyl E. Moses. Neptune, New Jersey, January 1987.

MITCHELL, SHARON L. 1961–

Personal Born on 1 July 1961 in Trenton, New Jersey; first child of Lucy Patten Mitchell (sexton) and Robert Ernest Mitchell, both of Trenton; granddaughter (maternal) of Leola Patten of Trenton and Timothy Patten of Philadelphia, Pennsylvania; granddaughter (paternal) of Jesse Mae Mitchell of Americus, Georgia; sisters: Teri Mitchell, Deborah Mitchell. Education: Our Lady of Divine Shepherd, Trenton; Notre Dame High School, Lawrenceville, New Jersey, 1975–1979; Monmouth College (now Monmouth University), West Long Branch, New Jersey, B.A., 1979–1983.

Residence in New Jersey   Trenton, 1961–1975, 1984–1993; Lawrenceville, 1975–1979, 1983–1984; West Long Branch, 1979–1983; Plainsboro, 1993 to present.

Career   Part-time basketball coach, Notre Dame High School, Lawrenceville, New Jersey, 1983–1992; nighttime supervisor, Princeton University Library Security, 1985 to present; associate head basketball coach, Notre Dame High School, Lawrenceville, 1989–1992.

Awards, Honors, Other Certificates   Member, Girls Athletic Association, 1975–1979; Women's Basketball Scholarship; Black Student Union, Monmouth College, 1979.

Memberships   Executive board member, shop steward, and negotiating team for Princeton University Library Assistants Union, Princeton.

Reflections

> "My first poem was read in church. I was in high school at the time. I read during an afternoon service when we were asked to testify. The response by the congregation frightened me to the point of throwing the piece away. It wasn't a negative response; just the opposite. Today, I still wonder why I threw the piece away. The only reason I've come up with is fear. I guess I never expected the positive response. I regret the action I took after reading the poem aloud. Today I'm grateful that my sister, Teri (Mitchell), encouraged me to take my writing to another level. I continue to work towards submissions to publications, and I'm attempting to write short stories that will eventually take me into a novel or two."

Publication

Mitchell, Sharon L. *Shades of My Being: Poems.* [Princeton, N.J.]: Slam Productions, 1999. 32, illus.

Bio-Bibliographical Source:

Mitchell, Sharon L. "African American Women Writers in New Jersey: Biographical Questionnaire." Completed by Sharon L. Mitchell, March 2001.

MOORE, BETTY JEAN GREEN 1937–

Personal   Born on 4 February 1937 in Arron, Florida; seventh child of Ethel Collins Green (seamstress) of Malone, Florida, and Robert Green (railroad worker) of Bristol, Florida; granddaughter (maternal) of Amanda Martin and Rev. P. R. Collins; granddaughter (paternal) of Sylvia Allen and Bruce Moore; sisters: Autra Simpson and Notra Goodson; brothers: Shedrick Green, Joseph Green, and Collins Green; children: W. Basirah Taha, James A. Moore, and Norma J. Moore. Education: Douglas Brown High School, Okeechobee, Florida; further studies: Essex County College of Business, Newark, New Jersey; Rutgers University, Newark (writing seminar). Religion: African Methodist Episcopal; St. Paul A.M.E. Church, East Orange, New Jersey.

Residence in New Jersey Newark, 1960–1983; East Orange, 1983 to present.
Career Writer.
Memberships Outreach Ministry and Alabama/Florida/West Indies Circle, St. Paul A.M.E. Church, East Orange; Women Dedicated to Making a Difference, East Orange.
Publications
Moore, B. J. *Poetry: Telling It Like It Is.* New York: Vantage Press [1995]. 83.
———. *Poetry: Telling It Like It Is-II.* New York: Vantage Press [1999]. 87.
Bio-Bibliographical Source
Moore, Betty Jean. Telephone conversation with Sibyl E. Moses, 13 August 2001.

MORRIS, MARGARET LEE HICKS 1920–

Personal Born on 23 November 1920 in Goldsboro, North Carolina; sixth child of Georgia Thornton Hicks (housewife and field worker) of Rocky Mount, North Carolina, and Quinn Lewis Hicks (farmer, factory and millworker) of Goldsboro; granddaughter (maternal) of Dolly Hicks and Giles Hicks; brothers: Octarvius (deceased) and Charles Dortch (deceased); sisters: Eleanor (deceased), Odell (deceased), Leatha (twin, deceased), Vivian (deceased), Lula Mae, and Retha (twin); husband: John R. Morris (deceased); children: Peggy Anne Evans, John Morris, Jr. (deceased), Donald Bruce Morris, and Kimberly Dionne Hernandez. Education:

Margaret Hicks Morris.
Photograph by Jaclyn Vosko,
courtesy of The Picture People.

Goldsboro (grades 1–2), 1927–1928; Progress St. Elementary School, Riverside, New Jersey (grades 5–8); Riverside High School, Riverside (grades 9–10); Burlington High School, Burlington, New Jersey (grades 11–12), 1939; Junto (night school), Philadelphia, Pennsylvania; Glassboro State College; Bayada School of Nursing, Cherry Hill, New Jersey; Manna Bible School, 1973; Main Bible Institute, 1976. Religion: Baptist; St. James Baptist Church, Beverly, New Jersey.
Residence in New Jersey Riverside, 1929–1934; Beverly, 1934 to present.
Career Director, Youth of Burlington County, 1960s; practical nurse, Burlington County, New Jersey, 1970; director of welfare, Beverly, 1972; teacher substitute and aid; provided articles and assistance for the homeless; home health aide, 1980; minister/evangelist, 1986 to present.
Memberships Vice president, Burlington County NAACP, 1960s; chairperson for religious affairs, Burlington County NAACP; deaconess and former Sunday School teacher, St. James Baptist Church, Beverly.

Reflections
"I was always trying to learn. I had a great hunger to learn as much as I could. My desire was to serve people and that is why I pursued every subject I could. All of the studies helped me in my ability to write. I always would write about everything I saw in prose, poetry, or drama, and books.

I had a teacher in elementary school by the name of Mrs. Edna Hines Tillery (deceased). She took an interest in me and told me I was going to be somebody, and I never forgot it. There was another teacher who told me to keep my mind and brains busy. A minister by the name of Rev. Robert Jackson told me I was a very good writer, because I wrote poems for the Christmas and Easter programs at my church when I was in elementary school. My mother told me anyone who does not learn something everyday was a fool. I had a doctor by the name of George Flaman. He also encouraged me to keep on writing and suggested that I should start with writing a children's book, which I did. The title was "Marissa and the Little Snow Flake." It was written about my beautiful granddaughter at the age of four, but it was never published. My greatest Christian growth came under the Christian tutoring of one of the most dynamic teachers of "the Holy Spirit" that I have ever known. He taught two students at a time. His name is Rev. Alvin A. Jackson, pastor of Saint Paul Baptist Church, Cinnaminson, New Jersey."

Publication
Morris, Margret Hicks. *My Meadow.* Mystic Island, N.J.: PenRose Publishing Company, 1996. 135, illus.

Bio-Bibliographical Source
Morris, Margaret Lee Hicks. "African American Women Writers in New Jersey: Biographical Questionnaire." Completed by Margaret Lee Hicks Morris, November 1999.

MURRAY, EVELYN STALLING 1937–

Personal Born in 1937, in New York, New York; married and divorced; two children. Education: Mays Landing Junior High School, Mays Landing, New Jersey; Pleasantville High School, Pleasantville, New Jersey, 1951–1955.

Residence in New Jersey Atlantic City.

Career Clerical work, nursing, modeling, banking, beauty culture.

Publication
Murray, Evelyn. *Showers of Blessings.* New York: Vantage Press, 1983. 188.

Bio-Bibliographical Source
Murray, Evelyn. Letter to Sibyl E. Moses, 16 September 1986.

Neals, Betty Elizabeth Harris
1934–

Personal Born on 27 March 1934 in
Newark, New Jersey; third child of Louise
Williams Mauran (homemaker), of South
Carolina and Otis Harris (farmer), of
Jacksonville, Florida; granddaughter
(maternal) of India Nix Williams and Jen-
nings Beauregard Williams, both of South
Carolina; granddaughter (paternal) of
Elizabeth Kato Harris and Lawyer Harris,
both of Key West, Florida (originally from
St. Vincents, Virgin Islands); sister: Gloria
Mauran Jones; brothers: Otis Harris, Jr.,
Emanuel Harris, and Lloyd Shallal Harris;
husband: Felix-Ramon Neals, Esq. (attor-
ney); children: Felice Inma Neals, Felix-
Reynold Neals, and Julien-Xavier Neals.
Education: Morton Street Elementary
School, Newark, 1940; Monmouth Street

Betty Harris Neals.
Photograph by William W. May,
courtesy of Bill May/Omnivision.

School, Newark, graduated 1949; South Side High School, Newark,
1949–1950; West Side High School, Newark, 1950–1952; Newark
State Teachers College, B.S., elementary education and speech therapy,
1956; New York University, New York, New York, M.A., educational
theater, 1974. Religion: Roman Catholic; Queen of Angels Church,
Newark.

Residence in New Jersey Newark, 1934–1965; East Orange 1965 to present.

Career Secretary, Sonnabend and Beron, Esqs., Newark; secretary,
Board of Education, Newark, summers of 1951 and 1952; teacher, Nassau Elementary School, East Orange, 1956–1963; math teacher, Rutledge
Avenue Intermediate School, East Orange, 1965–1973; creative dramat-
ics teacher, John L. Costley School, East Orange, 1973 to present; lyricist
for Rashaan Roland Kirk, distinguished jazz musician, on album *Return
of the 5,000 lb. Man;* wrote words to "Theme for the Eulipians" and "Giant
Steps," John Coltrane compositions recorded by Kirk on aforesaid
album.

Memberships National Honor Society, Kappa Delta Pi; historian during
high school and college, Leaguer's Inc., Newark; ASCAP; Delta Sigma
Theta Sorority, Inc.

Awards, Honors, Other Certificates Performance awards for oratory and acting, Catholic diocesan competitions, late 1940s and early 1950s; mini

grant, New Jersey State Department of Education, 1977; writing fellowship, New Jersey State Council of the Arts, 1983.

Reflections

"Influenced by grandmother, an extraordinary storyteller, whose stories about her life on the sea were fascinating. Both my parents were creative in music and art, [with] poetry, music, [and] art [being] a normal part of life within the walls of our apartment. Gwendolyn Brooks is [my] mentor as a writer. Influenced by my husband, a brilliant writer, though not extensively published. [I] was a ward of Dr. and Mrs. Reynolds Edward Burch, 1952–1960, residing in Newark [and was] greatly influenced by them. Educational career directed and guided by Mrs. Kathryn Bill Banks, teacher, West Side High School, Newark, New Jersey."

Publications

Books

Neals, Betty H. *Spirit Weaving.* 1ˢᵗ ed. New York: Sesame Press, 1977. 59.

———. *Move the Air.* East Orange, N.J.: Stonecart Press, 1983. 63.

Broadside, Recording

Neals, Betty H. *The Great Gittin' Down.* Broadside Series, no. 92. Detroit: Broadside Press, 1975.

———. *Soul, Alleluia.* [Poems read by author], 1973. Audiocassette. [East Orange, N.J., n.d.].

Bio-Bibliographical Sources

Neals, Betty H. "African American Women Writers in New Jersey Project: Biographical Questionnaire." Completed by Betty Neals, 1985.

———. Telephone conversation with Sibyl E. Moses, September 2000.

Gladys Cannon Nunery,
courtesy of Genevieve Nunery Vaughn.

NUNERY, GLADYS CANNON
1904–1992

Personal Born on 7 September 1904 in Jersey City, New Jersey; joined the ancestors on 26 November 1992. The second child of Elizabeth Genevieve Wilkinson Cannon (school teacher) of Washington, D.C., and George E. Cannon, M.D. (physician) of Columbia, South Carolina; granddaughter (maternal) of John F. Wilkinson (assistant librarian in the Supreme Court Section of the United States, 1871–1905) of Washington, D.C.; granddaughter (paternal) of Mary Cannon of South Carolina and Mr. Cannon; brother: George D. Cannon, M.D. (deceased, 1985); husband: Clarence

James Nunery (electrical engineer, divorced); child: Genevieve Nunery Vaughan. Education: Lincoln High School, Jersey City; Jersey City State College, Jersey City, B.A.; New York University, New York, New York, M.A.; Jersey City State College, doctorate; Lee Ballard School of Music. Religion: Presbyterian, Lafayette Presbyterian Church, Jersey City, 1904–1985; First United Presbyterian Church, Richmond, Virginia, 1985–1992.

Residence in New Jersey   Jersey City, 1904–1985.

Career   Teacher, Public School #9, Jersey City, 1923–1964; head, Federal "CAN-DO" tutoring program, Jersey City; senior congressional intern, Office of Congressman Frank Guarini of New Jersey, 1984.

Memberships   National President, National Sorority of Phi Delta Kappa, Inc., 1925; member, National Sorority of Phi Delta Kappa, Inc., Alpha Chapter, 1923–1992; church elder, 1965–1985, superintendent of church school (25 years), treasurer, planning committee member, Westminster Fellowship, Ladies Aid and Mothers Club, Lafayette Presbyterian Church, Jersey City; member, Synod; member, Commission on Christian Education; member, Jersey City Council of Churches; NAACP; The College Women of Jersey City, New Jersey; charter member, YWCA; member, The Liberal Arts Guild; member, The Loyal Temperance League.

Awards, Honors, Other Certificates   First woman elder, Lafayette Presbyterian Church, Jersey City, 1965; honored for devotion to church by gold communion chalice engraved with her name and twenty gold pins for each year of perfect attendance, Lafayette Presbyterian Church, Jersey City; "WOMAN of Achievement" award, *Jersey Journal Newspaper,* 1965; citation for outstanding education contribution to humanity, Operation Push; *Who's Who Among Black Americans,* 1975–1976 and 1977–1978; various awards, Hudson County School Board; citation for outstanding service on the board of education (twelve years), Jersey City City Council; award, New Jersey Federation of Colored Women; dedication of a section of The Afro-American Historical Society Museum, Jersey City to the achievements and contributions of the Cannon family to their city, state, and country.

Reflections

"After reading about so many pleasant incidents in my life, you might think I'm awfully conceited. Well, I'm awfully proud—of every life I've been privileged to touch and benefit, with the gifts given me by the Great Teacher. In relating these experiences to others, I acknowledge that my Maker has permitted me to be a farmer in his field—sowing seeds of inspiration to young people. My fervent hope is that readers of these pages will see their own possibilities and serve humanity.

From my early childhood aspirations to be a teacher, through all my classroom experiences and other phases of my work, God has been my Guiding Hand. My motto has been: 1-2-3. 1=God, 2=Others, and 3=Self.

Or, as one of my students said one Monday morning, "I learned something new yesterday in Church School—how to spell JOY! It's spelled—Jesus, Others, and You." I truly believe I would not have had such lovely memoirs of so many years without the Great Teacher pointing the way. Many, many rough spots showed up along the way, but I endeavored to overcome them and was blessed to continue along the path I had chosen."

Publication

Nunery, Gladys Cannon. *Memoirs of a Valiant Teacher*. [Jersey City, N.J.: Kitabu Press Publishers, 1982]. 46, illus.

Bio-Bibliographical Sources

Celenza, Regina G. "Women in the News: Lasting Rewards in Work with Children." *Jersey City Hudson Dispatch*, 18 February 1965, 23.

"Gladys (Cannon) Nunery, 88, Woman of Achievement." *Jersey City The Jersey Journal*, 28 November 1992, 12.

"Home Going Celebration for Dr. Gladys Cannon Nunery, 1904–1992." [obituary]. Richmond, Virginia: First United Presbyterian Church, 1992.

Nunery, Gladys Cannon. "African American Women Writers in New Jersey: Biographical Questionnaire." Completed by Genevieve Nunery Vaughan (Gladys Cannon Nunery's daughter), Richmond, Virginia, 18 October 1996.

PAYNE, J. JOYCE COLEMAN 1938–

Personal Born on 28 August 1938 in Burlington, New Jersey; youngest child of Katie Powell Coleman (domestic worker) and James Coleman (cook), both of Burlington; granddaughter (maternal) of Martha Powell of Maryland and Edward Powell; brothers: Roger (deceased), Maurie (deceased), Spearin (deceased), Richard (deceased), James (deceased); sisters: Ruth (deceased), Beatrice (deceased), Louise (deceased), and Majorie; husband: Robert Charles Payne (retired educator and media specialist); children: Robert, Jr., Gregory, and Michael. Education: James Fenimore Cooper Elementary School, Burlington; William R. Allen Elementary School, Burlington; Robert Stacy Junior High School, Burlington; Wilbur Watts High School, Burlington, 1952–1956; Trenton State College, Trenton, New Jersey, B.A., 1956–1960; Drexel Institute of Technology, Philadelphia, Pennsylvania, (library courses), 1963–1965; Rutgers University, New Brunswick, New Jersey, M.A. education, 1978–1980. Religion: Methodist; Wesley A.M.E. Zion Church.

Residence in New Jersey Burlington, 1938 to present.

Career English teacher, Burlington, 1960–1966; English teacher, Burlington Township, Burlington, 1967; vice principal, Hopkins Middle School, 1981–1986; adjunct professor, Trenton State, EOF program, 1983–1985; principal, B. Bernice Young Elementary School, Burlington Township, New Jersey, and Springside Elementary School, Burlington Township, 1986–1992; director of education, Willingboro, New Jersey, 1992–1995; adjunct professor, LaSalle University, Philadelphia, 1993; superintendent, Lawnside School District, 1996 to present.

Memberships Alpha Kappa Alpha Sorority, Inc.; Wesley A.M.E. Zion Church: choir, church schoolteacher, building committee, Young Adult Club.

Awards, Honors, Other Certificates Sponsor of cheerleaders, yearbook dedicatee, Burlington High School, 1966; Burlington Township: Founder and sponsor of S.U.R.E. (Students United for Racial Equality), 1971–1981; Burlington Township Yearbook Dedicatee, 1971, 1982; Outstanding Secondary Educator Award, 1974; Middlestates Evaluation Participant, Englewood School for Boys, Englewood, 1975; Woman of the Year, National Association of University Women, Central New Jersey Branch, 1979; Citizen of the Year for services to youth and humanities, Alpha Phi Alpha Fraternity, 1981; community service award, National Council of Negro Woman Award, 1983; Delta Sigma Theta Sorority Distinguished Educator's Award, 1990; participation in Black History Month activities, Burlington County College, 1991; award for dedicated church service, Wesley AME Zion Church, 1991; mayor's proclamation for outstanding service and contributions to the children of Burlington Township, 1992; community service to family, church, and community, St. Mary's Chapter #3 OES, 1993; plaque, New Jersey Fire Department, Burlington Township, 1993; named as one of the state's top seventeen educational leaders, New Jersey Alliance of Black School Educators, 1994; achievement and service to education, A. Philip Randolph Institute Award, 1998.

Reflections

"Other than my mother, who was a constant influence in my life, my second grade teacher, Mrs. Cora Pollard, always remained a positive influence in my life until her death. She would let me stay after school and help her straighten up the room. It was during those times she planted the seeds in my heart and mind that I was smart, that I would make a great teacher, that I should allow no one to keep me from my dream. She watched me over the years and always kept her hand on me. She allowed me to practice my handwriting and consistently praised me as I improved. I began writing little notes that evolved into poetry and now a full novel. My short stories are an outgrowth of many of the childhood memories—thanks Mrs. Pollard. The person in my adult life came in the person of my high school principal, John Marker. He came to my door when I was teaching verbs one afternoon and politely asked me how I would like to go to Africa. My life has never been the same. My first published work of poetry was an outgrowth of my first trip to Kenya, Africa. My subsequent trips to Kenya in 1981, Ivory Coast in 1990, and South Africa in 1994 have only cemented more deeply how similar we all are—no matter the color."

Publications

Book

Payne, Joyce C. *Kenya Safari: An African Love Affair, A Collection of Poetry.* Burlington, N.J.: R/J Enterprises, 1990. 26. Designed by Connie-Mac Graphics.

Article

Payne, Joyce C. "Mahalia Atcheson." In The Women's Project of New Jersey, Inc. *Past and Promise: Lives of New Jersey Women,* n.p. Metuchen, N.J.: Scarecrow Press, 1990.

Bio-Bibliographical Sources

Payne, Joyce C. "African American Women Writers in New Jersey: Biographical Questionnaire." Completed by Joyce C. Payne, March 2000.
———. Telephone interview with Sibyl E. Moses, 27 March 2000.

Payton, Vanessa *see* Flournoy, Vanessa

Pitts, Gertrude Williams 1903–1960

Personal   Born on 27 December 1903 in Perry, Georgia; joined the ancestors on 21 November 1960 in Newark, New Jersey. The youngest child of about thirteen children born to Elizabeth Williams and Bill Williams, both of Georgia; sister: Mattie Belle Palmer; husband: Dorsey Pitts (truck driver; deceased) of Macon, Georgia; child: James Douglas Pitts (deceased). Education: Elementary and secondary schools in Georgia; University of Chicago, Department of Physiotherapy, Chicago, Illinois. Religion: Missionary Baptist, Zion Hill Baptist Church, Newark,.

Residence in New Jersey Newark, 1932–1960.

Career Owner, Pitts Swedish Massage, Newark, 1949–1960; district leader, Republican Committee, Third Ward, Newark, ca. 1949.

Gertrude Williams Pitts,
courtesy of Ophelia Pasley.

Memberships Executive committee member, International Garments Union; organizer, founder, and supervisor, Nurses Unit, Zion Hill Baptist Church, 1955–1960; senior choir and J. P. Gospel Chorus, Zion Hill Baptist Church; vice president, Newark Student Camp Fund.

Reflections (by Mrs. Ophelia Pasley)

"Gertrude Pitts organized the Nurses Unit in her church as a charity group. She would visit the sick, and took money from the treasury to buy members nightgowns and help people get their prescriptions filled when they did not have the money. She did this because she had noticed when she visited the sick that they did not have appropriate bedclothes. She started the Nurses Unit because she felt a group of women knew how to take care of the family. She asked people to meet her at the Red Cross School of Nursing on High Street in Newark. Only nine women graduated, and classes lasted eight weeks. She used to talk a lot about Dr. Walter T. Darden; she had worked with him."

Publication

Pitts, Gertrude. *Tragedies of Life*. Newark, New Jersey: The Author, 1939. 62. Reprint, in African American Women Writers, 1910–1940 series, n.p. New York: G. K. Hall, 1997.

Bio-Bibliographical Sources

"Funeral Service: Mrs. Gertrude Pitts, Zion Hill Baptist Church, Saturday, November 26th, 1960." [obituary]. Newark, New Jersey, 1960. 4.

Pasley, Ophelia. Interview by Sibyl E. Moses. East Orange, New Jersey, 30 December 1993.

PORTER, DOROTHY BURNETT *SEE* WESLEY, DOROTHY PORTER

POUNCY, MATTIE HUNTER 1924–

Personal Born on 20 July 1924 in Sardis, Alabama; one of eleven children; husband: Hillard Warren Pouncy, Jr. (scientist); child: Hillard Warren

Mattie Hunter Pouncy,
courtesy of Mattie Hunter Pouncy.

Pouncy III. Education: Tuskegee Institute, Tuskegee, Alabama, B.S., 1944–1948; Tuskegee Institute, Tuskegee, B.S., education, 1950–1955; Rutgers, The State University, New Brunswick, New Jersey, 1961–1963; Newark State College, Union, New Jersey, special education certificate, 1964–1966; Trenton State College, Trenton, New Jersey, M.A., urban education, 1975–1977. Religion: Baptist.

Residence in New Jersey Somerset, 1961–1972; Princeton, 1972 to present.

Career Teacher, elementary school, Apalachicola, Florida, 1949–1952; teacher, elementary school, Union Springs, Alabama, 1952–1955; teacher (special education), Gary, Indiana, 1959–1961; teacher, elementary school, New Brunswick, 1962–1967; teacher, elementary school, Franklin Township, New Jersey, 1967–1973; cofounder and supervisor, Princeton Training School, Princeton, 1973–1974; teacher, elementary school, Plainfield School District, Plainfield, 1974 to present.

Memberships Kappa Delta Pi; National Education Association; New Jersey Education Association; National Historical Society; The Executive Female; Nassau Christian Center, Princeton; The Progressive Baptist Women of New Jersey; Historical Society of Washington, D.C.; Union County Education Association; New Jersey Republican State Committee; Republican Presidential Task Force.

Publication

Pouncy, Mattie Hunter. *Reach a Little Deeper*. New York: Vantage Press, Inc., 1985. 229.

Bio-Bibliographical Source

Pouncy, Mattie Hunter. "Biographical Sketch and Resume." [1986]. 4.

RILEY, MAURICE LEE FICKLIN
1927–1996

Personal Born on 19 September 1927 in Newark, New Jersey; fifth child of Grace E. Ficklin (housewife) of Savannah, Georgia, and Davis L. Ficklin (master carpenter) of South Carolina; brothers: Curtis Ficklin, Parnell Ficklin, Ira Ficklin (deceased), Sylvanus Ficklin (deceased), and Eugene Ficklin (deceased); husband: Fred Riley; children: Cheryl Laverne Freeman-Lutz, Marsha Brennette Riley, Kenneth Brian Riley (deceased), and Jilletta Denise Riley Pitt. Education: Central High School, Newark, high school diploma, 1946; Shaw University, Raleigh, North Carolina, B.A., magna cum laude, behavioral science, 1975; Baltimore College of Bible, Baltimore, Maryland, honorary doctorate in humane letters. Religion: Baptist; Mount Calvary Baptist Church, Newark.

Maurice Ficklin Riley.
Photograph by Samuel E. Fleming.

Residence in New Jersey Newark, 1927–1996.

Career Office Secretary, Mount Calvary Baptist Church, Newark (more than 27 years); assistant director, Martin Luther King Community Center, Newark, 1975–1977; positions in the following agencies: Agape Group Home, East Orange Young Men's Christian Association, Cornell University Medical School, Essex County Division for Employment and Training.

Memberships Director, Christian Youth Ministry; president, Missionary Society; Pastor's Aide Club; teacher, adult women's Sunday School class; president, Church Women United (Newark Unit); first vice president, Women's Department, New England Missionary Baptist Convention; president elect, Women's Auxiliary, National Baptist Deacon's Convention, Inc., USA; Member, City National Bank Advisory Board, Newark; secretary, board of trustees, Northern Baptist School of Religion.

Awards, Honors, Other Certificates Woman of the Year, Baltimore College of Bible, Honorary Doctorate of Humane Letters, 1975; National Sojourner Truth Meritorious Service, National Association of Negro Business and Professional Women's Clubs, 1982.

Publications

Riley, Maurice. *The Deaconess: Walking in the Newness of Life.* 2nd ed. Newark,
    N.J.: Christian Associates Publications [1993]. 148.

————. *The Deaconess: Walking in the Newness of Life: Workbook.* Compiled
    and illustrated by Cheryl, Marsha, and Jill Riley. [Newark, N.J.: Chris-
    tian Associates Publications, 1997]. 56.

————. *The Deaconess: Walking in the Newness of Life: Instructor's Workbook.*
    Compiled and illustrated by Cheryl, Marsha, and Jill Riley. [Newark,
    N.J.: Christian Associates Publications, 1997]. [iv] 57 [17]. illus.

————. *Lost at the Pool: A Challenging Ministry for Deaconesses, Mothers' Boards,
    Missionaries, and All Saints to the New Convert.* [Newark, N.J.: Christian
    Associates Publications, n.d.]. 49.

Bio-Bibliographical Sources

"A Worship Celebration of Triumph for Dr. Maurice L. Riley, September
    19, 1927–April 8, 1996. Monday, April 15, 1996, 11:00 AM, Mount
    Calvary Baptist Church . . ." [obituary]. Newark, N.J., 1996. 9.

Riley, Marsha. Telephone conversation with Sibyl E. Moses, 8 June 2000.

Riley, Maurice Lee Ficklin. "African American Women Writers In New Jer-
    sey: Biographical Questionnaire." Completed by Marsha Riley (daugh-
    ter of Maurice L. Riley), December 1999.

ROBERTS, IROSE FERNELLA ADAMS 1945–

Personal   Born on 10 September 1945 in Potters Village, Antigua, West
Indies; first child of Mary Magdalene Jacobs Adams (housekeeper and
short order cook) and George Alexander Adams (building contractor,
retired), both of Potters Village; granddaughter (maternal) of Agatha
Spenser Jacobs and Edmund Jacobs, both of Antigua; granddaughter
(paternal) of Rebecca Frances Jarvis of Antigua; sisters: Esther Adams,
Catherine Adams Sutton, Rosaly Adams Smith, Francine Adams Judge,
and Michelle Adams; brothers: Leroy Adams, Clevon Adams, Grantley
Adams, George "Miles" Ernesto Adams; husband: Virgil George Roberts
(building contractor; divorced); child: Virgil George Rycott Roberts. Education: Potters Village Government School, Potters Village, Antigua,
1950–1962; Antigua Pilgrim High School, St. Johns, Antigua, 1962–1964;
Manpower Vocational Training Program in practical nursing, Government
of Virgin Islands, Insular Board of Vocational Education, St. Croix, Virgin
Islands, certificate, 1974; Essex County College, Newark, New Jersey,
A.A., nursing, 1980–1985. Religion: Baptist; Mount Zion Baptist Church,
East Orange, New Jersey.

Residence in New Jersey: East Orange, 1976 to present.

Career   Nurse's aide, St. Croix; licensed practical nurse, Veterans Administration Medical Center, East Orange.

Memberships   ASCAP (Association of Songwriters, Authors and Publishers); National Association of Female Executives; International Society of Poetry.

Awards, Honors, Other Certificates   Award for "outstanding practical nurse trainee," Manpower Vocational Training Program, Government of Virgin Islands, Insular Board of Vocational Education, St. Croix, 1974; award for excellence in nursing, Veterans Administration Medical Center, East Orange, 1991; Hands and Heart Award for "your compassionate attitude and unselfish service on behalf of veterans [which] is exemplary and a credit not only to the Veterans Health Administration, but also to the Department of Veterans Affairs," Office of the Chief Medical Director, Department of Veterans Affairs, Washington, D.C., 1992; award for excellence in nursing, Department of Veterans Affairs Commendation for Administrators, VA Medical Center, East Orange, 1992; performance awards, Veterans Administration Medical Center, East Orange, 1986, 1989, 1990, 1993; "poet of merit" award, American Poetry Association, 1989; *Who's Who Among Women,* 1992; *Who's Who in the East,* 1989/1990.

Reflections

"I have experienced some rewarding moments in my life. From a child I have been touched by Dr. Martin Luther King, Jr. I believed in what he stands for and also for what he believed in. I have also known the Lord Jesus Christ as my lord and savior. Maya Angelou also inspires me to write, she's a very outstanding Black woman. My other influence is Alice Walker; *The Color Purple* touched my life. As a young girl growing up in my native country I was always creating a poem, but not just any poem it always [had] a religious theme. Relatives that write, my sister, Rosaly Smith Adams writes poems, songs, etc."

Publications

Book

Roberts, Irose. *Faith, Hope and Love.* New York: Vantage Press, 1984. 206.

Poetry

Roberts, Irose. "Somebody Loves Me," In *Hearts on Fire: A Treasury of Poems on Love,* vol. 2, edited by John Frost, 332. Santa Cruz, Calif.: American Poetry Association, 1985.

———. "Life's Lonely Road." In *American Poetry Anthology,* vol. 4, no. 1, edited by John Frost, 217. Santa Cruz, Calif.: American Poetry Association, 1985.

———. "Together We'll Make It." In *The National Poetry Anthology,* 2. [New York: Poetry Anthology, Inc.], 1989.

Bio-Bibliographical Source

Roberts, Irose. "African American Women Writers in New Jersey: Biographical Questionnaire." Completed by Irose Roberts, fall 1993.

RODGERS-ROSE, LA FRANCIS AUDREY 1936–

Personal   Born on 19 July 1936 in Norfolk, Virginia; fifth child of Beulah Polly Smith Rodgers (domestic worker, insurance agent, and outreach worker for older adults) of Scotland Neck, North Carolina, and Carroll Mathias Rodgers (minister) of Norfolk; granddaughter (maternal) of Cynthia Hill Smith and Thomas Smith, both of Scotland Neck; granddaughter (paternal) of Fannie Hunter Rodgers of Henderson, North Carolina, and Rev. James E. Rodgers of Princess Anne County, Virginia; sisters: Lois Rodgers (deceased), Cynthia Beulah Rodgers (deceased), and Cynthia Leola Rodgers; brothers: Carleton Rodgers (deceased), Carroll Rodgers, Jr., and James Rodgers; husband: Dr. Vattel T. Rose (divorced); children: Henry David Rose and Valija C. Rose. Education: George Peabody Elementary School, Portsmouth, Virginia, 1942–1949; I. C. Norcom High School, Portsmouth, 1949–1954; Morgan State University, Baltimore, Maryland, B.A., sociology and history, 1954–1958; Fisk University, Nashville, Tennessee, M.A., sociology and anthropology, 1958–1960; University of Iowa, Ph.D., sociology and social psychology, 1961–1964. Religion: Church of God; previous memberships: Baptist and United Methodist.
Residence in New Jersey   Plainfield, 1972–1982; Newark, 1982 to present.
Career   Research assistant, Department of Sociology and Race Relations Institute, Fisk University, Nashville, 1958–1960; teaching assistant, Department of Sociology, University of Iowa, Iowa City, Iowa, 1961–1964; assistant professor, Department of Sociology, St. Olaf College, Northfield, Minnesota, 1964–1969; assistant professor, Department of Sociology, Case Western Reserve University, Cleveland, Ohio, 1970–1972; associate research sociologist/consultant, Educational Studies Division, Educational Testing Services, Princeton, New Jersey, 1972–1974; lecturer, Afro-American Studies Department, Fordham University, Rose Hill Campus, Bronx, New York, 1981–1985; lecturer, Department of Africana Studies, Rutgers University, New Brunswick, New Jersey, 1974–1985; lecturer, Women Studies Program, University of Pennsylvania, Philadelphia, Pennsylvania, 1983–1985; lecturer, Afro-American Studies Program, Princeton University, Princeton, 1973–1989; social psychologist, Hope for Pregnant Teens, Hillside, New Jersey, 1982–1990; director, National Volunteer Program, National Black United Fund, Newark, New Jersey, 1991–1994; lecturer, Afro-American Studies, Drew University, Madison, New Jersey, 1987–1994; president and founder, International Black Women's Congress, Newark, 1983–present.
Memberships   President, Association of Social and Behavioral Scientists, 1994; president and founder, International Black Women's Congress, 1983; president, Association of Black Sociologists, 1976; Association for the Study of Afro-American Life and History; National Council for Black Studies; African Studies Association; United Nations Association of the USA; Sociologists for Women in Society; American Sociological Association; New Jersey Black Educators Association; National Black Child Devel-

opment Institute; National Council of Negro Women; Delta Sigma Theta Sorority, Inc.

Awards, Honors, Other Certificates   Fannie Lou Hammer Award, US Organization, Los Angeles, California, 1995; Outstanding Educator Award, Concerned African American Men of New Jersey, 1994; Oni Award, International Black Women's Congress, 1993; Enstooled: Nana Obaapanyin Akosua Asantewa Ofusua I, 1993; Ella Baker Award, California State University at Long Beach, 1992; Aiyekoo Award, Newark, 1990; Newark Municipal Council Resolution, October 1990; National Black Wholistic Retreat Cultural Consistency and Support Award, 1989; QUEST, Essex County CYO Service Award, 1989; *Essence Magazine* Woman of the Month, July 1985; Fulbright Fellow, 1986; Distinguished Service Award, New Jersey Life Member's Guild, National Council of Negro Women, 1981; Distinguished Sociology Scholar, American Sociological Association, 1972; Outstanding Sociology Graduate Student, University of Iowa, 1963; president, Alpha Kappa Delta, Sociology Honor Society, Fisk University Chapter, 1959–1960; Danforth Fellow, Fisk University, 1959–1960.

Reflections

"I really don't consider myself a writer in the true sense of the word. As a scholar, you are expected to write and publish. The person who influenced me the most was my mother. With a seventh grade education, I saw her do so much. I did not know any writer while growing up."

Publications

Rodgers-Rose, La Francis. *The Dominant Values of Black Culture.* New York: Afram Associates, 1972. 27, 3,; Plainfield, N.J.: Pyramid Publishing Company, 1972.

———, ed. *The Black Woman.* Sage Focus Edition, 21. Beverly Hills, Calif.: Sage Publications, 1980. 316p.

Rodgers-Rose, La Francis, and James T. Rodgers, eds. *Strategies for Resolving Conflict in Black Male and Female Relationships.* Newark, N.J.: Traces Institute Publications, 1983. v, 73.

Aldridge, Delores P., and La Francis Rodgers-Rose, eds. *River of Tears: The Politics of Black Women's Health.* Newark,N.J.: Traces Institute Publications, 1993. 175.

Bio-Bibliographical Sources

Rodgers-Rose, La Francis. "African American Women Writers in New Jersey: Biographical Questionnaire." Completed by La Francis Rodgers-Rose, 5 October 1996.

———. [Résumé]. 13.

ROPER, GRACE ARIADNE TROTT 1925–

Personal   Born on 8 September 1925 in New York, New York; first child of Erma Gwendolyn Clinton Trott (housewife) of Nassau, Bahamas, and

Edwin Elliot Trott (laborer and teacher) of New York; granddaughter (maternal) of Carolyn Wallace Sweeting and Reuban Clinton, both of Nassau; granddaughter (paternal) of Elvira Warner Trott, of Puerto Rico, and Alfred Trott, of Bermuda; sister: Eleanor Gwendolyn Trott McBride (deceased); husband: Ivan Joseph Roper (government computer analyst, retired); children: James Anthony, Eric Ashley, Johanna Edwina, and Robert Ramsey. Education: Public School #186, Manhattan, New York, 1932–1938; Junior High School #136, Manhattan, 1938–1941; George Washington High School, Manhattan, 1941–January 1944; YWCA Secretarial Course, New York, certificate, 1945; City College of New York, New York, 1945–1948; Clark College, Atlanta, Georgia, 1948–1949; Newark State College, Newark, New Jersey, 1960–1961;. Religion: Episcopal; St. Augustine's Episcopal Church, Asbury Park, New Jersey.

Residence in New Jersey   Belmar, 1956 to present.

Career   Clerk, New York Public Library, New York, 1950–1954; library director, Belmar Public Library, Belmar, New Jersey, 1962–1995.

Memberships   Belmar Women's Club; Red Bank Chapter, Alpha Wives, Inc.; Officers Wives Club, Fort Monmouth New Jersey; secretary, Monmouth Librarians Association, 1976–1977; vice president, 1981, and president, 1983–1984, Belmar Board of Education; Sunday school teacher, superintendent, choir member, Vestry Women, St. Augustine's Episcopal Church, Asbury Park, New Jersey; Girl Scouts; Brownie leader; Cadette leader; member, Central Jersey Business and Professional Women.

Awards, Honors, Other Certificates   Ten-year award, National School Board Association, 1985; "Woman of Many Talents" recognition, *Asbury Park Press,* 1976.

Reflections

"I remember being twelve and having my father say I'd never be able to go to college as there wasn't enough money. I remember how I cried and vowed within myself that somehow I'd go. I owe so much to the people who practically adopted me at Countee Cullen Branch [of The New York Public Library]. For it was their help, guidance, and encouragement that caused me to work eight hours, go to school at night, and sit up till 2 and 3 A.M. with homework. . . . I have made many attempts at writing, but my only publication is *Belmar In Retrospect,* the history of our town written and published because the need was great. The young people were constantly asking for information that was scattered all over."

Publication

Roper, Grace T. *Belmar in Retrospect.* Belmar, N.J.: Hoffman Press, 1978. 33.

Bio-Bibliographical Source

Roper, Grace Trott. "African American Women Writers in New Jersey: Biographical Questionnaire." Completed by Grace T. Roper, 21 September 1986.

RUFF, PHONTELLA CLOTEAL BUTCHER 1928–

Personal   Born on 22 November 1928 in Birmingham, Alabama; first child of Allean Perry Butcher Cutler (seamstress) of Sprott, Alabama, and Henry Cornelius Butcher (tailor/cleaners business owner) of Birmingham; grand-daughter (maternal) of Estelle Perry and Rev. Morgan Perry, both of Sprott; granddaughter (paternal) of Rev. David A. Butcher of Birmingham; sisters: Blanche Marvella Cutler and Claraleata Cutler; brothers: Henry Lee Butcher (deceased) and David Alphonso Butler; husband: Amos Warren Ruff (computer programmer); child: Mark Warren Ruff. Education: First Baptist Church School, Birmingham (grades K-1), 1934–1936; Selma University Laboratory School, Selma, Alabama (grades 2–4), 1936–1939; Whittier Elementary School, Camden, New Jersey (grades 5–7), 1939–1942; Hatch Middle School, Camden (grades 8–9), 1942–1944; Camden High School, Camden (grades 10–12), 1944–1947; Glassboro State College, Glassboro, New Jersey, B.S., 1951; Glassboro State College, Glassboro, M.A., educational administration, 1972; further studies: Rutgers University, New Brunswick, New Jersey. Religion: Jehovah's Witness.
Residence in New Jersey   Camden, 1937–1952; Willingboro, 1952 to present.
Career   Teacher (grade 5), Cooper-Grant School, Camden, 1951–1952; teacher (grades 4–5), Stevens School, Camden, 1952–1954; teacher (grades 5–6), Broadway School, 1954–1956; teacher/reading teacher, teacher in charge of school for unwed mothers, Hatch Middle School, 1966–1969; principal, Powell School/Read School, Camden, 1969–1972; principal, Parkside School, Camden, 1972–1991; teacher and director of Head Start Program, Camden; adjunct professor (vocational education), Glassboro State College, Glassboro.
Memberships   Life member, National Education Association; life member, New Jersey Education Association; Camden County Educational Association; Camden Administrators' Association; Camden County Principals' Association; cofounder and president, NAACP Youth Council, Camden City Chapter, early 1940s; founder, Willingboro Business and Professional Women's Club.
Reflections
   "The late Dr. William Dinkins, the president of Selma University, and Pastor David V. Jemison, pastor of Tabernacle Baptist Church in Selma, Alabama, along with Dr. Howard W. Brown, the principal of Whittier School, Dr. Rebecca Batts Butler, U.S. Wiggins, M.D., president of the New Jersey State NAACP and Camden City Chapter, Dr. Lottie Johnson, my aunt Catherine Cunningham, and my mother Allean Cutler, all encouraged me to write about the experiences I vividly remembered of the sites and sounds of the South, where I lived as a child."
Publications
Ruff, Phontella. *How to Conduct and Administer T4C Conferences in the Elementary School.* Publication no. 0043. Trenton, N.J.: State of New Jersey

Department of Education, Division of Vocational Education, Bureau of Occupational Research, 1976. 50.

———. *So Rich*. [Willingboro, N.J.: The Author, 1989]. [19].

Bio-Bibliographical Source

Ruff, Phontella. Telephone conversations with Sibyl E. Moses, 7 and 8 August 2001.

RUSHIN, KATE 1951–

Kate Rushin.
Photograph by Milardo Photography.

Personal   Name at birth: Donna Kaye Rushin. Born on 7 July 1951 in Syracuse, New York; only child of Beatrice Elizabeth "Lizzy" Williams Rushin (social worker and first Black caseworker for New Jersey State Board of Child Welfare) of Lawnside, New Jersey, and Frank Davenport Rushin (electroplater and tailor) of Macon, Georgia; granddaughter (maternal) of Addie Olivier Arthur Williams of Lawnside and George E. (Edward Harrison Horseman, Noah, Surrender) Williams, Sr. of Lawnside; granddaughter (paternal) of Roxie Wiggins Rushin Edwards of Americus, Georgia, and William G. Rushin of Georgia. Education: Parkside Elementary School, Camden, New Jersey, 1955–1962; Lawnside Public School, Lawnside, 1962–1965; Hadddon Heights High School, Haddon Heights, New Jersey, 1965–1969; Oberlin College, Oberlin, Ohio, B.A., theater/communications, 1973; Brown University, Providence Rhode Island, M.F.A., creative writing, 1994.

Residence in New Jersey   Camden, 1952–1962 and 1973–1975; Lawnside, 1962–1969.

Career   Editorial assistant trainee, The Chilton Company, Radnor, Pennsylvania, 1973; instructor, English, women's studies, Urban Scholars, and Upward Bound, University of Massachusetts-Boston/Harbor Campus, 1980–1990; poet-in-residence, South Boston High School, The Artists' Foundation, and The Theater Company of Boston, Boston, Massachusetts, 1980–1983; bookseller, New Words Bookstore, 1982–1992; instructor, Black women writers, Massachusetts Institute of Technology, Cambridge, Massachusetts, 1991–1993; director, Center for African American Studies Program and visiting writer, English and African American Studies Program, Wesleyan University, Middletown, Connecticut, 1994–2000; visiting writer and adjunct assistant professor, African American Studies Program, Wesleyan University, Middletown, Connecticut, 2000 to present.

Publication

Rushin, Kate. *The Black Back-Ups: Poetry.* Ithaca, N.Y.: Firebrand Books, 1993. 93.

Bio-Bibliographical Source

Rushin, Kate. "African American Women Writers in New Jersey: Biographical Questionnaire." Completed by Kate Rushin, 21 June 2001.

SALAAM, NEFETERRI 1946–

Personal Former name Patricia Ann Nicely Simon; born on 6 June 1946 in Newark, New Jersey; second child of Daisy Lee Gentle Nicely (housewife and domestic engineer) of Damascus, Georgia, and Meritt Heath Nicely (truck driver, deceased) of Alabama; granddaughter (maternal) of Otis Gentle; sisters: Barbara Nicely (deceased) and Olivia Noel Nicely; husband: Eddie Simon (housing superintendent); children: Rhamenia Elisha Simon and Ansiric Hammid Simon. Education: Peshine Avenue School, Newark, New Jersey (K–2), 1950–1952; Bergen Street School, Newark (grades 3–4), 1953–1954; Miller Street School, Newark (grades 5–7); Cleveland Street School, Newark (grades 8–9), 1958–1959; Central High School (night division), Newark, ca. 1961–1962; Essex County College, New Jersey, 1984–1985. Religion: Al-Islam.
Residence in New Jersey Newark, 1946–1957, 1962 to present; East Orange, 1958–1961.
Career Owner and operator, "Sister Pat's House of Seafood," Bergen St. and Shephard Ave., Newark, 1968–1975; writer; manager, Essex Plaza Complexes (senior citizens housing), Newark, 1984.
Memberships Unity in the Community (community-based organization Salaam established to open communication between and to unite the elderly and youth in Newark), 1984–1985; Neophyte, Inc. (established by Betty Alston), 1982–1984/1985.
Awards, Honors, Other Certificates Acknowledgment from Nancy and Ronald Reagan.
Publication
Simon, Patricia Nicely. *The Longest Rent Strike in History*. New York: Carlton Press, Inc., 1980. 159.
Bio-Bibliographical Source
Simon, Patricia Nicely. Interview with Sibyl E. Moses, Newark, New Jersey, 3 January 1987.

SANDERS, VIOLA HARRIS 1946–

Personal Born on 8 May 1946 in Wilson, North Carolina; daughter of Sarah D. Harris and Mr. Harris, both of North Carolina; husband: Richard Sanders; child: Maurice R. Sanders. Education: Adams School, Wilson; C. H. Darden High School, Wilson; Middlesex College, Edison, New Jersey.
Residence in New Jersey Newark; East Orange; Plainfield; Piscataway, 1964 to present.
Career Owner, Vii's Services, Inc., Piscataway.

Memberships   NAACP; executive board, Metuchen-Edison Branch, NAACP; The Minority Interchange; Toastmaster International, Inc.; Newark Metropolitan Business and Professional Women; Alliance of Concerned Citizens of Piscataway; National Association of Female Executives; National Coalition of 100 Black Women, Inc.; board member, Piscataway Township Historic Advisory Commission; advisory board, Katherine Gibbs School, Piscataway.

Awards, Honors, Other Certificates   Award for Outstanding Leadership in Presenting Authentic African American History, Piscataway African American Senior Club; Award of Appreciation for Outstanding and Dedicated Service, NAACP, Metuchen-Edison Branch, 1995.

Publication

Sanders, Viola H. *African American Inventors.* [Piscataway, N.J.]: Vii's Services, Inc., [1998]. 60, illus.

Bio-Bibliographical Source

Sanders, Viola H. "African American Women Writers in New Jersey: Biographical Questionnaire." Completed by Viola H. Sanders, 1 August 2000.

SAUNDERS, ESTHER "HETTY" CA. 1793–1862

Personal   Born in Delaware, ca. 1793; joined the ancestors on 15 December 1862.

Residence in New Jersey   Elsinboro; Claysville, Mannington Township, ca. 1800–1862.

Career   Caretaker, John Denn family and James Woodnutt family.

Publication

Pierce, Donald L, editor. *I Love to Live Alone: The Poems of Esther "Hetty" Saunders.* Salem, N.J.: Salem County Historical Society, 2001. 48, illus.

Poem

Saunders, Hetty. "The Hill of Age." In *The New Jersey Scrap Book of Women Writers,* Margaret Tufts Yardley, published by the Board of Lady Managers for New Jersey to represent the many writers who are not bookmakers at the World's Columbia Exposition. Newark, N.J.: Board of Women Managers for the State of New Jersey, 1893.

Bio-Bibliograhpical Source

Pierce, Donald L, editor. *I Love to Live Alone: The Poems of Esther "Hetty" Saunders.* Salem, N.J.: Salem County Historical Society, 2001. 48, illus.

SHAKIR, QADRIYYAH BUTEEN 1932–2000

Personal   Former name Lola Buteen (Burke) Wiggins. Born on 1 February 1932 in Pulaski, Candler County, Georgia; joined the ancestors on 3 December 2000 in Plainfield, New Jersey. The ninth child of Lillie (Dekle)

Qadriyyah Buteen Shakir,
courtesy of Chadia Shakir-Saleem.

Burke (housewife) and Benjamin Franklin Burke, Sr. (farmer), both of Metter, Candler County, Georgia; sisters: Henrietta Holloway, Lola Buteen Burke Wiggins, Eula Holloway, and Lillie M. Nelson; brothers: Wallace Burke (deceased), Irvin E. Burke, Roosevelt Burke, Bernard Talmadge Burke, Earlie Burke (deceased), Benjamin Franklin Burke, Jr. (deceased), William Burke (deceased), George Burke (deceased), Eulus Burke (deceased), Carl Wilkson Burke (deceased), and Felix Landis Burke (deceased); husband: Earnest Cardell Shakir (former name Wiggins) July 1977; children: Earnest Ibn (Wiggins) Shakir, Jemil Rahman (Wiggins) Shakir, Chadia Amenah (Wiggins) Shakir Saleem. Education: Aline Elementary School, Aline, Georgia, 1938–1941; Dekle Branch Elementary School, 1942–1946; Candler County Training School, Metter, 1947–1952; Fort Valley State College, Fort Valley, Georgia, 1952–1956; Newark State Teachers College, Newark, New Jersey, B.S., elementary education, 1963; New Jersey Elementary Education Certificate, 1970. Religion: Al Islam.
Residence in New Jersey   Plainfield, 1957–2000.
Career   Elementary school teacher (fifth grade), Susie Dasher Elementary School, Dublin, Georgia, 1956–June 1957; substitute teacher, Plainfield, 1959–1964; teacher (all grades), Sister Clara Muhammad School (formerly The University of Islam), Newark, 1965–1990; teacher, Sister Clara Muhammad Weekend School, Masjidullah, Inc., Plainfield, 1975–1999.
Awards, Honors, Other Certificates   Certificate of achievement for "outstanding work in the Nation of Islam," Muhammad University of Islam, 1973; certificate of appreciation in "recognition of the valuable and devoted services rendered to this school," Sister Clara Muhammad Elementary and Secondary School, Newark, 1977; achievement award for "outstanding and dedicated service," Sister Clara Muhammad Elementary and Secondary School, Newark; certificate of appreciation for "outstanding work in the World Community of Al-Islam in the West," American Muslim Mission, Al-Masjid Muhammad, Plainfield, 1978; certificate for regular attendance and progress, Plainfield Adult School, Board of Education, Plainfield, 1979; certificate of appreciation for "Devoted and Invaluable Services," American Muslim Mission, Al-Masjid Muhammad, Plainfield, 1980; certificate of merit for "goodness, worth, quality, value, and commendable service rendered to this school," Sister Clara Muhammad Elementary School, Newark, 1983; award for "significant contributions to the City of Plainfield in civic pride, business, religion and economic

development," American Muslim Mission, Al-Masjid Muhammad, Plainfield, 1983; certificate of appreciation for "having graciously and generously given yourself to the Muslim community," Masjid Muhammad, Newark, 1986; certificate of appreciation for "having graciously and generously given of [herself] for the betterment of our Masjid, School and community," 1989; award for "consistent patience and sacrifice in helping to develop notable intellects and well mannered, rational thinking students," 1992.

Reflections

"As a youngster growing up it was my greatest desire to become a teacher. It was my firm belief that I could help the young people of today become better educated tomorrow. The most influential people in my life are as follows: parents, grandfather, [and] my aunt and uncle, Professor Z. B. Anderson and Neppie Anderson, retired educators in Columbus, Georgia, who also paid for my college education. The Honorable Elijah Muhammad, his son Warith D. Muhammad, the American spokesman for Human Salvation who says 'we must educate our own, and write our own books.' Also my husband who has been very supportive.

My most unique experience as an adult is the pilgrimage to Mecca in June of 1992. My statement upon my return from Mecca: 'Hajj 1992. Hajj Erases All Doubt and Assures Paradise.' As Saleem Mu Alaikum. The key to success in making up one's mind to attend Hajj is to fear no one or nothing, besides Allah, and be flexible and open to change. There is no experience equal to experience itself. I had desired for many years to make the pilgrimage to Mecca. I kept putting it off in the name of problems that really didn't exist. The mind is a powerful mechanism and will play tricks on you if you don't persist with the Name Allah. I began to do some serious thinking and cleansed my mind and decided I was not going to keep delaying this important invitation from Allah the Most High. I had heard many times some people journey to Hajj just to die there because it assures paradise in the event it does happen. Highly praised is Allah and Glorified is He for permitting me to have successfully completed all rites of Umrah and Hajj without actual death although I did dream I had died while there, but I have come to the conclusion that the dream is a revelation to inform me that Paradise has been granted for my pure intentions and sacrifices. In-Sha-Allah.

I thank Allah much for my Husband who traveled on the trip with me and was very helpful. Three other sisters were my personal guests, namely: Wakeelah Rahman, Faheemah El-Amin of Plainfield, N.J., and Dr. Maryam Suluki of Willingboro, N.J. We, the sisters, were very elated and excited to have kissed the Ka'aba, the House that Abraham and his son Is'mail built for the sake of Allah. Hajj has left the imprint of true happiness on my heart. The

Prophet Muhammad says, (SAS) a Muslim is not a Muslim unless he or she desires for his Brother or Sister that which he desires for him or herself. I am making an international appeal to all who have not yet made Hajj to begin planning today because tomorrow may be too late to make Hajj in the near future and remember the journey of a thousand miles begin with the first step. I now can say with confidence a friend will see you through when others see you are through. The Best Friendship one can have is the Friendship with Allah. La-illah-il-lal Allah Wal-la-hu akbar. "There is no God but Allah and Allah is the Greatest." El Hajjah Qadriyyah Shakir

Publications

Shakir, Qadriyyah Buteen. *My Book of the States and Their Capitals.* [Jersey City], N.J.: New Mind Productions [1985]. 66, illus.

———. *My Qur'anic Reader and Work Study Book.* [Jersey City]: New Mind Productions, 1990. iv, 124.

Bio-Bibliographical Sources

[Obituary for Hajjah Qadriyyah Shakir. Plainfield, N.J., The Shakir Family, December 2000, 4].

Shakir, Qadriyyah Buteen. "African American Women Writers in New Jersey: Biographical Questionnaire." Completed by Qadriyyah Buteen Shakir, September 1985.

———. Supplementary unpublished materials: copies of certificates, awards, diplomas, and "Hajj 1992," the author's statement upon return from Mecca.

SHANGE, NTOZAKE 1948–

Personal   Former name Paulette Linda Williams. Born on 18 October 1948 in Trenton, New Jersey; daughter of Eloise Owens Williams (psychiatric social worker) and Paul Towbin Williams (physician); granddaughter (paternal) of Ida Bolles Williams (housewife) of Drummondville, Ontario, Canada, and Charles Williams (window cleaner) of New York, New York; husband: David Murray (divorced); child: Savannah Thulani Eloisa. Education: Morristown High School, Morristown, New Jersey; Barnard College, B.A., American studies, cum laude, 1966–1970; University of Southern California, Los Angeles, California, M.A.,

Ntozake Shange.
Photograph by Jiri Weiss,
courtesy of the Library of Congress.

American studies, 1973; further study: contemporary Afro-American dance, San Francisco.

Residence in New Jersey   Trenton; Lawrenceville

Career   Faculty member, Sonoma State College, Rohnert Park, California, 1973–1975; Mills College, Oakland, California, 1975, and the University of California Extension, 1972–1975; creative writing instructor, City College, New York, 1975; artist-in-residence, Equinox Theatre, Houston, 1981 to present; New Jersey State Council on the Arts; lecturer, Douglass College, New Brunswick, New Jersey, 1978; professor of drama and creative writing, University of Houston, Houston, Texas, 1983 to present.

Memberships   Women Against Violence Against Women and Children; Actors Equity; National Academy of Television Arts and Sciences; Dramatists Guild; PEN American Center; Academy of American Poets; Poets and Writers, Inc.; Women's Institute for Freedom of the Press; New York Feminist Arts Guild; Writer's Guild.

Awards, Honors, and Other Certificates   New York Drama Critics Award, 1977; Obie, Outer Critics Circle, Audelco, and *Mademoiselle* awards and Tony, Grammy, and Emmy Award nominations, all in 1977, for *for colored girls who have considered suicide/when the rainbow is enuf: a choreopoem;* Frank Silvera Writers' Workshop award, 1978; Obie Award, 1981, for *Mother Courage and Her Children; Los Angeles Times* Book Prize for Poetry, 1981, for *Three Pieces;* Guggenheim fellowship, 1981; Columbia University Medal of Excellence, 1981; Nori Eboraci Award, Bernard College, 1988; Lila Wallace-Reader's Digest Fund Annual Writer's Award, 1992; Paul Robeson Achievement Award, National Coalition of 100 Black Women, 1992; Living Legend Award, National Black Theater Festival, 1993; Claim Your Life Award, 1993; Monarch Merit Award Pushcart Prize.

Publications

Books

Shange, Ntozake. *For Colored Girls Who Have Considered Suicide When the Rainbow is Enuf.* San Lorenzo, Calif.: Shameless Hussy Press, 1975. 27. Reprint, New York: Macmillan, 1977. Translated (Italian) in 1977 by Simonetta Franceschetti as *Per Ragazze di Colore che Hanno Pensato al Suicidio quando l'Arcobaleno Basta.* Rome: Stampa Alternativa, 1977.

———. *Nappy Edges.* New York: St. Martin's Press, 1975. 148. Reprint, New York: Bantam Books, 1980.

———. *Melissa & Smith.* St. Paul, Minn.: Bookslinger, 1976. [19].

———. *Natural Disasters and Other Festive Occasions.* San Francisco: Heirs, 1977.

———. *Sassafrass.* Berkeley, Calif.: Shameless Hussy Press, 1977. 60.

———. *A Photograph: Lovers in Motion, a Drama.* New York: French, 1981. 50.

———. *Three Pieces.* New York: St. Martin's, 1981. xv, 142. Reprint, New York: Penguin Books, 1982.

———. *A Daughter's Geography.* New York: St. Martin's Press, 1982. 77.

———. *Sassafras, Cypress & Indigo: A Novel*. New York: St. Martin's Press, 1982. 224.

———. *From Okra to Greens: Poems*. St. Paul, Minn.: Coffee House Press, 1984. [30].

———. *See No Evil: Prefaces, Reviews & Essays, 1976–1983*. San Francisco: Momo's Press, 1984. 72.

———. *Betsey Brown*. New York: St. Martin's Press, 1985. 207.

———. *From Okra to Greens: A Different Kinda Love Story*. New York: S. French, 1985. 58.

———. *Spell Number Seven*. London: Methuen, in association with the Women's Playhouse Trust, 1985. 52.

———. *Ridin' the Moon in Texas: Word Paintings*. New York: St. Martin's, 1987. xiii, 81, illus.

———. *The Love Space Demands: A Continuing Saga*. New York: St. Martin's Press, 1991. 64.

———. *Liliane: Resurrection of the Daughter*. New York: St. Martin's, 1994. xii, 288. Reprint London: Methuen, 1995.

———. *I Live in Music: Poem*. Paintings by Romare Bearden; edited by Linda Sunshine. New York: Welcome Enterprises [1994]. [32], illus.

———. *If I Can Cook, You Know God Can*. Foreword by Vertamae Grosvenor. Boston: Beacon Press, 1998. xiv, 113.

———. *Whitewash*. Illustrated by Michael Sporn. New York: Walker & Co., 1997. 1v. (unpaged), illus.

Poetry

Shange, Ntozake. "Like the Fog and the Sun Teasin the Rapids." *Mademoiselle* 82, no. 9 (September 1976): 28.

———. "Memory (for Phillip Wilson, Oliver Lake, David Murray, & Julius Hemphill)." *Mademoiselle* 82, no. 9 (September 1976): 28.

———. "On Becoming Successful." *Mademoiselle* 82, no. 9 (September 1976): 28.

———. "Yo U Tu." *Little Magazine* 10, no. 1 (1976): 27–29.

———. "Sue-Jean." *Little Magazine* 11, no. 1 (1977): 26–28.

———. "Cross Oceans into My Heart." In *The Next World: Poems by Thirty-Two Third World Americans*, edited by Joseph Bruchac, 167–170. Trumansburg, N.Y.: Crossing, 1978.

———. "Graduation Nite." In *The Next World: Poems by Thirty-Two Third World Americans*, edited by Joseph Bruchac, 170–172. Trumansburg, N.Y.: Crossing, 1978.

———. "Oh She Got a Head Fulla Hair." *Black Scholar* 10, no. 3–4 (November–December 1978): 13–14.

———. "We Are Just Kinda That Way." *Beloit Poetry Journal* 29, no. 2 (winter 1978–1979): 22.

———. "With No Immediate Cause." *Heresies* 6 (1978): 12.

———. "Wow, Yr Just Like a Man!" *Ms* 7, no. 6 (December 1978): 50,52.

———. "Aw, Babee, You So Pretty." *Essence* 9, no. 12 (April 1979): 87, 145–146.

———. "Black and White Two-Dimensional Planes." *Callaloo* 5, no. 2 (1979): 56–62.

———. "Gray." *Callaloo* 5, no. 2 (1979): 63.

———. "Is Not So Gd to be Born a Girl." *Black Scholar* 10, no. 8–9 (May–June 1979): 28–29.

———. "Otherwise I Would Think It Odd to Have Rape Prevention Month." *Black Scholar* 10, no. 8–9 (May–June 1979): 29–30.

———. "Unrecovered Losses/Black Theatre Traditions." *Black Scholar* 10, no. 10 (July–August 1979): 7–9.

———. "With No Immediate Cause." *Radical America* 13, no. 6 (November 1979): 48.

———. "Aw, Babee, You So Pretty." In *Midnight Birds: Stories of Contemporary Black Women Writers,* edited by Mary Helen Washington, 87–92. New York: Anchor-Doubleday, 1980.

———. "Comin to Terms." In *Midnight Birds: Stories of Contemporary Black Women Writers,* edited by Mary Helen Washington, 251–254. New York: Anchor-Doubleday, 1980.

———. "Cypress-Sassafras [sic]." In *The Third World Woman: Minority Women Writers of the United States,* edited by Dexter Fisher, 281–286. Boston: Houghton-Mifflin, 1980.

———. "Jonestown or the Disco." In *Women Poet, the East,* edited by Elaine Dallman, 74–75. Reno, Nev.: Women-in-Literature, 1980.

———. "Nappy Edges (A Cross Country Sojourn)." In *Black Sister: Poetry by Black American Women, 1746–1980,* edited by Erlene Stetson, 268–269. Bloomington: Indiana University Press, 1980.

———. "No More Love Poems No. 1." In *Black Sister: Poetry by Black American Women, 1746–1980,* edited by Erlene Stetson, 268–269. Bloomington: Indiana University Press, 1980.

———. "She Bleeds." *Essence* 11, no. 1 (May 1980): 103.

———. "Dark Phrases." In *Black Sister: Poetry by Black American Women, 1746–1980,* edited by Erlene Stetson, 270–272. Bloomington: Indiana University Press, 1981.

———. "Frank Albert and Viola Benzena Owens." In *Black Sister: Poetry by Black American Women, 1746–1980,* edited by Erlene Stetson, 273–276. Bloomington: Indiana University Press, 1981.

———. "Get It and Feel Good." *Essence* 13, no. 1 (May 1982): 22.

———. "Moon Journey." *Heresies* 4, no. 2 (1982): 34.

Bio-Bibliographical Sources

"Ntozake Shange." *Contemporary Black Biography.* Vol. 8. Detroit: Gale Research, 1994. Reproduced in Biography Resource Center. Farmington Hills, Mich.: The Gale Group. 2001. Available: <http://www.galenet.com/servlet/BioRC>

"Ntozake Shange." *St. James Guide to Young Adult Writers.* 2nd ed. St. James Press, 1999. Reproduced in Biography Resource Center. Farmington Hills, Mich.: The Gale Group. 2001. Available: <http://www.galenet.com/servlet/BioRC>

Shange, Ntozake. "The Race Today." *Review* 16, no. 3 (January 1985): 10–14.
Williams, Ruby Ora. "African American Women Writers in New Jersey: Biographical Questionnaire." Completed by Ruby Ora Williams (Ntozake Shange's aunt), December 1996.

SHARIF, UMMIL-KHAIR ZAKIYYAH 1926–

Ummil-Khair Sharif,
courtesy of Ummil-Khair Sharif.

Personal   Former name Doris Mae Venable Gartrell Laws; born on 10 April 1926 in Plainfield, New Jersey; third child of Olivia Rebecca Flannagan Venable (teacher), of Charlottesville (formerly Profit), Virginia, and William Arthur Venable (postal worker) of Plainfield, New Jersey; granddaughter (maternal) of Liza Martin Flanagan and Wash Flannagan, both of Charlottesville (Profit); sisters: Frances Elizabeth (Pam) Venable, Alma Louse Venable Davis, and Marion Olivia Venable Williams; brothers: Cecil Carlton Venable, Clarence Cornelius Venable, and William Arthur Venable II. Married in 1945; children: Bernadette Alma Gartrell, Janice Christine Gartrell Clark, Demetrious Barnet Gartrell, Jamal Laws Sharif, Khalilah Almeria Sharif, and Melande Awatif Sharif Carter. Education: 7th Washington School, Plainfield, New Jersey, 1931–1938; Hubbard School, Plainfield, 1938; Plainfield High School, Plainfield, graduated 1944; program for private school teachers, Jersey State College; science and math program for inner-city private school teachers, NJIT; certificate, Arabic Language Workshop, North East Region Department of Islamic Education, Sister Clara Muhammed Schools, 1989; certificate in word processing, Plainfield Adult School, Plainfield, 1990; certificate in sewing, Plainfield Adult School, Plainfield; certificate in typing, Plainfield Adult School, Plainfield. Religion: Al-Islam.

Residence in New Jersey   Plainfield, 1926–1945 and 1948 to present.

Career   Factory (condenser) worker, Cornell Dubilier, South Plainfield, 1942; Chock Full of Nuts, New York, 1945–1946; factory (pocketbook) worker, Plainfield, 1948; Westinghouse, Edison, New Jersey, 1950–1959; teacher (grade school and preschool), Muhammad University of Islam, Newark, 1967 to present.

Memberships   Mayor's Education Task Force, headed by Superintendent of Schools Ron Lewis, 1980; secretary, New Jersey State Department of

Islamic Education, 1980–present; secretary, Northeast Region Department of Islamic Education, 1980 to present.

Awards, Honors, Other Certificates   Acknowledgment from Nancy and Ronald Reagan; certificate of appreciation "in recognition of the valuable and devoted services rendered to this School," Sister Clara Muhammad Elementary School, 1977; certificate of appreciation for "devoted and invaluable services rendered," American Muslim Mission, Plainfield, 1980; certificate of appreciation for "outstanding support of school fund raising projects," Sister Clara Muhammad Elementary School #25, 1980; certificate of appreciation for "outstanding support of candy drive," Sister Clara Muhammad Elementary School #25, 1980; commendation for "unselfish and unwavering commitment to community service and the field of education," The Muslim Organization Committee, 1980; award of appreciation for "outstanding services rendered to this institution of learning," Clara Muhammad Elementary School, 1981; certificates of appreciation for "having graciously and generously given of themselves for the betterment of our Masjid, School, and community," Sister Clara Muhammad Elementary School, 1983, 1985, 1986, 1988, 1989, 1990; certificate of appreciation for "the valuable contribution given to Sister Clara Muhammad Pre School," 1985; certificate of merit for "goodness, worth, quality, value, and commendable service rendered to this school," Sister Clara Muhammad Elementary School, 1986; certificate of achievement for "demonstrating and exemplifying moral excellence in their character and behavior," Sister Clara Muhammad School, 1987; certificate of attendance for "your consistent presence throughout the school year," Sister Clara Muhammad School, 1989; certificate of appreciation for "having graciously and generously given of themselves for the betterment of our Masjid, School, and community," Masjid Mohammad-Newark, 1989, 1990, 1991; pioneer award for "long and dedicated service of 25 Golden years or more towards the upliftment of Al-Islam in the Northern New Jersey area," from Masjid Mohammed Newark Passaic Islamic Center, Islamic Senior Citizens Co., Masjid Mohammed Jersey City, Masjid Iman, Jersey City, and IDEA.

Reflections

"Lived in New York when I got married in 1945, lived in New Britain, Connecticut, from 1946 until 1947, then back to Plainfield until now, 1992. No one in [my] family has written anything. My mother influenced me most in childhood; she taught school in Virginia before coming to Plainfield where she married and had her family. She always made us read the dictionary and taught us at home when we returned from school. We always had to go to Sunday School and church. My parents were the foundation builders of Shiloh Baptist Church, one of the oldest churches in Plainfield. The most influential person [in my life] was Malcolm X, El Hajji Malcolm Shabazz. I first heard him in 1959 in New York and immediately joined the Nation of Islam. After the Honorable

Elijah Muhammad died, his son Imam W. D. Mohammed influenced me to write. Working in our school, the University of Islam, now renamed Sister Clara Muhammad School in memory of his mother, he said [that] as long as we continue to use the public school textbooks we will be teaching Christianity; in every book there is a philosophy. We must write our books based in the Quran, we are Muslims.

The most dynamic experience in my life is when I made Hajj. In 1982, with 300 other Pilgrims we made the Journey of a lifetime. I witness[ed] Muslims from all over the world, Caucasians, Africans, Asians, you name the country, wall-to-wall people all giving Praise and thanks to the Creator, Allah, marching around the Kaaba, the House built by Prophet Abraham and Prophet Ismail [sic]. It was a sight to behold and an experience never to be matched nor to be equaled. Allah u Akbar." Al Hajjah Ummil-Khair Sharif

Publications

Sharif, Ummil-Khair Z. *ABC's in Al Quran.* [Jersey City, N.J.]: New Mind Productions, 1983. [32].

———. *Iqraa! . . .; Qur'an Based Curriculum Guide.* [Jersey City: N.J.: New Mind Productions]. ii, 47.

Bio-Bibliographical Sources

Sharif, Ummil-Khair Zakiyyah. "African American Women Writers in New Jersey: Biographical Questionnaire." Completed by the Ummil-Khair Zakiyyah Sharif, March 1993.

———. Supplemental materials provided by Al Hajjah Sharif, consisting of copies of numerous awards and an adult education certificate.

Helen Shaw.
Photograph by Joseph Turner,
Turner Studios.

SHAW, HELEN 1938–

Personal Born on 4 December 1938 in Linden, New Jersey; eighth child of Obie L. Coleman Shaw of Montezuma, Georgia, and Henry J. Shaw (1903–1965; minister, Sunlight Baptist Church, Edison, New Jersey) of Cordele, Georgia; granddaughter (maternal) of Eva and Neil Coleman, both of Georgia; granddaughter (paternal) of Elnora McKenzie and B. K. Shaw, both of Georgia; sisters: Evelyn Shaw Higgins (deceased) and Dorothy Shaw Edwards; brothers: Robert Shaw, Henry Shaw, Jr. (deceased), Benjamin Shaw (deceased), Harry

Shaw (deceased), Herman Shaw, William Shaw, and David Shaw (deceased); children: Kether A. Hassan, Julie R. Freeman, Heather S. Rogers, Jacquelyn R. Gilliam, and Timothy A. Fields. Education: Elementary School #5, Linden, New Jersey; Linden Junior High, Linden; Linden High School, Linden, 1956; attended Middlesex County College, Edison, New Jersey, and Union County College, Cranford and Plainfield, New Jersey. Religion: Baptist.

Residence in New Jersey   Linden, 1938–1958; Plainfield, 1967–1983 and 1985–1994.

Career   Secretary, Stewart Air Force Base, Newburgh, New York, 1957–1958; secretary, Norton Air Force Base, San Bernardino, California, 1958–1960; psychiatric technician trainee, Patton State Hospital, San Bernardino, California, 1960–1961; manhours analysis clerk, Lockheed Electronics, North Plainfield, New Jersey, 1968–1969; secretary, Bell Labs, and later AT&T, Murray Hill and Basking Ridge, New Jersey, 1970–1971 and 1971–1976; secretary to Superintendent of Schools, Plainfield Board of Education, Plainfield, 1985–1989; secretary, New Jersey Transit, Newark, New Jersey, 1988–1990; secretary, R. W. Johnson Pharmaceutical Research, Raritan, New Jersey, 1990–1998.

Awards, Honors, Other Certificates   New Jersey Writers' Award, New Jersey Institute of Technology, Newark, 1986.

Reflections

"Poetry and writing have always been a natural part of who I am. My father loved poetry and was always attentive when I shared my 'right off the drawing board creations' with him. He always encouraged me to write. During my school years in Linden, I was encouraged to continue writing by my English teachers, specifically Mrs. McCormick, who always sought perfection in her students, and Mrs. Sarah Light, who took me aside one day after class and said, 'Miss Shaw, someday, you are going to be a great writer!'

However, it was during the next sixteen years after 1967, while I remained in New Jersey, that my gears locked into the writing mode and poetry and prose [became] my driver. While raising my children in Plainfield, New Jersey, I continued to write poetry, inspired by the experiences and feelings brought about by everyday living."

Publications

Books

Hooks, Helen Shaw. *Through the Brown Eyes of Black Me: Inspirational Poetry.* 1st ed. Sacramento, Calif.: Quotes and Footnotes Publications, 1984. 99, illus.

Shaw, Helen. *When There Was Only Space God Spoke! The Creation Story for All God's Children.* Augusta, Ga.: PoetShaw Inspirational Publications [2001]. 20.

Bio-Bibliographical Source

Shaw, Helen. "African American Women Writers in New Jersey: Bio-graphical Questionnaire." Completed by Helen Shaw, April 1985 and 15 July 2001.

———. Correspondence with Sibyl E. Moses, 20 July 2001.

SHIVERS, RUBY WILLIAMS 1941–

Personal Born on 21 February 1941 in Lake Butler, Florida; eighth child and third daughter of Lula Hedgeman Williams (housewife) of Lake Butler, and Cary McCoy Williams (hacker) of Winfield, Florida; granddaughter (maternal) of Viola Hedgeman and Philip Hedgeman; granddaughter (paternal) of Mary Williams and James Williams; sisters: Mary Jane, Lula Mae, and Rose Marie; brothers: James Carey, Haywood, Eugene, Clarence, Bland, John Henry, and William Floyd; husband: Lloyd G. Shivers, Jr.; sons: Lloyd III (Rashan), Walter Doyle (Sabir), and Bland Capece (Waheed). Education: Consolidated Elementary School, Lake Butler; Union County High School, Lake Butler; Seton Hall University, B.A., communications, 1976, South Orange, New Jersey; Drake Business College, Elizabeth, New Jersey. Religion: African Methodist Episcopal; Mount Teman A.M.E. Church, Elizabeth, New Jersey.

Residence in New Jersey Elizabeth, 1959–1979; Plainfield, 1979 to present.

Career Salad Girl, Manara Italian Restaurant, Gainesville, Florida, 1959; Dave's Dress Factory, Roselle Park, New Jersey, 1960–1961; legal secretary, Newark, New Jersey; branch administrative manager trainee and later manager, Burroughs Corporation; administrative assistant, Pretty Purdie Productions (owner, Bernard Purdie, former music director for Areatha Franklin), 1980; secretary, Bellcore Communications, 1984–1992; account assistant, PLI Brokerage, Inc., Warren, New Jersey.

Memberships Trustee, choir member, and president, African Cultural Awareness Committee, Mt. Teman A.M.E. Church, Elizabeth, New Jersey; board member and cofounder of Women in Support of the Million Man March, Inc. (WISOMMM); cofounder, Cary Williams Memorial Scholarship Foundation.

Awards, Honors, Other Certificates Black Book Award, U.B. & U.S. Communications Systems, Inc., 7 June 1997.

Publications

Shivers, Ruby. *Verbal Healing: We Must Reject Tired, Trite, Tasteless, and Other Nonsensical Expressions that Keep Us Damaged.* Plainfield, N.J.: ChaAski [1996]. 166; as *We Must Reject Tired, Trite, Tasteless, and Other Nonsensical Expressions that Keep Us Damaged.* Plainfield, N.J.: ChaAski [1996]. 177.

———. *Victims of Confusion: The 15 Step Program to Reverse the Damage of Slavery.* [Plainfield, N.J.: ChaAski Publishing, 2000]. 32.

Bio-Bibliographical Source
Shivers, Ruby Williams. "African American Women Writers in New Jersey: Biographical Questionnaire." Completed by Ruby W. Shivers, 1 September 2000.

SIMON, PATRICIA NICELY *SEE* SALAAM, NEFETERRI

SPINNER, BETTYE DELORES TYSON 1936–

Personal Born on 12 April 1936 in Rocky Mount, North Carolina; the eighth child of Alma Louise Anthony Tyson (housewife, educated as a teacher) of Tarboro, North Carolina, and Hubert Daniel Tyson, Sr. (hospital attendant, small business owner) of Kinston, North Carolina; granddaughter (maternal) of Isabelle and Henry Anthony, both of Tarboro; granddaughter (paternal) of Martha and Alonzo Tyson, both of Kinston; sisters: Martha, Alma (deceased), Thelma, Dorothy (deceased), Ruby, and Sylvia; brother: Hubert Tyson, Jr. (deceased); husband: Charles Ralph Spinner, Jr. (Lt. Colonel, U.S. Army, Ret.); children: Charles Ralph Spinner, III, Kay S. Thompson, and Stephen Anthony Spinner. Education: Edward Evans Elementary School, Fayetteville, North Carolina, 1942–1944; Newbold Training School, Fayetteville, 1944–1949; E. E.

Bettye T. Spinner.
Photograph by Charles R. Spinner.

Smith High School, Fayetteville, 1949–1953; Hampton Institute, Hampton, Virginia, B.S., Speech and Drama, 1953–1957 and M.A., English Education, 1958; Oberlin College, Oberlin, Ohio, 1956; Brooklyn College, CUNY, Brooklyn, New York, 1959–1961; Johns Hopkins University, Baltimore, Maryland, 1966–1968; Rutgers University, New Brunswick, New Jersey, Ed.D. (English Education), 1986–1990. Religion: Presbyterian; The Presbyterian Church of Willingboro, Willingboro, New Jersey.
Residence in New Jersey Willingboro, 1978 to present.
Career Clerk-typist, Student Employment Office, Hampton Institute, Hampton, 1953–1957; clerk-typist, Federal Trade Commission, Washington, D.C., 1953–1957 (summers); teacher of English, Speech, and Drama in Cleveland, Ohio, 1959, Brooklyn, New York, 1959–1961, Verdun, France, 1962–1963, and Heidelberg, Germany, 1970–1973; teacher, junior high school and high school, Chesterfield County, Virginia; teacher of

junior and senior honors and advanced placement English, humanities, electives in speech, and creative writing, Moorestown High School, Moorestown, New Jersey, 1977–1997.

Memberships Teacher Advisory Committee, Geraldine R. Dodge Foundation, 1986 to present; associate chair, NCTE Resolutions Committee, 1987–1988, chair, 1988–1989; NCTE National Achievement Awards in Writing Advisory Committee, 1990–1996, chair, 1992–1996; Executive Board, New Jersey Council of Teachers of English, 1993 to present; Planning Council, New Jersey Governor's Awards in Arts Education, 1994 to present; New Jersey Alliance for Arts Education, 1994 to present; served at various times as elder, deacon, and director of Christian education, The Presbyterian Church of Willingboro.

Awards, Honors, Other Certificates Directing Award, USAREUR, Dependent Schools Drama Festival, Munich, Germany, 1972; Sustained Superior Performance Teaching Award, Heidelberg American High School, 1973; NJ Artist-Teacher Institute, 1983, 1985; grant recipient, National Endowment for the Humanities, 1986–1989, 1992–1994; Best Poem by a County Poet, Burlington County Cultural and Heritage Commission, 1987–1989; president, Burlington County Poets, 1987–1990, 1996 to present; featured reader, Geraldine R. Dodge Poetry Festival, 1988 and the NJ Governor's Conference on the Arts, 1995; Geraldine R. Dodge Poet, 1988 to present; vice president (Anthologies), New Jersey Poetry Society, 1989–1995; local coordinator, Delaware Valley, National African American Read-In Chain, 1990 to present; English Institute, Wellesley College Center for Research on Women, 1993; visiting teacher/diversity consultant, American College Testing, 1995 to present; featured poetry teacher, NJEA "Classroom Close-up, NJ," NJN, Channel 5, 1996; New Jersey Governor's Award, NJCTE Outstanding English Educator Award 2000.

Reflections

"I cannot recall a time in my life when words were not important. The youngest in a family of eight, I needed them desperately for self defense once I could speak! I grew up awed by my brother and sister's skill at reciting poems for classes and singing lyrics learned for school choir. As years passed, I would often 'hold the book' while they memorized or harmonize with them as they serenaded our mother at night or sing with them their newly created lyrics for songs they had taught me. Although my mother died when I was eleven, I credit her with instilling in all her children the love of music and language that led me to creative writing. I have no siblings or children who are professional writers but several whose gift with words is obvious whenever, wherever they speak and write. And from the beginning, my school teachers echoed my family's earlier lesson, that words have life and music: Miss Avant in first grade when she enchanted me by turning nursery rhymes into acting scripts; Miss McIver, who challenged our grammar grade chorus to sing Handel and influenced my writing lyrics to "O Sole Mio" as our class song when we graduated from elementary school; and in high school Miss Lennon, who coached me to state victory in public speaking, and Mrs. Fowler, whose whisper inspired me through Shakespeare to valedictory and on to college at Hampton where novelist and teacher, Jay Saunders Redding, taught me in Literature and Creative Writing classes, that words are also mirrors of the world, reflecting all its beauty and its flaws."

Publications

Books

Spinner, Bettye T. *Review for High School Equivalency Examination.* Mendham, N.J.: EDEX Associates, Inc., 1978.

———. *Whispers of Generations.* Southhampton, N.Y.: Luke Press, 1988. 32.

———. *In the Dark Hush: Poems.* Southhampton, N.Y.: Luke Press, 1992. 65.

Poetry

Poetry in magazines, journals, and anthologies: *English Journal; Bitterroot; Anthology of American Poetry; Writer Magazine; Lutheran Women; Western Ohio Journal; Footworks; NJ English Journal; Paterson Literary Review; WordSpinners,* all 1985–1987, 1989–1990; *New Jersey Poetry Society Anthology, 1986–1992; Seeding the Process of Multicultural Education,* editors Nelson and Walters, Minnesota Inclusiveness Program, 1998.

Articles

Spinner, Bettye T. "Re-Vision: The Student as Poet." (ERIC Document Reproduction Service No. 290–170), 1989.

———. "Using Latin American Poetry in English Translation." *Latin America.* New York: Queens College/CUNY Press, 1989.

———. "Teacher to Teacher: Approach and Reflection." *Starling with Delight.* Geraldine R. Dodge Poetry Program Newsletter, 1995.

———. "Sustaining the Wonder of Teaching." In *A Passion for Teaching,* n.p. Washington, D.C.: Association for Supervision and Curriculum Development, 1999.

———. "Harvest Home." In *A Passion for Teaching,* n.p. Washington, D.C.: Association for Supervision and Curriculum Development, 1999.

Bio-Bibliographical Sources

Spinner, Bettye T. "African American Women Writers in New Jersey: Biographical Questionnaire." Completed by Bettye T. Spinner on 19 June 2000.

———. "Resume." [ca. 19 June 2000].

STONE, ELBERTA WILHELMINIA HAYES 1922–

Personal Born on 20 March 1922 in Montclair, New Jersey; only child of Alice Gwendolyn Franciso Hayes (nurse's aide) of Brooklyn, New York,

Elberta Wilhelminia Stone,
courtesy of Elberta Wilhelminia Stone.

and William Elbert Hayes (waiter and butler) of Lynchburg, Virginia; husband: Richard Herbert Stone (welfare investigator); child: Valerie Ellen Stone, M.D. Education: Glenfield Elementary School, Montclair, 1927–1936; Montclair High School, Montclair, 1936–1940; Morgan State College, Baltimore, Maryland, B.A., 1944; Rutgers University, New Brunswick, New Jersey, M.L.S., 1956. Religion: Episcopal, St. Phillip's and Trinity (Episcopal) Cathedral, Newark, New Jersey.

Residence in New Jersey   Montclair, 1922–1939; 1951 to present.

Career   Control clerk, U.S. Social Security Administration, Baltimore, 1944–1946; library assistant, Enoch Pratt Public Library, Baltimore, 1946–1950; preprofessional librarian, Brooklyn Public Library, Brooklyn, New York, 1950–1952; library assistant (1952–1956), junior business librarian (1956–1958), senior librarian (1958–1960), Newark Public Library, Newark, 1952–1960; children's librarian, West Orange Public Library, West Orange, New Jersey, 1960–1962; educational media specialist, Newark Board of Education, Newark, 1962–present; school librarian, Newton Elementary School, Newark and Cleveland Elementary School, Newark, 1962–1972; central office librarian, Newark Board of Education, Newark, 1972 to present.

Memberships   St. Phillip's and Trinity (Episcopal) Cathedral, Newark: vestry and junior warder, 1982–1985; various other church-related activities.

Awards, Honors, Other Certificates   Writer's Award, Phyllis Wheatly Society.

Reflections

"Am a great reader and have always had a vivid imagination, probably developed by aunts Dollie and Carrie Allen, who made my life interesting, can't think of any one person who influenced me. Since I developed a talent for storytelling, I suppose the book was an outgrowth of that."

Publication

Stone, Elberta H. *I'm Glad I'm Me.* New York: G. P. Putnam [1971]. [32]. Braille edition, American Printing House for the Blind, Louisville, Ky., 1971.

Bio-Bibliographical Source

Stone, Elberta H. "African American Women Writers in New Jersey: Biographical Questionnaire." Completed by Elberta H. Stone, 1986.

STRICKLAND, DOROTHY MAE SALLEY 1933–

Personal   Born on 29 September 1933 in Newark, New Jersey; youngest of four children born to Evelyn Elizabeth Daniels Salley and LeRoy Salley, Sr., both of Blackville, South Carolina; granddaughter (maternal) of Maggie Haygood Daniels and Cass Daniels; granddaughter (paternal) of Mary Metheny Salley and Jacob Salley; sister: Barbara Salley Drew (deceased); brothers: Leroy Sally, Jr. (deceased) and Edward Salley (deceased); husband: Maurice Raymond Strickland (attorney; deceased); children: Mark Raymond, Maurice Randall, and Michael Raymond. Education: Jefferson Elementary and Junior High Schools, Union, New Jersey, 1938–1948; Union High School, Union, 1948–1951; Newark State College, Newark, B.S., general elementary education, 1951–1955; New York University, New York, New York, M.A., educational psychology, 1956–1958; New York University, New York, Ph.D., Division of Early Childhood and Elementary Education, 1967–1971; Honorary Doctorate of Humane Letters, Bank Street College of Education, New York, 1991. Religion: Roman Catholic; St. Peter Claver's Church, Montclair, New Jersey.

Residence in New Jersey   Union; Newark; Orange; West Orange.

Career   Telephone operator (part-time), New Jersey Bell Telephone Co., 1951–1955; elementary classroom teacher, East Orange Public Schools, 1955–1961; reading consultant and learning disability specialist, East Orange Public Schools, 1961–1966; assistant professor, Jersey City State College, Jersey City, New Jersey, 1966–1970; associate professor, 1970–1973, professor, 1973–1980, chairperson (1973–1976), Kean College, New Jersey, 1970–1980; professor of education, 1980–1990, and Arthur I. Gates Professor of Education, Teachers College, Columbia University, New York, 1985–1990; The State of New Jersey Professor of Reading, Rutgers University, New Brunswick, New Jersey, 1990 to present.

Memberships   New Jersey Reading Teachers Association; International Reading Association; National Council Teachers of English; American Association of Elementary-Kindergarten-Nursery Educators; National Association for the Education of Young Children; Day Care and Child Development Council; National Council of Research in English; American Educational Research Association; American Association of Colleges for Teacher Education; National Reading Conference. Other professional activities: National Advisory Panel of the National Center on Adult Literacy University of Pennsylvania; National Advisory Board of the National Center on the Study of Literature; Committee on Establishment of Non-Profit Affiliation for Research, National Reading Conference; Middle Childhood/Generalist Standards Committee, National Board for Professional Teaching Standards; Board of Directors, New Jersey Center for the Book; Selection Committee, Ezra Jack Keats Award for Outstanding Children's Book; Consultant, WGBH, Long Ago & Far Away.

Awards, Honors, Other Certificates   Promising Researcher Award, National Council Teachers of English, 1972; Founder's Day recognition, University

Honors Scholar, New York University, 1971; award for Dedication to Literacy, Manhattan Council, International Reading Association, 1983; Outstanding Teacher Educator of Reading Award from International Reading Association, 1985; Outstanding Contribution to Education, National Association of University Women, 1987; elected to Reading Hall of Fame, International Reading Association, 1990; Distinguished Alumnus Award, New York University, 1990; Outstanding Alumnus Award, Kean College of New Jersey, 1990; American Association of Education Press Award for distinguished publication, for *Emerging Literacy: Young Children Learning to Read and Write,* coedited with Lesley Morrow, 1990; Rewey Belle Inglis Award for Outstanding Woman in English, National Council of Teachers of English, 1994; Jubilee Medal *Pro Meritis* for distinguished service within the archdiocese of Newark, 1997; Indiana University citation for Outstanding Contributions to Literacy, 1998; Outstanding Educator in the Language Arts, National Council of Teachers of English, 1998; Kappa Delta Pi, honorary society for teachers; Pi Lambda Theta, international honorary society; Phi Delta Kappa, professional fraternity in education; Phi Delta Phi, national honorary society.

Reflections

"Mrs. Luex, the local librarian in the very small storefront branch library in my neighborhood, was a major influence on me as a reader. I enjoyed reading and she took a special interest in me. Each time I entered the library, she always appeared to be delighted to see me. She would reach under her desk and pull out a book that she said she had simply waiting for me. It wasn't until many years later, as an adult, that I realized that she probably did that for many children. She had the gift of making a child feel very special.

Since most of my writing is professional writing for teachers, it is a natural extension of my work. I am fortunate to be able to write about the areas of my work that I care most about: using literature in the classroom, teaching children to write, and the emergent literacy of young children. I am inspired by the energetic, caring teachers with whom I work and I hope that my work inspires them to do even better things for children."

Publications

Books

Goodman, Yetta M., Myna M. Haussler, and Dorothy S. Strickland, editors. *Oral and Written Language Development Research: Impact on the Schools: Proceedings from the 1979 and 1980 IMPACT Conferences Sponsored by the International Reading Association and the National Council of Teachers of English.* Washington, D.C.: International Institute of Education, 1981. 180.

Strickland, Dorothy S., ed. *The Role of Literature in Reading Instruction: Cross-Cultural Views.* Newark, Delaware: International Reading Association, 1981. x, 42.

———, ed. *Listen Children: An Anthology of Black Literature.* New York: Bantam, 1982. 120 p.

Strickland, Dorothy S., Joan T. Feeley, and Shelly B. Wepner. *Using Computers in the Teaching of Reading.* New York: Teachers College Press, 1986. xiv, 240.

Taylor, Denny, and Dorothy S. Strickland. *Family Storybook Reading.* Portsmouth, N.H.: Heinemann, 1986. xv, 116.

Strickland, Dorothy S., Joan T. Feeley, and Shelley B. Wepner. *Using Computers in the Teaching of Reading.* New York: Teachers College Press, 1987. xiv, 240, illus.

Strickland, Dorothy S., and Eric J. Cooper, eds. *Educating Black Children: America's Challenge.* Washington, D.C.: Bureau of Educational Research, School of Education, Howard University, 1987. ix, 134.

Kullisaid, Eleanor R., and Dorothy S. Strickland. *Literature, Literacy and Learning: Classroom Teachers, Library Media Specialists, and the Literature-Based Curriculum.* Chicago: American Library Association, 1989. vii, 44, illus.

Strickland, Dorothy S., and Lesley Mandel Morrow, eds. *Emerging Literacy: Young Children Learn to Read and Write.* Newark, Del.: International Reading Association, 1989. x, 161.

Wepner, Shelley B., Joan T. Feeley, and Dorothy S. Strickland, eds. *The Administration and Supervision of Reading Programs.* New York: Teachers College Press, 1989. xi, 284.

Feeley, J., Dorothy S. Strickland, and S. Wepner. *Process Reading and Writing: A Literature-Based Approach.* New York: Teachers College Press, 1991.

Galda, L., B. Cullinan, and Dorothy S. Strickland. *Language, Literacy, and the Child.* Fort Worth, Tex.: Harcourt Brace Jovanovich, 1992.

Strickland, Dorothy S., and M. Strickland, editors. *Families: Poems Celebrating the African American Experience.* Honesdale, Pa.: Boyds Mills Press, 1994.

Wepner, S., Dorothy S. Strickland, and J. Feeley. *The Administration and Supervision of Reading Programs.* 2nd ed. New York: Teachers College Press, 1995.

Galda, L., B. Cullinan, and Dorothy S. Strickland. *Language, Literacy, and the Child.* 2nd ed. Fort Worth, Tex.: Harcourt Brace Jovanovich, 1997.

Morrow, L.M., Dorothy S. Strickland, and D. Woo. *Literacy Instruction in Half Day and Full Day Kindergartens.* Newark, Del.: International Reading Association, 1998.

Strickland, Dorothy S. *Teaching Phonics Today.* Newark, Del.: International Reading Association, 1998.

Strickland, Dorothy S., and L. M. Morrow, eds. *Beginning Reading and Writing.* New York: Teachers College Press; Newark, Del.: International Reading Association, 2000.

Articles and Book Chapters

Strickland, Dorothy Salley, B. Cullinan, and A. Jaggar. "Teaching Them to Read When They Speak A Different English." *Early Years* 2, no. 3 (November 1971):15.

Strickland, Dorothy Salley. "The Black Experience in Paperback." In *New Perspectives on Paperbacks,* edited by M.J. Weiss, J. Brunner, and W. Heiss, n.p. Monograph no. 1, College Reading Association. [Easton, Pa: College Reading Association , 1972?].

Strickland, Dorothy Salley. "Black is Beautiful vs. White is Right." *Elementary English.* (February 1972): n.p.

———. "Expanding Language Power of Young Black Children: A Literature Approach." In *Better Reading in Urban Schools,* edited by J. Allen Figurel, n.p. Newark, Del.: International Reading Association, 1972.

———. "Reading: A Language Experience." *The Reading Instruction Journal* 15, no. 2 (January 1972): n.p.

Strickland, Dorothy Salley, and William Stewart. "Issues and Debate: The Use of Dialect Readers." *The Reading Instruction Journal* (February/March 1973): n.p.

Strickland, Dorothy Salley. "A Program for Linguistically Different, Black Children." *Research in the Teaching of English.* National Council Teachers of English 7 (spring 1973): 79–86.

———. "Educators Responses." In *Black Dialects and Reading,* edited by B. Cullinan, n.p. ERIC Clearinghouse on Reading and Communication Skills and NCTE, 1974.

———. "Fostering Reading in the Gifted and Creative: Specific Materials and Resources in Early Childhood Education." In *Reading for the Creative and Gifted,* edited by M. Labuda, n.p. Newark, Del.: International Reading Association, 1974.

Strickland, Dorothy Salley, B. Cullinan, and A. Jaggar. "Language Expansion for Black Children in the Primary Grades: A Research Report." *Young Children* 29 (January 1974): 98–112.

Strickland, Dorothy Salley. "Developing Children's Language." In *Survival Through Language: The Basics and Beyond,* edited by R. Bean, A. Berger, and A. Petrosky, n.p. Pittsburgh, Pa.: University of Pittsburgh, 1977.

———. "A Language Experience: Tool for Content Reading in the Middle Grades." *The Reading Instruction Journal* 21, no. 1 (January 1977): 2–5.

———. "Preschool Programs Should Balance Cognitive and Affective Learning." *Right to Read '77.* (International Reading Association) 3, no. 4 (April 1977): n.p.

———. "Promoting Language and Concept Development." In *Literature and Young Children,* edited by B. Cullinan and C. Carmichael, n.p. [Champaign, Ill.]:National Council Teachers of English, 1977.

Strickland, Dorothy Salley, Robinson, and B. Cullinana. "Reading and the Young Child: Ready or Not." In *Reading in the Kindergarten,* edited by L. Ollila, 13–39. Newark, Del.: International Reading Association, 1977.

Strickland, Dorothy Salley. "Talk . . . Talk . . . Talk." *Early Years* 6 (February 1977): 68–76.

———. "Learning Failure and Unused Learning Potential." In *Report of the Task Panel, President Carter's Commission on Mental Health,* 661–729. Washington, D.C.: U.S. Government Printing Office, 1978.

————. "Parent Involvement in Reading Instruction." *Georgia Journal of Reading* 3, no. 2 (spring 1978): 64–69.

————. "Pre-elementary School Reading" In *Projections for Reading: Preschool Through Adulthood,* edited by B. Calkings, F. Hesser, G. Schiffman, and R. Staiger, 7–16. Washington, D.C.: U.S. Department of Health, Education, and Welfare, 1978.

————. "The Sooner-the-Better, More-the Merrier Syndrome." *Early Years* 8, no. 9 (May 1978): 38–40.

Strickland, Dorothy Salley, and C. Dorsey-Gaines. "What Teachers Do and What They Say They Do." *Early Years* 9, no. 1 (September 1978): 40–41, 48.

Strickland, Dorothy Salley. "How Parents Can Help in Reading Development." *Curriculum Products Review* 14, no. 1 (September 1979): 22.

Strickland, Dorothy Salley, J. Algozzine, E. Gotts, and G. Schiffman. "Improving Basic Education Skills of Appalachian Children" *Journal of the Appalachian Regional Commission* 12, no. 3 (January–February 1979): 32–37.

Strickland, Dorothy Salley. "Integrating the Basic Skills." *Early Years* 9, no. 9 (May 1979): 30–31.

————. "Reflections on Reading in the 1970's." *Language Arts* no. 8 (November December 1979): 886–887.

————. "Basic Skills Focus on Reading." *The Reading Instruction Journal,* 23, no. 3 (spring–summer 1980): 53–56.

Strickland, Dorothy Salley, et al. "Gold Nugget Teaching Tips." *Early Years* 10, no. 9 (May 1980): 28–29, 74.

Strickland, Dorothy Salley. "Nurturing the Gifts and Talents of Young Learners." In *Strategies for Educational Change,* edited by Walter Marks and R. Nystrand, n.p. New York: Macmillan, 1981.

————. "Integrating the Basic Skills Through the Content Areas." In *Basic Skills: Issues and Choices,* 41–47. Washington, D.C.: National Institute of Education, Department of Education, 1982.

————. "Know the Learner: First Step in Planning the Early Childhood Language/Reading Curriculum." In *Early Childhood Resource Guide,* edited by Hannah Scheffler, Bernice Cullinan, Dorothy Strickland, Rene Queen, 286–288. New York: Garland Press, 1982.

————. "Language and Literacy Development: Essential Knowledge for Beginning Teachers." In *Essential Knowledge for Beginning Educators,* edited by D. Smith, 112–123. [Washington, D.C.]: AACTE, 1983.

————. "Building Children's Knowledge of Stories." In *Research Foundations for a Literate America,* 163–176. [Lexington, Ky.]: Lexington Books, 1984.

————. "Early Childhood Foundations for Learning to Read in China." In *Reading in China,* n.p. [Washington, D.C.]: U.S. Department of Education, 1985.

Strickland, Dorothy Salley, and Denny Taylor. "Family Literacy: Myths and Magic." In *The Pursuit of Literacy,* 30–48. [Dubuque, Iowa]: Kendall/Hunt, 1985.

Strickland, Dorothy Salley, and J. Feeley. "Using Children's Concept of Story to Improve Reading and Writing." *Reading Thinking and Concept Development,* 163–176. New York: College Board Publications, 1985.

Strickland, Dorothy Salley, and B. Cullinan. "Language, Literature and Literacy in Classroom Research." *The Reading Teacher* (1986).

———. "Literature and Language." *Language Arts* (1986).

Strickland, Dorothy Salley. "Literature as a Key Element in Language Arts and Reading Programs." In *Children's Books in the Reading Program,* edited by B. Cullinan, 68–76. Newark, Del., 1987.

———. "Sharing Books with Young Children." *Scholastic Pre-K Today* (January 1987).

———. "Whole Language: What Does It Mean? How Does It Work?" *Scholastic News* 44, no. 8 (1987).

———. "Family Storybook Reading: Implications for Children, Families, and Curriculum." In *Emerging Literacy: Young Children Learn to Read and Write,* edited by Dorothy Strickland and Lesley Morrow, 27–34. Newark, Del.: International Reading Association, 1989.

———. "A Model for Change: Framework for an Emergent Literacy Curriculum." In *Emerging Literacy: Young Children Learn to Read and Write,* edited by Lesley Morrow, 135–146. Newark, Del.: International Reading Association, 1989.

———. "Pre-Kindergarten." In *Administration and Supervision of Reading Programs,* edited by Shelley Wepner and Joan Feeley, 41–58. New York: Teachers College Press, 1989.

———. "Teachers Coping with Change." In *The Role of Assessment in Early Literacy,* edited by Lesley Morrow and Jeffrey Smith, 205–218. New York: Prentice Hall, 1989.

———. "Emergent Literacy: New Perspective on How Young Children Learn to Read and Write." *Educational Leadership* 57 (March 1990): 18–23.

———. "Interview: The Past, Present, and Future of Literacy Education: Comments from a Panel of Distinguished Educators, Part I." *The Reading Teacher* 43 (1990): 302–311.

———. "Interview: The Past, Present, and Future of Literacy Education: Comments from a Panel of Distinguished Educators, Part II." *The Reading Teacher* 43 (1990): 370–381.

Strickland, Dorothy Salley, and J. Feeley. "Research on Language Learners: Development in the Elementary School Years." In *Handbook on Learning and Teaching the English Language Arts,* edited by J. Flood, J. Jensen, D. Lapp, and J. Squire, 286–302. New York: Macmillan, 1991.

Strickland, Dorothy. "Organizing a Literature-Based Curriculum." In *Invitation to Read,* edited by B. Cullinan, 110–121. Newark, Del.: International Reading Association, 1992.

———. "Educating African American Learners at Risk: Finding a Better Way." *Language Arts* 71 (1994): 328–336.

———. "Educating Low Income Black Children." In *Literacy Among Afro-*

American Youth, edited by V. Gadsden, 69–73. Cresskill, N.J.: Hampton Press, Inc., 1994.

———. "Meeting the Needs of Families in Family Literacy Programs." In *Family Literacy: Directions in Research and Implications for Practice,* edited by A. Benjamin and J. Lord, 89–96. Washington, D.C.: U.S. Department of Education, Office of Educational Research and Improvement, 1995.

———. "Pre-Elementary Programs: A Model for Professional Development." In *The Administration and Supervision of Reading Programs,* edited by S. Wepner, D. Strickland, and J. Feeley, 41–58. New York: Teachers College Press, 1995.

———. "Reinventing our Literacy Programs: Books, Basics, Balance." *The Reading Teacher* (December–January 1995): 294–303.

Weiss, S., Dorothy Salley Strickland, and G. Bronco. "Reader Response: It's Okay to Talk in the Classroom." *The Language and Literacy Spectrum* 5 (1995): 65–70.

Strickland, Dorothy Salley, and M.R. Strickland. "Language and Litercay: The Poetry Connection." *Language Arts* 74 (1997): 201–206.

Strickland, Dorothy Salley. "What's Basic in Reading? Finding Common Ground." *Educational Leadership* 55 (March 1998): 7–10.

———. "Principles of Instruction." In *Literacy Instruction for Culturally and Linguistically Diverse Students,* edited by M. Obitz, 50–53. Newark, Del.: International Reading Association, 1999.

———. "Classroom Intervention Strategies: Supporting the Literacy Development of Young Learners at Risk." In *Beginning Reading and Writing,* edited by D. Strickland and L. Morrow, 99–110. New York: Teachers College Press and Newark, Del.: International Reading Association, 2000.

Bio-Bibliographical Sources

Strickland, Dorothy S. "African American Women Writers in New Jersey: Biographical Questionnaire." Completed by Dorothy S. Strickland, 27 December 1993.

———. Correspondence with Sibyl E. Moses, 27 December 1993.

———. [Résumé]. Rev. September 2001. 33.

Talley, Jere Elaine 1947–

Personal   Born on 11 January 1947 in Washington, D.C.; oldest child of Geraldine Elaine Coleman Talley Turnstall (administrative assistant) of Atlantic City, New Jersey, and Leroy Talley (carpenter) of Cheraw, South Carolina; granddaughter (maternal) of Ruth Ann Coleman of Downingtown, Pennsylvania, and Cornelius Coleman of Washington, D.C.; granddaughter (paternal) of Corrette Minnie Talley of Cheraw and Solomon Talley; great granddaughter of Rosetta Johnson of Atlantic City; brother: Otearle Keith Tunstall. Education: Massachusetts Avenue School, Atlantic City, 1954–1959; Atlantic City High School, Atlantic City, 1962–1965; Wilberforce University, Wilberforce, Ohio, B.S., Elementary Education, 1965–1969; University of Illinois, Champaign, Illinois, M.Ed., Educational Psychology, 1969–1970; University of Arkansas, Fayetteville, Arkansas, 1974–1977. Religion: African Methodist Episcopal; St. James A.M.E. Church, Atlantic City.

Residence in New Jersey   Atlantic City, 1949–1965.

Career   Lead consultant, Science Research Associates, Chicago, Illinois, 1970–1973; administrative assistant, State of Illinois, Springfield, 1973–1974; career development consultant, Houston, Texas, 1980–1981; training analyst, First City Bancorporation, Houston, 1981–1985; president, board of directors, 1989 to present, Amistad Bookplace, Houston, 1984 to present; instructor, Mansfield Business School, Houston, 1986–1988; counselor, University of Houston, College of Technology Center for Applied Technology, Job Search Center, Texas, 1987 to present.

Reflections

"I grew up surrounded by family which included my grandmother, aunts and an uncle as well as myself, my mother, and brother. Each summer, cousins and more visiting relatives and friends swelled our household. Growing up in the huge, old house that was my grandmother's was wonderful. There were enough adults so that there was always an ear to listen and many family rituals to be part of. The house was so large, seven bedrooms, two baths plus three full-sized apartments on the street level plus a huge back yard that there was always a place to curl up with a book. The women in my family influence me through their unwavering strength. 'My ladies' instilled by example the importance of the family without suffocating individuality. I was encouraged to explore my interests, dance, art, athletics, rock collecting and yes, writing. When I left home I was secure enough in myself to test what the world had to offer. I seriously started writing poetry in April of 1967 and have never stopped. I started writing fiction in

1985 because I wanted to see if I could be any good at that. Poetry is easier for me for some reason but, actually I took on both purely for the challenge and the satisfaction the end product each genre gives me."

Publications
Books
Talley, Jere. *Sweet Bitch: Poems.* Houston, Tex.: Oceansun Publications [1984]. 62.

Talley, Jere. *Matters of the Heart: Poems.* [Houston, Tex.] Oceansun Publications [1985]. 41 [i].

Poetry
Talley, Jere. "Juggling." *Essence* 16 (August 1985): 100.

———. "Love." *Essence* 19 (April 1989): 123.

Broadsides
———. "An African American Woman's Praisesong Celebration." [Houston, Tex.]: Oceansun Publications, 1986.

———. "Another Woman Has Been Found Dead . . . In Memory of Mrs. Betty J. Mayes." [Houston, Tex.]: Oceansun Publications, 1987.

———. "Refuse to be Lonely." [Houston, Tex.]: Oceansun Publications, 1988.

———. "Sisters." [Houston, Tex.]: Oceansun Publications, 1989.

———. *"Freedom and Justice: Now, What About Clarence Brandley."* [Houston, Tex.]: Oceansun Publications, 1989.

Bio-Bibliographical Sources
Duran, Mary. "A.C. Native's Poetry Published." *The Press* (Atlantic City, N.J.) 11 April 1984, 9.

Talley, Jere. "African American Women Writers in New Jersey: Biographical Questionnaire." Completed by Jere Talley, 3 September 1989.

———. Letter to Sibyl E. Moses, 3 September 1989.

TATE, CLAUDIA C. 1946–2002

Personal Born on 14 December 1946 in Long Branch, New Jersey; daughter of Mary Austin Tate (mathematician) and Harold Tate (electronic engineer); children: Read Hubbard and Jerome Lindsey, III. Education: River Street School, Red Bank, New Jersey, 1952–1958; Knollwood School, Fair Haven, New Jersey, 1958–1961; Rumson-Fair Haven Regional School, Fair Haven, 1961–1965; University of Michigan, Ann Arbor, Michigan, B.A., English and American literature, 1968; Harvard University, Cambridge,

Claudia C. Tate.
Photograph by Ron Carter.

Massachusetts, M.A., English and American literature and language, 1971; Harvard University, Cambridge, Massachusetts, Ph.D., English and American literature and language, 1977.

Residence in New Jersey   Long Branch, 1946–1950; Red Bank, 1950–1958; Fair Haven, 1958–1968, 1997–2002.

Memberships   Modern Language Association; College Language Association; American Association of University Women; Association of Women's Studies; D.C. Commission on the Arts and the Humanities, literature panel, 1984–1985; D.C. Community Humanities Council, 1986; Alpha Kappa Alpha Sorority, Inc.

Career   Part-time instructor, English Department, Wheelock College, Boston, 1972; Massachusetts; teaching fellow, Department of English and American Literature, Harvard University, 1972–1975; part-time instructor, English Department, Lesley College, Cambridge, Massachusetts, 1973–1975; part-time instructor, English department, University of Massachusetts at Boston, 1973–1975; assistant professor of English, 1977–1983, associate professor of English, 1983–1989, Department of English, Howard University, Washington, D.C.; instructor, Afro-American Studies, Department of Afro-American Studies, Harvard University, Cambridge, 1975–1976; professor of English, George Washington University, Washington, D.C., 1989–1997; Professor of English, Princeton University, Princeton, New Jersey, 1997–2002.

Awards, Honors, Other Certificates   Graduate fellow, Harvard University, 1969–1972; fellow, DuBois Institute for Afro-American Research, Harvard University, 1976–1977; member, Faculty Advisory Committee of the University Sponsored Research Program, 1978–1979; Howard University Faculty Development Grant, 1978–1979, 1979–1980; Andrew Mellon Incentive Award, 1978–1979, 1982–1983, 1983–1984; National Endowment for the Humanities Postdoctoral Fellowship for Independent Study, 1979–1980; Outstanding Young Woman of America, 1980; Member, Modern Language Association Delegate Assembly, 1984–1986.

Publications

  Books

Tate, Claudia, ed. *Black Women Writers at Work.* New York: Continuum, 1983. xxvi, 213. British edition: Oldcastle Books, Great Britain, 1985; Spanish edition: Noema Editores, S.A. Mexico, 1986; Japanese edition: Shobun-Sha, Tokyo, 1987.

———, ed. *The Works of Katherine Davis Chapman Tillman.* New York: Oxford University Press, 1991. xxxv, 437.

———. *Domestic Allegories of Political Desire: The Black Heroine's Text at the Turn of the Century.* New York: Oxford University Press, 1992. x, 302, illus.

———. *The Selected Works of Georgia Douglas Johnson.* New York: G. K. Hall; London: Prentice Hall International, 1997. lxxii, 448.

———. *Psychoanalysis and Black Novels: Desire and the Protocols of Race.* New York: Oxford University Press, 1998. xvi, 238, illus.

Articles and Book Chapters

Tate, Claudia. "*Black Boy:* Richard Wright's 'Tragic Sense of Life,' " *Black American Literature Forum* 10, no. 4 (winter 1976): 117–119.

———. "Corregidora: Ursa's Blues Medley," *Black American Literature Forum,* 13, no. 4 (winter, 1979): 139–141.

———. "An Interview with Gayl Jones." *Black American Literature Forum* 13, no. 4 (winter 1979): 142–149.

———. "On White Critics and Black Aestheticians." *C.L.A. Journal* 12, no. 4 (June 1979): 383–389.

———. "Nella Larsen's *Passing:* A Problem of Interpretation." *Black American Literature Forum* 14, no. 4 (winter 1980): 142–146. Reprinted in *Contemporary Literary Criticism: Volume 37,* edited by Daniel G. Marowski, 216–218. Detroit: Gale Research Company, 1986.

———. "Christian Existentialism in Richard Wright's *The Outsider.*" *C.L.A. Journal,* 25, no. 4 (June 1982): 371–395.

———. " 'In Her Own Right,' excerpt from *Black Women Writers at Work.*" *Essence* (October 1983): 24–27.

———. "Black Women Writers—An Emerging Voice." *Topic,* no. 153. USIA (1984): 59–61.

———. "Should We Expect Black Women To Be Supermothers?" *Ebony* 39, no. 11 (September 1984): 84–86, 88, 90.

———. "An Introduction to Gayl Jones." *An Anthology of Short Stories Written by Women in the United States,* edited by Susan Koppleman. Bloomington: University of Indiana Press, 1985.

———. "Anger So Flat: Gwendolyn Brooks' *Annie Allen.*" In *A Life Distilled: Critical Essays on the Poetry of Gwendolyn Brooks,* edited by Maria Mootry and Gary Smith, 140–150. Urbana: University of Illinois Press, 1985.

———. "Notes on the Invisible Women in Ralph Ellison's *Invisible Man.*" In *Speaking for You Ralph: A Collection of Essays on Invisible Man,* edited by Kimberly Benston, 163–172. Washington, D.C.: Howard University Press, 1985.

———. "Pauline Elizabeth Hopkins: Our Literary Foremother." In *Conjuring: Black Women, Fiction and Literary Tradition,* edited by Marjorie Pryse and Hortense Spillers, 53–66. Bloomington: University of Indiana Press, 1985. Reprinted in *Black Women in the United States History,* edited by Darlene Clark Hine, 1345–1358. Brooklyn: Carlson Publishing Inc., 1990.

———. "The Pondered Moment: May Miller's Meditative Poetry," *New Directions,* 12, no. 1 (January 1985): 30–33.

———. "On Black Literary Women and the Evolution of Critical Discourse," Review Essay. *Tulsa Studies in Women's Literature* 5, no. 1 (spring 1986): 111–123.

———. "Uncovering Female Cultures," Review Essay. *Women's Review of Books,* III, no. 1 (July 1986): 17–18.

———. "Gwendolyn Brooks." In *Encyclopedia of Contemporary Biography: Volume 13,* 209–210. Illinois: McGraw-Hill, 1987.

———. "Maya Angelou." In *Encyclopedia of Contemporary Biography: Volume 13*, 50–51. Illinois: McGraw-Hill, 1987.

———. "Introduction." In *The Flagellants*, by Carlene Hatcher Polite, vii–xxxi. Boston: Beacon Press, 1987.

———. "Laying the Floor; or, the History of the Formation of the Afro-American Canon." *Book Research Quarterly* 3, no. 2 (summer 1987): 60–78. Reprinted in *The New Calvacade: African American Writing from 1790 to the Present, volume II*, edited by Arthur P. Davis, J. Sunders Redding, and Joyce Ann Joyce, 752–775. Washington, D.C.: Howard University Press, 1992.

———. "Alice Walker." In *Encyclopedia of Contemporary Biography: Volume 15*, 506–508. Illinois: McGraw-Hill, 1988.

———. "Margaret Walker." In *Encyclopedia of Contemporary Biography: Volume 15*, 508–510. Illinois: McGraw-Hill, 1988.

———. "Nella Larsen." In *Encyclopedia of Contemporary Biography: Volume 14*, 366–367. Illinois: McGraw-Hill, 1988.

———. "Toni Morrison." In *Encyclopedia of Contemporary Biography: Volume 14*, 523–525. Illinois: McGraw-Hill, 1988.

———. "Zora Neale Hurston." In *Encyclopedia of Contemporary Biography: Volume 14*, 203–204. Illinois: McGraw-Hill, 1988.

———. "Reshuffling the Deck; or, (Re)Reading Race and Gender in Black Women's Writing." *Tulsa Studies in Women's Literature* 7, no. 1 (spring 1988): 119–132.

———. "Allegories of Black Female Desire; or ReReading Nineteenth-Century Narratives of Black Female Authority." In *Changing Our Own Words*, edited by Cheryl Wall, 98–126, 230–234. New Brunswick, N.J.: Rutgers University Press, 1989.

———. "Audre Lorde." In *The Heath Anthology*, edited by Paul Lauter, et al., 2935–2938. Atlanta: D.C. Heath, 1989.

———. "Alice Walker." In *Modern American Writers*, edited by Elaine Showater, 511–520. New York: Scribners, 1990.

———. "Desire and Death in *Quicksand* by Nella Larson." *American Literary History* 7, no. 2 (summer 1995): 234–260.

———. "Introduction." In *Dark Princess: A Romance*, by William E. B. DuBois, ix–xxviii. Jackson, Miss.: Banner Books, 1995.

———. "Freud and His 'Negro': Psychoanalysis as Ally and Enemy of African Americans." *Journal for the Psychoanalysis of Culture & Society* 1, no. 1 (spring 1996): 53–62.

———. "Hitting 'A Straight Lick with a Crooked Stick': *Seraph on the Suwanee*, Zora Neale Hurston's Whiteface Novel." *Discourse: A Journal for Theoretical Studies in Media and Culture* 19, no. 1 (fall 1996): 72–87. Rev. version of essay published in *The Psychoanalysis of Race*, edited by Christopher Lane, 380–394. New York: Columbia University Press, 1998.

———. "The Personal in Scholarship: The Inevitability of the Personal." *PMLA* 111, no. 5 (October 1996): 1147–1148.

————. Entries on Katherine Davis Chapman Tillman, Pauline Elizabeth Hopkins, *Contending Forces*, Kristin Hunter, and *Women's Era*. In *The Oxford Companion to African American Literature*, 366–367, 170–171, 375–376, 785–786. New York: Oxford University Press, 1997.

Book Reviews

Tate, Claudia. Review of *The Song of Solomon*, by Toni Morrison. *C.L.A. Journal* 21, no. 2 (December 1977): 327–329.

————. Review of *Images of Africa in American Literature* by Marion Berghahn. *Black American Literature Forum* 12, no. 3 (fall 1978): 131–132.

————. Review of *Afro-American Literature: The Reconstruction of Instruction*, edited by Dexter Fisher and Robert Stepto. *Black American Literature Forum* 13, no. 4 (winter 1979): 152–153.

————. "The Tragic Mulatto Revisited," review article of *Neither White Nor Black: The Tragic Mulatto Character in American Fiction*, by Judith R. Berzon. *Black American Literature Forum* 13, no. 4 (winter 1979): 152–153.

————. Review article of *Black Foremothers: Three Lives*, by Dorothy Sterling. *Black American Literature Forum* 14, no. 3 (fall 1980): 131–132.

————. "Growing Up Colored," Review of *Betsy Brown*, by Ntozake Shange. *The Washington Post* (17 June 1985): D9.

————. "Triple-Forged Trinity." Review of *The Bone People*, by Keri Hulme. *The New York Times Book Review* (17 November 1985): 11.

————. "Great Expectations." Review of Barbara Christian's *Black Feminist Criticism*. *Belles Lettres* (November–December 1985): 4.

————. Review of *Linden Hills*. *San Francisco Review of Books* (May/June 1985): 11.

————. "All the Preacher's Women." Review of *Almost Midnight*, by Don Belton. *The New York Times Book Review* (17 August 1986): 24.

————. "Recovery, Race, and Sisterhood." Review of *Prologue: The Novels of Black American Women, 1891–1965*, by Carole Watson; *Black and White Women of the Old South: The Peculiar Sisterhood in American Literature*, by Minrose C. Gwin. *Belles Lettres*. (March–April 1986): 4.

————. Review of *Beloved*, by Toni Morrison. *Sisters: A National Council of Negro Women, Inc. Publication* (spring 1988): 40 and 46.

————. Review of *Reconstructing Womanhood: The Emergence of the Afro-American Woman Novelist*, by Hazel V. Carby. *Legacy* 4, no. 2 (fall 1988): 57–58.

————. Short Reviews of *A Spy in the Enemies Country*, by Donald A. Petesch, and *The Poems of Phillis Wheatley*, by Phillis Wheatley. In *American Studies International* 37, no. 2 (October 1989): 103–104.

————. Short Reviews of *Black Women Writing Autobiography*, by Joanne M. Braxton, and *Afro-American Literary Study in the 1990s*, edited by Houston A. Baker, Jr. and Patricia Redmond. *American Studies International* 28, no. 2 (1990): 106–107.

————. Review of *Inspiring Influences*, by Michael Awkward, *Critical Essays on Toni Morrison*, by Nellie McKay, and *Afro-American Women Writers*,

1746–1933, by Ann Allen Shockley. In *Tulsa Studies of Women's Literature* 9, no. 2 (fall 1990): 317–321.

————. Review of *Down From the Mountaintop—Black Women's Novels in the Wake of the Civil Rights Movement, 1966–1989*, by Melissa Walker. *American Studies International* 30, no. 1 (April 1992): 130–131.

————. Review of *The Other Side of the Story—Structures and Strategies of Contemporary Feminist Narrative*, by Molly Hite; *Race, Gender, and Desire—Narrative Strategies in the Fiction of Toni Cade Bambara, Toni Morrison, and Alice Walker*, by Elliott Butler-Evans; *Wild Women in the Whirlwind—Afra-American Culture and the Contemporary Literary Renaissance*, edited by Joanne M. Braxton and Andrée Nicola McLaughlin. *Tulsa Studies in Women's Literature* 11, no. 1 (spring 1992): 125–128.

————. Review of *Plotting Change—Contemporary Women's Fiction*, by Linda Anderson. *American Studies International* 31, no. 1 (April 1993): 144.

————. "Reconstructing the Renaissance of U.S. Literature." Review of *To Wake the Nations—Race in the Making of American Literature*, by E. J. Sundquist. *American Quarterly* 46, no. 4 (December 1994): 589–594.

————. Review of *"Everyday Use" by Alice Walker*, edited and with an introduction by Barbara T. Christian. *African American Review* 30, no. 2 (winter 1996): 308–309.

————. Review of *The Harlem Renaissance in Black and White*, by George Hutchinson. *African American Review* 31, no. 3 (fall 1997): 517–518.

————. Review of *The Harlem Renaissance in Black and White*, by George Hutchinson. *American Literature* 69, no. 3 (September 1997): 636–637.

————. Review of *Theorizing Black Feminisms: The Visionary Pragmatism of Black Women*, edited by Stanlie M. James and Abena P. A. Busia; *Black Women Novelists and the Nationalist Aesthetic*, by Madhu Dubney; and *Discarded Legacy: Politics and Poetics in the Life of Frances E. W. Harper 1825–1911*, by Melba Joyce Boyd. *Signs* 22, no. 2 (winter 1997): 462–465.

Bio-Bibliographical Sources

May, Hal, ed. *Contemporary Authors: A Bio-Bibliographical Guide to Current Writers in Fiction, General Nonfiction, Poetry, Journalism, Drama, Motion Pictures, Television, and Other Fields, vol. 121*. Detroit: Gale Research Co., 1987.

Tate, Claudia. Correspondence with Sibyl E. Moses. 15 August 1985.

————. [Résumé], 2000. 6.

TAYLOR, HOPE ROSEMARY 1955–

Personal   Born on 1 December 1955 in Tucson, Arizona; youngest child of Gladys Wade Powell Taylor (social worker) of Milton, Massachusetts, and John Anderson Taylor (U.S. Army) of Tucson, Arizona; granddaughter (maternal) of Gladys Powell of Louisville, Kentucky, and Lawrence Powell of Milton, Massachusetts; granddaughter (paternal) of Louise and John Taylor; sister: Anne Powell and Taylor Felton. Education: Manhattanville College, Purchase, New York, B.A., political science, 1977; Kean University, Union, New Jersey, graduate studies in education administration. Religion: Roman Catholic. Residence in New Jersey: Orange, East Orange, and South Orange, 1960–1999; Hillsborough, 1999 to present. Career: Teacher, Maplewood Middle School, Maplewood, New Jersey.

Reflections

"My mother was and remains the strongest guiding influence in my life. Although she is deceased, her presence is vibrant and constant. A graduate of Howard University in the early 1940s, she was published in the Howard University Press. She spent her life in community and social service work. Her encouragement has allowed me to always strive for the best.

The life experience which has most altered my path was being diagnosed ten years ago with SLE, Systemic Lupus Erythematosus. Although I have had every major organ affected and have undergone chemotherapy several times, I have continued to write, write, and live! [I am] an activist for human rights, in general, and for gay, lesbian, and transgender rights."

Publications

Taylor-McGriff, Hope. *Overflow.* Orange, N.J.: Bryant & Dillon Publishers, 1993. 103.

Taylor-McGriff, Hope. *To the Tune of Hope.* Orange, N.J.: Bryant & Dillon Publishers, 1996. 197. illus.

Bio-Bibliographical Sources

Durbach, Elaine. "Giving Them Wings: Maplewood Middle School Helps Kids Become Teens." *Maplewood Matters Magazine.* Available: <http://www.maplewoodonline.com/matters/middle_school.shtml> Accessed 5 July 2001.

Taylor, Hope Rosemary. "African American Women Writers in New Jersey: Biographical Questionnaire." Completed by Hope R. Taylor, 3 July 2001.

THANDEKA 1946–

Personal   Former name, 1946–1984, Sue Booker. Born on 25 March 1946 in Jersey City, New Jersey; only child of Erma Barbour Booker (art teacher) of Washington, D.C. and Merrel Daniel Booker (Baptist minister) of Hoboken, New Jersey. Education: University of Chicago Laboratory High School, Chicago Illinois, 1963; University of Illinois, Champaign, Illinois, B.S., journalism, 1967; Columbia University, New York, New York, M.S., journalism, 1968; University of California at Los Angeles, Los Angeles, California, M.A., history of religions, 1982; Clare-

Thandeka.
Photograph © Ellen Levine Ebert
Portrait Photography.

mont Graduate School, Claremont, California, Ph.D., philosophy of religion/theology, 1988. Religion: Unitarian Universalist.

Residence in New Jersey   Summit.

Career: Production assistant, Children's Television Workshop (*Sesame Street*) New York, 1968–1969; producer, writer, director of *The Black Frontier*, a docudrama series for PBS, KUON-TV, Lincoln, Nebraska, 1969–1970; staff producer and writer, KCET-TV, Los Angeles, 1970–1973; associate professor of journalism, California State University, Long Beach, 1973; staff producer and writer, KNBC-TV, Los Angeles, 1975–1984; assistant professor of philosophy, San Francisco State University, San Francisco, 1987–1991; affiliate minister, The Community Church of New York, New York, 1990–1991; assistant professor of religion, Williams College, Williamstown, Massachusetts, 1991–1997; visiting scholar, Union Theological Seminary, New York, 1996–1998; associate professor of theology and culture, Meadville Lombard Theological School, Chicago, Illinois, 1998 to present; community minister, Rockford Unitarian Universalist Church, Rockford, Illinois, 2001 to present; director, The Center for Community Values, Chicago.

Memberships   The American Academy of Religion; Society for the Study of Black Religion; The Unitarian Universalist Ministers Association; Directors Guild of America, Inc.

Awards, Honors, Other Certificates   Travel fellowship to the Soviet Union, University of Illinois, 1965; KCET-TV playwriting fellowship, Eugene O'Neill Playwrights' Conference, 1973; one Emmy award, six Emmy nominations, Grand Prize: Atlanta International Film Festival, 1971–1977; National Winner, NBC Employee Playwriting Competition, 1983; Goethe Institute Fellowship, Bremen, Germany, 1985; First Place Prize, Jean Fairfax-Muskiwinni Fellowship for African-American Women in Doctoral Programs in Religion, 1985; research fellowship, San Francisco State University, 1989; fellow, Stanford Humanities Center, Stanford, University, 1990–1991; Kate-Connolly-Weinert Award, the American Academy of Religion, for the panel "The Courage to be Human: White Racial Induction and Christian Shame Theology," 1998.

Publications

  Books

Booker, Merrel Daniel, et al., comp. *Cry at Birth: Collected and Edited by the Bookers.* New York: McGraw-Hill [1971]. xviii, 172, illus.

Thandeka. *The Embodied Self: Friedrich Schleiermacher's Solution to Kant's Problem of the Empirical Self.* SUNY Series in Philosophy. Albany: State University of New York Press, 1995. xiv, 151.

———. *Learning to Be White: Money, Race, and God in America.* New York: Continuum, 1999. x, 169.

  Articles/Short Essays

Booker, Sue. "Paul Tillich's Earth Mother." *Epoche* 6, no.1–2 (1978): 33–47.

Thandeka. "I've Known Rivers: Black Theology's Response to Process Theology." [Reply to W.R. Jones, T. Walker, and H. J. Young, 240–281] *Process Studies* 18, no.4 (winter 1989): 282–293.

―――. "Schleiermacher's *Dialektik:* The Discovery of the Self that Kant Lost." *Harvard Theological Review* 85, no.4 (1992): 433–452.

―――. "The Fate of African Americans." *Tikkun: A Bimonthly Jewish Critique of Politics, Culture & Society* 11 (September/October 1996): 38–44.

―――. "The Self Between Feminist Theory and Theology." *Horizons in Feminist Theology: Identity, Tradition, and Norms* (1997): 79–98, 237–244.

―――. "The Whiting of Euro-Americans: A Divide and Conquer Strategy." *The World* XII: no.4 (July/August 1998): 14–20.

―――. "The Cost of Whiteness." *Tikkun: A Bimonthly Jewish Critique of Politics, Culture & Society* (May/June 1999):33–38.

―――. "Middle-Class Poverty." *The World* XII, no.5 (September/October 1999):16–23.

―――. "Why Anti-Racism Will Fail." *The Journal of Liberal Religion* I, no.1 (October 1999): 1–11.

―――. "Genesis 1:1." *Tikkun: A Bimonthly Jewish Critique of Politics, Culture & Society* (January/February 2000): 48.

―――. "Counting Our Blessings." In *Thematic Preaching: An Introduction,* by Jane Rzepka and Kenneth Sawyer, n.p. St. Louis, Mo.: Chalice Press, 2001.

Book Reviews

Thandeka. Review of *Fundamentals of Buddhist Ethics,* by Gunapala Dharmasin. *The Pacific World: Journal of the Institute of Buddhist Studies* no. 6 (fall 1990): 115–117.

―――. Review of *Hope in Progress: A Theology of Social Pluralism,* by Henry James Young. *Process Studies* no. 22 (summer 1993): 111–112

―――. Review of *Facing Up to the American Dream: Race, Class, and the Soul of the Nation,* by Jennifer L. Hochschild. *The World: Journal of the Unitarian Universalist Association* 11, no.1 (1997): 57–58.

―――. Review of *Religious Imagination and the Body: A Feminist Analysis,* by Paula M. Cooey. *Religion and Health* 36, no.1 (1997): 99.

―――. Review of *Apocalypse Now and Then: A Feminist Guide to the End of the World,* by Catherine Keller. *The World* 11, no. 5 (July/August 1997): 42.

―――. Review of *Class Warfare: Interviews with David Barsamian,* by David Barsamian and Noam Chomsky. *The World* 12, no. 3 (May/June 1998): 51.

―――. Review of *Don't Call Us Out of Name: The Untold Lives of Women and Girls in Poor America,* by Lisa Dobson. *The World* 13, no. 1 (January/February 1999): 47–48.

―――. Review of *Rich Man's War: Class, Caste, and Confederate Defeat in the Lower Chattahoochee Valley,* by David Williams. *The World* 13, no. 6 (November/December 1999): 53–55.

Bio-Bibliographical Sources:

Thandeka. "Curriculum Vitae." [Rev. 2001], 11.

"The Rev. Dr. Thandeka, Associate Professor of Theology and Culture." Available: *http://www.meadville.edu/thandeka.html* Accessed 11 July 2001.

THOMAS, NATURI SONGHAI 197?

Naturi Songhai Thomas.
Photograph by Kevin Fox.

Personal   Born on 4 May 197? in Los Angeles, California; oldest child of Donna R. Wells-Thomas (interior decorator) of Dijon, France, and William John Thomas (home restorer) of Cape May, New Jersey; granddaughter (maternal) of Geraldine Wells of Dijon, France, and Donald R. Wells of Irvington, New Jersey; granddaughter (paternal) of Cleopatra Mae Thomas of New Orleans, Louisiana, and Tommy Lee Thomas of Harlem, New York; brother: Darius Alan Thomas. Education: The Looking Glass School, Bloomfield, New Jersey; St. Michael's Parochial School, Union, New Jersey; Columbia High School, Maplewood, New Jersey. Religion: Roman Catholic.

Residence in New Jersey   Maplewood; South Orange; Tom's River; West New York; Clifton.

Career   Actress (theater, film, television, video).

Memberships   Screen Actors Guild, New York.

Awards, Honors, Other Certificates   Featured speaker, "Read To Me" Conference, St. Peter's College, Jersey City, 1999.

Reflections

"I can easily name the two writers who've most influenced me, Toni Morrison, with *The Bluest Eye*, and Maya Angelou's *I Know Why the Caged Bird Sings*. My parents are to be thanked as well. My father, for teaching me to read at two. He said it saved him money on toys, and my mother for treating all my childish ramblings and girlish meanderings as literary second comings."

Publication

Thomas, Naturi. *Uh-oh! It's Mama's Birthday!* Illustrated by Keinyo White. Morton Grove, Ill.: Albert Whitman & Co., 1997. [22].

Bio-Bibliographical Source

Thomas, Naturi. "African American Women Writers in New Jersey: Biographical Questionnaire." Completed by Naturi Thomas, April 2001.

THOMAS, VEONA YOUNG 194?–

Personal   Born on 19 December 194? in Harlem, New York; third child of Elizabeth and Vernon Young; granddaughter (paternal) of Elizabeth Robinson (minister); husband: John R. Thomas, Sr.; children: John R.

Thomas, Jr. and Timothy D. Thomas. Education: Lehman College, Bronx, New York, B.A., magna cum laude, black studies and education, with special studies in theater, 1993.

Residence in New Jersey Englewood; Hackensack, 1949–1996; Teaneck, 1996 to present.

Career Entrepreneur, owner of first African-American boutique in Bergen County, New Jersey; created "Shades of Delight" Models; organized first Black Book Fair, Black Art Exhibit, and others,

Veona Young Thomas.
Photograph by Jim Edmonds.

1969–1985; staff writer and columnist, *Black Masks* (theater magazine) and *The Torchbearer* (newspaper), 1988–1992; publisher and editor, *Write on Newsletter* for aspiring writers; creator, REJOTI Productions; cooriginator and guide, Performing Writers Workshop, National Black Theater, New York; founder and director, The Creative Process Dramatic Group; founder and director, Black Writer's Weekend Retreat, Catskill Mountains, New York; founder, "Write On" Annual Contest; dramaturg, Frank Silvera Writers Workshop, New York; playwright, Frederick Douglas Cultural Arts Center, New York; playwright, Negro Ensemble Playwright Workshop, New York; playwright, Frank Silvera Writers Workshop, New York; playwright, Frank Silvera Musical Symposium, New York, 1983 to present.

Memberships Morani Shujaa Honor Society, Lehman College, Bronx, New York; The Dramatist Guild; National Black Theater Network; Audience Development Committee, Inc. (AUDELCO), Harlem, New York.

Awards, Honors, Other Certificates Jacob Hammer Memorial Prize for writing *Like Father Like Son,* English Department, Lehman College, Bronx, New York; Alice Heniger Prize in Literature for Children, English Department, Lehman College, Bronx; Jane Harris Award, Lehman College, Bronx; award for academic excellence, Department of Black Studies, Lehman College, Bronx; award for Black Studies, Morani Shujaa Honor Society, Lehman College, Bronx; winner of Drew University one-act play competition, *For Sistahs Only,* Madison, New Jersey, 1988; Dean's List, Lehman College, Bronx, 1992; listed in *Contemporary Black American Playwrights and Their Plays* . . .

Reflections

"My mother, Elizabeth Young, was always supportive of whatever I did. Later on, my eldest sister became my cheerleader. In the late 1980s, playwright Shauneille Perry encouraged me to go back to college and complete my degree."

Publications

Books

Thomas, Veona. *Laughter, Lyrics & Tears, A Collection of Prose and Poetry.* [Saddlebrook, N.J.: Rejoti Publications, 1983]. 48 [1].

———. *The Way We Feel and the Way It Is.* [Saddlebrook, N.J.: Rejoti Publications, 1984]. 16 [1].

———. *Never Too Late To Love.* Teaneck, N.J.: Rejoti Publishing and Productions, 1987. 77 [2], illus. Third printing, 1996.

Produced Plays

Raisin' Canaan. Black Spectrum Theater, Queens, New York, 1991; Knoxville, Tenn., 1996.

Like Father Like Son. Riant Theater, New York, 1996.

Tuesday In No Man's Land. Riant Theater, New York, 1991; complete season at the Majestic Lodge #153, New Jersey, 1994–1995.

Mattie Two Braids. A complete season at the Majestic Lodge #153, New Jersey, 1994–1995.

Nana's Got the Blues. A complete season at the Majestic Lodge #153, New Jersey, 1994–1995; Riant Theater, New York, 1992.

Heaven Sent. Premier, National Black Theater, New York, 1989–1990; H.A.D.L.E.Y. Players, New York, 1990; Ad Hoc Committee, Orrie de Nuyer, New Jersey, 1991; REJOTI Productions, The Theater of Riverside Church, New York, 1992: Encore Theater, Baltimore, Md., 1994.

Teamwork. Teaneck Women's Club, Teaneck, New Jersey, 1991; REJOTI Productions, N.J., 1994.

Chocolate Memories. REJOTI Productions, New Jersey, 1994.

A Watch On Martin Luther King. Board of Education Magnet School Program, Teaneck, New Jersey, 1987; Thomas Jefferson School, New Jersey, 1991; Benjamin Franklin School, New Jersey, 1991; REJOTI Productions, New Jersey, 1994.

Girlfriends. John Harms Cultural Center, Englewood, New Jersey, 1986; Black Social Workers, Jersey City College, New Jersey, 1987; Black Health Project, Paterson, New Jersey, 1987; 100 Black Women, Englewood, New Jersey, 1987; Oz Theater Company, New York, New York, 1989; Avalon Theater, New York, 1990. Women's Day. Passaic County Day Care Center, New Jersey, 1986; Jersey City State College, 1987; Englewood Hospital Theater, 1987; Oz Theater Company, New York, 1989.

For Sistahs Only. Drew University Theological School, Madison, New Jersey, 1988.

Nzinga's Children. World premier, National Black Theater, 1985; McCree Theater, Flint, Michigan, 1986; New World Theater, University of Massachusetts, 1988.

A Matter of Conscience. National Black Theater, New York, 1987.

This Younger Generation. Board of Education Magnet School Program, Teaneck, New Jersey,

Television

Raisin' Canaan. TCI Cable, New Jersey, 1993.

Second Best. Filmscript writer/project director for YOUSA; produced by UA Columbia Cable TV, New Jersey, 1989.

Radio

Never Too Late To Love, A Soap Opera. WBAI-FM, New York, 1996.
Forever Friends. One-act play. WBAI-FM, New York, 1994.

Bio-Bibliographical Sources

Thomas, Veona. "African American Women Writers in New Jersey: Bio-graphical Questionnaire." Completed by Veona Thomas, 12 November 1996.

————. Letter to Sibyl E. Moses. 7 May 1985.

————. "Resume—Veona Thomas: Playwright-Writer." 1996.

THOMPSON, MARY LOUISE 1943–

Personal   Born on 16 February 1943 in Pittsburgh, Pennsylvania; third child of Louise Scott Thompson Blanks (income tax consultant, notary public, and retired state supervisor) of Smithville Township, Marlboro County, South Carolina, and Fred Thompson (minister and house painter; deceased) of Gadston, Alabama; granddaughter (maternal) of Louise Short Scott of Marlboro County, and Eli Scott of Cheraw, South Carolina; grand-daughter (paternal) of Mattie Hollis and Charlie Thompson; sisters: Cecelia Marie and Gloria Jean; brothers: Raymond (deceased), Edward Lee, Gary, and Frances Malladew; Education: Manchester Elementary School, Pittsburgh, 1948–1951; Robert Memorial Junior High School, Vineland, New Jersey, 1951–1958; Vineland High School, New Jersey, 1958–1961; Mercer County Community College, Trenton, New Jersey, A.A., social sciences, 1971; Trenton State College, Trenton, New Jersey, B.S., elementary education, 1972; Rider College, Lawrenceville, New Jersey, M.A., graduate program for administrators, 1975–1977; Seattle University, Graduate School of Education, Seattle, Washington, 1984; University of Pennsylvania, Graduate School of Education, Philadelphia, Pennsylvania, 1985–1987. Religion: African Methodist Episcopal Zion.

Residence in New Jersey   Vineland, 1951–1962, 1985; Trenton, 1965–1978; Atlantic City, 1985–1986; Camden, 1986–1988; Eatontown, 1988 to present.

Career   Recreational attendant, Vineland State School, Vineland, 1961–1962; occupational therapy specialist, United States Women's Army Corps, U.S. and Landstuhl, Germany, 1962–1965; instructor, counselor, social worker, United Progress, Inc., Trenton, 1967–1972; prevocational instructor, Manpower Development Training Act, Mercer Skills Center, Trenton, 1972; various positions with the New Jersey state government, 1972–1978; program administrator, Department of Environmental Protection's Office of Youth Services; area coordinator, Department of Transportation's Office of Community Involvement; program development specialist, Division of Youth and Family Services' Social Services Planning Unit; coordinator, Department of Community Affairs' Office of Youth Services' Juvenile Justice Committee and the Governor's State Committee on Children and Youth; acting regional director and deputy regional director,

U.S. Department of the Interior, Office of the Secretary, Office of Youth Programs, Manhattan, New York, and Seattle, 1978–1982; executive director Mizpah Inland Human Services, Inc., Mizpah, New Jersey; founder, Mizpah Childcare Learning Center, Mizpah, 1985–1988. Pastor, Wesley Memorial A.M.E. Zion Church, Fairton, New Jersey; associate pastor, St. John A.M.E. Zion Church, Mizpah; founder and administrator, Sojourner Truth Child Care Learning Center and Emergency Feeding Program, Seattle; pastor, Sojourner Truth A.M.E. Zion Church, Seattle; associate minister, Ebenezer A.M.E. Zion Church, Seattle; pastor, Faith Chapel A.M.E. Zion Church, Mt. Holly, New Jersey; pastor, Mt. Zion A.M.E. Zion Church, Eatontown, New Jersey, 1972 to present.

Memberships   Alpha Kappa Alpha Sorority, Inc.; National Political Congress of Black Women; New Jersey Education Association; National Association of Clergy Women; National Council of Negro Women.

Awards, Honors, Other Certificates   First female pastor ever assigned to 143-year old Mt. Zion A.M.E. Zion Church, Eatontown, New Jersey; plaque in honor of 143rd anniversary of Mt. Zion A.M.E. Zion Church, Eatontown mayor and council, 1988; principal/supervisor certificate, New Jersey and Washington State, grades K–8; executive management certificate, Office of Personnel Management.

Reflections

"My mother, Mrs. Louise Scott Thompson Blanks, was the most influential person in my life with regard to everything. She always read stories to us, especially biblical stories for children. This sparked an early desire to read. She also taught us pre-school math, words, etc. I suppose I was in born with literary skills. I have been scribbling either poems or narratives since age 6 or 7. My first acceptable poem was one written as a 5th grade student. I received an A for this assignment. Historically, there were many writers, artists, musicians and other gifted talented relatives: My deceased aunt, Shady Scott Kollock, wrote a book, *True Historical Facts About Africa,* many years ago; my uncle, Bernard Scott, published biblical charts and Christmas cards; my mother is the author of *Between Earth and Sky,* This is truly a masterpiece. Perhaps, some day she will receive due recognition."

Publication

Thompson, Mary L. *Inspirational and Seasonal Poems for the Young at Heart.* Mizpah, N.J.: MLT MaLot Publishers [1985]. 67, illus.

Bio-Bibliographical Sources

Thompson, Mary L. "African American Women Writers in New Jersey: Biographical Questionnaire." Completed by Mary L. Thompson, February 1989.

———. Correspondence with Sibyl E. Moses. "Update and Corrected Information." 23 March 1989.

———. [Résumé]. N.d., 3 leaves.

THOMPSON, MINDY *SEE* FULLILOVE, MINDY THOMPSON

THORNTON, JEANETTE FRANCES 1945–

Personal Born on 13 July 1945 in New York City; second child of Itasker Frances Edmonds Thornton (housewife) of East Beckley, West Virginia, and Donald Everett Thornton (laborer) of Long Branch, New Jersey; granddaughter (maternal) of Lurendia Edmonds and Alfonzo Edmonds, both of West Virginia; granddaughter (paternal) of Fannie Jane Payne Thornton and James P. Thornton of Long Branch; sisters: Donna (deceased), Yvonne, Linda, Rita, and Joann; husband: Emile Allen Powe, M.D., education: Gregory School, Long Branch; Long Branch High School, Long Branch; Monmouth College, West Long Branch, New Jersey, B.A., 1963–1968; Newark State College (Kean College), Union, New Jersey, M.A., 1970–1972; Rutgers University, New Brunswick, New Jersey, Ed. D., 1972–1975; Boston University, Boston, Massachusetts, M.D., 1977–1981

Jeanette F. Thornton (left) *and Rita L. Thornton* (right), *courtesy of Jeanette F. Thornton and Rita L. Thornton.*

Residence in New Jersey Long Branch, 1948–1977.
Career Psychiatrist.
Reflections
   "My parents have influenced my life greatly although I didn't know this until recently (the past five years)."
Publication
Thornton, Jeanette F., and Rita L. Thornton. *A Suitcase Full of Dreams: the Untold Story of a Woman Who Dared to Dream.* Atlantic Highlands, N.J.: Thornton Sisters Publishing House, 1996. 219.
Bio-Bibliographical Source
Thornton, Jeanette. "African American Women Writers in New Jersey: Biographical Questionnaire." Completed by Jeanette Thornton, January 2000.

THORNTON, RITA LOUISE 1952–

Personal Born on 28 May 1952 in Long Branch, New Jersey; fifth child of Itasker Frances Edmonds Thornton (housewife) of East Beckley, West Virginia, and Donald Everett Thornton (laborer) of Long Branch; granddaughter (maternal) of Lurendia Edmonds and Alfonzo Edmonds, both of West

Jeanette F. Thornton (left) and Rita L. Thornton (right), courtesy of Jeanette F. Thornton and Rita L. Thornton.

Virginia; granddaughter (paternal) of Fannie Jane Payne Thornton of Virginia and James P. Thornton of Long Branch; sisters: Donna (deceased), Jeanette, Yvonne, Linda, JoAnn (half sister), and Betty (foster sister); husband: Rev. David Earl Reaves (registered nurse and minister). Education: Gregory School, Long Branch; Long Branch High School, Long Branch; Mamouth College, West Long Branch, New Jersey, B.A., 1970–1973; Seton Hall University, Law School, Newark, New Jersey, J.D., 1989–1993; Rutgers University Graduate School, Newark, Ph.D. program, 1999 to present. Religion: Baptist.

Residence in New Jersey   Long Branch.

Career   Environmental lawyer.

Reflections

"My sister, Jeanette, has greatly influenced my life in two ways: (1) She allowed me to get to really know and understand my parents when they were young and new at parenting. Being the youngest girl in a family of five or six girls caused me to be very far removed from my parents to the extent that I really didn't know them and they were too tired to want to get to know me. (2) Through Jeanette, I have recently seen how my parents have influenced me in their own special way."

Publication

Thornton, Jeanette F., and Rita L. Thornton. *A Suitcase Full of Dreams: The Untold Story of a Woman Who Dared to Dream.* Atlantic Highlands, N.J.: Thornton Sisters Publishing House, 1996. 219.

Bio-Bibliographical Source

Thornton, Rita. "African American Women Writers in New Jersey: Biographical Questionnaire." Completed by Rita Thornton, January 2000.

THORNTON, YVONNE SHIRLEY 1947–

Personal   Born on 21 November 1947 in Manhattan, New York; middle child of Itaskere Frances Edmonds (domestic) of East Beckley, West Virginia, and Donald Everett Thornton (laborer) of Long Branch, New Jersey; granddaughter (maternal) of Lurendia and Alfonzo "Flood" Edmonds, both of West Virginia; granddaughter (paternal) of Fannie Jane Payne Thornton of Virginia and James P. Thornton of Long Branch, New Jersey; sisters: Donna Thornton (deceased 1993), Jeanette, Linda, Rita, and Betty; husband: Shearwood J. McClelland, M.D. (orthopedic surgeon); children: Shearwood McClelland, III, Kimberly Itaska McCelland. Education:

Gregory School, Garfield School, Long Branch, 1952–1959; Long Branch Junior High School, Long Branch, 1959–1961; Long Branch Senior High School, 1961–1965; Monmouth College, West Long Branch, New Jersey, B.S., biology, 1965–1969; Columbia University, College of Physicians and Surgeons, New York, New York, M.D., 1969–1973; Columbia University School of Public Health, Division of Executive Health Policy and Management, M.P.H., 1994–1996. Monmouth University, Monmouth, New Jersey, honorary degree, Doctor of Humane Letters, 1995. Religion: Baptist.

Yvonne S. Thornton. Photograph by Fred Gary Target Photographers, courtesy of Yvonne S. Thornton.

Residence in New Jersey Long Branch, 1948–1969; Hackensack (six months in 1982); Teaneck, December 1982 to present.

Career Assistant professor, obstetrics and gynecology, Uniformed Services University of the Health Sciences, Bethesda, Maryland, 1979–1982; assistant professor, obstetrics and gynecology, Cornell University Medical College, 1982–1989; associate professor, 1989–1992; associate clinical professor, obstetrics and gynecology, Columbia University College of Physicians and Surgeons, 1995–1998: clinical professor, obstetrics and gynecology, University of Medicine and Dentistry of New Jersey-New Jersey Medical School, 1998 to present; director, The Perinatal Diagnostic Testing Center; staff perinatologist, full-time attending staff, Department of Obstetrics and Gynecology, Morristown Memorial Hospital, Morristown, New Jersey.

Memberships Diplomat, National Board of Medical Examiners; diplomat, American Board of Obstetrics and Gynecology; fellow, American College of Obstetricians and Gynecologists (F.A.C.O.G.); fellow, American College of Surgeons (F.A.C.S.); American College of Physician Executives (A.C.P.E.); American Society of Human Genetics; Association of Professors of Gynecology and Obstetrics (A.P.G.O.); life member, The New York Academy of Medicine; American Institute of Ultrasound in Medicine (AIUM); Association of Women Surgeons; Society for Maternal-Fatal Medicine; The New York Obstetrical Society; The New York Gynecological Society; Alpha Kappa Alpha Sorority, Inc.

Awards, Honors, Other Certificates Lambda Sigma Tau, Monmouth College Honor Society, 1968, and elected secretary, 1969; highest degree graduate in Biology, Monmouth College, June 1969; Joseph Garrison Parker Award, Columbia University, College of Physicians and Surgeons, 1973; Distinguished Alumni Award, Monmouth College, October, 1984; Distinguished Alumni Hall of Fame, Long Branch High School, October 1993; First Place Winner, Daniel Webster Oratorical Competition, International Platform

Association (founded 1831), 1996; Award of Excellence in Literature, New Jersey Education Association, November 1996; Best Books for Young Adults, award from the American Library Association, for *The Ditchdigger's Daughters,* 1996.

Publications

Books

Thornton, Yvonne S. [as told to Jo Coudert]. *The Ditchdigger's Daughters: A Black Family's Astonishing Success Story.* New York: Birch Lane Press, 1995. 261. Reprint, New York: Viking/Penguin, 1996.

————., editor. *Primary Care for the Obstetrician and Gynecologist.* New York: Igaku-Shoin, 1997. xii, 276. illus

————. [with Jo Coudert] *Woman to Woman.* New York: Dutton Publishing, 1997. 368.

Articles

Graziano J. H., Y. S. Thornton, J. K. Leong, and A. Cerami. "Pharmacology of Cyanate. II. Effects on the Endocrine System." *The Journal of Pharmacology and Experimental Therapeutics* 185, no. 3 (June 1973): 667–675.

Thau, R. B., K. Sundaram, Y. S. Thornton, and L. S. Seidman. "Effects of Immunization with β-subunit of Ovine Luteinizing Hormone on Corpus Luteum Function in the Rhesus Monkey." *Fertility and Sterility* 31, no. 2 (February 1979): 200–204.

Thornton Y. S. "Caution of Treatment for Gonorrhea in Pregnancy." *Journal of the Medical Society of New Jersey* 76 (1979): 479.

Thornton, Y. S., and A. Cerami. "Sickle Cell Crisis During Pregnancy in a Patient with Hemoglobin SD Disease." *American Journal of Obstetrics and Gynecology* 139, no. 6 (March 1981): 739–740.

Thornton Y. S., S. Y. Yeh, and R. H. Petrie. "Antepartum Fetal Heart Rate Testing and the Post-term Gestation." *Journal of Perinatal Medicine* 10, no. 4 (1982): 196–202.

Yeh S. Y., S. L. Bruce, and Y. S. Thornton. "Intrapartum Monitoring and Management of the Postdate Fetus." *Clinics in Perinatology* 9, no. 2 (June 1982): 381–386.

Edersheim T. G., Y. S. Thornton , M. L. Alonso, and E. Kazam. "Effect of Chorionic Villus Sampling on Serum Alpha Fetoprotein Levels." *American Journal of Perinatology* 2, no. 4 (October 1985): 328–329.

Thornton Y. S., S. J. Birnbaum, and N. Lebowitz. "A Viable Pregnancy in a Patient with Myositis Ossificans Progressiva." *American Journal of Obstetrics and Gynecology* 156, no. 3 (March 1987): 577–578.

Thornton, Y. S. "Therapeutic Management of Myasthenia Gravis during Pregnancy, Labor and Delivery." *Contemporary OB/GYN* 31 (1988): 157–175.

Thornton, Y. S. "The Gravid Myasthenic." In *Perinatal Pharmacology,* edited by R. H. Petrie, n.p. Oradell, New Jersey: Medical Economics Book Division, 1989.

Thornton, Y. S., and E. T. Bowie. "Neonatal Hyperbilirubinemia After

Treatment of Leprosy." *Southern Medical Journal* 82, no. 5 (May 1989): 668.

Thornton, Y. S. "Autonomic Hyperreflexia in a Gravid Paraplegic." In *Clinical Decisions in Obstetrics and Gynecology,* edited by Robert C. Cefalo, n.p. Rockville, Md.: Aspen Publications, 1990.

————. "Are We Hippocrats or Hypocrites?" *Medical Economics* 71, no. 16 (August 1994): 24, 29, 32.

————. "How a Ditchdigger Made Doctors of His Daughters." *Medical Economics* 72, no. 23 (December 1995): 114.

Bio-Bibliographical Sources

Thornton, Yvonne S. "African American Women Writers in New Jersey: Biographical Questionnaire." Completed by Yvonne Thornton, 15 August 1999.

————. "Curriculum Vitae." June 1999. 8.

TRAVIS, NANCY ELIZABETH 1962–

Personal   Born on 6 March 1962 in Newark, New Jersey; oldest child of Irene Elizabeth Sanders Travis (elementary school teacher) of Charlotte, North Carolina, and David Joseph Travis (army officer and high school teacher) of Newark, New Jersey; granddaughter (maternal) of Ida Brown Sanders of Philadelphia, Pennsylvania, and William Sanders of Charlotte; granddaughter (paternal) of Louise Wilson Travis of Opalocka, Alabama, and Samuel James Travis of Lawrenceville, Virginia; brother: David Joseph Travis, Jr.; husband: Nelson Kofie, Ph.D.; child: Omar. Education: Kentopp School, East Orange, New Jersey, 1967–1971; Lincoln School, East Orange, 1972–1975; Far Brook School, Short Hills, New Jersey, 1975–1977; Scotch Plains-Fanwood High School, Scotch Plains, New Jersey, 1977–1980; Spelman College, Atlanta, Georgia, B.A., English, 1984; Wellesley College, Welles-

Nancy Elizabeth Travis.
Photograph by Eric Wagman,
courtesy of Phyllis Wagman and
Eric Wagman Studio.

ley, Massachusetts, Exchange Program, 1983; George Washington University, Washington, D.C., M.A., women's studies. Religion: Baptist.

Residence in New Jersey   Elizabeth, 1962; Hanover, 1963–1964; East Orange, 1966–1976; Fanwood, 1976–1984; Newark, 1984–1985; South Orange, 1985–1987.

Career   Public relations staff, YMCA, East Orange, summer 1983; project director, Students' Summer Writing Project, Maplewood, New Jersey, summer 1983; coordinator for essay contest, NAACP, Orange and Maplewood, New Jersey, 1986; advertising assistant, CBS Educational Publishing, New York, 1984–1985; editorial secretary, Black Enterprise Magazine, New York, 1985–1986; secretary, Earle Palmer Brown Companies, Newark, 1986–1987.

Memberships   Newark (New Jersey) Writers Guild.

Awards, Honors, Other Certificates   Howard University Press Book Publishing Institute, Washington, D.C., certificate, 1984.

Reflections

> "Two teachers have influenced me the most. In fifth grade, Mr. St. Jacques read aloud to our class: *The Cross and the Switchblade* and *Soul Brothers and Sister Lou*, the book by Kristin Hunter. This experience motivated my interest in fiction. Later, in high school, I continued my interest by reading all the novels by black authors. In college, I became aware of my interest in writing because of a particular course taught by Judy Gebre-Hewit, called 'Woman as Writer.' I came to appreciate the fact that each individual brings unique perceptions and elements of personality to their work, which come to shape their own literary voice. When I did an oral report on Gwendolyn Brooks, I noticed the similarities in our personalities (shyness, appreciation of the ordinary), and began to believe that perhaps I could become a poet also."

Publications

Books

Travis, Nancy, ed. *Extensions*. Maplewood, N.J.: Students' Summer Writing Project, 1983.

———. *Me & Rosemary; Revolutionary Teens, a Memoir of 3rd World Girls*. [Newark, N.J.: The Author, 1986]. 29 [3].

———. *April & June*. Berkeley, Calif.: Shameless Hussy Press, 1987. 43.

Short Stories and Poetry

Travis, Nancy. "Danger for a Black Girl." *Brown Sister* (Wellesley, Mass.: Wellesley College, 1983), 9.

———. "Three at Kenneth's Wedding." *Brown Sister* (Wellesley, Mass.: Wellesley College, 1983), 11.

———. "4005 Delovan Avenue." *Focus*, Spring 1984, 30.

———. "Slum Analysis." *Focus*, Spring 1984, 31.

———. "South Bronx." *Focus*, Spring 1984, 32.

———. "(Un) Planned Parenthood." *Focus*, Spring 1984, 30.

———. "Her Golden Years." *Up Against the Wall, Mother* (Alexandria, Va.) 5, no. 2 (April 1985), 1.

———. "Poet." *New Directions: The Howard University Magazine* (April 1985), 36.

———. "People of Color." *Touchstone* 10, no. 1 (1985), 31.

———. "SAKS Ads." *The Village Voice*, 28 October 1986, 56.

———. "Rites." *Rebirth of Artemis,* 6, no. 1 (1987), 10.

———. "Swanson Experience." *Touchstone* 12, no. 1 (winter 1987), 35.

Bio-Bibliographical Sources

Travis, Nancy. "African American Women Writers in New Jersey: Bio-graphical Questionnaire." Completed by Nancy Travis, 3 January 1987.

———. Letter to Sibyl E. Moses, 13 February 1987.

TRUSTY, EMMA MARIE H. COOPER 1936–

Personal Born in 1936 in Hopewell, Cumberland County, New Jersey; child of Martha Harris Cooper and Leon Cooper; granddaughter (maternal) of Laura Bunting Harris and Robert Harris; granddaughter (paternal) of Edward Cooper and Emma Johnson Cooper; great-granddaughter (maternal) of Sarah Dorsey and Thomas Dorsey of Salem, New Jersey; descendant (paternal) of Ezekiel Cooper and Thomas Cooper of Cumberland County, New Jersey; husband: Andrew David Trusty; children: Andrew, Deborah, Nathan, and Daniel. Education: Bridgeton High School, Bridgeton, New Jersey, 1955; Martland Medical Center (Newark City Hospital), Newark, New Jersey, R. N., 1958; Temple University, Philadelphia, Pennsylvania, B.S., education, 1964; LaSalle University, Philadelphia, M.A., 1995.

Residence in New Jersey Hopewell, Cumberland County.

Career Registered Nurse, Martland Medical Center (earlier name Newark City Hospital), Newark, 1958–?.

Publication

Trusty, Emma Marie Cooper. *The Underground Railroad, Ties that Bound Unveiled: A History of the Underground Railroad in Southern Jersey from 1770 to 1861.* Philadelphia, Pa.: Amed Literary, 1999. 422.

Bio-Bibliographical Sources

Trusty, Emma Marie Cooper. "Dedication and Acknowledgments." In *The Underground Railroad, Ties that Bound Unveiled: A History of the Underground Railroad in Southern Jersey from 1770 to 1861.* Philadelphia, Pa.: Amed Literary, 1999. 7, 13, 105.

———. Telephone conversation with Sibyl E. Moses, 28 October 1999.

TUCK-PONDER, MICHELE LOIS 1958–

Personal Born on 11 April 1958 in New York, New York; third child of Anna Mable Powell Tuck (blue-collar worker) of Drewryville, Virginia, and William Achilles Tuck (postal machine mechanic) of South Boston, Virginia; granddaughter (maternal) of Anna Fields Powell and Joseph Norman Powell, both of Virginia; granddaughter (paternal) of Martha Jane Tuck and Willie Bruce Tuck, both of Virginia; sisters: Patricia and

Jacqueline; husband: Rhinold Lamar Ponder (attorney); child: Jamaica Sharon Ponder. Education: Washington Irving Elementary School, Teaneck, New Jersey; Hawthorne Elementary School, Teaneck; Bryant School, Teaneck; Thomas Jefferson Junior High School, Teaneck; Teaneck High School, Teaneck; Northwestern University, Evanston, Illinois, Journalism, B.S., 1976–1980; University of Pennsylvania Law School, Philadelphia, J.D., 1980–1983. Religion: United Methodist.

Residence in New Jersey: Teaneck, 1963–1976; Plainfield, 1989–1992; Princeton, 1992 to present.

Career   Press secretary/legislative assistant to Republican Louis Stokes, U.S. House of Representatives, Washington, D.C., 1986–1987; special assistant to Senator Frank Lautenberg, U.S. Senate, Washington, D.C., 1988–1990, 1994; State of New Jersey, Trenton, N.J., 1990–1994; assistant counsel to Governor, Office of the Governor, Deputy Director, Division on Women, Department of Community Affairs; assistant director, New Jersey Division on Civil Rights, Department of Law and Public Safety; president, Ponder Literary Properties, New Brunswick, New Jersey, 1995–1997; director of development and public affairs, University of Medicine and Dentistry-Robert Wood Johnson Medical School, 1997–1998; mayor, Princeton Township, Princeton, 1995–1997; Township Committee, 1994, 1998–1999; community builder fellowship, U.S. Department of Housing and Urban Development, Camden, New Jersey, 1998 to present.

Memberships   New York, Bar, 1984; New Jersey Bar, 1991; Leadership New Jersey, Class of 1995; National Black Congress of Local Elected Officials; board of directors, Center for Non-Profits; board of directors, The National Conference; board of directors, chairperson, advisory board, The New Jersey Organ and Tissue Sharing Network; board of directors, chairperson, facilities committee, Delaware Raritan Valley Girl Scout Council; board of directors, Regional Planning Partnership (formerly MSM, Mercer Somerset and Middlesex Housing Adv. Board, 1995–1996); Political Congress Black Women, Trenton, 1995–1996.

Awards, Honors, Other Certificates   "Women Making "Herstory" Award," National Organization for Women; "Upstream Navigator Award," William P. Heard Foundation; "Sadie T. Alexander Distinguished Alumni Award," University of Pennsylvania, Black Law Students Association; "Outstanding Legislator Award," Zeta Phi Beta Sorority, Inc.

Reflections

"My first realization that I was a talented writer came in 1968. After the assassinations of Martin Luther King and Robert Kennedy, my fourth grade teacher asked the class to write essays on both men. My essay was on the state of society and my hope for the future. My teacher called my mother after reading the essay at home that evening and told her that I was the most gifted writer she had ever seen in 15 years of teaching. My mother then encouraged my writing. A few years later, I won a creative writing contest sponsored by *Scholastic Magazine*. Upon receiving a phone call from

Scholastic telling him I was the winner, the principal called the entire school into an assembly to announce the award. I realized at that time that I could receive kudos for simply doing what I liked to do. I was fortunate to have two creative writing teachers, Mr. Sosland and Mrs. Barron, who encouraged my writing. I also was assigned the toughest English teachers who insisted upon perfect grammar and honed my writing skills. As a journalism major at Northwestern, appreciation of accuracy and writing structure were the main focus, while my analytical writing skills were sharpened as a law student at Penn. Writing is something that flows naturally for me, and a gift in which I have great pride."

Publications

Books

Ponder, Rhinold Lamar and Michele Tuck-Ponder, eds. *The Wisdom of the Word: Faith: Great African-American Sermons.* New York: Crown Publishers, 1996. 95.

———. *The Wisdom of the Word: Love: Great African-American Sermons.* New York: Crown Publishers, 1997. 95.

Bio-Bibliographical Sources

Shaping A Life, Douglass College, Rutgers University, Center for American Women and Politics. "Michele Tuck-Ponder." <http://sal.rutgers.edu/bios.html> Accessed 28 June 2000.

Tuck-Ponder, Michele. "African American Women Writers in New Jersey: Biographical Questionnaire." Completed by Michele Tuck-Ponder, 18 July 2000.

Who's Who in the East, 1997–1998. 26th ed. New Providence, N.J.: Marquis Who's Who, 1996.

TUCKER, WANDA REGINA BUGGS 1951–

Personal Born on 13 June 1951 in Newark, New Jersey; first child of Gloria Jacqueline Cleveland Buggs (school aide) of Staunton, Virginia, and Samuel Buggs, Jr. (maintenance worker; deceased) of Charleston, West Virginia; granddaughter (maternal) of Frances Juanita Cleveland Armour; granddaughter (paternal) of Pricilla Buggs (deceased) and Samuel Buggs (deceased); sister: Cheryl Lynn Buggs Seward; brothers: Michael Leon Buggs (deceased), Samuel Buggs III and Emanuel Charles Buggs; husbands: Frederick Mark Tucker (auto body repairman; divorced) and Ronald Eric Kemp (customer service supervisor, Jersey Central Power & Light Co.); children: Tanya Sarina Tucker and Mark Duane Tucker. Education: 18th Avenue Elementary School, Newark, 1956–1962; Dayton Street Elementary School, Newark, 1962–1965; West Side High School, Newark, 1965–1968; Bloomfield High School, Bloomfield, New Jersey, GED, 1975; College of St. Elizabeth, Convent Station, New Jersey, 1985. Religion: Previously Baptist; New Hope Baptist Church, Newark.

Residence in New Jersey Newark, 1951–1968; East Orange, 1969–1971; Belleville, 1972–1986; West Orange, 1987; Budd Lake, 1987 to present.
Career Receptionist in radiology office, James Brown, MD, 1980–1984; General Public Utilities Service Corp., 1984 to present: microfilm clerk, 1984, graphics administrator, 1984–1989, and communications administrator, 1989 to present.
Memberships New Hope Baptist Church: organized first teen choir; Brownie Scout troop leader; president, Belleville (New Jersey) Tenant Association; Rent Leveling Board; New Jersey Tenant Association; volunteer, Clara Maas Hospital, Belleville, New Jersey; board of directors, Essex County, New Jersey Big Brothers/Big Sisters; founding member of Friends in Deed, a group of General Public Utilities Service Corp. employees volunteering to perform projects within the Morris County, New Jersey community.
Reflections

> "I have independently published two books of poetry. They are love poems, but they also speak of being black. I first started writing poetry when in elementary school. I used to love to sing and would write songs. While in high school, I found that I had a knack of not only putting my feelings down on paper, but also [capturing the feelings of] others. I still have my original poems handwritten in my old notebook. The two writers that encouraged me were Nikki Giovanni and Rod McKuen. I think that writing kept me sane. The year that I entered high school, my father and mother had separated that summer. I found that writing took away a lot of the pain."

Publications

Tucker, Wanda R. *Love As I See It.* [Belleville, N.J.: The Author, 1976]. 24. Printed by FAS Publishing, Madison, Wisconsin.

———. *Sensuous Feelings.* [Belleville, N.J.: The Author, 1977]. 24. Printed by FAS Publishing, Madison, Wisconsin.

Bio-Bibliographical Sources

Tucker, Wanda. "African American Women Writers in New Jersey: Biographical Questionnaire." Completed by Wanda Tucker, July 1994.

———. Letter to Sibyl E. Moses, 19 August 1985.

———. Telephone conversation with Sibyl E. Moses, 6 June 1994.

WALKER, SHEILA SUZANNE 1944–

Sheila Suzanne Walker.
Photograph by Marsha Miller,
courtesy of University of Texas at Austin.

Personal Born on 5 November 1944 in Jersey City, New Jersey; daughter of Susan Robinson Walker Snell (receptionist) of Stewart County, Georgia, and James Oram Walker (chiropractor) of Newark, New Jersey; granddaughter (maternal) of Mattie Robinson and John Perry Robinson; granddaughter (paternal) of James Blaine Walker of Spotsylvania County, Virginia, and Manie White Walker of Haverstraw, New York. Education: Garfield School, Kearny, New Jersey, 1949–1951; Washington School, East Orange, New Jersey, 1951–1956; Vernon L. Davey Junior High School, East Orange, 1956–1958; East Orange High School, East Orange, 1958–1962; Bryn Mawr College, Bryn Mawr, Pennsylvania, B.A. cum laude, Political Science, 1966; Sorbonne and Institut d'Etudes Politiques, Paris, France, Junior Year Abroad, 1964–1965; University of Chicago, Chicago, Illinois, M.A., 1969 and Ph.D., anthropology, 1976.

Residence in New Jersey Kearny, 1944–1951; East Orange, 1951–1962.

Career Lecturer, cultural anthropology, Northwestern University, Evanston, Illinois, summer, 1968; lecturer, Departments of Sociology and Theology and Religion, Elmhurst College, Elmhurst, Illinois, 1969; research specialist, Chicago Urban League, Chicago, Illinois, 1970; research assistant, Divinity School, Harvard University, Boston, Massachusetts, 1972–1973; development consultant, Africare, Somolia, 1984; development consultant, U.S. Agency for International Development and United Nations Development Programme, Mali and Burkina Faso, 1985; assistant professor, 1973–1981, and later associate professor, 1981–1986, Graduate School of Education, and associate professor, Department of African American Studies, University of California at Berkeley, Berkeley, California, 1986–1989; visiting associate professor, Department of Anthropology, City College of the City University of New York, fall 1987; scholar-in-residence, Schomburg Center for Research in Black Culture, New York, 1987; development consultant; National Council of Negro Women, Senegal, Zimbabwe, Botswana, and Mozambique, 1990; William Allen Neilson Visiting Professor, Department of African American Studies, Smith College, Northampton, Massachusetts, Spring, 1992; professor, Department of Anthropology, College of William and Mary, Williamsburg, Virginia,

1989–1991; professor, Department of Anthropology and Annabel Irion Worsham Centennial Professor, College of Liberal Arts; The University of Texas at Austin, Austin, Texas, 1991 to present; director, Center for African and African American Studies, University of Texas at Austin, Texas, 1991–2001.

Awards, Honors, Other Certificates   NDEA Title IV; Kent Fellowship, Danforth Foundation; National Council of Negro Women, Mary McLeod Bethune Achievement Award, 1983; Regents Faculty Summer Fellowship, University of California, Berkeley; First Annual Black Women's Leadership Conference Achievement Award, University of California, Berkeley, 1988; African-American Scholars Council Research Grant; Faculty Development Grant, University of California, Berkeley; Social Science Research Council Postdoctoral Field Research Grant; Professional Development and Applied Research Center Grant, School of Education, University of California, Berkeley; Spencer Foundation Grant, School of Education, University of California, Berkeley; National Research Council Senior Postdoctoral Research Grant.

Reflections

"When I was a child, my parents and grandparents and I often visited my aunt in Manhattan's Chinatown, an environment and people that fascinated me. Those experiences, watching the surprisingly multicultural television programming of the early 50s, ignited my desire to discover the other peoples of the world. I enjoyed reading adventure books as a child, the only travel book that I remember reading in high school was by an African American, which stuck in my mind, being Langston Hughes' *I Wonder as I Wander.*

I began discovering the world beyond the United States after my sophomore year of college when I spent a summer living with a family and traveling in Cameroon in Central Africa as part of the Experiment in International Living exchange program. I continued by studying African anthropology during a junior year abroad spent in Paris.

In graduate school while studying anthropology, I wanted to share the information I was learning about African and African American culture with an African American readership in a popular format. I wrote articles for *Black World, Ebony,* and *Essence,* partially in response to questions people asked me about my experiences in Africa where I lived and traveled throughout much of the continent doing field research, consulting, and participating in cultural activities. So, I developed the habit of writing popular articles as well as scholarly books and articles necessary to advance in my academic career. I am currently working on popularly-oriented books on my experiences in Cameroon, both my initial discovery experience and a subsequent fieldwork experience, and on my experiences doing development consulting in Somalia."

Publications
Books

Walker, Sheila S. *Ceremonial Spirit Possession in Africa and Afro-America.* Leiden, Holland: E.J. Brill, 1972. xii, 179.

———. "New Perspectives on Black Education," Special Issue, *Anthropology and Education Quarterly* 9, no.2 (summer 1978).

Bond, George, Walton Johnson, and Sheila S. Walker, eds. *African Christianity: Patterns of Religious Continuity.* Studies in Anthropology. New York; Academic Press, 1979. xvi, 175.

Walker, Sheila S., and Johnetta Cole, eds. "Black Anthropology," Two-volume Special Issue, *The Black Scholar* 11, nos. 7 & 8 (September–October) and (November–December 1980).

———. *The Religious Revolution in the Ivory Coast: The Prophet Harris and the Harrist Church.* Chapel Hill: University of North Carolina Press, 1983. xvii, 206.

———., editor. *African Roots/American Cultures: Africa in the Creation of the Americas.* Lanham, Md.: Rowman & Littlefield Publishers, 2001. xx, 375, ill.

Articles and Chapters in Books

Walker, Sheila S. "Ambivalence of U.S. Racial Feelings: The Black-Jewish Paradox," *Patterns of Prejudice* 7, no. 3 (May–June 1973): n.p.

———. "Abomey Tapestries: History of An African Kingdom." *A Current Bibliography on African Affairs* 9, no. 2 (1976–1977): n.p.

———. "Religion and Modernization in an African Context: The Harrist Church of the Ivory Coast." *Journal of African Studies* 4, no. 1 (spring 1977): n.p.

———. "Women, Education, and Rural Development in Cameroon: The Fulbé of the Garoua Region," *The African-American Scholar* 1, no. 5 (June 1977): n.p.

———. "A Challenge to Anthropology and Education." *Anthropology and Education Quarterly* 9, no. 2 (summer 1978): 75–84.

———. "Women and Walls: Architectural Reflections of Changing Patterns of Male-Female Interaction Among the Fulbé of Northern Cameroon." *Working Paper, Department of Architecture,* University of California, Berkeley, 1978.

———. "Afro-American Names and Identity" (Noms et Identité Chez Les Noirs-Américains"). *Ethiopiques: Revue de Culture Négro-Africaine* (Dakar, Senegal), April 1979. In English and French.

———. "Fulbé Women in Northern Cameroon: Their Place and How It's Changing, Albeit Slowly." *Women in Anthropology,* Sacramento Anthropological Society Sacramento, California, Publication no. 15 (spring 1979): 76–97.

———. "The Message as the Medium: The Harrist Churches of Ivory Coast and Ghana." In *African Christianity: Patterns of Religious Continuity,* edited by George Bond, Walton Johnson, and Sheila Walker, 9–64. New York: Academic Press, 1979.

―――. "Reflexions Architecturales sur les Femmes et les Murs: Les Fulbé du Nord-Cameroun." *Recherche, Pédagogie et Culture,* Paris 7, no. 41–42 (May–August 1979): n.p.

―――. "Women in the Harrist Movement." In *The New Religions of Africa,* edited by Bennetta Jules-Rosette, 87–97. Norwood, N.J.: Ablex Publishing Corporation, 1978.

―――. "African Gods in the Americas: The Black Religious Continuum." Special "Black Anthropology" issue, *The Black Scholar* 11, no. 8 (November–December 1980): n.p.

―――. "Afro-American Women and Higher Education," In *Looking Back at "A Second Look at the Second Sex,"* n.p. Berkeley: C.C.E.W. Women's Center, University of California, 1980.

―――. "From Cattle Camp to City: Fulbé Women in Northern Cameroon." *The Journal of African Studies* 7, no. 1 (spring 1980): n.p.

―――. "Witchcraft and Healing in an African Christian Church." *The Journal of Religion in Africa/ Religion en Afrique* 10, no. 2 (1980): 127–138.

―――. "Young Men, Old Men, and Devils in Aeroplanes: The Harrist Church, the Witchcraft Complex, and Social Change in the Ivory Coast." *The Journal of Religion in Africa* 11, no. 2 (1980): 106–123.

―――. "African Initiative and Indigenous Christianity in Ivory Coast." In *Transformation and Resiliency in Africa,* edited by Pearl T. Robinson and Elliot P. Skinner, 191–209. Washington, D.C.: Howard University Press, 1983.

―――. "The Bahian Carnival." *Black Art: An International Quarterly* 5, no. 4 (fall 1983): n.p.

―――. "Candomblé: A Spiritual Microcosm of Africa." *Black Art: An International Quarterly* 5, no. 4 (fall 1983), n.p.

―――. "Master Didi." *Black Art: An International Quarterly* 5, no. 4 (fall 1983): n.p.

―――. "Reflections on Becoming a Black Anthropologist." *Association of Black Anthropologists Occasional Papers* no. 1. Urbana: Afro-American Studies and Research Program, University of Illinois, 1983.

―――. "Systematic Mis-Education in California Public Schools: Teaching About Peoples of Africa, the African Diaspora, and the Third World Through Educational Media." *Black Perspectives: A Newsletter for Bay Area Black Professionals,* Bay Area Association of Black Psychologists 2, no. 6 (September 1985): n.p.; 3, no. 1 (November 1985): n.p.; 3, no. 2 (April–May 1986): n.p.

―――. "Création de Mythes au sujet de l'Afrique et la Mauvaise Education des Américains: l'Utilisation des Médias Educationnels en Vue d'Enseigner l'Ethnocentrisme dans les Ecoles Publiques de Californie." *Actes du Symposium International en Vue de la Création d'un Institut des Peuples Noirs,* Ouagadougou, Burkina Faso, April, 1986.

―――. "The Feast of Good Death: An Afro-Catholic Emancipation Celebration in Brazil." *Sage: A Scholarly Journal on Black Women* 3, no. 3 (fall

1986): n.p. Rev. and published in *Women in Africa and the African Diaspora: A Reader,* edited by Rosalyn Terborg Penn and Andrea Benton Rushing, n.p. Washington, D.C.: Howard University Press, 1996.

———. "William Wade Harris." In *The Encyclopedia of Religion,* edited by Mircea Eliade, n.p. New York: Macmillan Publishing Company, 1987.

———. "Africanity Versus Blackness: The Afro-Brazilian/ Afro-American Identity Conundrum." *Introspectives: Contemporary Art by Americans and Brazilians of African Descent,* California Afro-American Museum, Los Angeles, California. (February 1989).

———. "Everyday and Esoteric Reality in the Afro-Brazilian Candomblé." *History of Religions: An International Journal for Comparative Historical Studies* 30, no. 2 (November 1990): 103–128.

———. "Walled Women and Women Without Walls Among the Fulbé of Northern Cameroon." *Sage: A Scholarly Journal on Black Women* 7, no. 1 (summer 1990): 13.

———. "A Choreography of the Universe: The Afro-Brazilian Candomblé as a Microcosm of Yoruba Spiritual Geography." *Anthropology and Humanism Quarterly* 16, no. 1 (June 1991): n.p.

———. "The Saints Versus the Orishas in a Brazilian Catholic Church as an Expression of Afro-Brazilian Cultural Synthesis in the Feast of Good Death." *African Creative Expressions of the Divine,* edited by Kortwright Davis and Elias Farajaje-Jones, 84–98. Washington, D.C.: Howard University School of Divinity, 1991.

———. "The Virtues of Positive Ethnocentrism: Some Reflections of an Afrocentric Anthropologist." *Transforming Anthropology: A Publication of the Association of Black Anthropologists* 2, no. 2 (1991), n.p.

Walker, Sheila S., and Jennifer Rasamimanana. "Tarzan in the Classroom: How 'Educational' Films Mythologize Africa and Mis-Educate Americans." *The Journal of Negro History* 62, no. 1 (winter 1993): 3. Reprinted in *Cultural Portrayals of African Americans: Creating an Ethnic/ Racial Identity,* 27–48. Westport, Conn.: Bergin and Garvey, 1997.

———. "The All-Americas/ All-American African Diaspora." *Currents of the Spirit in the African Diaspora: Survivals, Innovations, and New Expressions.* Washington, D.C.: Program in African American Culture, National Museum of American History, Smithsonian Institution, 1994.

———. "Sailing My Fantasy." In *Go Girl: The Black Woman's Travel Book,* edited by Elaine Lee, n.p. Seattle, Wash.: Eighth Mountain Press, 1997.

———. "De l'Argentine au Canada, la Diaspora Africaine est Présente dans Toutes les Amériques et chez tous les Américains." In *La Chaine et le Lien: Une Vision de la Traite Négrière,* n.p. Mémoire des Peuples. Paris: UNESCO, 1998.

———. "Les Divinités Africains Dansent aux Amériques et au Maroc." In *La Transe,* edited by Abdelhafid Chlyeh. *Rencontres d'Essaouira,* n.p. Marrakesh, Morocco: Editions Marsam, 2000.

———. "Everyday Africa in New Jersey: Wondering and Wandering in the

African Diaspora." In *African Roots/American Cultures: Africa in the Creation of the Americas,* edited by Sheila S. Walker, n.p. Lanham, Md.: Rowman & Littlefield, 2001.

Anthropological Journalism/ Popular Anthropology

Walker, Sheila S. "Anthropology: What's That?" *Essence* 2 (June 1971): 15.

———. "Black English: Expression of the Afro-American Experience." *Black World* (June 1971): n.p.

———. "How You Eat Is How You Be." *Essence* 4 (September 1973): 62–63.

———. "Abomey Tapestries: History of an African Kingdom." *Essence* 5 (February 1974): 62–63.

———. "Growing Up As Daddy's Girl." *Essence* 7 (June 1976): 62–63.

———. "Climbing My Family Tree." *Essence* 7 (August 1976): 52–53.

———. "What's in a Name? Black Awareness Keeps the African Tradition of 'Meaningful Names' Alive." *Ebony* 32 (June 1977): 74+.

———. "Bahia: Africa in America." *Essence* 8 (July 1977): 42–43.

———. "Senegalese Women." *Essence* 9 (July 1978): 66–69, 125–126.

———. "A Senegalese Mosaic." *Essence* 9 (July 1978): 62, 118, 120, 122–125.

———. "The Sixth Pan-African Film Festival of Ouagadougou." *African Film Society Update* no. 4 (summer 1979), n.p.

———. "It Can Work (African/Afro-American Marriages)." *Essence* 10 (July 1979): 81.

———. "African Cinema: Surveying the Art." *Center for Southern Folklore Newsletter* 3, no. 1 (1980): n.p.

———. "A Festival Reflection on Faces and Places." *Paradise* (Air Niugini flight magazine, Port Moresby, Papua New Guinea) no. 28 (March 1981): n.p.

———. "Careers in Languages." *The Black Collegian* 11, no. 3 (December 1980–January 1981): n.p.

———. "Living the Songs Daddy Sang—Letter From Martinique, Summer 1984." *Genetic Dancers* 1, no. 1 (first quarter 1985): n.p.

———. "Africans and African Americans: Together into the Twenty-First Century." With His Excellency Ambassador Moumouni Djermakoye, First African/African American Summit, Abidjan, Côte d'Ivoire, April, 1991.

———. "The Significance of the First Summit Meeting of African Heads of State and African American Leaders." *The Amsterdam News* 82, no. 17 (27 April 1991), n.p.

———. "Africa on Our Minds and in Our Hearts." *Emerge* (October 1992): 75–76.

———. "An Honest View of the Columbus Legacy." *Emerge* (October 1992): 68.

———. "Breaking Away From 'Miseducation.'" *The Constituent: News from the Constituency for Africa* 1, no. 2 (July–September 1992): n.p.

———. "Our Natural Ties with Africa." *Emerge* (February 1992): 47–48.

———. "Returning to the Source." *Word: News from an Afro-American Per-*

spective, University of California, Berkeley, 2, no. 3 (December 1988): n.p.

———. "A Summit Fueled by a Common Past—A Reunion of Africans and African Americans." *African World* (November–December 1993): n.p.

Bio-Bibliographical Sources

Walker, Sheila S. "African American Women Writers in New Jersey: Biographical Questionnaire." Completed by Sheila Walker, 2000.

———. "Sheila S. Walker, Ph.D.: [Résumé]" 10.

WALL, CHERYL ANN 1948–

Personal   Born on 29 October 1948 in New York, New York; first child of Rennie Strayhorn Wall (teacher) of Meridian, Mississippi, and Monroe Wall (Baptist minister) of Latta, South Carolina; granddaughter (maternal) of Rosa Hunter Strayhorn of Eutaw, Alabama, and Henry Strayhorn of Hillsboro, North Carolina; granddaughter (paternal) of Anna Green Wall and Jerry Wall, both of South Carolina; sister: Gatsie H. Wall; brother: Henry Strayhorn Wall (deceased); daughter: Camara Rose Epps. Education: P.S. 160, Jamaica, New York (grades K–6); Shimer Junior High School, Jamaica (grade 7–8); Rhodes School, New York, New York (grades 8–12); Howard University, Washington, D.C., B.A., English, magna cum laude, 1970; Harvard University, Cambridge, Massachusetts, Ph.D., History of American Civilization, 1976.

Residence In New Jersey   New Brunswick and Highland Park, 1972 to present.

Career   Instructor of English, Douglass College, Rutgers University, New Brunswick, New Jersey, 1972–1976; assistant professor of English, Rutgers University, 1976–1982; associate professor of English, Rutgers University, 1982–1997; director of undergraduate studies in English, Rutgers University, New Brunswick, 1988–1991; professor of English, Rutgers University, 1997 to present; chair, Department of English, Rutgers University, 1997 to present.

Memberships   Toni Morrison Society; Zora Neale Hurston Society; College Language Association; Modern Language Association (Executive Committee, Division of Black American Literature and Culture); Crossroads Theatre, New Brunswick (Charter Member and Board of Directors), 1981–1985; president, 1981–1983; consultant, New Jersey Committee for the Humanities, 1992–1993; Black American Literature and Culture, 1992–1996; Highland Park (N.J.) Human Rights Commission, 1996 to present; American Studies Association (National Council), 1997–2000.

Awards, Honors, Other Certificates   Howard University Scholarship Recipient, 1966–1970; Phi Beta Kappa, 1969; Southern Fellowships Award, 1970; Woodrow Wilson Teaching Intern, 1972; Ford Foundation Fellow, Harvard University, Boston, Massachusetts, 1970–1972; Fulbright-Hays Award, Junior Lecturer, Technical University, Aachen, West Germany, 1978–1979;

Rutgers Research Council Summer Fellowship, 1980; Rutgers University Junior Faculty Fellowship, Spring 1981; Presidential Award for Distinguished Public Service, Rutgers University, 1986; Rutgers Faculty of Arts and Sciences Award for Undergraduate Teaching, 1995–1996; Outstanding Postdoctoral Scholar Fellowship, American Association of University Women Educational Foundation, 1996–1997; Warren I. Susman Award for Excellence in Teaching, 1997; New Jersey Women of Achievement Award, Douglass College, 2000.

Publications

Books

Wall, Cheryl A., ed. *Changing Our Own Words: Essays on Criticism, Theory, and Writing by Black Women.* New Brunswick, N.J.: Rutgers University Press, 1989. viii, 253.

Wall, Cheryl A. *Women of the Harlem Renaissance.* Bloomington: Indiana University Press, 1995. xx, 246, illus.

Wall, Cheryl A., ed. *Zora Neale Hurston: Novels and Stories.* New York: Library of America, 1995. 1041.

Wall, Cheryl A., ed. *Zora Neale Hurston: Folklore, Memoirs, and Other Writings.* New York: Library of America, 1995. 1001.

Wall, Cheryl A., ed. *Sweat: Zora Neale Hurston.* New Brunswick, N.J.: Rutgers University Press, 1997. viii, 233.

Wall, Cheryl A., ed. *Zora Neale Hurston's Their Eyes Were Watching God: A Casebook.* New York: Oxford University Press, 2000. x, 191, ill.

Chapters and Other Parts of Books

Wall, Cheryl A. "Gwendolyn Brooks." In *American Women Writers, Vol. I,* edited by Lina Mainiero, 241–243. New York: Frederick Unger Publishing Co., 1979. Reprinted in *American Women Writers, Abridged Edition, Vol. I,* edited by Lina Mainiero, 76–78.

———. "Frances Watkins Harper." In *American Women Writers, Vol. II,* edited by Lina Mainiero, 244–246. New York: Frederick Unger Publishing Co., 1980. Reprinted in *American Women Writers, Abridged Edition, Vol. I,* edited by Lina Mainiero, 295–297.

———. "Jessie Fauset." In *Notable American Women: The Modern Period,* edited by Barbara Sicherman, 225–227. Cambridge, Mass.: Belknap Press, 1980.

———. "Nella Larsen." In *American Women Writers, Vol. II,* edited by Lina Mainiero, 507–509. New York: Frederick Unger Publishing Co., 1980.

———. "Zora Neale Hurston." In *Notable American Women: The Modern Period,* edited by Barbara Sicherman, 361–363. Cambridge, Mass.: Belknap Press, 1980.

———. "Anne Spencer." In *American Women Writers, Vol. IV,* edited by Lina Mainiero, 135–137. New York: Frederick Unger, 1982.

———. "Poets and Versifiers, Signers and Signifiers: Women of the Harlem Renaissance." In *Women, the Arts, and the 1920's in Paris and New York,* edited by Kenneth W. Wheeler and Virginia Lee Lussier, 74–98. New Brunswick, N.J.: Transaction Books, 1982.

———. "Zora Neale Hurston: Changing Her Own Words." In *American Novelists Revisited: Essays in Feminist Criticism,* edited by Fritz Fleischmann, 371–393. Boston: G. K. Hall Publishing, 1982. Reprinted in *Black Literature Criticism,* edited by James Draper, 1073–1079. Detroit: Gale Research, 1992; *Zora Neale Hurston, Critical Perspectives Past and Present,* edited by Anthony Appiah and Henry L. Gates, 76–97. New York: Amistad/Penguin, 1993.

———. "Maya Angelou" (Interview). *Women Writers Talking,* edited by Janet Todd, 59–67. New York: Holmes & Meier, 1983.

———. "Jessie Fauset" and "Zora Neale Hurston." In *The Gender of Modernism,* edited by Bonnie Kime Scott, 155–195. Bloomington: Indiana University Press, 1990.

———. "Zora Neale Hurston." In *African American Writers,* edited by Valerie Smith, 205–218. New York: Charles Scribner's Sons, 1990.

———. "Gloria Naylor." In *American Women Writers, Vol. 5,* edited by Carol Hurd Green and Mary G. Mason, 330–332. New York: Continuum, 1994.

———. "On Freedom and the Will to Adorn: Debating Aesthetics and/as Ideology in African American Literature." In *Aesthetics and Ideology,* edited by George Levine, 283–303. New Brunswick, N.J.: Rutgers University Press, 1994.

———A. "Whose Sweet Angel Child? Blues Women, Langston Hughes, and Writing during the Harlem Renaissance." In *Langston Hughes: The Man, His Art, and His Continuing Influence,* edited by C. James Trotman, 37–50. New York: Garland, 1995. Reprinted in *GRAAT* ("Publication des Groupes de Recherches Anglo-Américaines de l'Université Francois Rabelais de Tours") no. 14 (1996): 63–72.

———. "Notes" [to Mules and Men, Tell My Horse, Dust Tracks on a Road, Selected Articles]. In *Folklore, Memoirs, and Other Writings,* 988–1001. New York: Library of America, 1995.

Wall, Cheryl A. "Jonah's Gourd Vine, Their Eyes Were Watching God, Moses, Man of the Mountain, Seraph on the Suwanee, Selected Stories." In *Novels and Stories, n.p.* New York: Library of America, 1995.

———. "Jessie Fauset." In *Encyclopedia of African-American Culture and History,* 939–940. New York: MacMillan, 1996.

———. "Afterword." In *The Pasteboard Bandit,* by Arna Bontemps and Langston Hughes, 87–93. New York: Oxford University Press, 1997.

———. "Zora Neale Hurston" and other related entries. In *The Oxford Companion to African American Literature,* edited by William Andrews, Frances Foster, and Trudier Harris, n.p. New York: Oxford, 1997.

Journal Articles

Wall, Cheryl A. "Paris and Harlem: Two Culture Capitals." *Phylon* 35 (March 1974): 64–73.

———. "Passing for What? Aspects of Identity in Nella Larsen's Novels." *Black American Literature Forum* 20 (spring–summer 1986): 97–111.

———. "Mules and Men and Women: Zora Neale Hurston's Strategies of

Narration and Visions of Female Empowerment." *Black American Literature Forum* 23, no. 4 (winter 1989): 661–680.

———. "'Speaking in Pieces, Instead of Telling One Long Thing': The Beacon Press Black Women Writers Series." *Iris* (spring 1990): 31–34.

———. "A Note on *The Weary Blues.*" *Lenox Avenue* 3 (1997): iii–iv.

———. "Sifting Legacies in Lucille Clifton's Generations." *Contemporary Literature* 40, no. 4 (winter 1999): 552–574.

Reviews

Wall, Cheryl A. Review of *Modernism and the Harlem Renaissance,* by Houston Baker and *Ride Out of Wilderness,* by Melvin Dixon. *American Literature* 60 (1988): 680–682.

———. "Black Women Writers: Journeying Along Motherlines." [Review of *The Character of Word,* by Karla Holloway and *Specifying: Black Women Writing the American Experience,* by Susan Willis]. *Callaloo* (spring 1989): 419–422.

———. Review of *Vicious Modernism: Black Harlem and the Literary Imagination,* by James de Jongh. *The Journal of American History* 78 (1992): 1488–1489.

———. "A Constellation of Women." [Review of *Daughters,* by Paule Marshall]. *Transformations* 3 (spring 1992): 40–42.

———. "A Sure Attention to Voice." [Review of *Liberating Voices,* by Gayl Jones]. *Novel* (winter 1993): 223–225.

———. Review of *Codes of Conduct: Race, Ethics, and the Color of Our Character,* by Karla Holloway; *Who Set You Flowin'? The African- American Migration Narrative,* by Farah Jasmine Griffin; *The Rooster's Egg: On the Persistence of Prejudice,* by Patricia Williams. *Signs* 23, no. 1 (1997): 217–220.

———. Review of *Black Women, Writing and Identity: Migrations of the Subject,* by Carole Boyce Davies. *Criticism* 39, no. 3 (1997): 456–457.

———. Review of *Borders, Boundaries and Frames: Cultural Studies and Cultural Criticism,* edited by Mae Henderson. *African American Review* 31, no. 3 (1997): 509–511.

Bio-Bibliographical Sources

Wall, Cheryl A. "African American Women Writers in New Jersey: Biographical Questionnaire." Completed by Cheryl A. Wall, November 2000.

———. "Curriculum Vitae: Cheryl A. Wall." June 2000. 8.

WESLEY, DOROTHY LOUISE BURNETT PORTER 1905–1995

Personal   Born on 25 May 1905 in Warrenton, Virginia; joined the ancestors on 17 December 1995, in Fort Lauderdale, Florida. The eldest child of Bertha (Roberta) Ball Burnett (1887–1961; housewife, professional tennis player, organizer of New Jersey Tennis Association) of Warrenton, Virginia (grew up in Roxbury, Massachusetts) and Hayes Joseph Burnett, M.D.

(1877–1922; physician); sisters: Alice Earnestine Burnett and Leonie Harper; brother: Hayes Joseph Burnett, Jr.; husbands: James Amos Porter (1905–1970; married from 1929 to 1970) and Charles Harris Wesley (1891–1987, married from 1979 to 1987); child: Constance Porter Uzelac. Education: Elementary schools, Montclair, New Jersey; Montclair High School, Montclair, graduated 1923; Miner Normal School, Washington, D.C., diploma, 1925; Howard University, Washington, D.C., A.B., 1928; Columbia University, New York, New York, B.S., library science, 1931n and M.S., library science, 1932; American University, Washington, D.C., Certificate in Preservation and Administration of Archives, 1957; Susquehanna University, Selinsgrove, Pennsylvania, Honorary Doctor of Letters, 1971; Syracuse University, Syra-

Dorothy Porter Wesley,
courtesy of the Moorland-Spingarn
Research Center, Howard University.

cuse, New York, Honorary Doctor of Humane Letters, 1989; Radcliffe College, Cambridge, Massachusetts, Honorary Doctor of Humane Letters, 1990. Religion: Episcopal.

Residence in New Jersey   Montclair, ca.1907–1923.

Career   Librarian, Miner Teachers' College, Washington, D.C., 1925; cataloger, Howard University, Carnegie Library, Washington, D.C., 1928–1930; curator, Howard University, Moorland Spingarn Research Center, Washington, D.C., 1930–1973; part-time library assistant, The New York Public Library 135th Street Branch, New York, summers 1930–1932;

Memberships   Association for the Study of Afro-American Life and History, Executive Council; African-American Institute (The Women's Advisory Committee); Africanist Society; American Antiquarian Society; American Library Association; Association of Afro-American Museums; Bibliographical Society of America; Black Academy of Arts and Letters; Boston Public Library Associates; Delta Sigma Theta Sorority, Inc.; District of Columbia Library Association; District of Columbia Historical Advisory Boards; Library Company of Philadelphia; National Caucus and Center on Black Aged Inc.; National Trust for the Preservation of Historic Sites; Nigerian Historical Society; Phi Beta Kappa Society; Smithsonian Associates; the Society of American Archivists; President's Committee on Employment of the Handicapped.

Awards, Honors Other Certificates   Julius Rosenwald Scholarship (for pursuit of M.L.S. at Columbia University), 1931–1932; Journal of Negro History Award for the second best article of the year [on David Ruggles], 1943; Julius Rosenwald Fellowship for Research in Latin American Literature,

1944–1945; Ford Foundation Fellowship to fund position as Acquisitions Librarian to build the collection at the National Library of Nigeria, 1962–1964; outstanding service in the area of human relations, D.C. Chapter of the National Barristers Wives, for, 1968; Ford Foundation Grant for research on the Remond family in England, Scotland, Ireland, and Italy, 1973; dedication of the Dorothy B. Porter Room in Founders Library, Howard University, for outstanding contributions to the University and to the world of scholarship, 1973; Alumni Award for Distinguished Achievements, Howard University, 1974; Delta Sigma Theta Sorority, Inc. Bicentennial Award, 1976; U.S. Department of the Interior, Heritage Conservation and Recreation Service's Cultural Achievement Award, for significant contributions to the preservation of America's cultural resources, 1976; Prince Hall Masons Charitable Foundation Grant for research on the Remond family, 1977; The Conover-Porter Award, established by the Africana Librarians Council of the (U.S.) African Studies Association, named in honor of Dorothy B. Porter; Olaudah Equiano Award for Excellence for Pioneering Achievements in African American Culture, University of Utah, 1989; Ford Foundation "Visiting Senior Scholar", The W.E.B. DuBois Institute for Afro-American Research at Harvard University, 1988–1989; National Endowment for the Humanities Charles Frankel Award presented by President William Clinton at the White House, 14 October 1994; Certificate of Recognition from the Alpha Wives of Washington, D.C., on the occasion of the installation of their archives at Howard University, Moorland Spingarn Research Center, 10 June 1994; "A Celebration of the Lives and Works of Dorothy Porter Wesley and Dorothy Sterling on the Occasion of the Publication of *The Abolitionist Sisterhood: Women's Political Culture in Antebellum America*," Cambridge, 18 May 1994; Association for the Study of Afro-American Life And History, October 1995.

Reflections (as reported to Avril J. Madison)

"Well, as I recall, my first year when I had been appointed as librarian, I had to work with Mrs. Emma [Green] Murray, who was the head librarian, and I had to learn the procedure for cataloging in a general collection and get a feeling of how the [Howard University] library worked itself, generally.

Then the next year, 1931, I was appointed to build a collection of books by and about the Negro, and that was my assignment that E. C. Williams gave me. He was pushed by [the Reverend] Jesse Moorland, who was a [Howard University] trustee member. He had given his collection in 1914, and it had stayed boxed up, most of it, and unused. He said, 'I want you to find someone to come in and work with the collection and build the collection.' You know, at that time, students weren't interested in their African heritage. They weren't interested in Africa or the Caribbean. They were really more interested in being like the white person. They wanted to go to white schools. They didn't even want to come to Howard. I heard a number of them, 'Oh, what am I going to go to Howard for?' You know? So nothing really had been done. Very little had been done, and it meant that I had just gathered together everything I could by and about the subject, acquire what I could, mainly by begging. You see, I had no staff, no money, but I had to beg, beg, beg, and clean up people's basements, and find books anywhere I could."

Publications

Books/Monographs/Pamphlets

Porter, Dorothy B., *North American Negro Poets: A Bibliographical Checklist of Their Writings. 1760–1944.* Hattiesburg, Miss: The Book Farm, 1945. 90.

Howard University. Graduate School. *Howard University Masters' Thesis Submitted in Partial Fulfillment of the Requiring for the Master's Degree at Howard University, 1918–1945,* compiled by Dorothy B. Porter. Washington, D.C.: Howard University Graduate School, 1946. 44.

Porter, Dorothy B., ed. *A Catalogue of the African Collection at Howard University,* compiled by students in the Program of African Studies. Washington, D.C.: Howard University Press, 1958.

Porter, Dorothy B., and Ethel M. Ellis, compilers. *Journal of Negro Education: Index to Volumes 1–31, 1932–1962.* Washington, D.C.: Howard University Press, 1963.

Porter, Dorothy B., comp. *The Negro in American Cities: A Selected and Annotated Bibliography.* Prepared for the National Advisory Commission of Civil Disorders. Washington, D.C.: Howard University Library, 1967. 200 leaves.

Porter, Dorothy B., ed. *Negro Protest Pamphlets: A Compendium.* New York: Arno Press, 1969.

Porter, Dorothy B., comp. *Working Bibliography on the Negro in the United States.* Ann Arbor, Mich.: Xerox, University Microfilms, 1969. 202.

———. *Early Negro Writing, 1760–1837.* Boston: Beacon Press, 1971. 658. Reprint,Baltimore, Md.: Black Classic Press, 1995.

Porter, Dorothy Burnett, comp. *The Negro in the United States: A Selected Bibliography.* Washington, D.C.: U. S. Government Printing Office, 1970. 313. Reprint, Detroit: Omnigraphics, 1999.

———. *Afro-Braziliana: A Working Bibliography.* Boston: G. K. Hall, 1978. 294.

Articles and Book Chapters

Porter, Dorothy B. "Daniel Jackson Sanders (Biographical Sketch)." In *Dictionary of American Biography, vol. 8,* edited by Dumas Malone, 332. New York: Charles Scribner's Sons, 1935.

———. "Sarah Parker Remond: Abolitionist and Physician." *The Journal of Negro History* 20, no. 3 (July 1935): 287–293.

———. "Some Recent Literature on the Negro." *Wilson Bulletin* 9 (June 1935): 569–570.

———. "Harriet Tubman (Biographical Sketch)." In *Dictionary of American Biography, vol. 10,* edited by Dumas Malone, 27. New York: Charles Scribner's Sons, 1936.

———. "Library Resources for the Study of Negro Life and History." *Journal of Negro Education* 5, no.2 (April 1936): 232–244.

———. "The Organized Educational Activities of Negro Literary Societies, 1828–1846." *The Journal of Negro Education* 5, no. 4 (October 1936): 555–576.

———. "Books with Negro Characters for Children." *National Educational Outlook Among Negroes* 1 (December 1937): 33–36.

———. "Some Books Featuring Negro Characters for Young Children." *National Educational Outlook Among Negroes* 1 (September 1937): 14–15.

———. "Books with Negro Characters for Children." *National Educational Outlook Among Negroes* 2 (1938): 27–29.

———. "A Library on the Negro." *American Scholar* 7 (winter 1938): 115–117.

———. "New Books for Children's Book Week." *National Educational Outlook Among Negroes* 2 (November 1938): 22–24.

———. "Charter Day Exercises." *Howard Bulletin* (April 1939): 4–6.

———. "Early Manuscript Letters Written by Negroes." *The Journal of Negro History* 24 (April 1939): 199–210.

———. "Recent Literature on the Negro." *Quarterly Review of Higher Education* 8 (July 1940): 118–122.

———. "The Preservation of University Documents: With Special References to Negro Colleges and Universities." *The Journal of Negro Education* 11, no. 4 (October 1942): 527–528.

———. "David Ruggles, An Apostle of Human Rights." *The Journal of Negro History* 28, no. 1 (January 1943): 23–50.

———. "Selected References on the American Negro in World War I and World War II." *The Journal of Negro Education* 12, no. 3 (summer 1943): 579–584.

———. "Negro Women in Our Wars." *Negro History Bulletin* 7 (June 1944): 195–96, 215.

———. "Early American Negro Writings: A Bibliographical Study." *The Papers of the Bibliographical Society of America* 39 (third quarter 1945): 192–268.

———. "Phylon Profile XIV: Edward Christopher Williams." *Phylon* 8 (fourth quarter 1947): 315–321.

———. "Luther Porter Jackson: Bibliographical Notes." *Bulletin of Negro History* 13 (June 1950): 213–215.

———. "Padre Domingo Caldas Barbosa, Afro-Brazilian Poet." *Phylon* 12 (third quarter 1951): 264–271.

———. "Maria Louise Baldwin, 1856–1922." *The Journal of Negro Education* 21, no.1 (winter 1952): 94–96.

———. "The Negro in the Brazilian Abolition Movement." *The Journal of Negro History* 37, no.1 (January 1952): 54–80.

———. "Bibliography." *Journal of Negro Education* 22, no. 1 (winter 1953): 61–67.

———. "Bibliography." *Journal of Negro Education* 22, no. 2 (spring 1953): 162–187.

———. "Bibliography." *Journal of Negro Education* 22, no. 4 (autumn 1953): 505–517.

———. "A Glimpse of Negro History." *Bulletin of Negro History* 26 (April 1953): 146, 164–165.

———. "Bibliography." *Journal of Negro Education* 23, no. 1 (winter 1954): 74–81.

———. "The Water Cure—David Ruggles." In *The Northampton Book; Chapters from 300 Years in the Life of a New England Town, 1654–1954,* compiled and edited by the Tercentenary History Committee, 121–126. Northampton: Northampton, Massachusetts, Tercentenary History Committee, 1954.

———. "Bibliography." *Journal of Negro Education* 25, no. 2 (spring 1956): 159–168.

———. "Bibliography." *Journal of Negro Education* 26, no. 4 (autumn 1957): 494–508.

———. "David Ruggles, 1810–1849; Hydropathic Practitioner." *Journal of the National Medical Association* 49 (January 1957): 67–72.

———. "David Ruggles, 1810–1849; Hydropathic Practitioner." *Journal of the National Medical Association* 49 (March 1957): 130–134.

———. "A Bibliographical Checklist of American Negro Writers about Africa." In *Africa Seen by American Negroes,* 79–99. [Paris]: Présence Africaine [1958].

———. "Bibliography." *Journal of Negro Education* 27, no. 4 (autumn 1958): 505–518.

———. "The African Collection at Howard University." *African Studies Bulletin* 2 (January 1959): 17–21.

———. "Bibliography." *Journal of Negro Education* 28, no. 2 (spring 1959): 154–162.

———. "The Anti-Slavery Movement in Northampton." *The Negro History Bulletin* 24 (November 1960): 33–34, 41.

———. "Bibliography." *Journal of Negro Education* 29, no. 4 (autumn 1960): 470–489.

Porter, Dorothy B., and Dolores C. Leffall. "Bibliography." *Journal of Negro Education* 29, no. 2 (spring 1960): 168–180.

Porter, Dorothy. "Research Centers and Sources for the Study of African History." *Journal of Human Relations* 8 (1960): 54–63.

Porter, Dorothy B., and Dolores C. Leffall. "Bibliography." *Journal of Negro Education* 30, no. 4 (autumn 1961): 416–425.

Porter, Dorothy B. "Bibliography." *Journal of Negro Education* 30, no. 2 (spring 1961): 127–137.

———. "Bibliography." *Journal of Negro Education* 30, no. 1 (winter 1961): 49–63.

———. "Bibliography." *Journal of Negro Education* 31, no. 1 (winter 1962): 51–64.

Porter, Dorothy B., and Chidnand Stephens. "Bibliography." *Journal of Negro Education* 31, no. 2 (spring 1962): 164–171.

Porter, Dorothy B., and Dolores C. Leffall. "Bibliography." *Journal of Negro Education* 31, no. 4 (autumn 1962): 488–502.

Porter, Dorothy. "Fiction by African Authors: A Preliminary Checklist." *African Studies Bulletin* 5 (May 1962): 54–66.

———. "First International Congress of Africanists." *Journal of Negro Education* 32, no. 2 (spring 1963): 198–204.

Porter, Dorothy B., and Georgia E. Whitmire. "Bibliography." *Journal of Negro Education* 32, no. 2 (spring 1963): 161–172.

———. "Bibliography." *Journal of Negro Education* 32, no. 3, A Valedictory Note (summer 1963): 258–275.

Porter, Dorothy B., and Robin Gregory. "Bibliography." *Journal of Negro Education* 32, no. 1 (winter 1963): 63–73.

Porter, Dorothy B. "African and Caribbean Creative Writing: A Bibliographic Survey." *African Forum* 1, no. 4 (spring 1966): 107–111.

———. "Africana at Howard University." In *Handbook of American Resources for African Studies,* edited by Peter Duigon, 33–39. Stanford, California: Stanford University, Hoover Institution on War, Revolution, and Peace, 1967.

———. "The Librarian and the Scholar: A Working Partnership." In *Proceedings of the Institute on Materials by and about the American Negro,* 71–80. Atlanta: Atlanta University, School of Librarianship, 1967.

———. "Documentation on the Afro-American: Familiar and Less Familiar Sources." *African Studies Bulletin* 12 (December 1969): 293–303.

———. "Bibliography and Research in African-American Scholarship." *The Journal of Academic Librarianship* 2, no. 2 (May 1976): 77–81.

———. "The Black Role During the Era of the Revolution: A Little Known Chapter of Afro-American History is the Subject of a Show at the Smithsonian's National Portrait Gallery." *Smithsonian* 4, no. 5 (August 1973): 52–57.

———. "Family Records: A Major Resource for Documenting the Black Experience in New England." *Old Time New England* 63, no. 3 (winter 1973): 69–72.

———. "Fifty Years and Collecting." Introduction. In *Black Access: A Bibliography of Afro-American Bibliographies,* compiled by Richard Newman, xvii–xxviii. Westport, Conn.: Greenwood Press, 1984.

———. "The Remonds of Salem, Massachusetts: A Nineteenth-Century Family Revisited." *Proceedings of the American Antiquarian Society* 95, part 2 (April 17–October 16, 1985): 259–294.

———. "Black Antiquarians and Bibliophiles Revisited, with a Glance at Today's Lovers of Books and Memorabilia." In *Black Bibliophiles and Collectors: Preservers of Black History,* edited by Elinor Des Verney Sinnette, W. Paul Coates, and Thomas C. Battle, 3–20. Washington, D.C.: Howard University Press, 1990.

Book Reviews

Porter, Dorothy B. Review of *Black Venus*, by A. Salmon. *Opportunity* 8 (June 1930): 185–186.

———. Review of *Mom de Jos*, by E. Berry. *Opportunity* 10 (February 1932): 58.

———. Review of *Classified Catalogue of Collections of Anti-Slavery Propaganda in Oberlin College Library*, by F. Hubbard. *Opportunity* 11 (February 1933): 57–58.

———. "Alabama." Review of *Stars Fell on Alabama*, by Care Carmer. *Journal of Negro Education* 3, no. 4 (October 1934): 632–634.

———. "Negro Migration." Review of *Bibliography of Negro Migration*, by Frank Alexander Ross and Louise Venable Kennedy. *Journal of Negro Education* 3, no. 4 (October 1934): 634–635.

———. Review of *Africa Dances*, by G. Gorer. *Crisis* 42 (November 1935): 346.

———. Review of *Arts of West Africa*, by Michael E. Sadler. *Journal of Negro History* 20, no. 4 (October 1935): 478–480.

———. Review of *The Musical Instruments of the Native Races of South Africa*, by Percival R. Kirby. *Journal of Negro History* 20, no. 4 (October 1935): 477–478.

———. Review of *County Library Service in the South: A Study of the Rosenwald County Library Demonstration*, by Louis R. Wilson and Edward A. Wight. *Journal of Negro Education* 6, no.1 (January 1937): 78–81.

———. Review of *Sad-Faced Boy*, by Arna Bontemps. *Negro History Bulletin* 1 (December 1937): 8.

———. Review of *Theodore Parker*, by Henry Steele. Commager. *Journal of Negro History* 22, no.1 (July 1937): 102–105.

———. Review of *Two Quaker Sisters*, from the original diaries of Elizabeth Buffum Chace and Lucy Buffum Lovell. *Journal of Negro History* 22, no. 3 (July 1937): 358–361.

———. Review of *Le Cameroun, 1937*, by Henri Labouret. *Journal of Negro Education* 7, no.2 (April 1938): 194–196.

———. "A Guide to the National Capital." Review of *Washington, City and Capital*, by the Works Progress Administration. *Journal of Negro Education* 7, no.2 (April 1938): 190–192.

———. "Two Source-Books on the Negro." Review of *Negro Year Book, An Annual Encyclopedia of the Negro, 1937–1938*, edited by Monroe Work. *Journal of Negro Education* 7, no.2 (April 1938): 192–193. Review of *Who's Who in Colored America: A Biographical Dictionary of Notable Living Persons of African Descent in America, 1933–1937*. *Journal of Negro Education* 7 (April 1938): 192–194.

———. Review of *Racial Proverbs: A Selection of the World's Proverbs Arranged Linguistically*, by Selwyn C. Champion. *Journal of Negro History* 24, no.1 (January 1939): 106–109.

———. Review of *The First Negro Medical Society: A History of the Medico-*

Chirurgical Society of the District of Columbia, 1884–1939, by William M. Cobb. *Journal of Negro Education* 9, no.2 (April 1940): 213–215.

———. Review of "A Library on the Negro." *Classified Catalogue of the Negro Collection in the Collis P. Huntington Library of Hampton Institute,* compiled by Mentor A. Howe and Roscoe E. Lewis. *Journal of Negro Education* 10, no. 2 (April 1941): 264–266.

———. Review of *Negro Education in New Jersey,* by Marion T. Wright. *Hayes Memorial Foundation Bulletin* (1942): n.p.

———. Review of *The Southern Negro and the Public Library,* by Eliza A. Gleason. *Social Forces* 20 (May 1942): 512–513.

———. Review of *The Negro Handbook,* edited by Florence Murray. *Journal of Negro Education* 12, no.2 (spring 1943): 220–222.

———. "An American Heroine." Review of *Harriet Tubman,* by Earl Conrad. *Journal of Negro Education* 13, no.1 (winter 1944): 91–93.

———. "Cuban Dramatic Literature." Review of *Historia de la Literatura Dramatica Cubana,* by Jose Juan Arrom. *Journal of Negro Education* 13, no. 4 (autumn 1944): 528–530.

———. Review of *Brazilian Literature,* by Erico Verrisimo. *Journal of Negro Education* 14, no. 4 (fall 1945): 602–604.

———. Review of *The Land Possessions of Howard University: A Study of the Original Ownership and Extent of the Holdings of Howard University in the District of Columbia,* by Beulah H. Melchor. *Journal of Negro History* 30, no. 4 (October 1945): 441–443.

———. "Journey to Accompong." Review of *Katherine Dunham's Journey to Accompong,* by Katherine Dunham. *Journal of Negro Education* 16, no.2 (spring 1947): 201–202.

———. "The Negro in the Americas." Review of *Slave and Citizen: the Negro in the Americas,* by Frank Tannenbaum. *Journal of Negro Education* 16, no.2 (spring 1947): 199–201.

———. Review of *Where the Sabia Sings,* by Henriqueta Chamberlain. *Journal of Negro Education* 16, no. 4 (autumn 1947): 550–551.

———. "1952 Negro Year Book." Review of *1952 Negro Year Book: A Review of Events Affecting Negro Life,* edited by Jessie Parkhurst Guzman. *Journal of Negro Education* 22, no. 4 (autumn 1953): 500–501.

———. Review of *Brazil's New Novel,* by Fred P. Ellison. *The Midwest Journal* 7 (1955): 111–113.

———. "Fiction by Negro Authors." Review of *A Century of Fiction by American Negroes, 1853–1952,* by Maxwell Whitemen. *Journal of Negro Education* 25, no. 2 (spring 1956): 146.

———. Review of *La Obra Afro-Uruguaya de Ildefonso Pereda Valdes,* by Paulo Carvalho Neto. *Journal of Negro History* 4, no.1 (January 1956): 78–80.

———. "Drum, A South African Periodical." Review of *Drum, The Newspaper that Won the Heart of Africa,* by Anthony Sampson. *Journal of Negro Education* 27, no.2 (spring 1958): 164–166.

Bio-Bibliographical Sources

Britton, Helen H. "Dorothy Porter Wesley: A Bibliographer, Curator, and Scholar." In *Reclaiming the American Library Past: Writing in the Women,* edited by Suzanne Hildenbrand, 163–186. Norwood, New Jersey: Ablex Publishing Company, 1996.

"Dorothy Burnett Porter Curriculum Vitae (1972)." [Washington, D.C., 1972]. [9].

"Dorothy Louise Burnett Porter Wesley (May 25, 1905–December 17, 1995)" . . . [Obituary]. [Washington, D.C., Howard University, 1995]. [4], illus.

Scarupa, Harriet Jackson. "The Energy-Charged Life of Dorothy Porter Wesley." *New Directions* (January 1990): 7–17.

Wesley, Dorothy Porter. "African American Women Writers in New Jersey: Biographical Questionnaire." Completed, in part, by Dorothy Porter Wesley's daughter, Constance Porter Uzelac, December 2000.

———. "Interview by Avril J. Madison." In *Transcript of an Oral History Interview with Dorothy Burnett Porter Wesley, Librarian, Bibliophile, Curator, Scholar, Bibliographer,* 14–15. Washington, D.C.: Moorland Spingarn Research Center, Oral History Department, Howard University, 1993.

WESLEY, VALERIE DEANE WILSON 1947–

Personal   Born on 22 November 1947 in Willimantic, Connecticut; daughter of Mary Evelyn Spurlock Wilson and Bertram Wadsworth Wilson (Tuskegee Airman), both of Salem, Virginia; granddaughter (maternal) of Willimena Spurlock and Thomas Spurlock, both of Salem, Virginia; granddaughter (paternal) of Carmen Griffin Wilson and Bertram W. Wilson, Sr., both of Salem, Virginia; sister: Patricia Wilson Coker; husband: Richard Wesley (screenwriter, playwright); children: two daughters. Education: Ashford Elementary School, Ashford, Connecticut; Madrid High School, Madrid Spain; Kaiserslautern Dependents High School, Kaiserslautern, Germany; Howard University, Washington, D.C., B.A., 1970; Columbia Univer-

Valerie Wilson Wesley.
Photograph by Dwight Carter.

sity, New York, New York, M.A., journalism, 1982; Bank Street College of Education, New York, M.A., early childhood education, ca. 1979.

Residence in New Jersey   Montclair; East Orange.

Career Associate editor, *Scholastic News,* New York, 1970–1972; senior editor (later executive editor and now contributing editor), *Essence,* New York, 1988 to present.

Memberships Board of directors, Montclair Art Museum, Montclair; board of directors, YWCA of North Essex County; board of directors, Aljira Center for Contemporary Art; board of directors, Newark Arts Council, Newark, New Jersey, 2000 to present; board of directors, Sisters of Crime; National Council of Negro Women; founding member, Metro-Manhattan Links, Inc.

Awards, Honors, Other Certificates Griot Award, National Association of Black Journalists, New York Chapter, 1993; Best Books for Reluctant Readers citation, American Library Association, for *Where Do I Go from Here?,* 1993; Shamus Award nomination for *When Death Comes Stealing,* 1994; Notable Children's Trade Books in the Field of Social Sciences, for *Freedom's Gifts: A Juneteenth Story,* 1998; Black Caucus of the American Library Association, Best Adult Fiction Award for *Ain't Nobody's Business If I Do,* 2000; Zora Neale Hurston Society Award, 2001.

Publications

Books

Hudson, Wade, and Valerie Wilson Wesley. *Afro-Bets Books of Black Heroes from A to Z: An Introduction to Important Black Achievers for Young Readers.* Orange, N.J.: Just Us Books, 1988. 54, illus.

Wesley, Valerie Wilson. *Where Do I Go from Here?* New York: Scholastic, 1993. 138.

———. *When Death Comes Stealing.* New York: Putnam, 1994. 221 (A Tamara Hayle Mystery). Reprint, London: Headline, 1994; New York: Avon [1995]. Translated (German) by Gertraude Krueger. *Ein Engel über deinem Grab.* Zurich: Diogenes Verlag, 1996 and 1998. 288. Translated (Polish) by Krzysztof Obłucki. *Gdy śmierć siê zakrada.* Warsaw: Noir sur Blanc, 2001. 212.

———. *Devil's Gonna Get Him.* A Tamara Hayle Mystery. New York: Putnam, 1995. 212. Reprint, London: Headline, 1995; New York: Putnam, 1996. Translated (German) by Gertraude Krueger. *In Teufels Küche.* Zürich: Diogenes Verlag [19], 98. 277. Translated (French) by Annie Hamel. *Si le Diable l'emporte.* Paris: Librairie des Champs-Élysées, 1997. Printed by Impr. Brodard et Taupin. 221.

———. *Where Evil Sleeps.* A Tamara Hayle Mystery. New York: G. P. Putnam's Sons, 1996. 208. Reprint, New York: Avon Books 1997. Translated (French) by Pascal Aubin. *Danse avec le Diable.* Paris: Librairie des Champs-Élysées, 1998. 281. Printed by Impr. Brodard et Taupin.

———. *Freedom's Gifts: A Juneteenth Story.* New York: Simon & Schuster Books for Young Readers, 1997. Illustrated by Sharon Wilson. (unpaged).

———. *No Hiding Place.* A Tamara Hayle Mystery. New York: G. P. Putnam's Sons, 1997. 207. Reprint, New York: Avon Twilight, 1997. Translated (French) by Pascal Loubet. *À Visage Découvert.* [Paris]: Librairie des

Champs Élysées, 2000. 258. Printed by Impr. Brodard et Taupin. Translated (German) by Gertraude Krueger. *Todesblues: Ein Fall fur Tamara Hayle.* Zurich: Diogenes-Verlag, 2001. 285.

―――. *Easier to Kill.* A Tamara Hayle Mystery. New York: G. P. Putnam's Sons, 1998. 193. Reprint, large print edition, Rockland, Mass.: Wheeler Publications, 1998; London: Robert Hale, 2000. Translated (German) by Gertraude Krueger. *Auf dem Weg nach Oben: Ein Fall fur Tamara Hayle.* Zurich: Diogenes Verlag [20]00. 267.

―――. *Ain't Nobody's Business If I Do.* New York: Avon Books, 1999. 323. Reprint, New York: Avon Books, 2000.

―――. *The Devil Riding.* A Tamara Hayle Mystery. New York: Putnam, 2000. 189. Reprint, London: Robert Hale, 2001.

―――. *Willimena and the Cookie Money.* New York: Hyperion Books for Children, 2001. 124.

Articles

Wesley, Valerie Wilson. "Children of Divorce: What the Law Says." *Essence* 14 (July 1983): 74+

―――. "Cost Cutting for Parents." *Essence* 14 (July 1983): 22.

―――. "She Hit Me First! How To Combat Sibling Rivalry." *Essence* 14 (October 1983): 138.

―――. "Dr. Comer's RX for Sick Schools." *Black Enterprise* 15 (September 1984): 38–39.

―――. "Making America's Classrooms Work." *Black Enterprise* 15 (September 1984): 34–39+.

―――. "Teaching Your Children about Bigotry." *Ms.* 13 (December 1984): 118–120.

―――. "Changing the Bad Rap On Black Fathers." *Essence* 16 (November 1985): 125.

―――. "Love Legacies." *Essence* 15 (February 1985): 72–74+.

―――. "No-Name Baby." *Essence* 17 (May 1986): 138.

―――. "Teaching Black Pride." *Essence* 18 (April 1988): 98+.

―――. "Atlanta: Our Slice of the Peach." *Essence* 19 (June 1988): 21+.

―――. "Tranquil Tropics." *Essence* 19 (September 1988): 23–24+.

―――. "Odessa's Gift." *American Visions* 3 (October 1988): 37–40.

―――. "Taking Back Our Schools." *Essence* 20 (February 1990): 102+.

―――. "Learning To Let Go." *Essence* 21 (May 1990): 188.

―――. "Vigil." *Essence* 22 (May 1991): 76–78+.

―――. "Back in Love By Monday." *Essence* 22 (August 1991): 108+.

Jones, Mandisa-Maia, and Valerie Wilson Wesley. "Anatomy of a Party Gone Wrong." *Essence* 22 (December 1991): 62–64+.

Wesley, Valerie Wilson. "Nights in Negril." *Essence* 23 (December 1992): 101–102+.

―――. "When Death Comes Stealing." *Essence* 25 (October 1994): 66–68+.

―――. "Devil's Gonna Get Him." *Essence* 26 (August 1995): 76–78+.

―――. "Understanding Black Anger." *Essence* 26 (October 1995): 102–103+.

———. "Where Evil Sleeps." *Essence* 27 (September 1996): 102+.
———. "Faith's Healing." *Essence* 28, no. 8 (December 1997): 74–76+.
Pirrie, Anne, Sheila Hamilton, and Valerie Wilson Wesley. "Multidisciplinary Education: Some Issues and Concerns." *Educational Research* 41, no. 3 (winter 1999): 301–314.
Wesley, Valerie Wilson, and Amy Du Bois Barnett. "Kindred: A Portrait of Our Families Today." *Essence* 30, no. 8 (December 1999): 112–114+.

Bio-Bibliographical Sources
Howard University Directory of Graduates, 1870–1980. White Plains, N.Y.: Bernard C. Harris Publishing Company, Inc., 1982.
"Valerie Wilson Wesley: Biography." Available: <http://www.tamarahayle.com/biography.htm> Accessed 11 May 2000.
"Valerie Wilson Wesley." *Contemporary Authors* (Gale Literary Databases). Available: <http://www.galenet.com> Accessed 5 May 2000.
Wesley, Valerie Wilson. Email communication with Sibyl E. Moses, 9 December 2000; 11 October 2001.

WHITE, CHERYL ANNE FISHER 1956–

Personal   Born on 6 May 1956 in Camden, New Jersey; daughter of Willie Mae Latimore of Orangeburg, South Carolina, and Ulysee Munderlyn; sisters: Beatrice Ann Clark (deceased), Gloria Jean Latimore Bermudez, and Henrietta Munderlyn Parsons; brothers: Ronnie Fisher (deceased), Charles Lee Fisher, Calvin Lee Fisher, Darryl Latimore, Kenneth Latimore, and Rodney Latimore; children: LeAnne, Isaiah Lee, Willie Lee III, Matthew Ranier, and Christopher Martin. Education: Landis Jr. High School, Vineland, New Jersey; Vineland Senior High School, Vineland; Cumberland County College, Office Automation Management Certificate, 1998. Religion: Baptist.
Residence in New Jersey   Vineland; Cedarville; Aura, 1975–1976; Pitman, 1996–1998; Bridgeton, 1998 to present.
Career   Senior Claims Examiner, 1980–1993 and 1996–1998, customer service representative, 1993–1996, Prudential Health Care, Millville, New Jersey; church secretary, Union Baptist Temple, Bridgeton, 1995 to present; secretary for Anger Management, Affirmative Action and Homelessness Coordination Departments, Board of Education, Bridgeton, 1999 to present.
Memberships   Sunday School secretary, pastor's secretary, choir president, Pastor's Aide Society, president and secretary for Jr. Ushers, Missionary Treasurer and Secretary, St. Paul Baptist Church, Vineland.
Awards   Best Poet of the 90s, National Library of Poetry; Harriet Tubman Award, 1992; Phi Theta Kappa (International Honor Society), 1999.
Publications
Fisher, Cheryl Anne. *The Waiting World.* [Bridgeton, N.J.]: L.I.M.C.W. Inspirational Ministries, 1990. 58 [ii].

White, Cheryl. *A Voice of Inspiration*. [Vineland, N.J.: The Author], 1993. 83, illus.

Fisher, Cheryl Anne. *Endless Joy*. [Vineland, N.J.]: L.I.M. C.W. Inspirational Ministries [1999]. 40.

———. *Thoughts of Inspirations*. Bridgeton, N.J.: L.I.M.C.W. Inspirational Ministries, n.d. 27.

Bio-Bibliographical Sources

White, Cheryl. Correspondence with Sibyl E. Moses, 20 September 2000.

———. "Resume." Bridgeton, N.J.: [2000]. 2.

———. *A Voice of Inspiration*. [Vineland, N.J.: The Author], 1993. 83.

WIGGINS, LOLA BUTEEN *SEE* SHAKIR, QADRIYYAH BUTEEN

WILLIAMS, RUBY ORA 1926–

Personal Born on 18 February 1926 in Lakewood, New Jersey; seventh of nine children born to Ida Bolles Williams (housewife, deceased) of Drummondville, Ontario, Canada, and Charles Williams (window cleaner, deceased) of New York City, New York; granddaughter (maternal) of Louisa Broady Bolles of Port Robinson, Canada, and James Bolles of Louisa, Virginia; granddaughter (paternal) of Martha Harris Williams of Brooklyn, New York, and Dan Williams of Bridgeton, New Jersey; brothers: Charles William Williams (deceased), Olyphant Greer Williams (deceased), Paul Towbin Williams (deceased), James Senator Williams; sisters: Martha Blanche Williams Wright (deceased), Thelma Olive Williams Davis, Barbara Elizabeth Williams, Dorothy Constance Williams (Green) Stallworth (deceased), Brittomarte Roach Hochoy

*Ruby Ora Williams,
courtesy of Ruby Ora Williams.*

(half-sister, deceased). Education: No. 5 School, Lakewood, New Jersey, 1930–1937; Lakewood Junior and Senior High Schools, Lakewood, 1937–1943; Virginia Union University, Richmond, Virginia, A.B., English, 1946–1950; Howard University, Washington, D.C., M.A., English, 1950–1953; University of California, Irvine, Ph.D., comparative culture, 1969–1974; Columbia University, summers 1955, 1956; New York University, Summer 1964; University of California, Berkeley, summer 1959. Religion: Episcopal

Residence in New Jersey Lakewood; Fort Lee.

Career   Clerk-typist, Department of Education, Health, and Welfare, Washington, D.C., 1952–1953; instructor, English, Southern University, Baton Rouge, Louisiana, 1953–1955; instructor, English, Tuskegee Institute, Tuskegee, Alabama, 1955–1967; instructor, English, Morgan State College, Baltimore, Maryland, 1957–1965; program advisor, Headquarters, National Camp Fire Girls, Inc., 1965–1968; professor of English, California State University, Long Beach, 1968–1988; visiting professor, Virginia Union University, 1991–1992.

Memberships   Member, All Saints Episcopal Choir, Long Beach, Ca.; member, BEEM (Black Experience as Expressed in Music); member, International Congress of Virginia Union Women Graduates; Consortium of Doctors.

Awards, Honors, Other Certificates   Vassie Wright Our Author's Study Club Award; Long Beach Community Award for Education; honored, Consortium of Doctors, 1993; honored, California Librarian's Black Caucus, 1974; *Who's Who in Black America; Who's Who in American Education; Who's Who in the West.*

Reflections

"Three major experiences during my high school years occurred in the same year. On Sunday, April 20, 1941, seven members of my family, which lived on a small farm, fled on foot for our lives from a forest fire. Our house was one of fifty in the town that burned. We lost everything. Whereas the fire was traumatic, the kindness of the townspeople was unbelievable. Four different families took our family of nine in and fed us. I, my mother, and two other sisters stayed with a family that had six children. I marveled that each morning my father and second brother drove to each house to see that each child was all right. They did the same thing each night. One lady took her furniture out of storage to furnish our temporary home which my father found two weeks after the fire.

Two months after the fire, my parents were one of the four families honored by the local chapter of the National Honor Society for sending the high school children who had reflected honorably on the high school and on them. Three months after my parents were honored, the principal of the same high school that honored them for having exemplary children, suspended my youngest sister from school. She had complained to my mother about her history teacher using the "N" word in class. Our mother wrote a note of protest. The principal asked a Caucasian classmate if the incident had occurred. When the child flushed red and said, "no," Dorothy was suspended until our father went in for a conference. Papa was sick in bed, but he arose; he and I walked two blocks to the high school. He said nothing as we walked the ten minutes to the school. When we got there, we could hear the principal yelling in a faculty meeting, "I don't want to ever hear anything like this again.""

After the meeting ended, the principal, very much in charge, took my father into his inner office. He talked first, then my father responded. The principal came out very red faced. When we walked home, Papa said he told the principal it was a recent phenomenon that Europeans stopped swinging in the trees and eating uncooked birds with feathers on. He may have even mentioned John Dillinger, the Dalton Brothers, and other notorious gangsters. There was no question about Dorothy's being reinstated. We realized the principal made a big mistake sending for our father—never at a loss for words—instead of our mother, who wrote the note. She would not have been as effective as Papa.

My parents and older siblings were highly influential in my becoming a writer. We had many books in our home, we were encouraged to use the local library and to participate in family discussions about issues. Each parent was an avid reader. When our mother died, she was reading five newspapers a day. I recall my father discussing Bigger Thomas's character deficit. Papa had an inclination to write, especially letters to the editor about a variety of issues. He wrote a letter noting a magazine misidentified a dog. Papa's letter was published in the national publication. We still have a letter he wrote the Post Master General James Farley and Farley's reply.

A cousin, professor of English, Anthony Grooms has published a book of poems, *Ice Poems,* and a book of short stories, *Trouble No More.* Another cousin, Bertha Branch Davis, writes poetry and short stories. A cousin, Kathy Barrett Carter, is a prominent New Jersey journalist. Two nieces are also writers, Ntozake Shange and Ifa Baeyza."

Publications

Books

Williams, Ora. *American Black Women in the Arts and Social Sciences: A Bibliographic Survey.* Rev. and expanded ed. Metuchen, N.J.: Scarecrow Press, 1973. xix, 141, illus.

———. *American Black Women in the Arts and Social Sciences: A Bibliographic Survey.* Rev. and expanded ed. Metuchen, N.J.: Scarecrow Press, 1978. xxi, 197, illus.

———, ed., *An Alice Dunbar-Nelson Reader.* Critical explorations by Agnes Moreland Jackson. Washington: University Press of America, 1979. xvi, 250.

———. *American Black Women in the Arts and Social Sciences: A Bibliographic Survey.* 3rd ed. Metuchen, N.J.: Scarecrow Press, 1994. li, 387, illus.

Articles

Williams, Ruby Ora. "Universal Kinship." *The Camp Fire Girl* 46 (February 1967): 3.

———. "In '68 Human Rights Come First." *The Camp Fire Girl* 47 (May 1968): 3–4.

———. "A Bibliography of Works Written by American Black Women." *CLA Journal* 15, no. 3 (March 1972).

———. "Works By and About Alice Ruth (Moore) Dunbar-Nelson: A Bibliography." *CLA Journal* 3 no. 19 (March 1976): 322–326.

———. "Alice Moore Dunbar-Nelson." *Dictionary of Literary Biography: Afro-American Writers before the Harlem Renaissance*. Edited by Trudier Harris and Thadious Davis, 50. Detroit: Gale Research, 1986.

———. "Eva Jessye: A Legacy in American Culture" *Goldmine: A New Tradition, I.* Long Beach: California State University, 1986.

———. "Miss Tempy's Watchers." *Masterplots II: Short Story Series.* Pasadena, Calif.: Salem Press, 1986.

———. "Alice Ruth (Moore) Dunbar-Nelson: Another Harlem Renaissance Poet." *The Zora Neale Hurston Forum* 1, no. 2 (spring 1987): 12–18.

———. "The Town Poor." In *Masterplots II: Short Story Series,* n.p. Pasadena, Calif.: Salem Press, 1987.

Book Chapters

Williams, Ruby Ora. "American Black Women Composers: An Annotated Bibliography." In *But Some of Us Are Brave,* n.p. Westbury, N.Y.: Feminist Press, 1981.

———. "Lorenzo Graham: A Bio-Bibliography." In *Dictionary of Literary Biography.* Edited by Trudier Harris and Thadious Davis, 76. Detroit: Gale Research, 1988.

Biographical Sources

Page, James A., and Jae Min Roh. *Selected Black American, African, and Caribbean Authors: A Bio-Bibliography.* Littleton, Colo.: Libraries Unlimited, 1985.

Williams, Ruby Ora. "African American Women Writers in New Jersey: Biographical Questionnaire." Completed by Ruby Ora Williams, December 1996.

———. *American Black Women in the Arts and Social Sciences: A Bibliographic Survey.* Rev. and expanded ed. Metuchen, N.J.: Scarecrow Press, 1978.

———. Letter to Sibyl E. Moses, 29 February 1988.

WOLFE, DEBORAH CANNON PARTRIDGE 1916–

Personal Born on 22 December 1916 in Cranford, New Jersey; third child of Gertrude Moody Cannon (high school principal, social worker, and public servant) and David Wadsworth Cannon, Sr. (minister); husbands: Henry Roy Partridge, Sr. (divorced)and Estemore Wolfe (divorced); child: Henry Roy Partridge, Jr. (deceased). Education: Cranford High School, Cranford, high school diploma, 1933; Jersey City State College, B.S., education and social studies, 1933–1937; Teachers College, Columbia University, New York, New York, M.A., teacher education, rural education, 1937–1938; Vassar College, summer 1944; Columbia University, News

York, Ed.D., 1945; Jewish Theological Seminary of America, 1952–1953; Teachers College, Columbia University (postdoctoral study), 1953–1954; Union Theological Study, theology, 1950–1951; University of Pennsylvania (advanced postdoctoral study, research in education statistics), 1950–1951. Religion: Baptist; First Baptist Church, Cranford.

Residence in New Jersey   Cranford.

Career   Principal and English teacher, Lincoln School, Cranford, 1936–1938; principal and teacher trainer, Prairie School (laboratory school for Tuskegee Institute), Tuskegee, Alabama, 1938–1941; principal and teacher, Mitchell's Mill School (laboratory for Tuskegee Institute), Tuskegee; director, community center, 1935–1936, summers 1936–1937; head, Department of Elementary Education, and director, Graduate Studies, Tuskegee Institute, Tuskegee, 1938–1950; professor, and director, Graduate Workshop, Grambling College, Grambling, Louisiana, summer 1944; visiting professor, summers 1951–1954, New York University; visiting professor, Fordham University, Long Island, New York, 1952–1953; visiting professor, University of Michigan, Ann Arbor, summer, June 1952; visiting professor, Columbia University, Teachers College, New York, 1953–1954; visiting professor, Texas College, Tyler, Texas, summer 1955; visiting professor, University of Illinois, Champaign, Illinois, summer 1956; visiting professor, Wayne State University, Detroit, Michigan, summer 1961; chief of education, U.S. House of Representatives' Committee on Education and Labor, 1962–1965; professor, Queens College, the City University of New York, 1951–1986.

Memberships   Secretary, Council of National Organization for Children and Youth; Leadership Services Committee, National YWCA; board member and chairman of Educational Advisory Committee, Lisle Fellowship; board of directors, American Council on Human Rights; Education Committee, National Conference of Christians and Jews; chairperson, Speaker's Bureau, National Association of Negro Business an Professional Women's Clubs; life member, National Congress of Colored Parents and Teachers; life member, American Teachers Association; Fellowship of Southern Churchman; American Association of University Women (National Legislative Chairman); American Association of University Professors; Internal Reading Association; Comprehensive Education Society; American Academy of Social and Political Science; National Education Association, life member since 1965; international president, Zeta Phi Beta Sorority,1954–1965; National Society for the Study of Education; Association of Childhood Education, International; trustee, Science Service (1969 to present); president, National Alliance of Black Educators; vice president, National Alliance for Safer Cities; Non-Governmental Organization Representative to United Nations for Church Women United.

Awards, Honors, Other Certificates   National Honor Society, Cranford High School, Cranford; Honor Society, New Jersey State Teachers College, Jersey City, New Jersey; Kappa Delta Pi Honor Society in Education, Columbia University; Pi Lambda Theta Honor Society, Columbia University;

fellowship, General Education Board; invitation from President Truman to White House Conference on Children and Youth; citation, outstanding contribution to the religious and civic welfare of America, National Baptist Convention; invitation from President Eisenhower to White House Conference on Education; Honorary Membership of National Society for the Prevention of Juvenile Delinquency, Inc.; appointed by President Eisenhower to Citizens Advisory Committee on Youth Fitness; invited to inauguration of President John F. Kennedy and President Lyndon Johnson; high school in Macon County, Alabama, named in her honor; dormitory, Trenton State College, Trenton, New Jersey, named in her honor; National Achievement Award, National Association of Negro Business and Professional Women's Club, Inc. 1958; Woman of the Year, Delta Beta Zeta Chapter, Zeta Phi Beta Sorority 1959; Women of the Year, Women of Morgan State College, Baltimore, Maryland, 1959; Phi Delta Kappa Fraternity (first woman initiated in Rutgers University Chapter); Amsterdam News Honoree, 1959; one of New York's Outstanding 10 Women, 1958; Atlantic Region Achievement Award, Zeta Phi Beta Sorority, 1957; Today's Makers of History Award, The Association of the Study of Negro Life and History, 1959.

Publications

Book

Wolfe, Deborah Partridge. *Interim Report on Education and Citizenship in the Public School System of Puerto Rico to Adam Clayton Powell, Committee on Education and Labor, House of Representatives, Eighty-seventh Congress, second session.* Washington, D.C.: U.S. Government Printing Office, 1962. ix, 47.

Articles

Cannon, Deborah. "A Migrant Center in Maryland." *Women and Missions* 13, no. 12 (March 1937): 397–398.

Partridge, Deborah Cannon. "Adult Education Projects Sponsored by Negro College Fraternities and Sororities." *Journal of Negro Education* 14 (July 1945): 374–380.

———. "Directives for Designing the Curriculum of Negro Rural Schools." *Journal of Negro Education* 17, no. 4 (fall 1948): 554–555.

———. "Helping Teachers Understand the Nature of Learning." *Understanding the Child* 17 (October 1948): 113–114.

———. "Guidelines for Curriculum Design." *School Executive* 68 (December 1948): 29–30.

———. "Bridging the Gap Between School and Community." *P.T.A. Bulletin* (March 1948).

———. "Faculty and Staff Responsibility for Instruction and Research." *Journal of Higher Education Among Negroes* (winter 1948).

———. "Verse-Speaking as a Creative Are." *Elementary English* 25, no. 7 (November 1948): 442–445.

———. "Student Teacher Participation in Community Living." In *Association for Student Teaching Yearbook, 27th Yearbook* (November 1948): 66–74.

————. "Utilizing All Resources or Better Living." *PTA Bulletin* 3 (April 1950): 1–4.

————. "Understanding Your Child." *Our National Family* 13, no. 2 (January–February 1951): 17–18.

————. "Studying the Individual Child." *Our National Family* 13, no. 3 (May–June 1951): 7–9.

————. "Improving Human Relations." *Our National Family* 14, no. 1 (December 1951): 20–21.

————. "Working Together for Better Human Relations." *Journal of Educational Sociology* 26, no. 7 (March 1953): 303–310.

————. "Introducing a Guidance Program In the Rural School." *Understanding the Child* 22, no. 4 (October 1953): 109–111.

————. "Teaching Beginning Reading." *School Executive* 73, no. 2 (December 1953): 54–56.

————. "What it Means To Be a 'Greek'." *Archon* 20, no. 2 (July 1955): 3, 7.

————. "35 Years of ZΦB Sorority—Its Past, Present, Future." *Archon* 20, no. 3–4 (October–December 1955): 3, 9, 18, 24.

————. "Scholarship Opportunities." *Responsibility* 13, no. 1 (fall 1956): 36–37.

————. "Youth—the Years from 10–16: A Book Review." *Understanding the Child & YWCA Journal* 26, no. 2 (fall 1956): 36–37.

————. "Prevention and Control of Juvenile Delinquency." *Archon* 22 (December 1957): 3, 34.

————. "Developing World-Mindedness." *Journal of Educational Sociology* 31, no. 8 (March 1958): 256–264.

————. "Working Towards Integration." *Archon* 23, no. 3 (October–December 1958): 3, 28–31.

————. "Prepare Your Teachers to Deal with Prejudice." *School Executive* 78 (November 1958): 50–52. Reprinted in *Education Digest* 24 (February 1959): 16–18.

————. "Student Life at Moscow State University." *SEANYS Newsletter* 2, no. 2 (March 1958): 5–6.

————. "Education in the U.S.S.R." *New York State Education* 46 (March 1959): 412–414.

————. "Women in Pace with Space." *Archon* 24, no. 2 (December 1959): 3–5.

Wolfe, Deborah Partridge. "The Modern Women—Her Spiritual Possibilities." *Archon* 25, no. 1 (May 1960): 3, 52.

————. "Curriculum Adaptations for the Culturally Deprived." *Journal of Negro Education* 31, no. 2 (spring 1962): 139–151.

————. "The School's Role in Preventing Juvenile Delinquency." *Journal of Educational Sociology* 36, no. 2 (October 1962): 89–92.

————. "African's Challenge to the Women of America." *Archon* (December 1962).

————. "Education's Challenge to American Negro Youth." *The Negro History Bulletin* 26, no. 3 (December 1962): 115–118.

———. "Education in Modern Society—It's Ever Changing Pattern." *Vital Speeches* 29 (October 15, 1962): 23–26.

———. "Foreign Language Teaching in the Schools of America." *Pioneer Ideals in Education* (December 1962).

———. "Utilizing American Womanpower." *Archon* (April 1962).

———. "Africa's Challenge to the Education American Negro." *The Quarterly Review of Higher Education Among Negroes* [hereafter *Quarterly Review*] 31, no. 1 (1963): 1–5.

———. " The Education Congress—1963–64." *Teacher Education News and Notes,* Division of Teacher Education, City University of New York, 16, no. 3 (January-February 1965): 1 and 4.

———. "Education for Service." *Quarterly Review* 33, no. 3 (July 1965): 178–182.

———. "Elementary and Secondary Education Act of 1965." *Childhood Education* 42, no. 1 (September 1965): 12–14.

———. "What the Economic Opportunity Act Means to the Negro." *Journal of Negro Education* 34, no. 1 (winter 1965): 88–92.

———. "Role of Reading in Improving Human Relationships." *Quarterly Review* 34, no. 2 (April 1966): 65–72.

———. "The United Nations; Unity in Diversity." *Quarterly Review* 34, no. 4 (October 1966).

———. "The Press-Guardian of Responsibilities, Freedom and Truth." *Quarterly Review* 35, no. 2 (April 1967): 59–63.

———. "Education for Responsible Freedom." *Quarterly Review* 35, no. 4 (October 1967): 153–158.

———. "The Teacher's Role in Maintaining Cultural Pluralism." *Quarterly Review* 36, no. 2 (April 1968): 69–73.

———. "The History of Educator's Participation in Government and Politics." *Quarterly Review* 36, no. 4 (October 1968).

———. "Needed: Training for Teachers of the Underprivileged." *Quarterly Review* 37, no. 2 (April 1969).

———. "The Origin of Prejudice." *Quarterly Review* 37, no. 2 (April 1969): 57–61.

———. "New Criteria and New Perspectives for Selection of the Marginally Qualified Disadvantaged Student." *Quarterly Review* 37, no. 3 (July 1969): 107–117.

———. "Trends in Science Education." *Science Education* 54, no. 1 (January–March 1970): 71–75.

———. "Valuing the Dignity of Black Children: A Black Teacher Speaks." *Childhood Education* 46, no. 7 (April 1970): 348–350. Reprinted in *Learning to Live as Neighbors. 1971–1972 Annual Bulletin,* edited by Monroe D. Cohen.

———. "Preservice Science Education." *Science for Children* 8, no. 2 (October 1970): 27–29.

Wolfe, Deborah P. "An American Educator Reports on the People's Republic of China." *Kappa Delta Pi Record* 13, no. 4 (April 1977): 107–8, 127.

Wolfe, Deborah Cannon Partridge. "American Democracy: Its Challenge from Abroad." *Phi Delta Kappan* 60, no. 3 (November 1978): 159–60.

Wolfe, Deborah Cannon Patridge [*sic*]. "Booker T. Washington: An Educator for All Ages." *Phi Delta Kappan* 63, no. 3 (November 1981):205, 222.

Wolfe, Deborah. "Teaching: A Lifetime Commitment." *Kappa Delta Pi Record* 35, no. 2 (winter 1999): 86–88.

Bio-Bibliographical Sources

Wolfe, Deborah Cannon Partridge. "Curriculum Vitae." [Cranford, N.J.: The Author, undated]. 18 leaves. Photocopy.

Wayman, Ellen J. "Deborah Cannon Partridge Wolfe." In The Women of New Jersey Project, Inc. *Past and Present,* 429–430. Metuchen, N.J. and London: The Scarecrow Press, Inc., 1990.

WRIGHT, MARION MANOLA THOMPSON **1905–1962**

Personal Born on 13 September 1905 in East Orange, New Jersey; joined the ancestors 26 October 1962, in Washington D.C. The fourth child of Minnie Holmes Thompson (housekeeper) and Moses R. Thompson; husband: William H. Moss (divorced) and Arthur M. Wright (divorced); children: Thelma Moss (deceased) and James A. Moss (deceased); Education: Barringer High School, Newark, New Jersey, high school diploma, 1923; Howard University, Washington, D.C., A.B., 1923–1927, magna cum laude and M.A., Education, 1928; New York School of Social Work, New York, New York, diploma; Columbia University, New York, Ph.D., 1940; Religion: Baptist.

Residence in New Jersey East Orange; Newark; Montclair.

Career Instructor, Howard University, Washington D.C., 1929–1931, 1939–1940; family visitor, senior worker, case

Marion M. Thompson Wright, courtesy of the Moorland-Spingarn Research Center, Howard University.

supervisor, New Jersey Emergency Relief Administration, 1939–1936; assistant professor, Howard University, 1940–1946; associate professor, Howard University, 1946–1950; professor, Howard University, 1950–1962; director of student teaching, Howard University, 1940–1946; organizer and acting director of Counseling Service, Howard University, 1946–1947; counselor (part-time), Howard University, 1947–1948; acting head, Department of Education, Howard University, 1952–1953. Memberships:

National Association of College Women; National Council of Negro
Women; Delta Sigma Theta Sorority; National Education Association;
American Association of University Professors; American Guidance and
Personnel Association; Association for the Study of Negro Life and History;
American Teachers Association; Pi Lambda Theta Educational Sorority;
American Association for the Advancement of Science; Society for the
Advancement of Education; Friend's Historical Association; New Jersey
Historical Society; National Association of College Women. Howard Uni-
versity: Freshman Advisory Board; Committee on Student Petitions;
Review Editor, *Journal of Negro Education;* University-Wide Committee on
Research and Scholarly Activity; Committee on Determining Criteria for
the Rank of Assistant Professor; Graduate Council, 1951–1953.

Awards, Honors, Other Certificates   Best book review submitted to the *Journal of Negro History* for the year ending September 1942; best article submitted to the *Journal of Negro History* for the year ending September 1942;
award "For outstanding achievement and contributing to the welfare and
progress of the Negro citizens of the state of New Jersey," *New Jersey Her-
ald News,* 29 October 1948; Faculty Research Grant, *Evening Star,* to complete a biographical study of the late Lucy Diggs Slowe, the first dean of
women at Howard University, 1961.

Publications

Book

Wright, Marion T. *The Education of Negroes in New Jersey.* New York: Teachers College Bureau of Publications, 1941. 237.

Articles

Wright, Marion T. "Negro Youth and the Federal Emergency Programs:
CCC and the NYA." *Journal of Negro Education* 9 (July 1940): 397–407.

———. "Mr. Baxter's School." *Proceedings of the New Jersey Historical Society*
59, no. 2 (April 1941): 116–152.

———. "The Quakers as Social Workers Among Negroes in New Jersey
from 1763–1804." *Bulletin of Friends' Historical Association* 30, no. 2
(autumn 1941): 79–87.

———. "Have You Met the Social Worker?" *School and Society* 55 (February
1942): 239–241.

———. "New Jersey Laws and the Negro." *The Journal of Negro History* 38,
no. 2 (April 1943): 156–199.

Wright, Marion T., and Walter G. Daniel. "The Role of Educational Agencies in Maintaining Morale Among Negroes." *The Journal of Negro Education* 12, no. 3 (summer 1943): 490–501.

Wright, Marion T. "Cooperation with the Attendance Officer." *Educational
Administration and Supervision* Supplement 30 (January 1944): 32–39.

———. "Challenge of the Juvenile Delinquency." *The Aframerican Women's
Journal* (spring 1944): 15–17.

———. "The National Council of Negro Women and the Schools." *The
Journal of Negro Education* (summer 1944): 12–14.

———. "Educational Programs for the Improvement of Race relations:

Negro Advancement Organizations." *The Journal of Negro Education* 13 (summer 1944): 349–360.

———. "Take the Mountain to Mohammed." *Journal of Delta Sigma Theta Sorority* (May 1945): 8, 37–38.

———. "The Availability of Higher Education for Negroes in Delaware." *Journal of Negro Education* 17, no. 3 (summer 1947): 265–271.

———. "Negro Suffrage in New Jersey, 1776–1875." *The Journal of Negro History.* (April, 1948): 168–224.

———. "Guidance—The Weak Link in the Educational Chain." *The Midwest Journal* 1, no. 1 (winter 1948): 32–44.

———. "Educational Problems and Needs of Negro Youth." *Journal of Negro Education* 19, no. 3 (summer 1950): 310–321.

———. "Extending Civil Rights in New Jersey through the New Jersey Division Against Discrimination." *The Journal of Negro History* 38, no. 1 (January 1953): 91–107. (Five thousand reprints purchased by the New Jersey Division Against Discrimination for distribution).

———. "Parents Improve human Relations in Education." *Journal of Human Relations* 1, no. 4 (spring 1953): 20–30.

———. "New Jersey Leads in the Struggle for Educational Integration." *The Journal of Educational Sociology* 26 (May 1953): 401–417.

———. "Racial Integration in the Public Schools of New Jersey." *The Journal of Negro Education* 23, no. 3 (summer 1954): 282–289. Cited in brief submitted to the Supreme Court by the NAACP in November, 1954.

Book Reviews

Wright, Marion T. Review of *An Appraisal of the Negro in Colonial South Carolina*, by Frank J. Klingburg. *The Journal of Negro History* 27, no. 3 (April 1942): 222–224.

———. Review of *Tenants of the Almighty*, by Arthur Rapor. *The Journal of Negro Education* 13, no. 2 (spring 1944): 200–201.

———. Review of *Strange Fruit*, by Lillian Smith. *Journal of Negro Education* 13, no. 4 (fall 1944): 520–522.

———. Review of *An Evaluation of the Accredited Secondary Schools for Negroes*, by Aaron Brown. *Journal of Negro Education* 14, no. 2 (spring 1945): 209–211.

———. Review of *All Born Sailors*, by John Beecher. *Journal of Negro Education* 15, no. 2 (spring 1946): 214–215.

———. Review of *The Negro and the Post-War World*, by Rayford Logan. *Journal of Negro Education* 15, no. 2 (spring 1946): 212–213.

———. Review of *If He Hollers, Let Him Go*, by Chester Himes. *Journal of Negro Education* 15, no. 2 (spring 1946): 213–214.

———. Review of *Anatomy of Racial Intolerance*, by George B. De Huszar. *Journal of Negro Education* 15, no. 4 (fall 1946): 661–662.

———. Review of *Needs of Negro High School Graduates*, by William H. Gray. *Journal of Negro Education* 15, no. 4 (fall 1946): 660–661.

———. Review of *Color and Democracy*, by William B. Du Bois. *Journal of Negro Education* 15, no. 1 (winter 1946): 63–65.

———. Review of *They Seek a City,* by Anna Bontemps and Jack Conroy. *Journal of Negro Education* 15, no. 1 (winter 1946): 65–66.

———. Review of *Kingsblood Royal,* by Sinclair Lewis. *Journal of Negro Education* 16, no. 4 (fall 1947): 561.

———. Review of *The Vixens,* by FrankYerby. *Journal of Negro Education* 16, no. 4 (fall 1947): 562.

———. Review of *The Other Room,* by Worth T. Hedden. *Journal of Negro Education* 17, no. 4 (fall 1948): 500–501.

———. Review of *Knock on Any Door,* by Willard Mottley. *Journal of Negro Education* 17, no. 1 (winter 1948): 73–74.

———. Review of *You Can't Build A Chimney From the Top,* by Joseph Holley. *The Midwest Journal* 1, no. 2 (summer 1949): 110–112.

———. Review of *Without Magnolias,* by Bucklin Moon. *Journal of Negro Education* 18, no. 4 (fall 1949): 499–500.

———. Review of *No Trumpet Before Him,* by Nelia G. White. *Journal of Negro Education* 18, no. 4 (fall 1949): 500–501.

———. Review of *Your Most Humble Servant,* by Shirley Graham. *Journal of Negro Education* 19, no. 4 (fall 1950): 487–488.

———. Review of *The Negro and the Schools,* by Harry S. Ashmore. *Journal of Negro History* 24, no. 4 (fall 1955): 466–468.

———. Review of *Schools in Transition,* by Robin M. Williams, Jr. and Margaret W. Ryan. *Journal of Negro Education* 24, no. 4 (fall 1955): 466–468.

Other

Wright, Marion T. "The Supreme Court Reverses Itself." Prepared at the request of U.S. Culture Attaché in Rome, Italy.

Bio-Bibliographical Sources

The Bison, 1927. Washington D.C.: Senior Class of the College of Liberal Arts and Sciences, Howard University, 1927.

"Dr. Wright, of Howard, Gets Star Fellowship." *Washington Evening Star News,* May 14, 1961, A–10.

Hayes, Margaret E., and Doris B. Armstrong. "Marion Manola Thompson Wright." In The Women's Project of New Jersey, Inc. *Past and Promise, Lives of New Jersey Women,* 435–437. Metuchen, N.J. and London: The Scarecrow Press, 1990.

"Professor Marion Wright Found Dead in Automobile." *Washington Evening Star News.* October 27, 1962, B–11.

[Wright, Marion Thompson] "Contributions and Activities of Marion Wright, 1946–1955." Mimeographed. Source: Howard University Archives, Moorland Spingarn Research Center, Howard University, Washington, D.C.

[Wright, Marion Thompson] "Education, Experience, and Contributions of Marion T. Wright." Mimeographed.

Wright, Marion Thompson. "Wright, Marion Thompson." Information Sheet, Publicity Department, Office of the Secretary, Howard University. 8 May 1947. Completed by Marion Thompson Wright. 2.

Appendix A: Distribution of African American Women Writers in New Jersey, by Geographical Affiliation (Town)

Allentown
Dorin, Lenora Allen

Asbury Park
McCray, Carrie Allen

Atlantic City
Butler, Anna Land
Mathis, Sharon Yvonne Bell
Murray, Evelyn Stalling
Talley, Jere Elaine
Thompson, Mary Louise

Aura
White, Cheryl Anne Fisher

Belleville
Tucker, Wanda Regina Buggs

Belmar
Roper, Grace Ariadne Trott

Beverly
Morris, Margaret Lee Hicks

Bridgeton
Brown, Martha Hursey
Lindsey, Helen Marie Tudos Lee
White, Cheryl Anne Fisher

Budd Lake
Tucker, Wanda Regina Buggs

Burlington
Payne, J. Joyce Coleman

Camden
Abdus-Samad, Ni'mat Mujahid
Burnett, Gracie Diane

Davis-Thompson, Esther Louise
Gaines, Kathryn Elizabeth
Hunter-Lattany, Kristin Elaine
　Eggleston
Hunt-Hill, Jeanette Mae
Khan, Lurey
Ruff, Phontella Cloteal Butcher
Rushin, Kate
Thompson, Mary Louise

Cape May/ Cape May County
Hunter-Lattany, Kristin Elaine
　Eggleston
Lee, Jarena

Carney's Point
Butler, Sally Central

Cedarville
White, Cheryl Anne Fisher

Cherry Hill
Butler, Rebecca Batts

Claysville, Mannington Township
Saunders, Esther "Hetty"

Clifton
Thomas, Naturi Songhai

Cranford
Wolfe, Deborah Cannon

East Orange
Brown, Margery Wheeler
Campbell, Bertha Georgetta Merritt
Gilmore-Scott, Monique
Haynes, Oona'o
Holmes, Linda Janet
Hudson, Cheryl AuVal Willis

Johnson, Alice Perry
Karriem, Jaleelah
Moore, Betty Jean Green
Neals, Betty Elizabeth Harris
Roberts, Irose Fernella Adams
Salaam, Nefeterri
Sanders, Viola Harris
Taylor, Hope Rosemary
Travis, Nancy Elizabeth
Tucker, Wanda Regina Buggs
Walker, Sheila Suzanne
Wesley, Valerie Deane Wilson
Wright, Marion Manola Thompson

Eatontown
Thompson, Mary Louise

Elizabeth
Hughes, Sally Page
Shivers, Ruby Williams
Travis, Nancy Elizabeth

Elsinboro
Saunders, Esther "Hetty"

Englewood
Amos, Gloria Lucille White
Thomas, Veona Young

Englishtown
Hailstock, Shirley T.

Ewing
Hinton, Maurita Miles

Fair Haven
Greene, Carolyn Jetter
Tate, Claudia C.

Fanwood
Travis, Nancy Elizabeth

Fort Lee
Williams, Ruby Ora

Glassboro
Williams, Ruby Ora

Hackensack
Coleman, Chrisena Anne
Thomas, Veona Young
Thornton, Yvonne Shirley

Hanover
Travis, Nancy Elizabeth

Highland Park
Wall, Cheryl Ann

Hillsborough
Taylor, Hope Rosemary

Hoboken
Fullilove, Mindy Thompson

Hopewell
Trusty, Emma Marie H. Cooper

Jersey City
Ahmad, Ameerah Hasin
Clarke, Cheryl Lynn
Hendley, Essie Lee Kirkland
Nunery, Gladys Cannon

Kearny
Walker, Sheila Suzanne

Lakewood
Williams, Ruby Ora

Laurenceville
Dorin, Lenora Allen

Lawnside
Fauset, Jessie Redmon
Hinton, Maurita Miles
Lee, Jarena
Rushin, Kate

Lawrenceville
Mitchell, Sharon L.

Leonia
Hayes, Leola Grant

Linden
Shaw, Helen

Long Branch
Freeland, Annabelle Robinson
Tate, Claudia C.
Thornton, Jeanette Frances
Thornton, Rita Louise
Thornton, Yvonne Shirley

Magnolia
Hunter-Lattany, Kristin Elaine
    Eggleston

Maplewood
Thomas, Naturi Songhai

Mendham
Bryant, Irene Martin

Montclair
Brown, Vashti Adelaide Proctor
Campbell, Bertha Georgetta Merritt
Darden, Norma Jean
Edge, Sylvia Clark
Holley, Mary Rose
Johnson, Birdie (Byerte) Wilson
Layne, Patricia
Lloyd, Carole Darden
McCray, Carrie Allen
Stone, Elberta Wilhelminia Hayes
Wesley, Dorothy Louise Burnett Porter
Wesley, Valerie Deane Wilson
Wright, Marion Manola Thompson

Mt. Holly
Burnett, Gracie Diane

Morristown
Bryant, Irene Martin

Neptune
Jarrett, Norma Lynn
McKay, Lenora Sylvia Walker

New Brunswick
Clarke, Cheryl Lynn
Howell, Christine Moore
Wall, Cheryl Ann

Newark
Baraka, Amina
Benyard, Daphne Haygood
Beyah, Islah
Brown, Margery Wheeler
Edge, Sylvia Clark
Flagg, E. Alma Williams
Gilmore-Scott, Monique
Grant, Gwendolyn Goldsby
Johnson, Alice Perry
Karriem, Jaleelah
Kenyatta, Janice Green
Little, Benilde Elease
Livingston, Eddiemae
Lowery, Pauline Mason
Moore, Betty Jean Green
Neals, Betty Elizabeth Harris
Pitts, Gertrude Williams
Riley, Maurice Lee Ficklin
Rodgers-Rose, La Frances Audrey
Salaam, Nefeterri
Sanders, Viola Harris
Strickland, Dorothy Mae Salley
Travis, Nancy Elizabeth
Tucker, Wanda Regina Buggs
Wright, Marion Manola Thompson

Newtonville
Blanks, Louise Scott Thompson

Orange
Beyah, Islah
Brown, Margery Wheeler
Campbell, Bertha Georgetta Merritt
Fullilove, Mindy Thompson
Hinton, Maurita Miles

Kenyatta, Janice Green
Strickland, Dorothy Mae Salley
Taylor, Hope Rosemary

Palmyra
Flournoy, Valerie Rose
Flournoy, Vanessa

Piscataway
Kenyatta, Janice Green
Sanders, Viola Harris

Pitman
White, Cheryl Anne Fisher

Plainfield
Hendley, Essie Lee Kirkland
Hughes, Sally Page
Rodgers-Rose, La Francis Audrey
Sanders, Viola Harris
Shakir, Qadriyyah Buteen
Sharif, Ummil-Khair Zakiyyah
Shaw, Helen
Shivers, Ruby Williams
Tuck-Ponder, Michele Lois

Plainsboro
Hailstock, Shirley T.
Mitchell, Sharon L.

Port Norris
Carmichael, Mary Elizabeth Cornish

Princeton
Drewry, Cecelia Hodges
Howell, Christine Moore
Kenyatta, Janice Green
Pouncy, Mattie Hunter
Tuck-Ponder, Michele Lois

Red Bank
Freeland, Annabelle Robinson
Tate, Claudia C.

Riverside
Morris, Margaret Lee Hicks

Rockaway
Edge, Sylvia Clark

Salem
Butler, Sally Central
Lindsey, Helen Marie Tudos Lee

Somerset
Kenyatta, Janice Green
Pouncy, Mattie Hunter

South Orange
Little, Benilde Elease
Taylor, Hope Rosemary
Thomas, Naturi Songhai
Travis, Nancy Elizabeth

Summit
Thandeka

Teaneck
Clyburn, Evelyn
Thomas, Veona Young
Thornton, Yvonne Shirley
Tuck-Ponder, Michele Lois

Tinton Falls
Freeland, Annabelle Robinson

Toms River
Thomas, Naturi Songhai

Trenton
Biggs, Undra Elissa Clay
Collins, Elsie McIntosh
Dorin, Lenora Allen
Downing, Theresa Ann Bowman
Hailstock, Shirley T.
Hinton, Maurita Miles
Jackson, Mary Jane Ray
Lee, Helen Corinne Jackson
Mitchell, Sharon L.
Shange, Ntozake
Thompson, Mary Louise

Union
Strickland, Dorothy Mae Salley

Vauxhall
Kearse, Amalya Lyle

Vineland
Blanks, Louise Scott Thompson
Thompson, Mary Louise
White, Cheryl Anne Fisher

West Long Branch
Mitchell, Sharon L.

West New York
Thomas, Naturi Songhai

West Orange
Strickland, Dorothy Mae Salley
Tucker, Wanda Regina Buggs

Wildwood
Davis-Thompson, Esther Louise

Willingboro
Dudley, Frankie W.
Ruff, Phontella Cloteal Butcher
Spinner, Bettye Delores Tyson

Woodstown
Butler, Sally Central

Appendix B: Distribution of African American Women Writers in New Jersey, by Genre

Autobiography/Memoir
Abdus-Samad, Ni'mat Mujahid
Fullilove, Mindy Thompson
Hinton, Maurita Miles
Lee, Helen Jackson
Lee, Jarena

Bibliography/Index
Campbell, Georgetta Merritt
Wesley, Dorothy Louise Burnett Porter
Williams, Ruby Ora

Biography
Bryant, Irene Martin
Butler, Rebecca Batts
Collins, Elsie McIntosh
Holley, Mary Rose
Holmes, Linda Janet
Johnson, Birdie (Byerte) Wilson
Khan, Lurey
McCray, Carrie Allen
Nunery, Gladys Cannon
Tate, Claudia C.
Thornton, Jeanette Frances
Thornton, Rita Louise
Thornton, Yvonne Shirley
Wall, Cheryl A.
Wesley, Dorothy Louise Burnett Porter
Williams, Ruby Ora

Child/Juvenile Literature
Ahmad, Ameerah Hasin
Brown, Margery Wheeler
Brown, Vashti Proctor
Carmichael, Mary Elizabeth Cornish
Fauset, Jessie Redmon
Flournoy, Valerie Rose
Flournoy, Vanessa
Hudson, Cheryl AuVal Willis

Hunter-Lattany, Kristin Elaine
  Eggleston
Khan, Lurey
Layne, Patricia
Lindsey, Helen Marie
Mathis, Sharon Yvonne Bell
Shakir, Qadriyyah Buteen
Sharif, Ummil-Khair Zakiyyah
Stone, Elberta Wilhelminia Hayes
Thomas, Naturi Songhai

Comic Strip/Cartoon/Satire/Humor
Greene, Carolyn Jetter

Cookbook
Darden, Norma Jean
Jackson, Mary Jane Ray
Lloyd, Carole Darden

Criticism/Anthology
Baraka, Amina
Clarke, Cheryl Lynn
Tate, Claudia C.
Wall, Cheryl Ann
Wesley, Dorothy Louise Burnett Porter

Nonfiction Article, Essay, and Book
Brown, Martha Hursey
Clarke, Cheryl Lynn
Coleman, Chrisena Anne
Collins, Elsie McIntosh
Davis-Thompson, Esther
Fauset, Jessie Redmon
Freeland, Annabelle Robinson
Fullilove, Mindy Thompson
Grant, Gwendolyn Goldsby
Greene, Carolyn Jetter
Hayes, Leola Grant
Haynes, Oona'o

Hendley, Essie Kirkland
Holley, Mary Rose
Holmes, Linda Janet
Howell, Christine Moore
Johnson, Birdie Wilson
Kearse, Amalya Lyle
Kenyatta, Janice Green
Little, Benilde Elease
Mathis, Sharon Yvonne Bell
McKay, Lenora Walker
Riley, Maurice Lee Ficklin
Rodgers-Rose, La Francis Audrey
Roper, Grace Ariadne Trott
Sanders, Viola Harris
Shakir, Qadriyyah Buteen
Sharif, Ummil-Khair Zakiyyah
Shivers, Ruby Williams
Spinner, Bettye Delores Tyson
Strickland, Dorothy Mae Salley
Tate, Claudia C.
Thandeka
Thornton, Yvonne Shirley
Trusty, Emma Marie H. Cooper
Walker, Sheila Suzanne
Wall, Cheryl Ann
Wesley, Dorothy Louise Burnett Porter
Wesley, Valerie Deane Wilson
Williams, Ruby Ora
Wolfe, Deborah Cannon
Wright, Marion Manola Thompson
McCray, Carrie Allen

Novel

Amos, Gloria Lucille White
Biggs, Undra Elissa Clay
Blanks, Louise Thompson
Coleman, Chrisena Anne
Dorin, Lenora Allen
Fauset, Jessie Redmon
Flournoy, Vanessa
Gilmore-Scott, Monique
Hailstock, Shirley T.
Hunter-Lattany, Kristin Elaine
    Eggleston
Jarrett, Norma Lynn
Little, Benilde Elease

Morris, Margaret Lee Hicks
Murray, Evelyn Stalling
Pitts, Gertrude Williams
Pouncy, Mattie Hunter
Roberts, Irose Adams
Salaam, Nefeterri
Shange, Ntozake
Thomas, Veona Young
Wesley, Valerie Deane Wilson

Opinion: Editorial/Political Commentary

Greene, Carolyn Jetter
Haynes, Oona'o

Play/Screenplay/Documentary Script

Hunter-Lattany, Kristin Elaine
    Eggleston
Shange, Ntozake
Thomas, Veona Young

Poetry

Ahmad, Ameerah Hasin
Baraka, Amina
Benyard, Daphne
Beyah, Islah
Burnett, Gracie Diane
Butler, Anna Land
Butler, Sally Central
Clarke, Cheryl Lynn
Clyburn, Evelyn
Downing, Theresa Bowman
Dudley, Frankie W.
Flagg, E. Alma Williams
Gaines, Katheryn Elizabeth
Haynes, Oona'o
Hughes, Sally Page
Hunt-Hill, Jeanette Mae
Johnson, Alice Perry
Karriem, Jaleelah
Livingston, Eddiemae
Lowery, Pauline Mason
McCray, Carrie Allen
Mitchell, Sharon L
Moore, Betty Jean Green
Neals, Betty Elizabeth Harris

Payne, J. Joyce Coleman
Ruff, Phontella Cloteal Butcher
Rushin, Kate
Saunders, Esther "Hetty"
Shange, Ntozake
Shaw, Helen
Spinner, Bettye Delores Tyson
Talley, Jere Elaine
Taylor, Hope Rosemary
Thomas, Veona Young
Thompson, Mary Louise
Travis, Nancy Elizabeth
Tucker, Wanda Regina Buggs
White, Cheryl Fisher

Scholarly Writing
Campbell, Georgetta Merritt
Edge, Sylvia Clark
Fullilove, Mindy Thompson
Hayes, Leola Grant
Holley, Mary Rose
Holmes, Linda Janet
Strickland, Dorothy Mae Salley
Tate, Claudia C.
Thandeka
Thornton, Yvonne Shirley

Walker, Sheila Suzanne
Wall, Cheryl Ann
Wesley, Dorothy Louise Burnett Porter
Williams, Ruby Ora
Wright, Marion Manola Thompson

Short Story/Sketch
Shange, Ntozake
Fauset, Jessie Redmon
Hunter-Lattany, Kristin Elaine
    Eggleston
Mathis, Sharon Yvonne Bell

Songs and Libretti
Hughes, Sally Page

Speech/Sermon
Tuck-Ponder, Michele Lois

Textbook
Brown, Martha Hursey
Brown, Vashti Proctor
Edge, Sylvia Clark
Drewry, Cecelia Hodges
Shakir, Qadriyyah Buteen
Sharif, Ummil-Khair Zakiyyah

About the Author

Sibyl E. Moses, Ph.D., a native of Newark, New Jersey, is the Reference Specialist in African American History and Culture at the Library of Congress in Washington, D.C. Formerly an associate professor in the School of Library and Information Science, The Catholic University of America in Washington, D.C., she has directed the African American Women Writers in New Jersey Project since 1985. She received her B.A., magna cum laude, from Spelman College, Atlanta, Georgia, the M.P.A. from the University of Ife (now Obafemi Awolowo University), Ife-Ife, Nigeria, and her M.S. and Ph.D. from the University of Illinois, Urbana-Champaign. Her experience includes several years as an academic librarian in Nigeria. She was also director of the Office for Library Outreach Services at the American Library Association, and the project archivist at the Schomburg Center for Research in Black Culture, The New York Public Libraries. A member of Alpha Kappa Alpha Sorority, Inc., she is also the Imperial Directress for Archives and History in the Imperial Court, Daughters of Isis, P.H.A. She resides in Newark, New Jersey, and Silver Spring, Maryland.